Russia and the Dutch Republic, 1566–1725

Jordan E. Kurland (1928–2016).

Russia and the Dutch Republic, 1566–1725

A Forgotten Friendship

Kees Boterbloem

LEXINGTON BOOKS
Lanham • Boulder • New York • London

Published by Lexington Books
An imprint of The Rowman & Littlefield Publishing Group, Inc.
4501 Forbes Boulevard, Suite 200, Lanham, Maryland 20706
www.rowman.com

6 Tinworth Street, London SE11 5AL, United Kingdom

Copyright © 2021 The Rowman & Littlefield Publishing Group, Inc.

All rights reserved. No part of this book may be reproduced in any form or by any electronic or mechanical means, including information storage and retrieval systems, without written permission from the publisher, except by a reviewer who may quote passages in a review.

British Library Cataloguing in Publication Information Available

Library of Congress Cataloging-in-Publication Data

Library of Congress Control Number: 2021933225

ISBN 978-1-7936-4858-7 (cloth)
ISBN 978-1-7936-4860-0 (pbk)
ISBN 978-1-7936-4859-4 (electronic)

Contents

Foreword: Jordan E. Kurland (1928–2016)   vii
Preface   xi
Acknowledgments   xiii

Introduction   1
Chronology   23
Maps   33
1   The Prehistory of Dutch-Russian Relations; the English Pioneers   35
2   Flemish Trailblazers   41
3   New States on Europe's Fringe   51
4   De Vogelaer and Van Klenck   55
5   The Russian and Dutch Other   59
6   Diplomatic Ties   67
7   Isaac Massa   73
8   Business Opportunities   79
9   Guns and Grain   85
10   Medicine   91
11   Dutch Entrepreneurs   99

12	Pivot: Boreel's Embassy	103
13	Dutch Mercenaries in the Tsar's Service	113
14	The Western *Sloboda*	121
15	The New Commercial Statute of 1667	127
16	Envoys	133
17	The *Oryol*	143
18	Becoming Russian?	147
19	Koenraad van Klenck's Embassy	151
20	The Interregnum, 1676–1689	159
21	Peter the Great	169
22	Patrick Gordon and François Lefort	175
23	Russians in the Republic	181
24	A Final Blaze of Business: Lups and Brants	187
25	Cornelis Cruys and the Russian Exchange Students	193
26	An Era Closes: The Eighteenth Century	197

Epilogue	201
Glossary	209
Bibliography	211
Index	229
About the Author	251

Foreword

Jordan E. Kurland (1928–2016)

Figure 0.1. Anita and Jordan Kurland aboard the Queen Mary, September 18, 1959.

In a photograph taken in mid-September 1959, aboard RMS *Queen Mary* steaming toward Cherbourg, Jordan, and Anita Kurland are pictured relaxing in a lounge, he in a suit and tie, she in a dress and heels. Jordan, age 31, is about to begin a year's sabbatical leave from his faculty position at the Woman's College of the University of North Carolina (now UNC-Greensboro). Supported by a US–Soviet exchange program, he will be able to conduct research in the Archive of Ancient Acts (*TsGADA*, nowadays

RGADA) in Moscow for his Ph.D. dissertation on the Dutch influence on Russia in the late seventeenth century. While Jordan will stay in a dormitory at Moscow State University, Anita will spend the year in Leyden with three small children and a former student of Jordan's, Jackie Long, alternating childcare and travel. The Netherlands is familiar, since Jordan and Anita had lived there a half dozen years earlier, when Jordan was researching the dissertation, on a Fulbright fellowship, in the Dutch National Archives in The Hague. At the time this photograph was taken, though neither of them can know it, he is at approximately the midpoint of his career as a history professor—and the dissertation will never be finished.

This volume originates in the research and writing Jordan Kurland conducted in the 1950s and early 1960s on his dissertation project, "The Dutch in Russia: 1664–1689: A Study of the Influence of the Netherlands upon Muscovite Political and Economic Life."

Among the materials from the dissertation research, some of them now 65 years old, that Jordan left behind at his death in 2016 were three completed chapters tracing Russian-Dutch relations through the Boreel Embassy to Moscow of 1664–1665 and portions of a fourth, on the impact of Russia's new economic policy in the late 1660s. There were approximately 3,000 4 × 6 note cards (primarily transcriptions of sources) and 500 3 × 5 bibliography cards. A Table of Contents hints at the original design, through 1689, and a single-page outline indicates in somewhat more detail the shape of the argument through 1665.

Many of the raw materials for this volume were assembled by Jordan Kurland, who laid its original foundation. The final design and construction—not to mention a great many of the details and most of the writing—are the work of Professor Kees Boterbloem. This study pushes well beyond the dissertation's original bounds and incorporates research produced by other scholars active in the half-century this project lay dormant.

*

Jordan Kurland matriculated at Dartmouth College in 1945. During a vacation term at home in Boston, he met Anita Siegel. They would be married for 69 years, producing four children and eight grandchildren. With housing for married students at a premium in Hanover, NH, he transferred to Boston University, graduating in 1949 and earning his MA in History a year later. He then started work on his Ph.D. at Columbia's Russian Institute (now the Harriman Institute), completing the requirements for his Certificate with a 200-page essay on "The History and Destiny of Russia According to Konstantin Leontiev," a portion of which was published in *The American Slavic and East European Review* in 1957.[1]

Jordan's original interest in Russian history was stimulated by medieval Muscovy. In the early days of the Cold War, with the energies at the Russian Institute primarily focused on modern history and politics, notably revolutionary Russia and the Soviet Union, he decided to move forward in time, settling in the seventeenth century. Presumably, his interest in the Dutch Republic followed from his study of seventeenth-century Russia. His teaching career began, in the academic year 1954–1955, with a Visiting Instructorship at the Woman's College. At the end of that year, the family moved back to New York, returning to Greensboro the following year when a permanent position opened. He earned tenure, as A.B.D., with the rank of Assistant Professor.

As a faculty member (in 1954 and 1955, and then from 1956 to 1965), Jordan Kurland taught European history and offered introductory courses in the Russian language. He also became involved in academic freedom and free speech issues, serving as president of the UNC-G chapter of the American Association of University Professors (AAUP) and as executive secretary of the North Carolina AAUP conference. The AAUP was particularly active in opposing a 1963 law banning outside speakers identified with Communism from North Carolina's state university campuses. These efforts put him in contact with representatives of the national AAUP, and he was invited to join the AAUP's professional staff, which he did, in mid-1965, taking a leave of absence and relocating the family to Washington, DC, with every expectation of returning to his teaching position a couple of years later. He remained with the AAUP for over 50 years, working primarily on matters related to academic freedom and tenure. In 2000, he retired as director of staff for the Association's Committee A on Academic Freedom and Tenure but remained at the AAUP, ostensibly on a part-time basis, for the rest of his life. The photograph at the top of this Foreword was taken at the 2015 Annual Meeting of the AAUP, when Jordan, age 86, was honored for over half a century of service to the Association.

Even after he left the classroom, in 1965, Jordan remained interested in Russian history. He maintained his memberships in scholarly associations, skimmed their journals, and contributed several book reviews to *The American Historical Review* and *Slavic Review*. In the early 1970s, he returned to his dissertation during a year-long sabbatical from AAUP, which he spent at the Library of Congress. The dissertation had begun under the direction of Philip E. Mosely, who died in 1972. Mosely's successor as dissertation director, Geroid Tanquary Robinson (1893–1971), urged a different direction for bringing the project to a close. The details have been lost, but it seems to have involved wrapping up with the Boreel Embassy in 1664 and 1665 and writing a new introduction and conclusion. Jordan may have pursued that approach during this sabbatical but without completing it to his satisfaction. Professor Boterbloem estimates that it would have taken another year to finish the project.

*

In the summer of 2016, an email to the staff of the Association for Slavic, East European, and Eurasian Studies led to a posting on the H-Net Early Slavic discussion Board inviting inquiries from scholars who might be interested in assessing the dissertation materials and possibly working with them. A number of well-qualified scholars generously offered to go through these materials, and Professor Boterbloem was asked to take possession of them. He has made use of them in producing the present study, earning the appreciation and gratitude of the entire Kurland family.

Stuart M. Kurland

NOTES

1. See Jordan E. Kurland, "Leont'ev's View on the Course of Russian Literature," *American Slavic and East European Review* 3, 1957, 260–74.

Preface

This book finds its inspiration in a dissertation project undertaken in the 1950s at Columbia University in New York, which was left incomplete. In the midst of the Cold War, Jordan Kurland (1928–2016) decided to investigate a topic that seemed underresearched, even if pivotal in understanding the roots of the Soviet empire. Kurland decided to turn to the relationship between the United Provinces (after 1648, the Dutch Republic) and Muscovy, as Russia was still known before Peter the Great took its helm in 1689. His vantage point was going to be in particular the visit of Dutch Embassy led by Jacob Boreel to Moscow in 1665. It appears as if Kurland believed this moment to be the high point in the relationship between the early Dutch Republic and early Romanov Muscovy, which before all was economic. The evidential base to make this case seemed promising: The Dutch archives preserved not just the lengthy written report Boreel (*Verbael*) submitted to it after the ambassador had returned to Holland, but his report could be contextualized by the plentiful correspondence surrounding it that survived and was traceable. Furthermore, the Soviet authorities were willing to allow Kurland to conduct some research into archival and other sources about the Boreel mission in Moscow. Permission to Western scholars to work—however restricted—in Soviet archives was then still a recent phenomenon: It had only been been granted for the first time in the middle of the 1950s. This all seemed to augur well for a successful completion of Mr. Kurland's dissertation.

But when the project seemed to near its conclusion, Mr. Kurland—after some years of teaching as a faculty member—found a different calling, and became instead, in 1965, an indefatigable advocate for the rights of US university faculty, as a leader of the AAUP. He served the AAUP for half a century, and never found sufficient time again to turn to his dissertation and finish it.

The following pages endeavor in part to complete Kurland's project, although they aspire to something else as well: A much more exhaustive outline of the fascinating and rather significant relationship between the Russia and the Netherlands when this relationship mattered most to the course of world history. As I will try to show, Jordan Kurland's hunch about the moment of Boreel Embassy's pivotal significance was correct, if not for the reason he thought.

Acknowledgments

This book would not have been written without the materials gathered by Jordan Kurland for his unfinished dissertation, kindly made available to me by the Kurland family members. I am very grateful to them and their patience, as this book should have been published in 2019, but a number of my other commitments delayed its completion. Otherwise the usual suspects deserve thanks, not least David Schimmelpenninck van der Oye who enthusiastically supported my candidacy to the Kurlands to resume (in a sense) Jordan Kurland's project. In person and in writing, Stuart Kurland, Bruno Naarden, Marion Peters, Rudolf Dekker, Rawil Fakhrullin, Rudi Matthee, Henk van Nierop, Philip Longworth, Valentin Boss, Chester Dunning, Peter Brown, Charles Halperin, Marc Jansen, Erik van Ree, and Golfo Alexopoulos have been helpful in shaping my thinking about this topic. Inspirational in more general terms have been Geoffrey Parker, Maarten Brands, Jan-Willem Bezemer, W. H. Roobol, Steven High, J. Scott Perry, Daniel Kaiser, Anne Clendinning, Joyce Goggin, Eugenio Bolongaro, Susan Mooney, Catherine Desbarats, Martin Stegeman, Paul Robinson, Karel Berkhoff, and too many others whom I undoubtedly forgot to mention here. And, as always, many thanks for all their love and support go out to Susan, Duncan, and Saskia Mooney.

Introduction

When Jordan Kurland began his dissertation research—some of its findings have found a place in the following pages—in the early 1950s, the historiography regarding the early modern Dutch relations with Russia was mostly outdated. There was presumably a historical reason for this. After Peter the Great's death in 1725, despite a continued high level of Dutch shipping on Russia, the once close ties between the two countries loosened. At sea, the Russian *Zeevaartreglement* (*morskoi ustav*), in force since 1721, ceased to be published in a bilingual version after the 1780s, a sign that until that time a good number of Dutch sailors had served the Russian red, white, and blue flag.[1] The last famous one among them was Admiral Jan Hendrik van Kinsbergen (1735–1819), a dare-devil mercenary, who was victorious against Ottoman squadrons in the Russo-Turkish war that raged from 1768 to 1774.[2] But Russia lost interest in Holland, a third-rate Power by the 1780s, and the Dutch interest in Russia waned in accordance with the diminishing Dutch influence in Russia after 1725.

With the emergence of modern historiography after the end of the Napoléonic Wars, Russian historians occasionally homed in on the Dutch role in their country's history, as Richter did in discussing medicine in early modern Russia, Tsvetaev regarding Protestantism in Russia, or Pekarskii in his investigation of Russian printing and publishing.[3] In Ustrialov's, Solov'ev's, or Kliuchevskii's survey-style historical works it often remained a bit nebulous how Peter the Great could have become so fascinated with the Dutch that he liked to be addressed as *Min Her Bombardir* by his correspondents, since little was said about their earlier influence and role in late Muscovy (as Russia was still often known before 1700).[4] Peter's tutors Frans Timmerman (f. 1700s) and Karsten Brandt (d. 1691) almost appeared in their histories as *dei ex machina*. Zabelin, who investigated the domestic life at the tsarist court, referred to the importation of exotic goods to Moscow, more often than not shipped by Dutch merchants who had also piqued the tsars' interest in such exotica.[5] Before 1900, several translated Dutch source publications appeared in Russian, but many of such texts were truncated, while they generated little interest within a veritable plethora of Western European accounts about pre-Petrine Russia that were translated and interpreted in the last decades of Imperial Russia's existence.[6] In published archival documents in Russian, various seventeenth-century Dutch protagonists appeared, but few nineteenth-century historians linked them together to explore the disproportionately large role played by the Dutch in seventeenth-century Russia.

Only in the last years of Romanov rule did Russian historians begin to explore in great detail some episodes in Russian history in which various Dutchmen seemed key actors, often through source publications that were painstakingly annotated: This effort started out with the chief of the Russian Historical Society Aleksandr Polovtsov (1832–1909)—together with A. Kh. Bek—and was then then continued by A. M. Loviagin, Veniamin Kordt (1860–1934), and I. P. Kozlovskii.[7] A. S. Muliukin studied the equally germane topic of the immigration of foreigners to Russia, a project only resumed by late- or post-Soviet scholars in Russia (even if Erik Amburger studied it in Germany with great zeal).[8] S. F. Platonov, the last of the great prerevolutionary Russian historians, weighed the influence of, and interaction with, Western Europe on Muscovy, but, like Kliuchevsky, was primarily a great synthesizer rather than a scholar minutely charting his findings.[9]

After 1917, though, this stream of publications turned again into a trickle. Soviet historians and historians of Russia elsewhere became preoccupied with the immediate past in efforts to find the roots of the epochal revolution that gave birth to the Soviet Union. The exception, of sorts, was work by Inna Lubimenko (1878–1959), who in a variety of languages contributed valuable studies regarding the Russian trade with both the English Muscovy Company and the Dutch, and explored the rivalry between the merchants of the two Western European countries.[10] Although she received her doctorate in 1908, much of her work was published after 1917. Mikhail Bogoslovskii's (1867–1929) research is even now invaluable, even if his biography of Peter was never written; his chronicling of Peter's whereabouts does nonetheless quite meticulously chart the Timmerman–Brandt–Vinius link with the young tsar.[11]

On the Dutch side, the publication during the 1810s of Jacob Scheltema's works on Russian-Dutch relations and on Peter the Great's Grand Embassy seems anomalous.[12] They hint at a sudden upsurge in interest in matters Russian. This was partially the consequence of the decisive role played by the Russians in defeating Napoléon, who was thoroughly detested in most of the northern Netherlands by 1813, after almost two decades of French rule. This heightened attention was furthermore connected to the wedding of the

Dutch hero of the 1815 Battle of Quatre-Bras (a subplot of the main event at Waterloo), Crown-Prince William of Orange-Nassau, with the sister of Tsar Alexander I, Anna Pavlovna, in 1816. Scheltema's work was voluminous, but, even if based on a good deal of primary-source study, his investigations were eclectic rather than exhaustive, and the contents of his tomes are episodic and descriptive rather than analytical, not quite yet a work of modern historiography.[13] With good grounds, then, even *in the early 1990s* Thomas Eekman could write that Scheltema's 1817 four-volume *Rusland en de Nederlanden* remained the "best, or rather the only, survey of [Dutch-Russian] relations."[14] Subsequent to Scheltema until the First World War, very little ink was indeed spent in the Netherlands on the Dutch moment in Russian history.[15] Russian-Dutch relations were only explored, it appears, as part of more general discussions about the explorations of the Republic's denizens and the expansion of the Dutch maritime empire after 1600, as in Dutch-sponsored or Dutch-led efforts to find the north-east passage to East Asia.[16]

While in Dutch and Russian little of substance was published, in English even less on Russo-Dutch ties was written. Among modern historians, it was Lubimenko, probably, who was the first to focus on the trade at Arkhangel'sk, even if only some of her work was written in the English language.[17] In addition, her focus was much more on the English—and to some extent the French—and the Muscovy trade than on the Dutch. And while the Muscovy Company was studied by others as well, mention of their Dutch competitors was sporadic or episodical, although the volume of Dutch trade with Russia vastly outstripped that of the English throughout the seventeenth century.[18]

The lack of study of Russian-Dutch relations may have been due in part because of the absence in late Romanov Russia of those who had a good command of (seventeenth-century) Dutch (including its handwritten version) and, vice versa, of Dutch scholars knowing Russian sufficiently (and able to read the late-Chancellery-Slavonic Russian manuscript) before 1900. Some Russian emigrés settled in the Netherlands before 1914, mainly Ashkenazi Jews, but the singular scholar among this group, Boris Raptschinsky, only began to publish after 1917.[19] Among indigenous Dutch academics, C. C. Uhlenbeck and Nicolaas van Wijk were rather Slavists (i.e., experts in linguistics and literature) than historians, even though Uhlenbeck was dispatched by the Dutch government in the early 1890s to Russia to investigate the archival record about the Dutch in early Romanov Muscovy.[20]

After a sort of interwar hiatus (when only nonexperts seem to have written about the *Soviet Union*, mainly in starkly positive or negative terms, with very little being written about Muscovy or early Imperial Russia), the Soviet victory in the Second World War and the Cold War's beginnings gave the scholarly study of the past of Russia and the Soviet Union a distinct impetus. Th. J. G. Locher (1900–1970) in Leyden and Bruno Becker (1885–1968) in

Amsterdam oversaw a quick growth of the study of "Eastern Europe," which was also boosted by the growth of Dutch universities and student numbers in general, especially after 1960, leading to departments (or chairs) of Eastern European Studies at the universities of Amsterdam, Leyden, Utrecht, and Groningen. But the Dutch Slavists, who excelled in various academic disciplines (while some, such as Karel van het Reve, became famous public intellectuals), rarely studied older Russian history.[21] De Buck was perhaps an exception, but while his publication of the Witsen diaries (with Locher) was an astounding feat of historiography, much of De Buck's yeoman research labor was never reflected in his publications.[22] Simon Hart, an Amsterdam archivist, published a number of useful articles during the postwar era, without however providing a comprehensive overview or synthesis.[23]

Indeed, before the 1990s, most of the interesting studies about the early modern Dutch and Russians came from a variety of places outside the Netherlands and Belgium, while inside the Soviet Union only Mikhail Ivanovich Belov's dissertation at Leningrad's Zhdanov University and his subsequent article investigated the early phase of the Dutch-Russian relationship.[24] But Belov turned in a different direction, probably because his topic did not generate much interest inside his country. Once in a while in Soviet scholarship the seventeenth-century Dutch suddenly appeared in an aside, as in their presence during the 1670–1671 Razin rebellion, about which the Dutchmen Struys, Butler, and Fabricius provided valuable eyewitness testimony.[25] But after the Kyiv university librarian Kordt ceased publishing any further scholarship in the 1920s, no substantial study of the Dutch presence in seventeenth-century Russia was undertaken until the very last days of the Soviet Union.

Most of the more scholarly study on the Dutch in Russia between 1945 and 1990 could be found in English- or German-language historiography, with pride of place belonging to Erik Amburger, even if he was more focused on Germans than Dutch expatriates in Russia.[26] But then, around 1990, the floodgates opened. It is moot whether this was linked to the greater access to archival documents in the early years after the proclamation of the Russian Federation's independence in 1991. Certainly, a number of scholars was able to explore in Moscow the Russian State Archive for Old Acts' (*Rossiiskii Gosudartsvennyi Arkhiv Drevnikh Aktov*, or *RGADA*) extensive collection at far greater leisure than in Soviet times, but Western scholars had been allowed into the Soviet incarnation of this archive since the 1950s (Jordan Kurland's sabbatical field trip to the Soviet Union in 1959–1960 was one example).[27] Other reasons may have added to this *hausse*, such as the ever greater availability of digitized material. From the 1990s onward, previously hard-to-unearth articles have been placed on line, revealing key evidence about the Dutch role in Muscovy.[28]

This growth, however, proved temporary: Across the Western world, the funding for Eastern European or Russian studies cratered toward 2000, and many academic positions for the study of Russia disappeared. In the Netherlands, the universities' Eastern European institutes closed. It remains to be seen if the renewed political interest in, or fear of, Russia reverses this process. In the Russian Federation, meanwhile, the study of history, reasonably well funded in the Soviet Union, a state that based itself on the philosophy of *historical* materialism, became a secondary concern in the 1990s. Massive budget cuts led to massive dismissals, and young scholars chose different professions instead of trying to eke out a spartan existence as an underpaid academic. With the turbulent economic seas calming under Vladimir Putin, history began to be studied again with some zeal (and money), but the focus has been mainly on the late Imperial and Soviet periods (not least on the Second World War).

Still, the quality and quantity of the scholarship on Russia and the Netherlands in the early modern age produced during the last generation has been impressive. Roger Tavernier has produced a fine overview, even if it needs further updating by now.[29] In Dutch, both Wijnroks and Veluwenkamp provided important pieces of the puzzle, but neither has provided a fully comprehensive overview of Dutch-Russian relations up to 1725.[30] Equally, Schade's treatise does not cover the story until Peter's death.[31] Kotilaine delivered a lasting contribution to our understanding of trade (especially foreign) with seventeenth-century Russia, especially in his massive dissertation and subsequent book.[32] In doing so, he seems to have severely challenged the idea of Immanuel Wallerstein or Fernand Braudel that Russia may not have belonged to the European economic "World System" of the period, but remained outside of its periphery.[33] Nonetheless, Kotilaine's studies have been almost purely economically oriented, to a great extent ignoring political or cultural matters.

Bushkovitch, Hughes, Zitser, and Cracraft all dedicated a good amount of space in their work on Peter the Great to the Dutch, but their main focus was on the tsar, not on the Dutch.[34] Driessen has explored Peter's scientific infatuation, which was fed by his visits to Dutch curiosity cabinets and operation theaters.[35] Travel accounts by Dutch and other travelers have been studied in depth as well.[36] Naarden, Wladimiroff, and Peters have written about Witsen and Russia.[37] Zandt's Master's thesis is excellent on Siberia.[38] Waegemans and Kreslins have said important things about language, adding to the earlier research of Van der Meulen and Croiset van der Kop.[39]

Great strides have been made as well with regards to military history in its sort of broader definition of the interaction of war and society. A pioneer was Richard Hellie in his *Enserfment and Military Change*, even if he did not note any particularly pronounced Dutch role.[40] Reger, Phillips, Fuhrmann,

Esper, Paul, and Floria certainly have aided to our insight into the Dutch role in Russian military modernization, while Brian Davies, Robert Frost, and Carol Belkin Stevens discussed warfare in Eastern Europe in broader terms.[41] Related to these studies are the earlier dissertations by Geraldine Phipps and Martha Lahana on foreigners in Russia, as many of those foreigners were mercenaries, who included a number of Dutch natives.[42] Kovrigina's work has added further detail to this topic, as has Orlenko's.[43] While numerous among mercenaries in Russia, the Dutch contingent among Western merchants and entrepreneurs was far more prominent. Kovrigina and Demkin studied this topic in some depth in the late Soviet and early post-Soviet years, coinciding with the main contributions by Wijnroks and Veluwenkamp (the latter two solely looking at Dutch merchants).[44] It should be noted that Joseph Fuhrmann already in the 1970s wrote an excellent book on the proto-industrial efforts by indeed almost exclusively Dutch entrepreneurs.[45] In Fuhrmann's and Longworth's biographies of Aleksei Mikhailovich, too, traces of the Dutch presence in Russia can be found, albeit more in the former than the latter.[46] Amburger, besides his numerous scholarly publications, has left us with a searchable database of all foreigners residing in prerevolutionary Russia, which is, however incomplete, of great value to the researcher.[47]

Ingrid Maier, Daniel Waugh, and Stepan Shamin (together with others) have helped us greatly to understand how information from the West was relayed to the tsar in what seemed to have been weekly summaries.[48] The sources for this information were more often than not Dutch newspapers (after an initial period, during which the tsar's clerks in the *posol'skii prikaz* frequently debriefed Dutch merchants arriving in Moscow). Even if the frequent wars with Poland or Sweden do not already prove this adequately, such close observation of what unfolded elsewhere in Europe further puts paid to the sort of dismissal of Russia being beyond the European pale as Braudel and Wallerstein would have it. Erika Monahan has added to our understanding about the exploration and exploitation of Siberia in which a number of Dutchmen were involved.[49]

Even if published source translations in Russian have become widely available (with many of them bundled on a website), both non-Russian-language and Russian ego-documents about seventeenth-century Russia have remained scarce: in the latter case, Avvakum's autobiography comes most readily to mind, as well as some of the tsars' correspondence; perhaps parts of the works by Krizhanich and Kotoshikhin might be counted as such; and a curious Russian travel account—of his travels to Central and Southern Europe in 1697 and 1698—is that by P. A. Tolstoi.[50] Among ego-documents and firsthand descriptions in non-Russian languages, though, the Dutch provide a fair number: Isaac Massa, Anthonis Goeteeris, Nicolaas Witsen, Jan Struys (when his ghostwriter did not plagiarize other texts), Balthasar Coyett, Johan

Willem van Keller, and Cornelis de Bruin were key eyewitnesses who wrote about—and sometimes illustrated or mapped—what they saw in Muscovy at some length.[51] Only recently issued in their entirety—at least that part that survived in manuscript—in print, Patrick Gordon's diaries are invaluable, and while its author was a Scot, he was married into the Dutch Van Bockhoven clan (as was François Lefort, who appears to have had no inclination to chart his wondrous escapades in a diary, but did leave substantial correspondence[52]), which makes many of his observations of use for our understanding of Russo-Dutch relations.[53]

It would take many pages to account for all the scholarship produced during the last half century, often exceptionally good, that has allowed us to get a deeper insight into the history as such of the United Provinces, and, albeit somewhat less, of Muscovy Russia. The Dutch Republic remains an endless source of fascination for historians and others since people such as Immanuel Wallerstein, Jan de Vries, and Geoffrey Parker began to investigate its history, and especially its precocious modernity, from a variety of perspectives (economic, military, cultural, political, etc.) in the early 1970s.[54] In English, early modern Russia has received considerably less attention despite the eventually towering significance of the Soviet Union in the twentieth century and of the Russian Federation today, which of course dwarfs that of the modern-day Netherlands. Still, some key studies have given us a far better understanding of how early Romanov Russia operated in a manner which Jordan Kurland could not have imagined around 1960; besides those historians already mentioned, work by Chester Dunning, Nancy Shields-Kollmann, Valerie Kivelson, Mikhail Khodarkovsky, Brian Boeck, Peter B. Brown, Simon Dixon, or Isolde Thyret has been outstanding and for many of these scholars the inspiration of Edward Keenan has been profound, despite his own somewhat halting scholarly production.[55] Considerations of space, too, prevent me from giving an overview of German-language or French-language historiography about seventeenth-century Russia, but more and more scholars attempt to publish in English in order to reach a larger audience, diminishing the traditionally robust output on Eastern Slavonic language and culture in those languages. Certainly, compared to the English-language scholarship of the last half century, even recent Russian-language work on Muscovy might be said to fall short of scholarly inspiration or quality, as well as number of significant monographs.[56] Economic causes appear key in understanding this development: There is not a shadow of a doubt that Russian scholars produce significant contributions to the field, but whereas the cost of book printing in Russia is much lower than in the West, we already saw how the support for scholarship in the Russian Federation and the other successor states has plummeted since the fall of the Soviet Union (even despite a slight upsurge in the Putin years before 2014). This has clearly led to a diminution of the volume of scholarly work about this period across the former Soviet region.

Much has been accomplished, then, yet gaps remain. Even if the accumulation of primary sources and scholarly writing would seem to allow for such an examination, no one yet has provided an overview of Dutch-Russian relations between the Republic's de facto "declaration of independence"—for which I will use the *Act of Abjuration* (*Plakkaat van Verlatinghe*) of 1581, which is debatable—and the end of the Great Northern War in 1721.[57] Dutch independence more or less coincides with the definitive shift of the economic center of gravity from the southern (Brabant and Flanders) to the northern (Holland and Zeeland) Netherlands, while it is around this very time that the Dutch presence in the White Sea becomes ever more apparent (in part through Muscovy's loss of Narva in 1583). I thus omit most of the story about the lively trade of the Narva-Antwerp era, which has been convincingly sketched by Wijnroks as a sort of prelude of the United Provinces' economic relationship with Muscovy.[58] Likewise, whereas the trade on the Baltic Sea in general (the *Moedernegotie*, certainly of key significance to Amsterdam before the 1560s) cannot be disentangled from that on Russia, going back to the heyday of the Hanseatic League and the flourishing of Novgorod in the later Middle Ages, I will only sporadically refer to it as far as it affects northern Netherlandic-Russian relations.[59]

The period on which Jordan Kurland homed in, that of the 1660s (and specifically of the Boreel embassy of 1664–1665), was pivotal for the history of both countries. The Dutch were at the height of their economic power and political might, but the relentless growth of their political and economic clout was cresting, its end arriving with a bang in 1672. Conversely, the Russians, confronted with a long sequence of crises that started a century earlier under Ivan IV in the 1560s, finally began to get their house in order, with 1667 being a particular signal year because of the Truce of Andrusovo, the New Commercial Code, Nikon's deposition as patriarch, and the first steps toward building a Russian navy (while Siberia had been brought under firmer control, all the way to the Pacific shore).

Kurland's focus on the Boreel embassy that unfolded during the middle of the 1660s was misdirected and too narrow, however, as will become evident in the following pages. Furthermore, in his notes no explicit evidence can be encountered why he identified this moment as a pivotal historical juncture that saw the Republic begin its decline and Russia begin its rise. The Boreel Embassy as such was a bland affair, hallmarked by petty quarrels between Muscovite officials and the Dutch ambassador having no significant consequences. Far more fascinating are the intrepid activities behind the scenes by one of Boreel's retainers, the young Nicolaas Witsen, who kept a highly revealing diary unencumbered by diplomatic formulae. That diary was long lost, but finally published in 1966 in its original Dutch, accompanied by a vast scholarly annotation.[60] It might have served as a far more compelling central piece around which Jordan Kurland might have built his dissertation, but it would have been a profound and time-consuming change of course even if he would have had the manuscript available to him.

As the 1660s are of considerable importance in the history of Dutch-Russian relations, a fair bit will be said about them in this book, but in order to arrive at a more comprehensive idea of these ties, the story needs to begin at the dawn of Dutch independence and end with the death of the greatest Russian "hollandophile." Only by surveying this much lengthier period the sometimes surprisingly great importance of these ties for the course of world history emerges.

By 1721, Imperial Russia (led by the newly minted Emperor Peter) had become a Great Power in Eastern Europe, replacing both Sweden and Poland. The role of Arkhangel'sk as port of entry for goods shipped overseas from the West diminished after the 1703 founding of St. Petersburg, which not only became a crucial Russian port for trade with the West (as conquered Riga and recovered Narva became as well), but the very capital of Russia in 1713. In that latter year, the Treaty of Utrecht was signed, bringing to a close almost 40 years of incessant warfare in Western Europe between Louis XIV's France and the Dutch Republic. The threat of a French hegemony in Western Europe seemed to have definitively been halted, but the effort exhausted the Dutch Republic. All vim and vigor that had been the country's hallmark in the previous one-and-a-half century had evaporated by 1713. The country remained powerful enough to maintain itself as a secondary player in Europe until the 1780s, but was no longer a Great Power, and the story of its subsequent relations with Russia is rather less significant to the course of world history than that of the previous 150 years.

Finally, the reader may note one peculiarity about the Dutch-Russian relations in this timeframe: It was one-way traffic. Before the Grand Embassy, traffic and communication between the two polities was largely driven by the Dutch. They conducted virtually all of the seaborne trade with Russia, they supplied the doctors, craftsmen, and mercenaries, and they supplied information, printed matter, cash, and high-in-demand manufactured goods (not least weapons) to Muscovy. Russians rarely visited the United Provinces. The few that tried seems to have been fooled by Dutch cunning in their efforts to trade, while the tsar's government preferred to work through Dutch (or Western) agents when in search of artisans, arms, or mercenaries.[61] The only exception were Russian diplomats who on a number of occasions came calling at The Hague. In other words, the following pages will say little about Russians in Holland or Zealand, certainly before 1697. Some awareness about the Republic existed in Muscovy, undoubtedly, thanks to the presence of Dutch people in Moscow and elsewhere in Russia, with the court being treated to summaries of Dutch newspapers since the early part of the seventeenth century, following the period mentioned above in which Dutch merchants calling at Moscow were routinely debriefed by Russian authorities about European developments.[62] Still, Vinius's report about the workings of the Dutch Republic (and England, France, and Spain) in the early 1670s shows a great amount of ignorance about Western Europe (Vinius himself, although a sort of Russified Dutchman, appears fairly nonplussed, although he may have sought to render his account in a simplistic fashion to cater to his audience and have feigned ignorance).[63]

While from the late 1690s onward Russians visited the Republic frequently, shipping between the two countries was almost exclusively conducted by Dutch (and other Western European) vessels and crews until the nineteenth century. This despite it having been one of Peter the Great's greatest ambitions to establish a large merchant marine. Certainly, this phenomenon had something to do with the absence of credit or capital available to Russian merchants even far into the eighteenth century.[64]

NOTES

1. *Kniga ustav' morskoi o vsem' chto kasaetsia dobromu upravleniiu, v' bytnosti flota na mor'*, St. Petersburg: Sankt-Peterburskoi tipografii, 1720. This flag, of course, was based on that of the Dutch Republic.

2. See R.B. Prud'homme van Reine, *Jan Hendrik van Kinsbergen, 1735–1819. Admiraal en filantroop*, Amsterdam: De Bataafsche Leeuw, 1990.

3. W.M. von Richter, *Geschichte der Medicin in Russland*, 4 vols, Moskva: Wsevolosjky, 1813–1817 [reprinted: Leipzig: Zentral-Antiquariat der Deutschen Demokratischen Republik, 1965]; P. Pekarskii, *Nauka i literatura v Rossii pri Petre Velikomu*, 2 vols, Sint-Petersburg: Obshchestvennaia pol'za, 1862; D. Tsvetaev, *Protestantstvo i protestanty v Rossii do epokhi preobrazovanii*, Moscow: Universitetskaia tipografiia, 1890; see also N. Bantysh-Kamenskii, *Obzor' vneshnikh' snoshenii Rossii po 1800 god'*, chast 1, Moscow: Lissner and Roman, 1894, 173–207. A good discussion and overview of the significance of this curious inventory of what Bantysh-Kamenskii deemed to be crucial Russian foreign-policy documents (which was largely compiled in the eighteenth century!) may be found in "Overzicht van de betrekkingen van Rusland tot Nederland tot aan het jaar 1800, door N.N. Bantys-Kamenskij. Medegedeeld door Dr. K. Heeringa," *Bijdragen en Mededeelingen van het Historisch Genootschap* 51, 1930, 35–103.

4. N.G. Ustrialov, *Istoriia Tsarstvovaniia Petra Velikogo*, 6 vols, St. Petersburg: Imperial Printing House, 1858–1863; S.M. Soloviev, *History of Russia*, vol. 26, ed. and trans. L. Hughes. Gulf Breeze, FL: Academic International Press, 1994; idem, *History of Russia*, vol. 28, ed. and trans, L.A.J. Hughes. Gulf Breeze, FL: Academic International P., 2007; V.O. Kliuchevskii, *Skazaniia inostrantsev o Moskvoskom gosudarstve*, second ed. Petrograd: Pervaia gosudarstvennaia tipografiia, 1918.

5. I. Zabelin, *Domashnii byt' Russkikh' tsarei*, 2 vols, second ed. Moskva: Grachev i kompaniia, 1872.

6. For A.A. Vinius as a diplomat, see, for example, *Pamiatniki diplomaticheskikh' snoshenii drevnei Rossii s' derzhavami inostrannymi*, vol. 4, St. Petersburg: V Tip. II Otd-niia Sobstvennoi E.I.V. kantseliarii, 1856, 754–1078.

7. A. Kh. Bek and A.A. Polovtsov, eds, *Otchet Niderlandskikh' poslannikov' Reinouta fan'-Brederode . . . v' Shvestiiu i Rossiiu v' 1615 i 1616 godakh*, Sankt-Peterburg: V.S. Balashev, 1878; I.P. Kozlovskii, *Andrei Vinius', sotrudnik Petra Velikogo (1641–1717 g.)*, Sankt-Peterburg: N. Ia. Stoikovoi, 1911; Balthasar Coyett, *Historisch Verhael of Beschryving van de Voyagie gedaan onder de Suite van den Heere Koenraad van Klenck*, Amsterdam: Jan Claesz. ten Hoorn, 1677 [Russian translation: *Posol'stvo Konraada fan Klenka k tsariam Alekseiu Mikhailovichu i Fedoru Alekseevichu*, tr. and ed. A.M. Loviagin. Sankt-Peterburg: Tipografiia Glav. upr. udelov, 1900; it has been reissued in recent years]; V. Kordt, *Chuzozemni podorozhi po skhidnii Evropi do 1701*, Kiev: Ukainska akademija nauk, 1926; idem, "Doneseniia poslannikov respubliki Soedinnenykh Niderlandov," *Sbornik Imperatorskogo Russkogo istoricheskogo obshchestva* 116, 1902; idem, "Ocherk snoshenii moskovskogo gosudarstva s Respublikoi Niderlandov do 1631 god," *Sbornik Imperatorskogo Russkogo istoricheskogo obshchestva* 116, 1902, iii–cccvii.

8. A.S. Muliukin, *Priezd inostrantsev v Moskovskoe gosudarstvo*, St. Petersburg: Trud, 1909; E. Amburger, *Die Familie Marselis*, Gießen: Wilhelm Schmitz, 1957.

9. For a relevant example, see S.F. Platonov, *Moscow and the West*, tr. J. Wieczynski, Hattiesburg, MS: Academic International Press, 1972.

10. Among her first works in English were Inna Lubimenko, "The Correspondence of Queen Elizabeth with the Russian Czars," *American Historical Review* 3, 1914, 525–42; idem, "Project for the Acquisition of Russia by James I," *English Historical Review* 29, April 1914, 246–56; idem, "Letters Illustrating the Relations of England and Russia in the Seventeenth Century," *English Historical Review* 32, January 1917, 92–103; but see, especially, idem, "Struggle of the Dutch with the English for the Russian Market in the Seventeenth Century," *Transactions of the Royal Historical Society*, December 1924, 27–51.

11. See M.M. Bogoslovskii, *Petr I. Materialy dlia biografii*, vols 1 and 2. Moskva: Nauka, 1941–1942.

12. J. Scheltema, *Peter de Groote, keizer van Rusland in Holland en te Zaandam in 1697 en 1717*. 2 vols. Amsterdam: Hendrik Gartman, 1814; idem, *Rusland en de Nederlanden*. 4 vols. Amsterdam: Hendrik Gartman, 1817.

13. An interesting, albeit equally dated (and lamentably brief), study about the Frisians in Russia is W. Eekhoff, "Friezen in Rusland vóór en onder Peter den Groote," *Nieuwe Friesche Volksalmanak* 7, 1859, 29–39.

14. Thomas Eekman, "Muscovy's International Relations in the Late Seventeenth Century," *California Slavic Studies* 14, 1992, 44–67: 64n4.

15. Only in 1913 did the University of Leyden establish a chair in Balto-Slavonic languages with particular attention to Russian, after several years of debate involving the Dutch education minister and other prominent politicians (see Jan Paul Hinrichs, "Nicolaas van Wijk [1880–1941]: Slavist, Linguist, Philanthropist," *Studies in*

Slavic and General Linguistics 31, 2006, 3 and 5–341: 85–93). Nicolaas van Wijk (1880–1941) was appointed to the post with strong support from the polyglot C.C. Uhlenbeck. A female candidate, Anna Croiset van der Kop (1859–1914), may have been much better suited for the position and enjoyed widespread support from foreign experts, but was bypassed (ibid., 98–101). Even today, women remain a minority at the highest levels of the Dutch academic world. Germane for our topic might be that one of the six pertinent reasons the university suggested in creating the post was that it would aid the study of Dutch trade in the early modern era (ibid., 86).

16. Thus, see S. Muller, *Geschiedenis der Noordsche Compagnie*, Utrecht: Van der Post, 1874; S.P. L'Honoré-Naber, ed., *Reizen van Jan Huyghen van Linschoten naar het Noorden (1594–1595)*. 's-Gravenhage: Nijhoff, 1914. For a more recent, albeit brief, account, see Louwrens Hacquebord, *De Noordse Compagnie (1614–1642): Opkomst, Bloei en Ondergang*. Zwolle: Walburg Pers, 2014. And for a more thorough study of a pioneer, see Marijke Spies, *Bij noorden om: Olivier Brunel en de doorvaart naar China en Cathay in de zestiende eeuw*. Amsterdam: Amsterdam UP, 1994, translated into English as idem, *Arctic Routes to Fabled Lands: Oliver Brunel and the Passage to China and Cathay in the Sixteenth Century*. Amsterdam: Amsterdam UP, 1996.

17. Lubimenko, "Correspondence of Queen Elizabeth"; idem, "Project for the Acquisition"; idem, "Letters Illustrating"; idem, "Struggle of the Dutch."

18. M.S. Anderson, *Britain's Discovery of Russia, 1553–1815*. New York: St. Martin's Press, 1958; T.S. Willan, *The Muscovy Merchants of 1555*. Manchester: Manchester UP, 1953; T.S. Willan, *The Early History of the Russia Company, 1553–1603*. Manchester: Manchester UP, 1968; S.H. Baron, "Osip Nepea and the Opening of Anglo-Russian Commercial Relations," *Oxford Slavonic Papers*, New Series 11, 1978, 42–63; see as well Maria Salomon Arel, "The Muscovy Company in the First Half of the Seventeenth Century: Trade and Position in the Russian State - A Reassessment," unpubl. Ph.D dissertation, Yale University, 1995; idem, *English Trade and Adventure to Russia in the Early Modern Era: The Muscovy Company, 1603–1649*, Lanham, MD: Lexington Books, 2019; G. Phipps, *Sir John Merrick, English Merchant-Diplomat in Seventeenth-Century Russia*, Newtonville, MA: Oriental Research Partners, 1983; and idem, "Britons in Seventeenth-Century Russia: A Study in the Origins of Modernization," unpublished Ph.D. diss., University of Pennsylvania, 1971. See, too, Paul Dukes, Graeme Herd and Jarmo Kotilaine, *Stuarts and Romanovs: The Rise and Fall of a Special Relationship*, Dundee: Dundee UP, 2009. Given this fairly copious literature—see also the previous note—I cannot really agree with Maria Salomon Arel's suggestions that this literature is "meager," even if quantity is not quality (and even if she argues this for the *later* Muscovy Company, which argument is not bereft of merit, see Arel, *English Trade*, 3–4). Kotilaine's dissertation clearly underlines how Dutch traders outstripped their English competitors throughout most of the seventeenth century (see Jarmo Kotilaine, "When the Twain Did Meet: Foreign Merchants and Russia's Economic Expansion in the Seventeenth Century," unpubl. Ph.D. diss. Harvard University, 2000, 104–79, 208). Arel refers to Kotilaine's book derived from the dissertation, but not to Kotiliane's much more detailed dissertation (see J. Kotilaine, *Russia's Foreign Trade and Economic Expansion in the Seventeenth Century*, Leiden: Brill, 2005).

19. Boris Raptschinsky, "Het Gezantschap van Koenraad van Klenk naar Moskou," *Jaarboek Amstelodamum* 36, 1939, 149–99. Some of Raptschinsky's work (not least his doctoral dissertation) was rather less than authentic; Knoppers dismissed it wholesale as plagiarism, a mere translation of Ustrialov and Venevitinov (see J.V.T. Knoppers, "The visits of Peter the Great to the United Provinces in 1697–98 and 1716–17 as seen in the light of the Dutch sources," unpubl. MA thesis, McGill University, 1970, 3; see Ustrialov, *Istoriia Tsarstvovaniia*; M.A. Venevitinov, *Russkie v Gollandii. Velikoe posol'stvo 1697–1698 goda*, Moscow: O.O. Gerben, 1897). While Knoppers is right about the dissertation, Raptschinsky did nonetheless contribute to a deeper understanding of the Dutch-Russian relations for those who did not read Russian (few did in the 1920s Netherlands). And, unfortunately, Knoppers's own thesis has a number of howlers, such as when suggesting that the volume of Dutch trade with Russia was less than that of the English before the mid-seventeenth century, or that Witsen traveled in Russia for three years and even sailed the Caspian Sea (ibid., 10–11). The Petersburger Bruno Becker was another expatriate of great influence on the Dutch study of Russia, but was actually an expert on the humanist Dirk Volkertszoon Coornhert, and left little of substance about Russia and the Netherlands in writing.

20. C.C. Uhlenbeck, *Verslag aangaande een onderzoek van de archieven van Rusland ten bate der Nederlandsche geschiedenis*, Den Haag: Nijhoff, 1891.

21. That is not to say that Van het Reve or Jan-Willem Bezemer were dilettantes regarding prerevolutionary Russian history, as is obvious from their two excellent textbooks on, respectively, literature and history; an exception is F. J. M. Feldbrugge, a legal expert, who wrote some outstanding works, including on the Russian Middle Ages and Early Modern era (see F.J.M. Feldbrugge, *A History of Russian Law: From Ancient Times to the Council Code [Ulozhenie] of Tsar Aleksei Mikhailovich of 1649*, Leiden: Brill, 2018; Bezemer's work was recently updated by Marc Jansen, see J.W. Bezemer and Marc Jansen, *Een geschiedenis van Rusland*, Amsterdam: Van Oorschot, 2014; and Karel van het Reve, *Geschiedenis van de Russische literatuur*, Amsterdam: Van Oorschot, 1985). Feldbrugge, however, never wrote anything much about Dutch-Russian relations. In Utrecht, the pivotal figure was Z. R. Dittrich (1923–2015), a native of (Czecho-) Slovakia, who fled to the West after the 1948 communist coup. Dittrich wrote a number of works on especially the Soviet Union.

22. See for his—Erik Amburger-like—spadework regarding the Dutch-Russian trade through Arkhangel'sk: "Notariele Akten over de Archangelvaart, 1594–1724," available at: http://resources.huygens.knaw.nl/archangel/app/voyages?language_of_user=nl, accessed September 10, 2019; N.C. Witsen, *Moscovische reyse 1664–5: Journaal en aentekeningen*, 3 vols, eds Th. Locher and P. de Buck, Den Haag: Nijhoff, 1966–1967. See further Piet de Buck, "De Russische uitvoer uit Archangel naar Amsterdam in het begin van de achttiende eeuw (1703 en 1709)," *Economisch- en Sociaal-Historisch Jaarboek* 51, 1988, 126–93; idem, "De Amsterdamse handel op Archangel (1600–1725)," in *Amsterdam, haven in de 17de en 18de eeuw*, eds Judica Krikke, Victor Enthoven, and Kees Mastenbroek, Amsterdam: Orionis, 1990, 28–33. Toward the end of his life, De Buck did produce an excellent radio series on the Dutch overseas trade on Eastern Europe: *De Moedernegotie*, radio documentary in eight parts, eds K. Amsberg and P. de Buck, Hilversum: VPRO, 1999. I am not sure whether this program has become available in any digitized fashion.

23. Simon Hart, *Geschrift en Getal: Een keuze uit de demografisch-, economisch- en sociaal-historische studiën op grond van Amsterdamse en Zaanse archivalia, 1600–1800*, Dordrecht: Historische Vereniging Holland, 1976. He had been preceded by Van Zuiden, see D.S. van Zuiden, *Bijdrage tot de kennis der Hollandsch-Russische relaties van de 16e tot de 18e eeuw*, Amsterdam: Gebroeders Binger, 1911; and idem, "Nieuwe bijdrage tot de kennis van de Hollandsch-Russische relaties in de 16e-18e eeuw," *Economisch-Historisch Jaarboek* 2, 1916, 258–95. The economic historian J. G. van Dillen occasionally wrote on this same topic as well (see J.G. van Dillen, ed., *Bronnen tot de geschiedenis van het bedrijfsleven en het gildewezen van Amsterdam*, vol. 3 [1633–1672], Den Haag: Nijhoff, 1974). For the eighteenth century, Van Brakel wrote what seems to have remained a single essay, see S. van Brakel, "Statistische en andere gegevens betreffende onzen handel en scheepvaart op Rusland gedurende de 18de eeuw," in *Bijdragen en Mededeelingen van het Historisch Genootschap* 34, 1913, 350–404; this was a topic to which Knoppers returned two generations later (see Jake V. Th. Knoppers, "Eighteenth Century Dutch Trade with Russia," unpubl. Ph.D. diss. McGill University, 1975).

24. M.I. Belov, "Rossiia i Gollandiia v poslednei chetverti XVII v.," in *Mezhdunarodnye sviazi Rossii v XVII-XVIII vv.*, ed. L. Beskrovnyi, Moskva: Nauka, 1966, 58–83.

25. *Krest'ianskaia voina pod predvoditel'stvom Stepana Razina*, 4 vols, Moscow: Institut istorii Akademii nauk SSSR, 1954–1976. Butler's letter (as well as an anonymous epistle) was published in Struys's 1676 book when it was fully translated into Russian in the 1930s, while Fabricius's memoirs (written at the request of Peter the Great, apparently) appeared among a variety of source publications regarding this Cossack revolt (A. Morozov, *Tri puteshestviia Ia.Ia. Streis*, trans. E. Borodina, Moscow: Sotsgiz, 1935; for an English translation of Fabricius's reminiscences, see S. Kovovalov, ed., "Ludwig Fabritius's Account of the Razin Rebellion," *Oxford Slavonic Papers* 6, 1955, 72–101).

26. Amburger, *Familie Marselis*; Joseph T. Fuhrmann, *The Origins of Capitalism in Russia*, Chicago, IL: Quadrangle Books, 1972; Reinhard Wittram, *Peter I, Czar und Kaiser: Zur Geschichte Peter des Grossen in seiner Zeit*, Göttingen: Vandenhoek und Ruprecht, 1964; P. Longworth, *Alexis: Tsar of All the Russias*, New York: Franklin Watts, 1984; Thomas Esper, "Military Self-Sufficiency in Muscovite Russia," *Slavic Review* 2, 1969, 185–208. A somewhat curious contribution was Harm Klueting, *Die niederländische Gesandtschaft nach Moscovien im Jahre 1630–1631: Edition der russischen Protokolle und ihrer niederländischen Übersetzungen. Mit paläographischer und sprachlicher Beschreibung. Ein Beitrag zur russischen Kanzleisprache (Prikaznyj Jazyk) des 17. Jahrhunderts*, Amsterdam: Hakkert, 1976.

27. A useful overview of what *RGADA* contains is T.B. Solov'eva, *Dokumenty o sviaziakh Rossii i Niderlandov v fondakh Rossiiskogo Gosudarstvennogo Arkhiva Drevnikh Aktov. Spravochnik*, Moscow: Manufaktura, 1999. Its inventory can be checked online through the University of Groningen, available at: https://www.archieven.nl/nl/zoeken?mivast=0&mizig=210&miadt=467&miaet=1&micode=RGADA&minr=738326&miview=inv2, accessed October 6, 2019. The actual documents, however, have not been digitized.

28. See, for example, the documents rendered in this overview of the Dutch presence at Arkhangel'sk, see Iu.N. Bespiatnikh, "Gollandtsy. 'Nemetskaia sloboda' v Arkhangel'ske v xvii-xviiivv.", available at: http://www.vostlit.info/Texts/Dokumenty/Russ/XVIII/1700-1720/Archangelsk/Archangelsk_inozemcy/text.htm, accessed September 28, 2019.

29. Roger Tavernier, *Russia and the Low Countries: An International Bibliography, 1500–2000*, Groningen: Barkhuis, 2006. And the book is somewhat plagued by a curious English transcription of Russian words. An earlier overview was F. Muller, *Essai d'une bibliographie Néerlando-Russe . . .*, Amsterdam: F. Muller, 1859.

30. E. Wijnroks, *Handel tussen Rusland en de Nederlanden 1560–1640: Een netwerkanalyse van de Antwerpse en Amsterdamse kooplieden, handelend op Rusland*, Hilversum: Verloren, 2003; among Veluwenkamp's works, see J.W. Veluwenkamp, "'N huis op Archangel'. De Amsterdamse koopmansfamilie Thesingh, 1650–1725," *Jaarboek Amstelodamum* 69, 1977, 123–39; idem, "Familienetwerken binnen de Nederlandse koopliedengemeenschap van Archangel in de eerste helft van de achttiende eeuw," *Bijdragen en Mededelingen betreffende de Geschiedenis der Nederlanden* 4, 1993, 655–72; idem, Archangel. Nederlandse ondernemers in Rusland, 1550–1785, Amsterdam: Balans, 2000; idem, "De Nederlandse wapenhandel op Rusland in de zeventiende eeuw," *Armamentaria* 31, 1996, 71–6; and idem, "Kaufmännisches Verhalten und Familiennetzwerke im niederländischen Russlandhandel (1590–1750)," in *Praktiken des Handels. Geschäfte und soziale Beziehungen europäischer Kaufleute in Mittelalter und früher Neuzeit*, eds M. Häberlein and C. Jeggle, Konstanz: UVK, 2010, 379–405. In Russian, see Ia.V. Veluvenkamp, "Kompaniia 'de Vogelar i Klenk' v gollandsko-russkikh kommercheskikh otnosheniiakh xvii v.," in *Niderlandy i Severnaia Rossiia*, eds Iu. N. Bespiatnikh et al., St. Petersburg: Russko-Baltiiskii informatsionnyi Tsentr, 2003, 37–73. See also the useful review by Kotilaine (J.T. Kotilaine, review of *Archangel* by J.W. Veluwenkamp, *Kritika* 3, 2002, 715–22).

31. Hans Schade, *Die Niederlande und Russland: Handel und Aufnahme diplomatischer Kontakte zu Anfang des 17. Jahrhunderts*, Frankfurt am Main: Peter Lang, 1992.

32. Kotilaine, *Russia's Foreign Trade*; idem, "When the Twain"; idem, "In Defense of the Realm: Russian Arms Trade and Production in the Seventeenth and Early Eighteenth Century," in *Military and Society in Russia*, eds M. Poe and E. Lohr, Leiden: Brill, 2002: 67–95.

33. See I. Wallerstein, *The Modern World-System*, second ed., vol. 2, Berkeley, CA: U. of California P., 2011, 218; F. Braudel, *Civilization and Capitalism: 15th to 18th Centuries*, vol. 3, New York: Harper and Row, 1981–1982, 442–3.

34. Bushkovitch, Hughes, and Cracraft were towering figures in the field of early modern Muscovy in the early post-Soviet era; the number of their publications is prodigious: See especially J. Cracraft, *The Revolution of Peter the Great*, Cambridge, MA: Harvard UP, 2003: idem, *The Petrine Revolution in Russian Culture*, Cambridge, MA: Harvard UP, 2004; L. Hughes, *Peter the Great: A Biography*, New Haven, CT: Yale UP, 2002; idem, *Russia in the Age of Peter the Great*, New Haven, CT: Yale UP, 1998; Paul Bushkovitch, *Peter the Great: The Struggle for Power (1671–1725)*,

Cambridge: Cambridge UP, 2007; Zitser's fine work is Ernest A. Zitser, *The Transfigured Kingdom: Sacred Parody and Charismatic Authority at the Court of Peter the Great*, Ithaca, NY: Cornell University Press, 2004. Hughes also wrote the first scholarly biography of a key political figure of the 1680s, see L. Hughes, *Sophia, Regent of Russia, 1657–1704*, New Haven, CT: Yale UP, 1990.

35. J.J. Driessen-van het Reve, *De Kunstkamera van Peter de Grote*, Hilversum: Verloren, 2006. Driessen has written far more on the Dutch-Russian connection that is of interest.

36. See Witsen, *Moscovische reyse*; I. Massa, *A Short History of the Beginnings and Origins of These Present Wars in Moscow*, ed. G. Edward Orchard, Toronto: U. of Toronto P., 1982; K. Boterbloem, *The Fiction and Reality of Jan Struys: A Seventeenth-Century Dutch Globetrotter*, Houndmills, Basingstoke: Palgrave Macmillan, 2008. I have written various other pieces on Struys in Dutch and English as well, the lengthiest of which can be found in Jan Struys, *Rampspoedige reizen door Rusland en Perzië in de zeventiende eeuw*, ed. Kees Boterbloem, Amsterdam: Panchaud, 2014. Marshall Poe has written both a fine analysis and made an attempt to list all Western travelers' accounts on Russia (see M. Poe, "*A People Born to Slavery": Russia in Early Modern European Ethnography, 1476–1748*, Ithaca, NY: Cornell UP, 2000; idem, *Foreign Descriptions of Muscovy: An Analytic Bibliography of Primary and Secondary Sources*, Columbus, OH: Slavica, 1995). Worthwhile as well is Stéphane Mund, *Orbis Russiarum: Genèse et développement de la représentation du monde "russe" en Occident à la Renaissance*, Genève: Droz, 2003.

37. Bruno Naarden, "Nicolaas Witsen en Tartarye," available at: http://resources.huygens.knaw.nl/retroboeken/witsen/dutch_intro.pdf, accessed May 4, 2019; I. Wladimiroff, *De kaart van een verzwegen vriendschap: Nicolaes Witsen en Andrej Winius en de Nederlandse cartografie van Rusland*, Groningen: Instituut voor Noord- en Oost-Europese Studies, 2008; Marion Peters, *De wijze koopman: Het wereldwijde onderzoek van Nicolaes Witsen (1641–1717), burgemeester en VOC-bewindhebber van Amsterdam*, Amsterdam: Bert Bakker, 2010.

38. Christiaan Zandt, "Nederlanders en Siberië 1665–1725," unpubl. MA thesis, University of Groningen, 1997.

39. E. Waegemans, "De taal van Peter de Grote: het Nederlands als wereldtaal— een gemiste kans?," in *De taal van Peter de Grote*, ed. E. Waegemans, Leuven: Acco, 2006, 11–15; idem, *De tsaar van Groot Rusland in de Republiek. De tweede reis van Peter de Grote naar Nederland (1716–1717)*. Groningen, Antwerpen: Benerus, 2013; Janis Kreslins, "Linguistic Landscapes in the Baltic," *Scandinavian Journal of History* 3–4, 2003, 165–74; A. Croiset van der Kop, "K voprosu o gollandskikh terminakh po morskomu delu v russkom jazyke," *Izvestiia otdeleniia Russkogo Iazika i Slovestnosti* 15, 4, 1911, 1–72; R. van der Meulen, "Peter de Groote en het Hollandsch," *Onze Eeuw* 13 (3), 1913, 117–38; idem, *Nederlandse woorden in het Russisch*, Amsterdam: Noord-Hollandsche Uitgeversmaatschappij, 1959.

40. R. Hellie, *Enserfment and Military Change in Muscovy*, Chicago, IL: U. of Chicago P., 1971.

41. W.M. Reger, "In the Service of the Tsar: European Mercenary Officers and the Reception of Military Reform in Russia, 1654–1667," unpubl. Ph.D. diss., U.

of Illinois at Urbana-Champaign, 1997; E.J. Phillips, *The Founding of Russia's Navy: Peter the Great and the Azov Fleet, 1688–1714*, Westport, CT: Praeger, 1995; Fuhrmann, *Origins*; Esper, "Military Self-Sufficiency"; Michael C. Paul, "The Military Revolution in Russia," *Journal of Military History* 1, 2004, 9–45; B.N. Floria, *Russkoe gosudarstvo i ego zapadnye sosedi (1655–1661 gg.)*, Moskva: Indrik, 2010; A.V. Malov, *Moskovskie vybornye polki soldatskogo stroia v nachal'nyi period svoei istorii 1656–1671 gg.*, Moscow: Drevlekhranilishche, 2006; Carol Belkin Stevens, *Russia's Wars of Emergence, 1460–1730*, New York: Harlow, Pearson, 2007; Robert Frost, *The Northern Wars: War, State and Society in Northeastern Europe, 1558–1721*, Harlow: Longman, 2000; Brian Davies, *Warfare, State and Society on the Black Sea Steppe, 1500–1700*, London: Routledge, 2007. See also Kees Boterbloem, "Dutch Mercenaries in the Tsar's Service: The Van Bockhoven Clan," *War and Society* 2, 2014, 59–78.

42. Phipps, "Britons in Seventeenth-Century Russia"; Martha Luby Lahana, "Novaia Nemetskaia Sloboda: Seventeenth Century Moscow's Foreign Suburb," unpubl. Ph.D. diss., University of North Carolina at Chapel Hill, 1983.

43. V.A. Kovrigina, *Nemetskaia sloboda Moskvy i ee zhiteli v kontse xvii-pervoi chetverti xviii vv.*. Moscow: Arkheograficheskii tsentr, 1998; S.P. Orlenko, *Vykhodtsy iz Zapadnoi Evropy v Rossii xvii veka*, Moscow: Drevlekhranilishche, 2004.

44. A.V. Demkin, *Zapadnoevropeiskoe kupechestvo v Rossii v xvii v.*, 2 vols, Moscow: Institut rossiiskoi istorii RAN, 1994; idem, "'Rospisi karablem' zapadnoevropeiskikh kuptsov, sostavlennye v Arkhangel'ske v 1658 g.,'" *Issledovaniia po istochnikovedeniiu SSSR dooktiabrskogo perioda*, Moscow: Akademii Nauk, 1987, 89–113; V.A. Kovrigina, "Inozemnye kuptsy-predprinimateli Moskvy Petrovskogo vremeni," in *Torgovlia i predprinimatel'stvo v feodal'noi Rossii*, eds L.A. Timoshina and I.A. Tikhoniuk, Moscow: Arkheograficheskii tsentr, 1994: 190–213; Veluwenkamp, *Archangel*; Wijnroks, *Handel*.

45. Fuhrmann, *Origins*.

46. Longworth, *Alexis*; Joseph T. Fuhrmann, *Tsar Alexis: His Reign and His Russia, Gulf Breeze*, FL: Academic International Press, 1981.

47. See *Erik-Amburger-Datenbank: Ausländer im vorrevolutionären Russland*, available at: https://amburger.ios-regensburg.de/, accessed September 20, 2019.

48. Daniel Clarke Waugh, "The Publication of Muscovite *Kuranty*," *Kritika: A Review of Current Soviet Books on Russian History* 3, 1973, 104–20; Ingrid Maier, *Vesti-Kuranty 1656 g., 1660–1662 gg., 1664–1670 gg.*, vol. 2: *Inostrannye originaly k russkim tekstam*. Moskva: Iazyki slavianskikh kul'tur, 2008; idem, "Zeventiende-eeuwse Nederlandse couranten vertaald voor de tsaar," *Tijdschrift voor Media Geschiedenis* 1, 2009, 27–49; Ingrid Maier et al., eds, *Vesti-Kuranty 1656 g., 1660–1662 gg., 1664–1670 gg.*, vol. 1: *Russkie teksty*, Moskva: Iazyki slavianskikh kul'tur, 2009; Ingrid Maier and V.B. Krys'ko, eds, *Vesti-Kuranty 1671–1672 gg.*, Moskva: Azbukovnik, 2017; S.M. Shamin, *Kuranty xvii stoletiia: Evropeiskaia pressa v Rossii i voznikovenie russkoi periodicheskoi pechati*, Moskva-Sankt-Peterburg: Al'ians-Arkheo, 2011.

49. Erika Monahan, *The Merchants of Siberia: Trade in Early Modern Eurasia*, Ithaca, NY: Cornell UP, 2016. Also of note is Alexandra M. Haugh, "Indigenous

Political Culture and Eurasian Empire: Russia in Siberia in the Seventeenth Century," unpubl. Ph.D. diss., University of California at Santa Cruz, 2005.

50. A good roadmap is the Russian-translated selection of texts that have been digitized as *Rossiia-Rossika*, available at: http://www.vostlit.info/Texts/Dokumenty/Russ/rossica.htm, accessed September 23, 2019. For Kotoshikhin's work, see G. Kotoshikhin, "O Rossii v tsarstvovanie Alekseia Mikhailovicha," available at: http://www.hist.msu.ru/ER/Etext/kotoshih.htm, accessed September 30, 2019 (the work has been translated and annotated into English as well); [Avvakum], "Zhitie Protopopa Avvakuma, im samim napisannoe," available at: http://old-russian.narod.ru/avvak.htm, accessed September 30, 2019 (which has also been translated and annotated into English); K.N. Brostrom, ed., *Archpriest Avvakum: The Life of Archpriest Avvakum Written By Himself*, Ann Arbor, MI: Michigan Slavic Publications, 1979; for Tsar Aleksei Mikhailovich's correspondence, and so on, see the digitized documents that are available at: http://www.vostlit.info/Texts/Dokumenty/Russ/XVII/1640-1660/AlexejI/index.htm, accessed September 30, 2019; for Krizhanich, see J.M. Letiche and B. Dmytryshyn, *Russian Statecraft: An Analysis and Translation of Iurii Krizhanich's "Politika,"* New York: Blackwell, 1985; and for Tolstoi, see P. Tolstoi, *The Travel Diary of Peter Tolstoi: A Muscovite in Early Modern Europe*, ed. and trans. M. Okenfuss, DeKalb, IL: Northern Illinois UP, 1987.

51. E. Ysbrants Ides, *Drie-Jaarige Reize naar China*, second ed., Amsterdam: F. Halma, 1704, perhaps also belongs to these accounts, as this manuscript, written in broken Dutch by a native Dane about an embassy to China for Peter the Great, was edited by Witsen and first published in Dutch. See previous notes for Massa, Struys, and Witsen. For Goeteeris, see F. Blom and P. Bas-Backer, *Op reis voor vrede*, Zutphen: Walburg, 2014; for Coyett, see [Coyett, Balthasar], *Historisch Verhael of Beschryving van de Voyagie gedaan onder de Suite van den Heere Koenraad van Klenck*, Amsterdam: Jan Claesz. ten Hoorn, 1677, which still awaits an English translation; Van Keller's letters are heavily used by researchers (see, e.g., Bushkovitch, *Peter*), but have not yet been printed either. De Bruin was studied intensively for a few years during the 1990s in the Netherlands, but interest in his work has started to fade, although Aidarova and Fakhrullin (with my aid) have begun to write in Russian about some aspects of his work (see G. Aidarova, R. Fakhrullin and K. Boterbloem, "Istoriko-arkhitekturnyi analiz izobrazheniia Kazani gollandskogo mastera Kornelisa de Breina," *Vestnik St. Peterburgskogo Universiteta, Seriia: Istoriia*, 2, 2020 [forthcoming]). His book is Cornelis de Bruin, *Reizen over Moskovie: door Persie en Indie*, Amsterdam: R. and G. Wetstein et al., 1714 (first ed.: Amsterdam: W. and D. Goeree, 1711); see, for an example of the 1990s *hausse*, Cornelis de Bruyn, *Reizen over Moskovie. Een Hollandse schilder ontmoet tsaar Peter de Grote*, Ed. Kiki Hannema, Amsterdam: Stichting Terra Incognita, 1996.

52. For Lefort, see Moritz Posselt, *Franz Lefort. Sein Leben und seine Zeit*, 2 vols, Frankfurt: Joseph Baer, 1866, vol. 2, 55.

53. See Patrick Gordon, *Diary of General Patrick Gordon of Auchleuchries 1635–1699*, 5 vols, ed. D. Fedosov, Aberdeen: Aberdeen UP, 2009–2014. For Lefort, see Moritz Posselt, *Franz Lefort* (Posselt already mined this correspondence).

54. Wallerstein, *Modern World System*, vol. 2; J. De Vries and A. van der Woude, *The First Modern Economy: Success, Failure and Perseverance of the Dutch Economy, 1500–1815*, Cambridge: Cambridge UP, 1997; G. Parker, *The Army of Flanders and the Spanish Road*, Cambridge: Cambridge UP, 1972; idem, *The Dutch Revolt*, London: Allen Lane, 1977; S. Schama, *The Embarrassment of Riches*, Berkeley, CA: U. of California P., 1988; Jonathan Israel, *The Dutch Republic*, Oxford: Oxford UP, 1995; idem, *Dutch Primacy in the World Trade, 1585–1740*, Oxford: Oxford UP, 1989; Jan Glete, *War and the State in Early Modern Europe*, New York: Routledge, 2002; Julia Adams, *The Familial State: Ruling Families and Merchant Capitalism in Early Modern Europe*, Ithaca, NY: Cornell UP, 2007; Wim Klooster, *The Dutch Moment: War, Trade and Settlement in the Seventeenth-Century Atlantic World*, Ithaca, NY: Cornell UP, 2016; A.Th. van Deursen, *Plain Lives in a Golden Age*, Cambridge: Cambridge UP, 1991; Oscar Gelderblom, *Zuid-Nederlandse kooplieden en de opkomst van de Amsterdamse stapelmarkt (1578–1630)*, Hilversum: Verloren, 2000; David Onnekink and Renger de Bruin, *De vrede van Utrecht (1713)*, Hilversum: Verloren, 2013; David Onnekink and Gijs Rommelse, *The Dutch in the Early Modern World: A History of a Global Power*, Cambridge: Cambridge UP, 2019; Donald Haks, *Vaderland en vrede: Publiciteit over de Nederlandse republiek in oorlog, 1672–1713*, Hilversum: Verloren, 2013; Pepijn Brandon, *War, Capital and the Dutch State (1588–1795)*, Leiden: Brill, 2015; Marjolein 't Hart, *The Dutch Wars of Independence: Warfare and Commerce in the Netherlands, 1570–1680*, London: Routledge, 2014; O. van Nimwegen, *The Dutch Army and the Military Revolutions, 1588–1688*, London: Boydell Press, 2010; Clé Lesger, *The Rise of the Amsterdam Market and Information Exchange*, Aldershot: Ashgate, 2006; Benjamin Roberts, "Marlboro Men of the Early Seventeenth Century: Masculine Role Models for Dutch Youth in the Seventeenth Century?," *Men and Masculinities*, July 2006, 76–94; Michiel de Jong, *"Staat van Oorlog,"* Hilversum: Verloren, 2005; Adam Clulow and Tristan Mostert, eds, *The Dutch and English East India Companies: Diplomacy, Trade and Violence in Early Modern Asia*, Amsterdam: Amsterdam UP, 2018; Erik Swart, *Krijgsvolk: Militaire professionalisering en het ontstaan van het Staatse leger, 1568–1590*, Amsterdam: Amsterdam UP, 2006; Rudolf Dekker, *Childhood, Memory and Autobiography in Holland*, Basingstoke: Palgrave, 1999; Lotte van der Pol, *The Burgher and the Whore: Prostitution in Early Modern Amsterdam*, Oxford: Oxford UP, 2011; Anne Goldgar, *Tulipmania*, Chicago, IL: U. of Chicago P., 2008; Benjamin Schmidt, *Innocence Abroad*, Cambridge: Cambridge UP, 2001; David Ormrod, *The Rise of Commercial Empires: England and the Netherlands in the Age of Mercantilism, 1650–1770*, Cambridge: Cambridge UP, 2003.

55. N. Shields-Kollmann, *By Honor Bound*, Ithaca, NY: Cornell UP, 1999; idem, *Crime and Punishment in Early Modern Russia*, Cambridge: Cambridge UP, 2012; idem "Law and Society in Early Modern Russia," in *The Cambridge History of Russia*, ed. Maureen Perrie, Cambridge: Cambridge UP, 2006, 559–78; M. Khodarkovsky, *Russia's Steppe Frontier*, Bloomington, IN: Indiana UP, 2002; Chester Dunning, *Russia's First Civil War*, Philadelphia, PA: Pennsylvania State UP, 2001; V. Kivelson, *Autocracy in the Provinces: The Muscovite Gentry and Political Culture in the Seventeenth-Century*, Stanford, CA: Stanford UP, 1996; idem, *Cartographies*

of Tsardom, Ithaca, NY: Cornell UP, 2006; Peter B. Brown, "Early Modern Russian Bureaucracy: The Evolution of the Chancellery System From Ivan III to Peter the Great, 1478–1717," unpubl. Ph.D. diss. Chicago, IL: University of Chicago, 1978; idem, "Tsar Aleksei Mikhailovich: Muscovite Military Command Style and Legacy to Russian Military History," in *Military and Society*, eds M. Poe and E. Lohr, Leiden: Brill, 2002, 119–46; Brian Boeck, *Imperial Boundaries*, Cambridge: Cambridge UP, 2009; S. Dixon, *The Modernisation of Russia, 1676–1825*, Cambridge: Cambridge UP, 1999; I. Thyret, *Between God and Tsar*, DeKalb, IL: Northern Illinois UP, 2001. For an overview of Keenan's work (not wholly complete), see "The Bibliography of Edward L. Keenan," *Harvard Ukrainian Studies* 1, 1995, 1–22.

56. One key exception was the work done by Skrynnikov, and to some extent by his fellow Petersburger Anisimov; see, for example, R.G. Skrynnikov, *Mikhail Romanov*, Moscow: AST, 2005; idem, *Velikii gosudar Ioann Vaislevich Groznyi*, 2 vols, Smolensk: Rusich, 1996; E. Anisimov, *The Reforms of Peter the Great*, Armonk, NY: M.E. Sharpe, 1993.

57. Despite a number of exhibitions suggesting otherwise, such as during the late 1990s in Amsterdam commemorating Peter the Great's Embassy of 1697–1698, or a Russo-Dutch exhibition in Moscow and Enkhuizen in 2013, celebrating the Russia Year ("*Rusland jaar*") of allegedly 400 years of trade relations in the Netherlands and the Russian Federation (see V.E. Bulatov et al., *Russia and the Netherlands: The Space of Interaction, from the Sixteenth to the First Third of the Nineteenth Century*, Moscow: Kuchkovo Pole, 2013). Four hundred years was not quite precise: 450 might have been closer to the mark, if Flanders is considered a historical part of the region called the Netherlands or Low Countries; if not, then perhaps 1581 should be seen as the starting point, and the celebrations should have been held a generation earlier than in 2013. See as well "Terugblik Nederland-Ruslandjaar 2013," available at: https://www.rijksoverheid.nl/documenten/brochures/2014/06/11/terugblik-nederland-ruslandjaar-2013, accessed January 8, 2020.

58. Wijnroks, *Handel*, 65–105.

59. A good fairly recent overview of its significance in English is Milja van Tielhof, *The "Mother of All Trades": The Baltic Grain Trade in Amsterdam from the Late Sixteenth to the Early Nineteenth Centuries*, Leiden: Brill, 2002.

60. Witsen, *Moscovische reyse*.

61. One possible exception was the visit by the merchant Nazar Chistoi (who died, after he had become a government official, in the 1648 Moscow riots) in the early 1620s (Kordt, "Ocherk," ccxcvii–ccxcviii). According to Kordt, Dutch sources suggest that his visit went well, but Russian merchants in 1649 declared that he had not been sold any Dutch goods in Holland and had been sent home empty-handed, only to be offered the goods in which he had expressed an interest in while in Holland once he was back in Arkhangel'sk; earlier, in the 1570s, some Russians may have visited Dordrecht (Wijnroks, *Handel*, 118).

62. Another sign of an early awareness of the Low Countries' significance and an intricate knowledge of the commodities that their merchants traded is evident from the *torgovaia kniga* as analyzed by Gromyko (M.M. Gromyko, "Russko-Niderlandskaia torgovlia na Murmanskom beregu v xvi v.," *Srednie Veka* 1 [17], 1960, 225–58). It

may very well be that much more of such handwritten manuals were used to guide Russian traders who negotiated with their Dutch counterparts at Arkhangel'sk and elsewhere, but nothing yet has been found. Similarly, we can merely guess at the manner by which Dutch trading houses managed to develop a sophisticated understanding of Russian culture and language, as no clear evidence about this process has surfaced; for example, we do not know how the Dutch learned the language; one suspects that this was done during apprenticeships of their agents in Russia (particularly of young men), but who tutored them, for example, and in how far they read, wrote, or spoke Russian competently is not known. Virtually the only clue in this regard is presented in Van Zuiden, *Bijdrage*, 11.

63. *Pamiatniki diplomaticheskikh' snoshenii,* vol. 4, 754–1078. Some more will be said about this report in a later chapter.

64. Kotilaine, "When the Twain," 51.

Chronology

1237–1240	Mongol conquest of Eastern Slavic settlements.
1250s	Willem van Rubroeck (sometimes Ruysbroeck, a native of Flanders), courtier of the French king Louis IX (1214–1270), travels to Karakorum, the Mongol capital, passing through the southern reaches of Eastern Slavonic settlement.
1347–1351	Black Death pandemic in Europe, but the pest may have arrived already earlier in Eastern Europe, carried by Mongol-Tatar soldiers and traders.
Fifteenth century	Growing trade between the Low Countries (towns such as Zwolle, Deventer, and Kampen) and the Baltic littoral, where the Russian-speaking city states of Novgorod and Pskov are affiliated with the Hanseatic League to which those Dutch towns belong. Novgorod is a virtually independent city-state before the 1470s (Pskov maintains its independence from Moscow even until 1510).
1419–1467	Philip III (the Good) is duke of Burgundy. He unites a significant number of the Netherlands under his rule (Holland, Brabant, Zealand, Limburg, Frisia, Flanders, Artois, Hainaut), and establishes an Estates-General to consult with the inhabitants of all these territories in a joint assembly in 1463.
1421	On behalf of Duke Philip, Gilbert de Lannoy travels in Poland-Lithuania, and passes clandestinely through some of Muscovy's western territory.
1438–1439	Attempt at reunification of western and eastern Christianity by Council of Florence.
1453	Fall of the last remnant of the Byzantine Empire, Constantinople, to Ottoman Turks.

1462–1505	Reign of Grand-Duke (*Velikii Kniaz*) Ivan III, known as Ivan the Great. Muscovy establishes independence from the Golden Horde, part of the Mongolian-Turkic (Tatar) empire that has ruled it for more than 200 years. Expansion of Muscovite rule across north-eastern European borderlands. Ivan III is the first Russian to occasionally use title of *tsar*.
1466–1472	The Tver' merchant Afanasii Nikitin travels to India. Although no lasting commercial ties are established between Muscovy and South Asia, Russian merchants trade with various regions around the Volga and Caspian Sea in subsequent centuries, and eventually penetrate Siberia. Very few travel westward beyond Muscovy's borders to trade with Europe, however. Instead, Western traders come to Muscovy's border towns such as Novgorod and Pskov, and, later, Narva, Kholmogory, and Arkhangel'sk.
1471	Novgorod surrenders to Muscovy: Its submission to Ivan III is formally confirmed in 1478.
1472	Ivan III marries Zoe (Sofia) Paleologos, niece of last Byzantine emperor.
1467–1477	Charles the Bold is duke of Burgundy.
1477–1482	Mary (the Rich) duchess of Burgundy. She marries Archduke Maximilian of Austria (1459–1519, a member of the Habsburg family) in Ghent in 1477. The fate of the Low Countries now becomes intertwined with that of the Habsburg dynasty.
1480	*Standing* at the Ugra river. A Muscovite army faces a Tatar army without giving battle and the Tatar army withdraws, which is often taken as the end of Mongol rule over Muscovy.
1482–1506	Philip IV the Fair (b. 1478) is duke of Burgundy.
1500–1558	Charles V of Habsburg, eventually proclaimed King of Spain (in 1516) and Holy Roman Emperor (in 1519), while being ruler of the Netherlands as Habsburg heir to the Burgundian lands (formally since 1506).
1505–1533	Vasily III is grand-duke of Russia.
1517	First visit of Habsburg diplomat Sigismund von Herberstein (1486–1566) to Muscovy.
1533–1584	Ivan IV (the Terrible) Russian monarch. After a regency, Ivan is officially crowned as tsar in 1547.
1549	First publication of Herberstein's Latin description of Muscovy.
Mid-sixteenth century	The population of the Low Countries amounts to approximately three million people, with as many as two-thirds of them living in the southern parts of Brabant, Flanders, Hainault, and Artois (nowadays Belgium). Muscovy, after the conquest of the Volga khanates in the 1550s, has likely no more than eight million inhabitants.

1551	Founding of forerunner of English Muscovy Company.
1553–1554	The English merchant Richard Chancellor in Moscow.
1555	Philip (V, better known as Philip II of Spain, 1527–1598) succeeds Charles V as lord of the seventeen Netherlands.
1558	The English trader Anthony Jenkinson travels down the Volga and reaches Bukhara.
1558–1583	Livonian Wars, eventually pitting both Poland-Lithuania and Sweden together against Muscovy.
1562	Setting out from Muscovite territory, Jenkinson visits Iran.
1565	First (?) Dutch ship (still licensed by King Philip II's government) anchors at Kola peninsula (perhaps Philips Winterkoning had already visited this area even a few years earlier). The Flemish trader Winterkoning is robbed and killed by locals. A (likely seasonal) Netherlandish settlement nonetheless arises here, which engages in trading with local Orthodox monks. From here, the southern Netherlander Olivier Brunel travels to Kholmogory at the northern Dvina's mouth; he subsequently lives for several years in Russia. Another Dutch merchant active in the region at this time is Simon van Salingen.
1566	Beginning of iconoclastic wave in the Low Countries, usually considered the beginning of the Dutch Revolt. Van Salingen and De Meyer travel in disguise to Moscow, to demand compensation from the tsar for Winterkoning's murder and his lost cargo, but decide not to seek a meeting with Ivan IV, on advice of a friendly Russian merchant.
From about 1570 onward	Despite English protests (based on the belief that their Muscovy Company had been granted the monopoly to trade with the Russian at the Dvina mouth), merchants from the Low Countries begin to make inroads into the overseas trade with Muscovy by way of the White Sea. Brunel is a pioneer here, perhaps capitalizing from his clout as an agent (*factor*) of the Russian entrepreneurial family of the Stroganovs. Additionally, Brunel is an early explorer of northern Siberia (around the Ob river delta).
1578	Jan van de Walle and others from the Low Countries arrive in Kholmogory; they are in the service of Antwerp merchants, including the firm owned by the De Moucherons. At first, the Dutch explorers are not quite sure about their purpose, for, similar to the English before them, they are most interested in finding a north-east passage to East Asia. Soon, though, the De Moucherons begin to shift their trade from Narva (which is captured by the Swedes at the end of the Livonian Wars in 1581) to the northern Dvina.

1580–c.1644	George (Jurriaan) van Klenck, son of a German retainer of the Prince of Orange-Nassau.
1581	Fall of Narva to the Poles. In the following years, most Western European trading with Russia shifts to Kholmogory-Arkhangel'sk, despite Danish attempts to raise toll on it at the northernmost point of Norway. In Western Europe, Brunel meets the cartographer Mercator as part of an effort to mount an expedition to find legendary Cathay by descending the Ob river in the direction of Central Asia (toward Karakalpakstan); among his sponsors appear to be the Stroganovs. Brunel probably dies during his explorations finding this route around 1584.
1582	Cossacks in service of Russian entrepreneur Stroganov, led by Yermak Timofeevich, establish first Muscovite foothold in Siberia.
1584	Arkhangel'sk founded at mouth of northern Dvina on the White Sea; chartered by Ivan IV, it seems to be established to rival English-dominated Kholmogory. Assassination of Prince William I of Orange-Nassau (1533–1584) in Delft, who is eventually succeeded by his son Maurice (1567–1625) as Dutch administrative and military chief (*stadtholder/stadhouder*); accession of Fyodor I in Muscovy (ruled 1584–1598).
1585	Fall of Antwerp to Spaniards. The 1580s see a massive exodus of southern Netherlanders from Brabant, Flanders, and Wallonia to the northern provinces.
1585–1586	Van de Walle establishes a factory (i.e., office and warehouse) in Arkhangel'sk, which becomes the staple and residence of Russian authorities as their White Sea port, instead of Kholmogory; eventually (by 1591), English merchants move to Arkhangel'sk as well.
1590s	Steady Dutch trade (from 1595 at least 10 ships per year) with Russia. Among key shippers on Arkhangel'sk are Dirck van Os, Isaac le Maire, Balthasar de Moucheron, and Marcus de Vogelaer, all natives of the southern Netherlands, as well as the Italian-born Sion Lus. In this early era, many ships originate in ports other than Amsterdam, such as Enkhuizen, Hoorn, Harlingen, Stavoren, Purmerend, or Kampen.
1598	Edict of Nantes: Religious tolerance of Calvinists (Huguenots) in France decreed by King Henri IV. Franco-Russian relations, meanwhile, remain ephemeral until the later years of Peter the Great's rule. After being a Dutch ally for almost a century, the French become their greatest foe after 1660.

1598–1605	Rule of Tsar Boris Godunov.
1600s	Despite the increasing unrest in Muscovy that eventually leads to a civil war that will be accompanied by foreign invasions, Dutch trade with Russia via Arkhangel'sk continues unabated. It is apparently too lucrative to abandon, despite the risk of trading in a country torn apart by turmoil. At this time, this trade mainly saw Dutch merchants pay cash for Russian goods such as furs, *iuft* (*juchtleer*, a sort of leather), other hides, naval stores, tar, potash, and saltpeter.
1602	Founding of *Vereenighde Oostindische Compagnie* (*VOC*), the Dutch East India Company.
1602–1672	Peter Gabriëlszoon Marselis, scion of a refugee family from the southern Netherlands, who, together with his father and his brothers, will lead a mighty multinational trading firm. Peter Marselis will head the Russian branch of this company.
c. 1603–1613	Height (or low point) of Muscovy's Time of Troubles (*Smutnoe vremya* or *Smuta*)
1605	First False Dmitrii (supported by Polish-Lithuanian army) proclaimed tsar.
1606–1610	Tsar Vasily IV Shuiskii.
1609–1621	Twelve Year Truce between Spain and United Provinces.
1610	Assassination of King Henri IV of France.
1610–1612	Polish occupation of Moscow.
1611–1632	Gustavus Adolphus king of Sweden.
1613–1645	Rule of Tsar Mikhail Romanov.
1614–1642	*Noordsche Compagnie*, culmination of Dutch wanderings in Arctic area. It is intended as a monopoly trade company focused on whaling.
1615–1616	Dutch mission of Van Brederode, Bas, and Joachimi to Baltic to mediate in the conflict between Sweden and Russia.
1617	Treaty of Stolbovo between Sweden and Muscovy.
1618	Truce of Deulino between Poland-Lithuania (*Rzeczpospolita*) and Muscovy. The foreign interference in Muscovy, which began in 1605, finally comes to a close.
1618–1648	Thirty Years' War.
1619	Filaret (Romanov), father of Mikhail, elected Russian patriarch.
1621	Dutch West India Company founded.
1625–1647	Frederick Henry (Frederik Hendrik) stadtholder of Holland and Zeeland.

1628–1691	Koenraad van Klenck, who will become the successor of his father in one of the most successful Dutch trading firms on Muscovy (partnering with De Vogelaer family).
1630–1631	Albert Burgh's and Johan van Veltdriel's Embassy in Moscow.
1632	Founding of blast-furnace arms manufactory at Tula by Andries Denijszoon Winius.
1632–1634	Smolensk War between Muscovy and *Rzeczpospolita*.
1633	Death of Filaret.
1634–1635	First Holstein embassy in Russia; Adam Olearius (1599–1671) is its secretary; building of first "Russian" seafaring ship for (future) travels of Holsteiners; several Dutch shipwrights and sailors work on this project, and the ship's pilot is Dutch-born Cornelis Kluyting.
1636–1639	Second Holstein Embassy, on which Olearius serves again, visits Russia and Iran.
1639	Sea Battle of the Downs: defeat of "second" Spanish armada.
c.1640–1649	British civil wars.
1641–1716	Andrei Andreevich Vinius (Andries Andrieszoon Winius, son of Andries Denijszoon Winius).
1641–1717	Nicolaas Witsen.
1643–1715	Louis XIV (b. 1638) is king of France.
1645–1676	Rule of Tsar Aleksei Mikhailovich (b. 1629).
1646–1647	The Russian nobleman Il'ia Danilovich Miloslavskii and the government secretary (*d'iak*) Ivan Baibakov's embassy to the United Provinces; they return to Arkhangel'sk with a group of officers who had served in the Dutch army, three of whom go by the last name of Van Bockhoven (Isaac, Cornelis, and Filips Albert/Albrecht), and are accompanied by the French-born officer François Souhay who is their in-law, as well as their families. Soon after his return, Miloslavskii's daughter Mariia marries Tsar Aleksei.
1647	First publication of Olearius's travel account in German; it is soon afterward published in Dutch in several editions; printing of first nonreligious book in Russian, an illustrated text on military drill derived from Jakob de Gheyn's work of the 1600s (made for Stadtholder Maurice of Orange-Nassau).
1647–1648	Coenraad Albertszoon Burgh's Embassy in Moscow. He will become the Dutch Republic's treasurer in the 1660s.
1647–1650	William II is stadtholder of Holland, Zeeland, Utrecht, Overijssel, and Guelders.

1648	Peace of Münster between Spain and the United Provinces (Dutch Republic); Aleksei Mikhailovich weds Mariia Miloslavskaia. Tax revolt in Moscow, killing hundreds of people.
1649	*Ulozhenie*—a set of basic laws for Muscovy—issued; beheading of King Charles I Stuart in London.
1650	After death of William II, no stadtholder succeeds in Holland, Zeeland, Utrecht, Overijssel, and Gelderland before 1672.
Mid-seventeenth century	The Dutch Republic has probably slightly fewer than two million inhabitants; by 1670, Russia, including by then northern Siberia, eastern Ukraine, and Kyiv, has about 10 million inhabitants.
1652	Ban on Western foreigners living within the confines of city of Moscow; foundation of the *nemetskaia sloboda*, the "Western" foreigners' suburb, as new residence for Western and Central Europeans.
1652–1654	First Anglo-Dutch War.
1653	Dutch-born Andries Winius, Russian subject since 1648, purchases great amounts of arms (almost 20,000 handheld firearms) and ammunition in Amsterdam as agent for Tsar Aleksei.
1654	Treaty of Westminster between England and the Republic. Dutch Estates-General permits further large arms sales to visiting Russian emissaries (Polivanov, Golovin, and Nashchokin).
1654–1667	Thirteen Years' War between *Rzeczpospolita* and Muscovy.
1655	New Russian mission (led by Ivan Amirev) buying arms in the Republic.
1656–1658	Russo-Swedish War.
1658–1659	John Hebdon purchases arms for the tsar in the Republic.
1659–1660	At least four further Russian missions arrive in the Republic in search of new arms' sales. Two are led by Jan van Sweeden.
1660	Treaty of Copenhagen between Denmark and Sweden; Denmark loses Scania.
1662	Riots in Moscow against use of copper coins as currency.
1664–1665	Jacob Boreel Embassy, in which Nicolaas Witsen participates; Witsen meets suspended Patriarch Nikon.
1665–1667	Second Anglo-Dutch War.
1666–1667	Church Council in Moscow, condemning schismatics (*staroobriadtsy* or Old Believers) and deposing Patriarch Nikon.
1667	Truce of Andrusovo: Eastern Ukraine and Kyiv under Russian suzerainty. New Commercial Statute introduced in Muscovy, increasing import tariffs at Arkhangel'sk and other fees placed on foreigners' trade. Beginning of building of *Oryol* (Eagle) at Dedinovo on the Oka river.

1668	Death of Jan van Sweeden, foremost Dutch entrepreneur in Russia of the 1660s.
1669	Manned by a Dutch crew (including Jan Struys and Karsten Brandt), the sailship *Oryol* travels from central Russia down the Oka and Volga rivers to Astrakhan. It is abandoned there in 1670, never to set sail on the Caspian Sea, for which it had originally been purposed.
1670–1671	Height of Stepan Razin's Cossack rebellion along the Volga shores.
1672	Dutch "Year of Disaster" (*Rampjaar*): Republic invaded by the armies of the French king and the Münster and Cologne bishops, and war at sea with British and French navies. Prince William III of Orange-Nassau proclaimed stadtholder; brothers Johan and Cornelis de Witt lynched in The Hague, and their followers purged from Holland's city councils. Birth of Peter, son of Tsar Aleksei Mikhailovich.
1674	(Second) Treaty of Westminster between England and the Republic.
1675–1676	Koenraad van Klenck's Embassy to Moscow, which has Jan Struys and Balthasar Coyett in its retinue. Their (? the authorship of both treatises is contested) descriptions of Russia are soon after published in Amsterdam. Tsar Aleksei dies when embassy is in Moscow. The tsar's last favorite, Artamon Matveev, banished to Pustozer'sk.
1676	Death of the Frisian Mennonite entrepreneur Lus Tieleman Ak(ck)ema (born c. 1600), a one-time partner of Winius and Marselis, in Moscow.
1676–1681	Russo-Turkish War.
1676–1682	Rule of Fyodor III Alekseevich (b. 1662).
1677	Stadtholder William III of Orange-Nassau weds Mary Stuart, niece of Charles II Stuart, king of England.
1678	Death of Cornelis van Bockhoven at second Turkish siege of Chyhyryn. Peace of Nijmegen between Dutch Republic and France.
1682	After Fyodor III's death, his half-brother Peter (1672–1725) is at first proclaimed sole tsar, but Fyodor's sister and her relatives, the Miloslavskiis, incite a *strel'tsy* rebellion that costs several boyars their lives. The episode ends with the physically and mentally afflicted Ivan V (1666–1696), son of Mariia Miloslavskaia, and Peter I, son of Natal'ia Naryshkina, ruling as co-tsars. In effect, the Miloslavskiis rule, with Sofiia, Ivan V's sister, eventually acting as regent, aided by the boyar Vasily V. Golitsyn.

1683	Siege of Vienna by Ottoman army.
1685	Edict of Fontainebleau: Last vestiges of tolerance of French Huguenots abolished by Louis XIV.
1686	Eternal Peace: Kyiv definitively Russian.
1687	Russian military campaign toward Crimea, which never reaches peninsula.
1688	Landing of Dutch expedition led by stadtholder William III at Torbay; King James II flees London. Peter begins to receive instructions in mathematics and science from the Dutch merchant Frans Timmerman and in sailing from the Dutch sailor and shipwright Karsten Brandt, both of whom have spent decades in Russia.
1688–1697	Nine Years' War: France at war with Britain and the Dutch Republic.
1689	William III and Mary (daughter of King James II) proclaimed king and queen of Great Britain. Execution of Quirinius Kuhlmann on Red Square. Second Muscovite campaign that fails to reach Crimea. Regent Sofiia Alekseevna attempts to gain firmer control over Muscovy but is rebuffed by her half-brother Tsar Peter and his supporters, and removed from power in September. Treaty of Nerchinsk between Qing China and Russia.
1692	First edition of Witsen's *North and East Tartary* published. Everhard IJsbrandt Ides (b. 1657), a merchant from Glückstadt of Dutch ancestry, departs Moscow on an embassy for the tsar to China.
1696	Death of Ivan V. Peter sole ruler and firmly holds the reins of power. Azov captured.
1697	Treaty of Ryswyck: It proves no more than a short truce, as the impending Spanish succession leads to a renewal of the French conflict with the Anglo-Dutch coalition (which includes Habsburg Austria).
1697–1698	Peter the Great's Grand Embassy (consisting of some 250 people) to Western Europe (mainly Dutch Republic and England, the visit to Austria is cut short); he is for almost one-and-a-half year absent from Moscow.
1698	*Strel'tsy* rebellion in Moscow, suppressed by the Scottish mercenary general Patrick Gordon.
1699	Treaty of Karlowitz between Austrian Habsburgs and Ottomans. Death of Patrick Gordon and François Lefort, Peter's favorite foreign courtiers.

1700–1721	Great Northern War between Sweden and Russia with several allies, who drift in and out of the Russian-led coalition. Battle of Narva: Russian army routed.
1701–1704	Cornelis de Bruin (1656–1727) travels in Russia, which he depicts in his writing and illustrations that are subsequently published.
1702	After death of William III, no new stadtholder is proclaimed in Holland, Zealand, Utrecht, Overijssel, and Guelders.
1702–1713	War of the Spanish Succession, with France fighting Great Britain, the Dutch Republic, and Austria.
1703	St. Petersburg founded, on formally Swedish territory.
1706	Andrei Vinius absconds to Holland after falling behind Swedish lines near Grodno; Nicolaas Witsen, a distant relative and life-long friend, serves as his host and supporter before the tsar.
1707–1708	Bulavin rebellion along lower reaches of Don and Volga rivers.
1708	Vinius returns to Russia.
1709	Battle of Poltava: Major Swedish defeat; King Charles XII flees to Ottoman territory.
1711	Battle of the Pruth: Russian army vanquished by Turks and Tatars; Peter the Great has to sign humiliating peace treaty, losing, among other things, Azov again.
1713	St. Petersburg proclaimed Russian capital. Soon most of the government offices and nobles (often reluctantly) move from Moscow to St. Petersburg. Treaty of Utrecht, ending virtually uninterrupted 40 years of warfare between France and the Dutch Republic.
1714	Battle of Gangut (Hangö): First Russian victory (over Sweden) in a sea battle.
1716–1717	Peter the Great's second visit to Western Europe; this time, he visits France as well.
1721	Treaty of Nystadt between Sweden and Russia.
1725	Foundation of Russian Academy of Sciences. Beginning of Vitus Bering's first trip to Kamchatka.
1725–1727	Rule of Tsarina Catherine I, Peter the Great's widow.

Map 1. Europe in the early eighteenth century.

Map 2. Map of the Burgundian lands, made in 1881. NB: Amsterdam is missing, reflective of its yet minor status in 1475.

Chapter 1

The Prehistory of Dutch-Russian Relations; the English Pioneers

Before the 1548 definition of the Burgundian Circle's territory by Holy Roman Emperor Charles V as a discrete polity within the many lands he ruled, it may be a stretch to argue that any clearly circumscribed, common Netherlandic identity existed in the Low Countries.[1] Evidently, various versions of Lower-German vernacular were spoken in the north-western extremity of the European continent that may have resembled each other more than other German dialects and that began to find their way into print, as presses were established in the Low Countries not long after Gutenberg's Bible. Nonetheless, other languages were in use as well in several of the Burgundian Circle's territories, such as Frisian or French. The nobility throughout the region was often multilingual, as was much of the clergy, which still often communicated in Latin, as in their writing or when celebrating mass. Itinerant merchants, too, mastered a number of tongues. And although Charles V (and before him his grandfather Emperor Maximilian I of Habsburg[2]) had tried to create a geographically contiguous polity, the archbishopric of Liège was left out of his "Burgundian" realm.

Since they had remained Catholic to an overwhelming degree before 1550, the Low Countries' inhabitants might have unified around these common religious beliefs.[3] The provinces that made up the Netherlands shared certain geographic and economic traits as well. Among them were a comparatively high level of urbanization (with a high number of artisans living in towns); a fairly dense network of transport routes on land and on water, reflective of a considerable amount of overseas, river, and overland trade (with a great number of ports and staples); and an unusual degree of agricultural specialization (including fisheries). This economic profile challenged religious uniformity in the course of the sixteenth century, however, as the Burgundian Circle was not an inward-looking region of closed-off communities, but rather marked by a significant degree of openness, within and with the outside world fueled by its dense communication network. In addition, the level of its population's schooling—often necessary for trade and manufacturing—was considerable, while rudimentary reading aptitude was stimulated by the rapid spread of printed matter produced by numerous printing presses. Thus, even if the anabaptist movement had been almost extinguished after its brief spell of popularity in the 1520s and 1530s, Calvinism could spread like wildfire in the 1560s, especially because it found significant support among the nobles and urban elite.

Differences among the Netherlanders were probably greater than similarities in the middle of the sixteenth century, though, and it might therefore be questioned whether the first natives of the Low Countries who traveled to Russia (and left an account of it) should be called Dutch.[4] Indeed, even by *1700* a clearly marked Dutch national identity can hardly be precisely defined among the northern Netherlanders. They moved around and switched their political allegiance, and routinely chose for the country that had offered them a better existence, like any modern-day immigrant does. In the early modern age, too, many people objected far more stridently to having to change their religion than their sovereign. And the importance of belonging to a particular region, or even a city, or being part of a certain professional group (a sense reinforced by artisan guilds, for example) may have been much more meaningful than being a denizen of the Republic of the Seven United Netherlands that was officially recognized by most European states in 1648. Nonetheless, a sense of national solidarity was developing, or strengthening, in the quarter millennium from the age of Philip the Good to that of the king-stadtholder William III.

If we do cast the net of Dutchness wide and far in chronological terms, Willem van Rubroeck (who lived in the middle of the thirteenth century) and Gilbert de Lannoy (1386–1462) might be considered as pioneering Netherlandic-Russian travelers. They journeyed to the eastern borderlands of Europe in the Middle Ages. In Rubroeck's case, this was part of a much longer voyage in the 1250s that saw him reach the capital of the then hegemonic Mongolian empire (which had subjugated the lands inhabited by the Eastern Slavs, not long before, around 1240), Karakorum.[5] Rubroeck's Latin manuscript, although read at the French court in his day, only became more widely known when it was printed (as an English translation by Richard Hakluyt) in the sixteenth century. In it, Rubroeck described how he met "Russians" on his way further east, while passing through the western Mongolian capital of Sarai on the Volga, but Rubroeck dedicates a scant few words to this people.

We know as well that in Rubroeck's time knights from the Low Countries joined the "crusades" then conducted against the last pagans of Europe, the Baltic peoples, who included the Prussians, Lithuanians, and Latvians.

Netherlandic knights were likely part of the Teutonic Knights who in 1242 were defeated at Lake Peipus (in the famous Battle of the Ice) by Eastern-Slavonic Novgorod's army commanded by Prince Alexander Nevsky (1221–1263), a battle evocatively depicted in Sergei Eisenstein's eponymous film of the 1930s. The engagement put a halt to any crusading deeper into Christian Slavic lands. But, as far as we know, none of these "German" Knights left any surviving substantial account of his encounter with their Orthodox foes.

Nor did the Lower-Germanic or Dutch merchants who settled in towns along the Baltic coast, or in the interior of the rising Polish-Lithuanian state (founded in 1385 through the Union of Krewo), leave us with any substantial discussion of the Eastern Slavs. This, even though both the Eastern Slavic towns of Novgorod and Pskov conducted a fairly brisk trade with the Hanseatic trading league, which included at its western extremities the Netherlandic towns of Bruges, Zwolle, Zutphen, Deventer, and Kampen. Indeed, evidence exists as well that in the later Middle Ages peasants from the Low Countries moved to the Eastern European territories ruled by Polish kings and Teutonic knights, but they neither left any account of their encounters with "Russians." Of course, a lack of written sources does not mean that no such meetings occurred.

The breakdown of the Mongolian empire after 1300 ended for a while the interest among Western Europeans to travel through the remote lands in which Russians lived, as trading opportunities with Asia declined. By the middle of the fourteenth century, the Black Death raged throughout much of Asia and Europe; for several generations after Rubroeck's travels, then, few in the Low Countries showed interest in long-distance travel to the remote corners of northern Europe. The principalities of Russia itself (apart from Novgorod) did not appear to harbor much of any significant value that was cherished by late medieval Western Europe. The end of the *Pax Mongolica* saw various parts of easternmost Europe meanwhile go their separate ways. Russians became more culturally and linguistically distinct from the Ukrainians and Belarusians around this time.[6] After 1300, the Kipchaq khanate of the Golden Horde ruled the entire length of the Volga river's shores, but other Eastern Slavs succumbed to new military conquerors (such as Lithuania's grand dukes).

When around 1420 an envoy of the Burgundian dukes, Gilbert de Lannoy, set out toward Poland, Europe and Asia were recovering from the previous century's devastation.[7] After 1385, the Polish monarchs had joined the most powerful rulers in Europe, at a time when the ambitious Burgundian court sought recognition of its full sovereignty in its numerous territories, and displayed a strong curiosity about the world beyond the theater of the Hundred Years' War in which it was embroiled (1337–1453).[8] This war witnessed the rise of Burgundy as a third power in Western Europe next to England

and France. Its dukes at first vied for the French throne, but, after John the Fearless's murder in 1419, his son and successor Philip the Good (r. 1419–1467) began to carve out another, de facto sovereign, realm next to the French monarchy. Although he did visit the Polish court as an official Burgundian emissary, Lannoy did not visit Muscovy in any formal capacity; traversing Muscovy, he was disguised as a local merchant to avoid being spotted, since he did not apparently receive permission to travel there.[9]

Lannoy's travels to Europe's eastern borderlands did not immediately lead to any more intensive sustained contacts between the Low Countries and Russia, which began to wrestle itself free from Qipchak tutelage after 1450. Undoubtedly, Dutch traders may have visited Novgorod or Pskov in the fifteenth century, but few ventured further east in what was still seen as Mongolian or Tatar land. Some Russian emissaries attended the Council of Florence, which in 1439 saw Orthodox prelates (the patriarch of Constantinople was desperate to enlist Western support against the Ottoman Turks who had encircled the Byzantine capital by that time) end the schism between Orthodoxy and Catholicism that went back to 1054. Here Russian-Orthodox clergy must have met their Dutch-Catholic counterparts. But the Eastern Slavic emissaries who agreed to church reunification were denounced upon their return to Moscow, and it remained a dead letter. Otherwise, until the second half of the fifteenth century Russia continued to be a virtually unknown faraway land for Netherlanders, while almost all Russians seemed to show neither time nor inclination to intensify contacts with Europe west of Poland.

Columbus's explorations westward and the suddenly much faster distribution of news that occurred around the same time with the spread of printing presses coincided with the establishment after 1480 of an independent Muscovy, which included Novgorod and Pskov, under Grand-Duke (*velikii kniaz*) Ivan III (r. 1462–1505). While facing down the Tatars (the name by which the Mongols were better by then better known), Ivan's international renown increased when he married the niece of the last Byzantine emperor who had died during Constantinople's capture by the Turks in 1453. For bold North-Western European traders and explorers, as well as for inquisitive Netherlandic humanists, Muscovy, the land of the Russians, suddenly became a place of interest.

Right around 1500, the travels of those Netherlandic traders and explorers into those hitherto unknown parts on Europe's outskirts were triggered by another felicitous coincidence. Thanks to the Burgundian house's deft marriage strategies, the newly unified kingdom of Spain was linked to the Burgundian lands (and, indeed, to further Habsburg territories, as well as to the Holy Roman Imperial succession). The scale of trade conducted by the Low Countries with other parts of the world now vastly increased.

The Habsburg-Burgundian union allowed the port of Antwerp to become much bigger than the mere Western European trading hub that it (and Bruges before it) had previously been. Rather than Seville, where the Spanish silver fleet arrived from the Americas, Antwerp became the center of an overseas web of commerce that linked the Americas to Europe, the Mediterranean, Asia, and the Baltic: It was the heart of the first global economy around 1550. By then, nearby Amsterdam had begun to compete with the Hanseatic League along the Baltic shores, beginning to surpass the League's ports as the foremost shipper of Baltic grain after 1500. A search for ever richer fishing grounds, as well as a desire to discover other seaborne trade routes to Asia, saw Antwerp-and-Amsterdam-based sailors explore further north along the Norwegian coast, eventually reaching the North Cape and moving further eastward beyond it.

Evidently, in humanist circles some awareness of the newcomer in Eastern Europe was being diffused around this time. Albert Pigge (c. 1490–1542), a denizen of Kampen—one of the Dutch Hanseatic Towns—whose importance declined with the growth of Antwerpen—, was one of those who spread word about Muscovy. This papal envoy, better known as Alberto Campense, knowledgeably wrote about Russia, even if he may not have traveled there himself.[10] He had good sources, though: His relatives, who traded on Novgorod from Kampen.

Russia's rising significance was confirmed in the sixteenth century under the rule of Grand Dukes Vasily III (r. 1505–1533) and Ivan IV (r. 1533–1584). While before 1550 the country grew relatively little in size, when it was embroiled in conflict—especially with the surviving Qipchak-Tatar khanates along the Volga and on the Crimea—it held its own in these hostilities, as it did in the simmering conflict with Poland-Lithuania. By the 1550s, the young Ivan IV (born in 1530) was engrossed in a program of strengthening his rule domestically and preparing for wars with the faltering neighboring polities (south-) east and (north-)west of Moscow. In the midst of Ivan's successful drive to conquer the khanates along the Volga, in late 1553, English traders arrived in Moscow. In a search for a north-eastern searoute to eastern Asia, they had stumbled on Russian settlers at the mouth of the northern Dvina river. Having already lost two of their three ships and unsure how to proceed eastward, the English merchants, led by Richard Chancellor (c. 1521–1556), decided that a journey overland southward to meet the Russian tsar in Moscow might at least salvage something from what would otherwise have been a vain trip. Tsar Ivan, whose country traded with Western Europe through the cumbersome route via Novgorod and Pskov (Russia had no functional Baltic port), was interested in opening up a new trading route with the West. Ivan's government and the English Muscovy Company thus became regular trading partners.

NOTES

1. I am leaving out the Franche-Comté (Free County of Burgundy) that was included as well in that cluster of territories, since it was geographically, historically, and culturally a region discrete from the Low Countries.

2. Maximilian abandoned the earlier efforts by his father-in-law, the Burgundian Duke Charles the Bold (and possibly his father Duke Philip the Good) to recreate a sort of Middle Kingdom as once ruled by Lotharius, the grandson of Charlemagne, in the ninth century.

3. Even if this had been a Catholicism that was laced with popular traditions that had little to do with the uniform Catholicism as the Council of Trent (1545–1563) was trying to standardize at the time.

4. I have written elsewhere about this at some length and I will return to this point below as well (see, e.g., Boterbloem, *Fiction*, 36–9, 48–9, 172–4; K. Boterbloem, *The Dirty Secret of Early Modern Capitalism: The Global Reach of the Dutch Arms Trade, Warfare and Mercenaries in the Seventeenth Century*, London: Routledge, 2019, 83–4, 88–97).

5. See William of Rubroek, *The Text and Versions of John de Plano Carpini and William de Rubruquis as Printed for the First Time by Hakluyt in 1598 together with Some Shorter Pieces*, ed. C. Raymond Beazley, London: Hakluyt Society, 1903. In Russian available as "Puteshestvie v Vostochnye strany Vil'gel'ma de Rubruk v leto Blagosti 1253," available at: http://www.hist.msu.ru/ER/Etext/rubruk.htm, accessed September 30, 2019.

6. Best recent discussion is Serhii Plokhy, *The Origins of the Slavic Nations: Premodern Identities in Russia, Ukraine, and Belarus*, Cambridge: Cambridge UP, 2006.

7. See for Lannoy, for example, Joachim Lelewel, *Guillebert de Lannoy et ses voyages en 1413, 1414 et 1421, commentés en français et en polonais*, Bruxelles: Vandale, 1843.

8. The Burgundian dynasty developed from a cadet branch of the French royal house of Valois.

9. "Lannoy, Ghillebert de," in *Biographie Nationale . . . de Belgique*, vol. 11, Brussels: Bruylant-Christophe, 1890–1891, 308–22: 310, 313–14.

10. Alberto Campense, "Lettera d'Alberto Campense intorno le cose di Moscovia. Al Beatissimo Padre Clemente VII Pontifice Massimo," in *Ramusio's Navigationi* II, Milano: Eunadi, 1978–1988; M.E. Kronenberg, "Albertus Pighius, proost van St. Jan te Utrecht, zijn geschriften en zijn bibliotheek," *Het Boek* 28, 1944–1946, 107–58 and 226; and C.N. Fehrmann, "Albert Pigge, een vermaard Kampenaar," *Kampener Almanak* 1955–1956, 169–213.

Chapter 2

Flemish Trailblazers

The ascendance of traders from the Low Countries among Western European merchants in the "Russia Trade" may have started earlier than the greater volume of historiography charting the early English Muscovy Company—which hardly mentions the Dutch—makes it appear.[1] Erik Wijnroks's findings in Antwerp, Russian, and Dutch archives show that this prominence was not the consequence of Amsterdam entrepreneurs' addition of northern Dvina's estuary to their traditional bulk "Eastland Trade" on the Baltic. For about two decades just after the middle of the sixteenth century, this trade on Danzig, Riga, and some other ports included trade with Russia through Narva.[2] The opening up of the Artic Russian port for Netherlandic traders instead primarily resulted from Antwerp merchants moving further afield. After the early 1570s, those Brabantine traders gradually moved the headquarters of their operations in the Low Countries from Antwerp to Amsterdam, a process completed toward 1600.[3] Evidently, both the economic havoc wrought by the war against Spain in Brabant (Antwerp was first devastated by a Spanish mutiny in 1576 and then fell to the Spaniards after a siege in 1585), and Holland succeeding Flanders and Brabant as the center of the rebellion and the refuge of Dutch Calvinism all informed this shift.

As a further revisionist point, Wijnroks's work suggests that historians have overestimated the significance for the Netherlandic economy of the volume and value of the so-called bulk trade—mainly grain for Dutch-caught fish—over the "rich trade"—of Dutch-transported manufactured goods, wines, spices, jewels, bullion for grain, caviar, furs, hides, tar, potash, or lumber—of the Low Countries with the Baltic Sea and the White Sea.[4] The trade with the Baltic ports and Arkhangel'sk was of a much greater variety in terms of the assortment of goods than earlier historians suggested, although evidence that Dutch ships sailed in ballast and paid with cash for Russian commodities around 1600 shows that the Russian demand for goods originating in Western Europe was initially fairly low.

While the Narva episode (during the 1560s and 1570s) of the Russia trade set the table for the subsequent Dutch trade on Arkhangel'sk, even before the early 1560s traders from Holland and Antwerpen operated along the Kola peninsula, gradually making their way down on its eastern side into the direction of the mouth of the northern Dvina.[5] After Filips Winterkoning and Simon van Salingen traded with Russian monks at the Kola peninsula during the 1560s, Brussels-born Olivier Brunel (c. 1551–1584) truly established a Dutch presence along the White Sea littoral.[6] Brunel was the first Netherlandic native who lived for long spells in Russia—if we consider Narva as temporarily occupied rather than legitimate long-term Russian territory—working as an agent for the entrepreneurial Stroganov family.[7] Many were to follow Brunel's path into Russian service before 1725, often Russifying in the process.

By 1577, the Antwerp merchant Jan van de Walle had joined Brunel on his trips to the north.[8] Van de Walle's involvement appears to show that the Russia trade began to attract "big business," for his brother Jacques Van de Walle was a colonel in Antwerp's civil guard on the eve of its fall in 1585 to the Spaniards, reflective of a very high position in the city's social hierarchy; likewise, Balthasar de Moucheron, another of the city's magnates, appears as a Russia trader in the records in 1582.[9] Jacques van de Walle was married to a sister of Isaac le Maire, an eventually famous Flemish-Dutch explorer and entrepreneur.[10] And Jacques van de Walle partnered in Antwerp with Jacques Hoefnagel, brother-in-law of Joost de Vogelaer, the *pater familias* of one of the most prominent Dutch merchant families in the seventeenth century.[11] Joost de Vogelaer's daughter Margaretha lived in Muscovy around 1580, when she was married to Zacharias Glissenberch (d. 1586), the commander of Tsar Ivan IV's Livonian Guard.[12] Glissenberch seems to have been the liaison who provided the Van de Walle group with lucrative ties with the tsar's court, with Jan van de Walle's prominence at the Russian court provoking English envy.[13] Tsar Ivan IV's personal physician was a Dutchman as well: Johan Eylof, who together with his son Joris loaded himself several ships for the trade on the north around this time, further indication of the close link of some Netherlandic traders to Moscow's court in Ivan the Terrible's last decade.[14] Despite this sudden irksome emergence of Netherlandic competitors, the English usually remained on friendly terms with the Dutch, perhaps because from the mid-1580s they allied with the Low Countries' rebels in fighting Spain. For example, after Glissenberch's death in 1586, his 10-year-old son was only allowed to leave to join his mother and her Vogelaer family in Holland after protracted negotiations with the tsarist authorities, in which the English merchant Jerome Horsey played a decisive role as mediator.[15]

Together with those of others, the signatures of the eventually key Russia traders Dirck van Os and Balthasar de Moucheron (both were subsequently among the first East India Company investors as well) appear on the act of surrender of the city to the Duke of Parma's armies in 1585, reflective of their status as some of Antwerp's most important citizens.[16] Already before 1585, Antwerp merchants chartered ships in Holland or Zeeland involved in the Russia trade; among those northern Dutch shipowners partnering with them was the Amsterdam resident Jacob Bicker, a forefather of this city's most powerful regent family of the middle of the seventeenth century.[17] The Bickers were in turn related to the De Bitter (called *Gor'kii* in Russian) family, soon to be important Russia traders as well.

The activities of Van de Walle, Brunel, or Eylof in Russia coincided with the transfer of the center of economic gravity from Antwerp to Amsterdam in the Low Countries. This process was accompanied by a feverish search among Netherlandic merchants for trading opportunities in places near and far. Among the potential eldorados being explored was Russia. The Dutch quest for a permanent trading port there became more immediate because of the demise of Narva as a hub of the Russia trade (and the Kola peninsula offering very limited opportunities for trade) in the early 1580s, and possibly because of Novgorod's sack at the hands of Ivan the Terrible's *oprichnina* before that (in 1570).[18] From 1578 onward at the latest, ever more Netherlandic ships annually anchored in the northern Dvina's mouth in search of the popular scarce commodities Muscovy had to offer.[19] Already in the early 1580s several dozen northern and southern Dutch merchants traded with Russia.[20] Wijnroks suggests that most of the Dutch traders active in northern Russia collaborated closely with each other, already forming a "large network" throughout the 1580s.[21] Looking for a better protected harbor than Kholmogory, which had been used by the English Muscovy Company, Dutch traders petitioned the tsar in 1583 for permission to load and unload their wares near a monastery dedicated to the Archangel Michael; a settlement arose on a plot of land there that became the port of Arkhangel'sk.[22] The trade with Russia, whether through Narva, Riga, or the Dvina ports, yielded decent profits for most of the last third of the sixteenth century.[23] One of those who capitalized on the opportunity was the earlier mentioned Balthasar de Moucheron, who had his hand in many pots. Moucheron shared an interest with Olivier Brunel in finding a northern sailing route to the East (the two may have partnered in mounting such an exploration as well as in some other projects).[24] After abandoning Antwerp for Middelburg in Zeeland, Moucheron at first partnered with several other southern Netherlanders in his dealings with Russia; like others he chartered northern Netherlandic ships fitted out by Jacob Bicker.[25]

Evidently, while some took the lead in chartering the ships, holds were often filled up with commodities dispatched by a number of (other) traders, who parceled out the space available among each other. Sometimes the ship's captains or agents—such as Brunel, or Melchior de Moucheron—loaded coin with which to purchase Russian wares after arrival in the north. Wijnroks discerns a fairly generous spirit of collaboration among the various Dutch traders on Russia, as expressed, too, in a willingness to represent each other's interests before Russian trading partners or authorities, or look after the affairs of other merchants when in situ.[26] Later, too, Dutch merchants might behave as a cartel, as when they opposed Russian price manipulation with *iufti* (leather hides) around 1670, effectively ending the seller's attempts to crank up prices.[27] And as we will see, Dutch diplomats in Moscow might represent the interest of all of the Dutch trading community engaging in commerce with Russia even more than that of the government they served, the Estates-General at The Hague.

Although such solidarity may have been of some importance in this process, it remains largely opaque how exactly the Dutch began to best their English competitors by the end of the quarter century after their first arrival at the northern Dvina's estuary. Kordt was surely right in suggesting that substantial bribery of key tsarist officials and lavish gifts bestowed on the tsar himself played a significant role in the Russians' eager amnesia about earlier promises of an English monopoly on the overseas trade with Muscovy at the White Sea.[28] Van de Walle or De Moucheron were already extremely wealthy, the assets of all ventures of each likely easily outstripping those of the entire English Muscovy Company. In addition, the Dutch proved that they could supply the Russians better than the English with highly sought-after commodities (including spices, jewels, and bullion) and could ship far more goods from Russia.[29] After Narva's and Novgorod's decline, rare imported goods were all the more coveted by the Russians with whom the Dutch traded at Arkhangel'sk, as is evident of a Russian guidebook (*torgovaia kniga*) used in the 1570s to help Russian merchants find their way among the merchandise on offer.[30]

Gradually, the number of Dutch ships anchoring at the Dvina estuary increased, reaching more than 10 per year when Arkhangel'sk was officially founded in 1585.[31] A lot of the increasing Netherlandic advantage over the English—which becomes incontrovertible after 1606, see below—may have been based as well on the sustained efforts by Dutch agents to familiarize themselves with Russian conditions. The De Moucherons had one of their own large family stationed in Arkhangel'sk, while members of the De la Dale family (related to the Moucherons by marriage) appear as Russian-based representatives of Dutch trading houses for several generations, from the 1580s to the 1660s.[32] The example of Koenraad van Klenck shows how a number of the leading merchants themselves mastered the Russian language and were eminently capable of reading Russian cultural signs throughout much of the period studied in this book.³³ No such sustained intense efforts to study their interlocutors can be discerned on the part of the British after 1600, even if some individual merchants, such as John Merrick and John Hebdon sr (and his sons), or mercenary officers like Paul Menzies or Patrick Gordon—albeit both Scots—became well versed in the Russian language.³⁴

English efforts to undermine the increasing prominence of the Dutch merchants grew more intense toward the end of the sixteenth century, when they persuaded the Russian authorities to bar most Dutch traders from regularly visiting Muscovite territory beyond Arkhangel'sk before 1600.³⁵ Soon after 1600, however, this prohibition was waived for an increasing number of Dutch traders, among whom the young Jurriaan van Klenck and Isaac Massa emerged.³⁶ By 1606, the Dutch surpassed their English competitors.

***

Economically and politically, Russia entered a volatile period in the 1560s. Russian historians have established that the economic crisis associated with the last years of Tsar Boris Godunov (r. 1598–1605), which set the table for the civil war and foreign invasions that devastated Muscovy from 1604 to 1618, may have found its roots in the 1560s.³⁷ In the 1580s, Giles Fletcher, part of an English mission that visited Tsar Fyodor I (r. 1584–1598), noticed on his way from the border to Moscow many ruined villages, whose population had disappeared, because it had succumbed to hunger, disease, or warfare, or at least fled its ancestral home during the Livonian Wars (1558–1583).³⁸ The climate change associated with the "Little Ice Age" that visited Europe in the early modern era had a particularly strong effect on Russia's northern environment, parts of which were located within the Arctic Circle. Marginally positioned lands proved no longer suitable to crop tillage, yields diminished, malnourishment increased, physical resistance weakened. All of these short-term and long-term trends affected Muscovy's inhabitants both in body and in mind, and human desperation burst out in the Time of Troubles.

The Dutch traders whose fortunes were made in the Russia trade benefited from the opportunities offered them by a Muscovy succumbing to turmoil around 1600. Immense human suffering caused by failed harvests, epidemics, and war did not lead to a steep decline in the Muscovite appetite for Dutch commodities, however, nor did the loading at Arkhangel'sk diminish of Russian goods craved in Western Europe. This may have been due in part because some of the wares (timber, tar, potash, saltpeter, hemp) originated in the relatively tranquil northern parts of Russia, which were spared the worst of the Time of Troubles.

It is moot whether this "surplus" of Russian wares was produced by squeezing more out of the Russian peasants than ever; if so, it might be linked to the introduction of serfdom across virtually all of Muscovy, a process that gathered particular momentum in the century prior to 1649 when all peasants were definitively tied to the land in Russia. One infers that the Muscovite lords and the tsar's government, who survived from the proceeds of serf labor and the taxes the peasants paid, could thus better afford the expensive Western-brought goods that were offered them, but evidence is scarce to prove this case (a kindred process may have been at work in neighboring Poland-Lithuania, where serfdom spread as well around this time). Be that as it may, what remains curious is the almost uninterrupted flow of commodities—even when this undoubtedly included cash—shipped by the Dutch traders to Arkhangel'sk even in the direst years of the Time of Troubles.

Conversely, the Dutch merchants needed to be able to benefit from the chances thus offered. As we saw, they could do so at first because of the flourishing of Antwerp as a center of the European world trade. This momentum was sustained even during Antwerp's demise between 1576 and 1585, when much of the Brabantine mercantile community emigrated from Antwerp northward, and, especially in the case of the Russia traders, to Amsterdam. There they teamed up with northern Netherlanders who sometimes already sailed on Russia (like the Bickers), even if most of the northern merchants and navigators were traditionally involved in the Baltic trade.

The Antwerp–Amsterdam linkage of merchants with shippers proved a happy marriage that was to explore ever further horizons, seemingly checked only by the remoteness or hostile climate of certain parts of the globe. Around 1590 most of the Antwerp contingent that had been key players in the Russia trade had moved their residences northward, primarily to Amsterdam.[39] Among them were Marcus de Vogelaer (sr), Jacques van de Walle, Dirck van Os, Isaac le Maire, Jacques Bernarts, Balthasar de Moucheron, and Jan de Bitter. They combined their efforts with the Amsterdam Bickers, and a few people who moved to Amsterdam from elsewhere, such as the German-born Poppen family.[40] Even before their relocation to the United Provinces, all of them formed part of an intricate trading network with agents in various ports across Europe and they succeeded in expanding their family businesses exponentially in the 1590s and 1600s, participating in the veritable economic boom of the Northern Netherlands during this era. They sponsored such ventures as the foundation of the East India Company (*Vereenighde Oostindische Compagnie* or *VOC*), the financing of Henry Hudson's expeditions, Olivier van Noort's circumnavigation of the globe, the Dutch shipments of grain to Italy, and the great expansion of the trade with Russia.[41]

With regards to Russia and other faraway parts of the world, growth was eventually checked by market conditions. Russian demand for Western goods was great, but not insatiable. Returns were beginning to level off after the first flourishing stage, that might be said to have begun around 1580 and lasted until about 1632. The Russians were only up to a certain level capable of buying, or exchanging for, the commodities brought by the Dutch; around 1630, it became obvious that Muscovy proved unwilling—and was most likely incapable—to supply the vast amounts of grain that the Dutch traditionally carried in bulk from the Baltic ports back to Holland.[42] Evidently, seventeenth-century Russian supply, or demand, was not infinitely elastic.

Toward 1650, another surge in trading volume did follow, however, in part driven by the Russian demand for weaponry. Indeed, for almost a century more both sides proved inventive in discovering new products which they could exchange with each other, but by the 1720s the Dutch trading volume hit a ceiling. Some of this resulted from the Dutch complacency that began to emerge in the first decades of the eighteenth century and forced a comparative retreat before foreign competitors, but some of this leveling out and eventual decline resulted from the successful replacement of foreign-made goods by domestic wares (or import substitution) by Russian enterprises (not in the least the manufacturing of arms), which had frequently been founded by Dutch expatriates in the previous century.[43] By its very nature, this Dutch export to Russia of know-how and expertise was bound to be a merely temporary phenomenon. We will explore this development in somewhat greater depth further down in these pages.

To return to the beginning of the seventeenth century, it is remarkable how the Dutch merchants rather stoically faced the havoc of the *Smuta* that tore Russia asunder. Exactly during some of Russia's darkest moments, Netherlanders entrenched themselves as the key suppliers of scarce foreign goods, not in the least bullion and arms (which were smuggled, since weapons' exports to Muscovy were formally prohibited by the United Provinces' authorities).[44] While the Time of Troubles laid waste to Russia in the years following 1600, Dutch trade continued almost unabated, even if various merchants and their agents (called *factors*) were occasionally caught in the crossfire.[45]

Many of the Dutch merchants had lived themselves at home through a similar existential crisis in their home country between 1566 and 1590 and had come up trumps: Was this the reason that they successfully managed to navigate the mayhem that overwhelmed Russia after 1600? Were they more used to taking unusual risks than their competitors as a consequence?

Wijnroks plausibly suggests as well that points were scored through the manner by which some Netherlandic merchants defied harassment by Polish-Lithuanian marauders; they thereby improved their standing in Russian eyes as steadfast allies facing down Muscovy's foreign foes.[46] Among those pillaged was Jurriaan van Klenck, who managed to cash in on his sufferings in 1613, when the new tsar granted him and his partners, the De Vogelaers, extensive trading privileges as a sort of compensation for the harm that had been done to him by plunderers identified as Polish-Lithuanians (rightly or not).[47]

Certainly, by the time of Mikhail Romanov's coronation in 1613, the Dutch outstripped the other Western Europeans, especially the English, trading with Russia by way of the White Sea harbor. Around 1606, the crucial shift occurred that saw the Dutch share in the trade on Arkhangel'sk surpass that of the English, an advantage they kept for the rest of the seventeenth century.[48] In part, the Dutch seemed most adept at changing the assortment of goods they brought to this northern port, especially once they began to transport arms and ammunition that were then in high demand in a Russia that was torn asunder.[49] After the worst of the domestic turmoil was overcome by 1613, Muscovy's armed conflict with Sweden and Poland that continued to flare up throughout the seventeenth century kept the Dutch busy in the arms trade.

By the mid-1610s, the domestic political crisis in Muscovy abated, even if the seventeenth century witnessed several more episodes of grave turmoil within the tsar's realm. Throughout it all, though, the Dutch staunchly continued to ship goods to and from Arkhangel'sk and explored and exploited the other lucrative economic opportunities early Romanov Russia seemed to offer them. Their prominence only faded when the economic boom of their own country itself began to wilt.

Of course, not all Dutch merchants made a fortune in the Russia trade, and some went bankrupt, as did the business of the Van de Walle brothers around 1590.[50] Its collapse was expensive as well for some of the other investors in their company, among whom were Joost de Vogelaer's widow, Jacques Bernarts, Balthasar de Moucheron, and Hendrick Fentsel (Fenzel).[51] Different from the Van de Walles, who had to sell most of their assets to their creditors, all of the others appear to have been able to survive their losses in the venture.

NOTES

1. Wijnroks, *Handel*, 27.
2. For Narva's temporary prominence, see Kordt, "Ocherk," xiv–xviii; and Wijnroks, *Handel*, 65–105. Wijnroks suggests that Ivan IV was interested in capturing Narva in part because he wanted to establish regular contacts with Antwerp (Wijnroks, *Handel*, 125). Wijnroks points out as well that, prior to Narva's rise as a hub for Russian exports (next to Riga), Muscovite commodities had been sluiced through Lübeck, which remained crucial as a destination for goods from Narva until 1581 (Wijnroks, *Handel*, 131–3).
3. Wijnroks, *Handel*, 21–7, 58, 61–3.
4. Ibid., 27, 52, 125–56.
5. Kordt, "Ocherk," xix–xvi; Wijnroks, *Handel*, 106.

6. T.S. Jansma, "Olivier Brunel te Dordrecht," *Tijdschrift voor Geschiedenis* 59, 1946, 337–62; Kordt, "Ocherk," xxx–xxxiii; Wijnroks, *Handel*, 106–11, 117–18. For his death, see Wijnroks, *Handel*, 124.

7. Kordt, "Ocherk," xxxiii, xxxvi–xlii; Wijnroks, *Handel*, 117–18, 149.

8. Wijnroks, *Handel*, 107.

9. Ibid., 63, 112–15, 120; J.H. de Stoppelaar, *Balthasar de Moucheron. Een bladzijde uit de Nederlandse handelsgeschiedenis tijdens den Tachtigjarigen oorlog*, 's-Gravenhage: Nijhoff, 1901; Kordt, "Ocherk," xlii–iii. Van de Walle's partners were father and son Gillis Hooftman.

10. Wijnroks, *Handel*, 116. See, too, Joost Jonker and Keetie Sluyterman, *At Home on the World Markets: Dutch International Trading Companies from the Sixteenth Century until the Present*, The Hague: SDU, 2000, 56–7.

11. Wijnroks, *Handel*, 116.

12. Ibid., *Handel*, 116–17, 244. Glissenberch was a veteran of the Dutch battlegrounds of the 1570s, where he had been involved on the Habsburg side in the siege of Amersfoort in 1572.

13. For the beginnings of this English suspicion as reflected in print, see Isabel de Madariaga, *Ivan the Terrible*, New Haven, CT: Yale UP, 2005, 348. See Wijnroks, *Handel*, 154–6.

14. Wijnroks, *Handel*, 119, 121.

15. Ibid., *Handel*, 244. See also Arel, *English Trade*, 8–10; as well, see Alison Games, *The Web of Empire: English Cosmopolitans in an Age of Expansion, 1560–1660*, Oxford: Oxford UP, 2008.

16. Wijnroks, *Handel*, 64, 251; Kordt, "Ocherk," c–ci.

17. Wijnroks, *Handel*, 121.

18. See the memorandum written in 1589 on the benefits of the trade with Russia that was unearthed by Kordt (Kordt, "Ocherk," lxx–lxxii); Wijnroks, *Handel*, 150.

19. Kordt, "Ocherk," xxxiii–iv. Initially, Van de Walle (at the Pudozhemskii mouth of the Dvina) and the Muscovy Company (which used the "Redrose Island") each used another location than where Arkhangel'sk arose after 1583 (see also ibid., lvi).

20. Wijnroks, *Handel*, 123.

21. Ibid., 112. See as well Jonker and Sluyterman, *At Home*, 39–40.

22. Kordt, "Ocherk," liv–lvi; see as well M.S. Arel, "The Archangelsk Trade," in *Modernizing Muscovy*, eds J. Kotilaine and M. Poe, London: Routledge, 2004, 175–201.

23. Wijnroks, *Handel*, 169.

24. Kordt, "Ocherk," xlii–xlv; Wijnroks, *Handel*, 120.

25. Wijnroks, *Handel*, 120–2; for a fairly typical contract drawn up in those early days, see that of Marcus de Vogelaer with captain Sybrandt Jacobsz, who hailed from the village of Akersloot, and sailed the ship *Jonas*, an agreement concluded in 1598; De Vogelaer rented the entire hold, but the trip was to include one or more stops at Kola and elsewhere on the way to Arkhangel'sk and back, where goods might be unloaded and loaded according to the merchant's (or his agent's) instructions (Van Zuiden, *Bijdrage*, 34–6).

26. Wijnroks, *Handel*, 123, 239.
27. Kotilaine, "When the Twain," 50.
28. Kordt, "Ocherk," lxiv–lxvii; Wijnroks, *Handel*, 154–5, 173–8. Meanwhile, some English merchants partnered with traders from the Low Countries, as did Jerome Horsey, who invested in Van de Walle's company (Wijnroks, *Handel*, 241).
29. Wijnroks, *Handel*, 150, 155, 173–7.
30. Ibid., 151–3. For an in-depth discussion of this text, see Gromyko, "Russko-Niderlandskaia torgovlia," 227, 229–38, 247–55.
31. Wijnroks, *Handel*, 154.
32. Ibid., 239.
33. See also ibid., 245, 249–50; and Van Zuiden, *Bijdrage*, 11.
34. See Phipps, *Sir John Merrick*; Gordon, *Diary*.
35. Kordt, "Ocherk," lxxiv; Van de Walle was an exception (see Wijnroks, *Handel*, 154–5).
36. Kordt, "Ocherk," lxxv–lxxvi, lxviii; Wijnroks, *Handel*, 245–6.
37. See E.I. Kolycheva, "The Economic Crisis in Sixteenth Century Russia," in Dan Kaiser and Gary Marker, eds *Reinterpreting Russian History: Readings, 860–1860s*, Oxford: Oxford UP, 1994, 165–70.
38. Giles Fletcher, *Of the Russe Commonwealth*, ed. R. Pipes, Cambridge, MA: Harvard UP, 1966 [London: Thomas Charde, 1591].
39. Wijnroks, *Handel*, 222–4.
40. Ibid., 254–5.
41. The *VOC*'s biggest initial shareholders were mainly emigrés from the southern Netherlands (see Wijnroks, *Handel*, 225).
42. Wijnroks, *Handel*, 303.
43. On this, see Boterbloem, *Dirty Secret*.
44. Kotilaine, "When the Twain," 104–15; Wijnroks, *Handel*, 216, 229.
45. Kordt, "Ocherk," lxxix–lxxx.
46. Wijnroks, *Handel*, 216. A key figure among the English merchants was John Merrick (c. 1560–c. 1638; see Phipps, *Sir John Merrick*).
47. Wijnroks, *Handel*, 247–8. For his petition to the tsar describing how he was plundered, see below.
48. Ibid., 306.
49. Kordt, "Ocherk," lxxx–lxxxi.
50. Wijnroks, *Handel*, 241.
51. Fenzel's nephew would be a key Russia trader in the 1640s and was an uncle of Jurriaan van Klenck's wife Geertruida (ibid., 241–3, 248, 256–7; Arel, *English Trade*, 116–17).

Chapter 3

New States on Europe's Fringe

The meteoric rise of the United Provinces and Muscovy to the ranks of Europe's most significant polities after 1600 indicates how the strength of early modern states was more apparent than real.[1] Perhaps this is why an expensive show was mounted when Dutch embassies visited foreign courts such as that of the tsar. Such costly forays were more about projecting than reflecting power. For all of the Dutch economic wealth, Louis XIV (1638–1715) might have vanquished the Republic in 1672, if the French king's military campaign had moved at slightly greater speed. This weakness can be likewise argued for the Russian case: In 1610, when Moscow was occupied by Polish-Lithuanian soldiers, the state of Muscovy teetered on the verge of extinction, after which it arose astonishingly swiftly from its ruin again. If the Polish king Sigismund III Wasa (1566–1632) had acted more decisively, however, the state of Muscovy might have definitively been erased from the map. Instead of vanishing, both early Romanov Russia and the United Provinces survived the grave threats to their existence. They meanwhile found each other in a mutually beneficial relationship, strengthening both sides, though in different respects: its prime beneficiaries were the Russian government (mainly the tsar and his entourage of high-ranking boyars, officials, and clergy), and Dutch private individuals (rather than its government).

Of course, the Low Countries had been a significant player in Western Europe in economic and cultural terms since at least the fourteenth century as part of a larger polity, but its political center tended to be outside the territory that would become the Dutch Republic. The sudden arrival of the northern Netherlands as a political and economic power was part of a larger shift around 1600 that saw Europe's center of economic gravity move from the Mediterranean Sea and its shores toward its north. It appeared as if places hitherto unnoticed, with little political clout or economic significance previously, moved on to the main stage of European affairs. England and the northern Netherlands forged ahead first, while Sweden temporarily acquired noticeable political importance as well. Muscovy, too, had been a mere secondary Power in northern Europe since the mid-fifteenth century. But this meager regional significance was suddenly magnified after 1600, catapulting the United Provinces to a temporary, and Russia into a longer-lasting, status of Great Power.

While Poland-Lithuania was formally a formidable empire, its economy was weak and its ostentatious political strengthening from 1568 onward through greater centralization proved ephemeral. This was in part because in this elective monarchy the newly ruling Wasa dynasty never quite acquired as firm a foothold as the preceding Jagiellonian dynasty. With the *Rzeczpospolita* ever more falling prey to internal strife in the seventeenth century (leading to its almost collapse in the mid-1650s), the power vacuum this created in this part of Europe was relatively quickly filled by the ascendant states of Brandenburg-Prussia and Russia. Perhaps newly significant states that emerged around 1650 such as the Dutch Republic, England (and Scotland), Sweden, Prussia, or Russia were not significantly stronger in politico-military terms than Spain, the Ottoman Empire, or Poland-Lithuania had been previously; after all, they were likewise equipped with infinitely small central bureaucracies and prone to sudden implosion when faced with internal or external challenges. But the governments of this quintet of states were all able to add territory (both inside and outside Europe), ramp up their military, and strengthen their political control over their realm.

The United Kingdom, Prussia, and Russia became major European players after 1700, whereas Sweden and the Republic faded, falling back into a second or even third tier of states joining the further declining Spain, Poland-Lithuania, and Ottoman Empire (which proved most resilient). But this was not a smooth or inevitable process, even if hindsight makes it seem this way. The fate of almost all these polities hung in the balance throughout the seventeenth century, however, as a study of any of the crises of this age appears to show. It is not inconceivable that the Dutch Republic might have remained a significant European power (especially if William III had not fallen from his horse in 1702), for example, if the southern Netherlands had been acquired in the course of the conflict best known as the War of the Spanish Succession (1700–1713). Meanwhile, Russia's road to greatness was by no means inevitable either. Had it not been faced by a feeble *Rzeczpospolita*, an overextended Ottoman Empire, and an overly cautious Prussia after Peter the Great's death in 1725, it might have faced another reckoning during the shaky period that ensued his passing.[2]

As it was, however, it was the Dutch who vanished and the Russians who emerged ever more emphatically on the European scene after the first quarter of the eighteenth century. It was a constant struggle to stay ahead in Europe throughout the early modern era: The Dutch managed for more than a century, perhaps for even 150 years, but eventually succumbed to a sort of collective exhaustion and a shared desire for a more peaceful existence in the Republic, a complacency which proved fatal in the 1780s and 1790s. The Russians managed to maintain the effort, but the price for their Great-Power status was steep in another way. Long before Peter's reign, Russia's political and military power was mainly achieved through squeezing almost every drop out of its population, obliging everyone to sacrifice themselves on behalf of the empire, from cruelly exploited serfs to the deployment of soldiers who served their country all their lives. The prime raison-d'être of all people, from high to low, was that of being the state's servants (as Peter the Great even admitted about himself) rather than existing as autonomous human beings.

NOTES

1. Arguing the opposite, to some degree, is Glete, *War and the State*.
2. Or if the Turks had not released Peter so easily after the disastrous Battle of the Pruth in 1711.

Chapter 4

De Vogelaer and Van Klenck

The late-Imperial-Russian historian Veniamin Kordt suggested that even before he was formally proclaimed tsar in Moscow, the teenaged Mikhail Romanov met Jurriaan van Klenck, who was among a group of Dutch merchants paying their respects to the new tsar in the town of Yaroslavl in 1613.[1] Van Klenck took the opportunity to explain to Russia's new ruler that he had suffered great losses because of "Lithuanians" having destroyed his goods (which were transported from Arkhangel'sk to Moscow) in Tot'ma during the Troubles; they had wounded him as well in a skirmish, while his company's warehouse in Moscow and its contents had been destroyed by fire during the city's recent Polish-Lithuanian occupation.[2] Together with his business partners, Marcus de Vogelaer's widow, Margaretha van Valckenburch (1565–1650), and her sons, Van Klenck was offered compensation for his damages by Mikhail's government through a reduction in the tolls and fees levied on his merchandise (Marcus De Vogelaer sr had enjoyed such a privilege previously[3]), while the looted warehouses in Arkhangel'sk, Kholmogory, and at Kola were returned to his firm.[4] Eventually, the De Vogelaer-Van Klenck company even received several years of full dispensation of paying any sales taxes to reimburse it for its severe losses during the Troubles. These privileges were among the most generous the tsar ever granted to Dutch merchants.[5]

The Van Klenck-De Vogelaer business was to remain one of the most significant trading partners of the Russians until the 1680s (when much of its business seems to have been taken over by Adolf Houtman).[6] Wijnroks suggests that they may have employed some 50 people in Russia alone in the 1630s.[7] Like De Vogelaer-Van Klenck, Karel du Moulin's (1588–c. 1655) consortium operated a number of warehouses along the route from Arkhangel'sk to Moscow.[8] Van Klenck and Du Moulin served as leading representatives of large companies almost in the manner of chief executive officers of businesses in today's United States. They were backed by a number of investors and managed a staff numbering dozens of people both in Holland and in Russia. They acquired great riches during the early decades of Romanov rule, currying favor with the tsar and ranking officials and boyars through lavish gifts and payments (even when tariffs were levied their trading volume seems to have hardly diminished).[9]

The Glissenberch-De Vogelaer marriage may have already reflected Joost de Vogelaer's significant early involvement in the Russia trade.[10] Russia traders such as Joost's son, Marcus de Vogelaer sr, his wife Margaretha, and their sons engaged in the marriage politics typical for the Dutch elite, which reinforced their business network. Sometimes that meant that daughters of one mercantile family wed sons of another; sometimes marriages were concluded with scions of regent families, which for the Brabantine immigrants to the north was a way of gaining access to the highest political circles in the United Provinces. While one of the elder Marcus de Vogelaer's sisters was married to Ivan the Terrible's chief bodyguard, his wife's sister Elisabeth van Valckenburch married Jacob Cats (1577–1660), the Dutch national poet and longtime chief administrator (*Raadspensionaris*) of the province of Holland.[11] Cats's son-in-law was the legendarily corrupt Recorder (*Griffier*) of the Dutch Estates-General, Cornelis Musch (c. 1592–1650), who served in that post from 1628 to 1650. The De Vogelaer-Van Valkenburch women evidently married men who occupied the highest positions in the country's economy and government. The hostility around 1630 that infected political The Hague against Isaac Massa, a formidable De Vogelaer-Van Klenck business rival, was therefore no accident (see below).

In this period, such nepotism and corruption were barely ever recognized as truly unethical practices in the search of mammon (even if Musch's behavior eventually did grate).[12] By 1600, the Dutch had moved far away from the medieval church's indictment of interest as usury. Especially in international transactions entrepreneurs were bereft of any legal recourse if things went wrong. Profit margins were substantial, for risk was high and loss could be crippling, as Jurriaan van Klenck found out at Tot'ma in the Time of Troubles (or might even lead to bankruptcy, as Jan van de Walle experienced before that). Some forms of insurance were developed, but none yet provided full coverage, a solid safeguard against adversity. Every means needed to be harnessed to ensure profit, and this included marriage politics and bribing politicians: Koenraad van Klenck undertook a somewhat clumsy and fruitless attempt to bribe the tsar's favorite Artamon Matveev in 1676 (although more out of a sense of obligation to the Republic's allies who urged him to do so than a genuine personal conviction it might work).[13] Patronage by the highest people in the land was sometimes brought into play: Jurriaan and Koenraad van Klenck enjoyed the support of the Orange-Nassau family. Their ancestors had already been Nassau retainers in Germany in the middle of the sixteenth century. This support occasionally proved quite useful. And it appears as well that Jurriaan on his visits to Moscow had few scruples in sharing what we would now call strategic information with the tsar: His first loyalty was to his business, not his country.

De Vogelaer and Van Klenck's modus operandi also included a willingness to sell or buy any commodity that might yield a return. Thus, Koenraad van Klenck sold arms to Russia and oversaw a restructuring of the administration of the Dutch slaveholding colony of Surinam in the 1680s without any pangs of conscience, even if he was a religious man who when Dutch ambassador to Muscovy made sure that he brought a Calvinist minister along with whom he worshipped on Sunday.[14]

Since little easily traceable evidence survives today of the once mighty De Vogelaer-Van Klenck business, historians tend to have overlooked its oversized power and influence in the seventeenth-century United Provinces, as they have with respect to some of the other firms that reaped the benefits of the Russia trade, such as those of Du Moulin, Marselis, Ruts, the Bernard (Bernarts) family, or even Massa.[15] Occasionally, Margaretha de Vogelaer-van Valckenburgh shows up as the anomalous—and therefore noteworthy—woman in the man's world of the *VOC* as one of the "Seventeen Gentlemen," the *Heeren XVII*, its 17-head strong board.[16] But it has remained opaque in much of the literature that, similar to many London merchants with global interests who first honed their skills in the Muscovy Company, the Dutch East India traders often started out on the path to fortune with trading on closer-by Russia (as had the de Vogelaer-Van Valckenburgh clan).[17]

What is furthermore remarkable about the firm of De Vogelaer and Van Klenck is its longevity.[18] While the *VOC* did indeed survive for almost 200 years, hardly any private Dutch business has ever been so successful. The lifespan of this family venture encompassed four generations, respectively, that of Joost, of Marcus sr and Margaretha, of their sons and Jurriaan van Klenck, and, finally, of Koenraad. From 1672 onward, Koenraad van Klenck seems to have withdrawn from his business when, as Amsterdam council member, Dutch ambassador, or Amsterdam's judge and commissary of naval affairs, he became too preoccupied with his city's government, but even then he transferred many of his Russian assets to Adolf Houtman, who continued to reap their substantial benefits. From Joost de Vogelaer in the 1570s to Adolf Houtman in the 1700s, the existence of the firm almost exactly coincides with the time period with which this book is concerned. Such a length of time is significant for any private company in capitalism's history. The Russia trade as, we will see further below, was indeed remarkably lucrative and the Russian connection made many a Dutchman's (and occasionally Dutch woman's) fortune.

NOTES

1. In *The Dirty Secret*, I have explained why "George" van Klenck went by the name of "Jurriaan" (see Boterbloem, *Dirty Secret;* Kordt, "Ocherk," cii–ciii).
2. Kordt, "Ocherk," cccxix–cccxxiii; Arel, *English Trade*, 26–7.
3. More on him may be found in Wijnroks, *Handel*, 244–5.
4. Ibid., 247–8, 294–5. They also involved the De la Dales in their firm. For more on Van Valkenburch, see *Digitaal Vrouwenlexicon van Nederland*, available at: http://resources.huygens.knaw.nl/vrouwenlexicon/lemmata/data/Valkenburch, accessed January 14, 2020.
5. Only the arms trader Hendrick van Ringen seems to have enjoyed full dispensation from paying tariffs—the privilege enjoyed for a long period by the English Muscovy Company—in the 1630s (Wijnroks, *Handel*, 285).
6. Wijnroks, *Handel*, 248–9.
7. Ibid., 250.
8. Wijnroks, *Handel*, 285, 299.
9. Kordt, "Ocherk," civ; Wijnroks, *Handel*, 267, 269–72.
10. See Adams, *Familial State*.
11. Wijnroks, *Handel*, 380.
12. The Dutch, following the lead of various Enlightenment thinkers elsewhere, only began to be troubled by the entanglement of business and politics and their regents' shameless rigging of the system after the middle of the eighteenth century, when the country's elite had become significantly ossified.
13. See K. Boterbloem, "Russia and Europe: The Koenraad van Klenk Embassy to Moscow (1675–76)," *Journal of Early Modern History* 3, 2010, 187–217.
14. Boterbloem, *Dirty Secret*, 193–6.
15. The Bernards/Bernarts were everywhere in the seventeenth century: See Daniel Bernard's 1669 portrait by Van der Helst in Jonker and Sluyterman, *At Home*, 68.
16. See *Digitaal Vrouwenlexicon van Nederland*.
17. See Arel, *English Trade*, 67–8.
18. For some illustration of the short lifespan of businesses, see the graphics provided by JP Morgan, Chase and Company, available at: https://www.jpmorganchase.com/corporate/institute/small-business-longevity.htm, accessed January 26, 2020.

Chapter 5

The Russian and Dutch Other

Before any original account was published about Muscovy itself in Dutch, a description of Siberia had appeared under Hessel Gerritsz(oon)'s name.[1] To learn about the heartland of the tsar's realm, however, Dutch readers might have perused translations of works published before the late 1610s in languages other than Dutch.[2] Of course, much of the readership for which printed travel accounts were intended read at least Latin still with some ease in the early 1600s. And this audience was altogether small, because most people lacked the money and time to engage in such a frivolous pastime as reading.

Gerritsz's 1612 account of the Samoyeds and Siberia was likely based on information he had acquired from Isaac Massa[3] and some of his fellow Russia traders; it was fairly accurate, even if it emphasized the lurid, as in its account of Siberian exile:

> Because all those banished, including murderers, traitors and thieves, and all sort of human scum who deserved to die were exiled there according to the scope of their crime, with some being confined there for a while, while others were ordered to [permanently] reside there, . . . when the name of Siberia first came into use in Moscow the criminals feared it as much as those of Amsterdam were initially afraid of its prison. [*Tuchthuys*, which dated from 1595, KB][4]

Among the employees of De Vogelaer and Van Klenck, for a while, was the once renowned but nowadays forgotten bard of seafaring, Elias Herckmans (1596–1644).[5] Around 1625, Herckmans penned an overview of the Time of Troubles, but unlike his long epic about the history of seafaring (*Der Zeevaert Lof*) of the early 1630s, it did not find its way into print.[6] Perhaps this was because writing never became a full-time occupation for Herckmans, who died in Brazil as a high-ranking official in the West India Company.

Not long before Herckmans's manuscript on Russia was completed, works by Danckaert and Goeteeris had appeared as the first authentic (and realistic rather than fantastic) Dutch printed books about Russia, but both authors had only visited the region along the Swedish-held Baltic border with Muscovy when they wrote their accounts; they never visited the country's interior.[7] More than half a century later followed the more or less realistic Struys and the dry-as-dust Coyett followed with more fulsome descriptions of Russia, while Cornelis de Bruin was to write a most comprehensive and accurate travel account in the 1700s.[8] Around the same time as De Bruin—who was sponsored by Witsen—Nicolaas Witsen, to whom we will return later, wrote the first scholarly description of Siberia, but both editions of his work were exclusively published for his own private use and never sold on the market.[9] For a country with such a large publishing industry, which maintained close economic ties with Russia, the amount of published books originally written in Dutch on Muscovy remained therefore oddly small.

The number of Latin descriptions of Russia available in the Republic was considerable, however, and reiterates the point that not merely academics in those days still read Latin texts next to those in the vernacular. In 1630, for example, a Latin description of Muscovy published by the then still fledgling publishing house of Elsevier in Leyden.[10] It joined the widely available book by Herberstein, which was continental Europe's authoritative text on Russia for a century (only in Britain, Fletcher's work—in English—surpassed it in popularity, it seems).[11] By the 1650s, Olearius's work replaced Herberstein's as the standard, and, rather than in Latin, it was besides in its author's German original best known in translations in a number of other languages, sign of a paradigmatic change with regards to the language of European writing.[12] By the second half of the seventeenth century, the fondness for Latin publications receded outside academe, with descriptions in the vernacular becoming the norm. Meanwhile, since an authoritative text such as Olearius's was published in Dutch translations, it may have reduced the demand for authentic Dutch accounts about Russia.[13] In terms of their contents, meanwhile, rather than being accurate, the descriptions of Muscovy that were popular excelled in repeating often questionable tropes in their rendition of this "rude and barbarous" kingdom.[14] No particularly specific Dutch slant can indeed be distinguished in the accounts by Goeteeris, Danckaert, Struys, or Coyett.

In addition to books, pamphlets or broadsheets about Muscovy were issued, such as that describing the triumphant description of progress of the Van Klenck embassy in 1676.[15] Altogether, though, readership of all texts was small; Herberstein, Danckaert, the Dutch translation of both versions of Olearius's account, as well as Struys's *Reysen* went through reprints, but otherwise none of the other works mentioned were, or so it appears.[16] Estimates are that the print-run for this sort of book was approximately 500 copies; therefore, even those that were reprinted did not exactly reach a large number of readers, even if people may have borrowed books from each other. As said previously, this audience consisted of a select group of those having the money and time to consider purchasing such books.

Reading, thus, was not necessarily the means by which most people in the Republic found out about Russia. Far fewer Dutch people read about Russia than visited it in the seventeenth century. Those visitors became the key source of knowledge about the place for most back in the Republic: Information about the tsar's realm was in the main orally transmitted. And that information went beyond the literary caricatures of printed texts, we can surmise, as a never-ending trickle of Dutch artisans, soldiers, and medical personnel went to Russia, often enticed by attractive wages and apparently unfazed by any negative reports about Russian savagery, crudeness, or superstitions with which printed texts were replete.[17]

The Dutch elite might have been increasingly offended by some of the Russian customs that routinely found their way to the pages of travel descriptions keen to present salacious details. The Dutch resident Johan Willem van Keller (c. 1620–1698), who resided in Russia for two decades and was therefore intimately familiar with Muscovite habits, wrote the following to the Estates-General at The Hague in March 1690:

> Since the birth of the young [tsarevich Aleksei] they have not done much else here as having banquets and [party]; on top of which the annual shrovetide revelry has come, which has very much added to the celebrations. But since such times and parties rarely pass without confusion, quarrels, murder and manslaughter (especially among people of such mindset and behaviour as they have here), a good number of people have been badly abused and even murdered in dreadful fashion. One very much desires that such bacchanalia will be abolished, since pious and honest people cannot safely make use of the public roads and alleys without being in danger of being assaulted and hurt, even if at various points guards have been ordered to stave off drunken violence.[18]

Whereas it may be a bit far-fetched to suggest that this illustrates how much further Norbert Elias's "civilisation process" had progressed among the Dutch elite (and Van Keller was a nobleman) than among the Russian populace (it seems meanwhile that Van Keller conflates the behavior of Russians from various social strata here), one can at least read something of a reflection of the classical dichotomy of civilized versus barbaric in this passage.[19] In how far Van Keller's view of Russia was molded by the tropes about savage Muscovy in published Western texts is moot. And it is unclear whether or not Van Keller might have been equally appalled at the carousing that was rampant in most of the Dutch Republic.

The published works about Russia were doubtlessly framed to reinforce the Dutch elite's sense of superiority over uncouth barbarians, but this disgust existed outside of those texts. Russians were only one iteration of the savages with which the "civilized" Dutch had to contend in their lives, as such buffoons were just as prevalent in the Republic itself. A difference may have been that someone like Van Keller was dismissive of the Russian *elite*'s carousing and that may reflect a more Eliasian refinement of manners, as straying from the refined standard expected from nobles. As is evident from the Heinsius scandal in the 1660s (see below), the Dutch elite subscribed to a more straight-laced concept of the norms of elite public behavior.

Conversely, in far less literate Russia (in the United Provinces likely more than a third of women and men could read, even if this reading was for most people limited to the Bible, primers, and the like), any knowledge about the Dutch and their Republic was almost exclusively based on hearsay and personal encounters with Dutch people. Dutch traders had been present in areas bordering Muscovy since the late Middle Ages, when some at least appeared in Novgorod. Their economic significance became so marked that it left a Dutch cultural imprint on north-eastern Europe. Along the Baltic shores, as Janis Kreslins has argued, Dutch played the same role as common language of communication as Italian in the Mediterranean around 1600, but for the Russians the distinction between *nemtsy* (all Western Europeans, or sometimes all Germans) and *galantsy* ("Hollanders") only gradually acquired significance in the seventeenth century.[20]

The image of the Dutch among those few Russians who encountered them, or knew about them otherwise (as the clerks or courtiers), can be approximated by inference only. They were often grouped together with other Western Europeans as the rather undifferentiated community of *nemtsy*. This name eventually became limited to mean exclusively "Germans" in Russian, although its original meaning was something such as "those who cannot speak," or "dumb ones." *Nemtsy* tended to include both English and sometimes Danes or Swedes as well, so one might suggest that it included all those who spoke a Germanic language. The name of the foreigners' suburb near Moscow, the *nemetskaia sloboda*, reflects this generic usage.

In the records of the Muscovite foreign office the Dutch were separately distinguished; some of the papers on Russian interaction with the Dutch have been preserved in the *galan(t)skaia kniga*, the "Holland book."[21] Indeed, for officials in Moscow and employed along the route to the north to Arkhangel'sk, it was impossible not to differentiate among the Western Europeans, as it must have been for many Russian merchants with whom the Western Europeans traded.

Before 1697, besides the tsar, his inner circle—not in the least thanks to the information provided in the *kuranty*—and a few government clerks, only a select few other native Russians knew anything about the Netherlands from which these *galantsy* hailed. Glissenberch, or Eyloff and other doctors employed by the tsar's court may have refined some of the courtiers' and their sovereign's awareness of the fledgling upstart country taking shape on the shores of the North Sea. After 1613, the Romanov court's understanding of much of Europe and the wider world was shaped through the prism of Dutch newspapers that began ever more regularly to arrive in Moscow, especially after Jan van Sweeden set up the postal service with Western Europe in the 1660s; in the 1680s, the Dutchman Witsen's map gave the young tsar Peter a more proportional idea of Siberia's layout.[22]

That the use of the Dutch language persisted in international communication along the Baltic Sea seems evident from what is written on an envelope containing one of the Scot Patrick Gordon's letters in 1692; Gordon himself, or the Moscow postmaster (possibly Andrei or Matvei Andreevich Vinius), wrote in Dutch ("*Ick versoecke deses te expediren* . . .") a note to the postmen in Narva (or Novgorod) to expedite the delivery of Gordon's letter to his cousin William in Riga.[23] Driessen renders a telling list of Dutch-derived words in Russian that were adopted somewhere during (or even before) Peter the Great's reign.[24] As already suggested in the first chapter, this cultural impact faded after the same tsar's death in 1725.

Before 1690 Russian society was predominantly inward-looking and suspicious of foreigners, not least of non-Orthodox Christians, which the *sloboda*'s creation in the middle of the 1650s reflects. Certainly, Dutch Protestants were not deemed as dangerous as the Catholics who tried to lead the Orthodox astray, but they were heretics, banished from entry into Russian houses of worship. Russian women (who went out heavily veiled) were sheltered from any contact with such foreigners, who were forbidden as well to employ Orthodox servants in their households. The *sloboda*'s strict segregation (about which more below) reflected a more general desire to maintain the purity of the Orthodox believers. It was hard to enforce such strict segregation: Tobacco, initially brought for personal consumption by the pipe-smoking Dutch, quickly grew in popularity even if the Orthodox hierarchy condemned smoking, sniffing, or chewing it as sinful before Peter took over as sole ruler in 1689.[25] Before that pivotal moment, most Russians tried to avoid the Westerners, who were seen as aliens in their midst.

NOTES

1. Hessel Gerritsz, *Beschryvinghe van der Samoyeden landt in Tartarien*, Amsterdam: Hessel Gerritsz, 1612. Isaac Massa's authentic handwritten account of what he witnessed during the Time of Troubles was not published before

the mid-nineteenth century (*Skazaniia inostrannykh pisatelei o Rossii, izdannye Arkheograficheskoiu komisseiu*, vol. 2: *Izvestiia gollandtsev Isaaka Massy i Il'i Gerkmanna* [St. Petersburg], 1868, 129–76, available at: http://www.vostlit.info/Texts/rus13/Gerkman/text1.phtml?id=337, accessed November 12, 2019 and http://www.vostlit.info/Texts/rus13/Gerkman/text2.phtml?id=338, accessed November 12, 2019; and [Dutch originals] at https://www.prlib.ru/item/445751, accessed November 12, 2019).

2. Such as S. von Herberstein, *Rerum moscoviticarum commentarii* . . ., Basel: Oporinus, 1551; Olaus Magnus, *A Description of the Northern Peoples, 1555*, ed. Peter Foote, Burlington, VT: Ashgate, 2010.

3. Clearest sign may be on B4v [following the page numbering used in the electronic transcription], where the narrator tells how he had some friends at the court when he lived in Moscow (see Hessel Gerritsz, *Beschryvinghe van der Samoyeden landt in Tartarien*, Amsterdam: Hessel Gerritsz, 1612, B4v; available at: https://www.dbnl.org/tekst/gerr049besc01_01/, accessed January 2, 2020).

4. Gerritsz, *Beschryvinghe*, B4r and B4v [translation my own].

5. See J.A. van Worp, "Herckmans, Elias," in *Nieuw Nederlandsch Biografisch Woordenboek*, eds P.J. Blok and P.C Mohlhuysen, Leiden: Sijthoff, 1911, vol. 3, 579–80; and J.A. van Worp, "Elias Herckmans," *Oud Holland* 11, 1893, 162–78.

6. E. Herckmans, *Een historischen verhael van de voornaamste beroerten des keyserrychs van Russia, onstaen door den Demetrium Ivanowyts* . . ., c. 1625 [manuscript]; E. Herckmans, *Der zee-vaert lof, handelende vande gedenckwaerdighste zee-vaerden met de daeraenklevende op en ondergangen der voornaemste heerschappijen der gantscher wereld* . . ., Amsterdam: Wachter, 1634. His manuscript on the Time of Troubles was published for the first time in the mid-nineteenth century in Dutch and Russian, and paired with Massa's account (see *Skazaniia inostrannykh pisatelei o Rossii*, vol. 2: *Izvestiia gollandtsev Isaaka Massy i Il'i Gerkmanna*; Van Worp, "Elias Herckmans," 165). Massa's work remained in manuscript as well before the mid-nineteenth century (see Massa, *Short History*).

7. Anthonis Goeteeris, *Journael der Legatie ghedaen inde Jaren 1615 ende 1616* . . ., 's-Gravenhage: Aert Meuris, 1619; J.P. Danckaert, *Beschrijvinghe van Moscovien ofte Ruslandt*, Amsterdam: Broer Jansz, 1615.

8. J.J. Struys, *Drie aanmerkelijke en seer rampspoedige reysen*. Amsterdam: J. van Meurs en J. Van Someren, 1676; [Balthasar Coyett], *Historisch Verhael*; De Bruin, *Reizen over Moskovie*.

9. N. Witsen, *Noord en Oost Tartarye, ofte bondig ontwerp van eenige dier landen en volken, welke voormaels bekent zijn geweest* . . ., Amsterdam: N.p., 1692 (second ed.: Amsterdam: F. Halma, 1705). See as well P. Bartenev, ed., "Delo tsarevicha Alekseia Petrovicha po izvestiiam gollandskogo rezidenta de-Bie," *Russkii Arkhiv* 7, 1907, 314–39. Jacob de Bie (1681–1728), the Dutch envoy—by then stationed in St. Petersburg—reported extensively on the trial and execution of Peter the Great's son-and-heir Aleksei.

10. *Russia seu Moskovia itemque Tartaria commentario topographico atque politico illustratae*, Leiden: Elzevier, 1630.

11. See Herberstein, *Rerum moscoviticarum*; G. Fletcher, *Of the Russe commonwealth*..., London: Thomas Charde, 1591.

12. A. Olearius, *Offt begehrte beschreibung der neuen orientalischen Reise*..., Schleswig: Zur Glocken, 1647; and A. Olearius, *Vermehrte Neue Beschreibung der Moskowitischen und Persischen reise*..., Schleswig: J. Holwein, 1656. Herberstein was never translated into Dutch, but in 1657 an edition of his Latin work appeared in Antwerp (published by Johannes Steels).

13. Adam Olearius, *Beschrijvingh vande nieuwe Parciaensche, ofte orientaelsche reyse, welck door gelegentheyt van een Holsteynsche ambassade, aen den koningh in Persien geschiet is*..., trans. Dirck van Wageninge, Amsterdam: Lambert Roeck, 1651. There were several editions issued by a number of publishers.

14. M. Poe, *"A People Born to Slavery": Russia in Early Modern European Ethnography, 1476–1748*, Ithaca, NY: Cornell UP, 2000; see, too, L.E. Berry and Robert O. Crummey, eds, *Rude and Barbarous Kingdom: Russia in the Accounts of Sixteenth-Century English Voyagers*, Madison, WI: U. of Wisconsin P., 1968.

15. *Relaes van't gepasseerde voor ende op de Inkomste ende Receptie van den Heere van Klenck Haer Hoogh. Mog Extraordinaris Ambassadeur binnen der Moscou, geschiet den January 11/21, 1676*, 's Gravenhage: N.p., 1676 [*National Library of the Netherlands*, The Hague: Knuttel 7442].

16. Boterbloem, *Fiction and Reality*, 155–6.

17. See ibid., 74.

18. *Nationaal Archief*, Archief der Staten-Generaal, Lias Moskoviën, Secrete Brieven (letter from Van Keller to Estates-General), March 30, 1690.

19. Norbert Elias, *The Civilizing Process*, rev. ed., Oxford: Blackwell, 2000, 164–9.

20. Janis Kreslins, "Linguistic Landscapes in the Baltic," *Scandinavian Journal of History* 3–4, 2003, 165–74.

21. *RGADA*, fond 50 (*snosheniia Rossii s Gollandiei*).

22. See the various publications mentioned in note 47.

23. Paul Dukes, ed., "Patrick Gordon and His Family: Some Additional Letters," *Journal of Irish and Scottish Studies* 2, 2014, 125–51: 145.

24. Jozien Driessen(-van het Reve), *Tsaar Peter de Grote en zijn Amsterdamse vrienden*, Amsterdam: Amsterdams Historisch Museum, 1996, 110–11.

25. Shields Kollmann, *Crime*, 143, 221.

Chapter 6

Diplomatic Ties

In 1614, for the first time an official Russian delegation, led by the *dvor'ianin* Stepan Ushakov and the *d'iak* Semyon Zaborovskii, visited The Hague.[1] They arrived to announce to the Dutch government the elevation of Mikhail Romanov to the tsarship. More substantially, though, the Russian emissaries requested military aid from the person whom they thought ruled the United Provinces, Stadtholder Prince Maurice of Orange-Nassau (1567–1625). The Russians wrongly believed Maurice, by then a military commander whose fame had reached Moscow, to be the Dutch sovereign, as a true monarch; this he was not, however, as he shared power with the United Provinces' Estates-General (to which he was strictly speaking subordinate).[2] The exact nature of the division of power between Estates-General and the two stadtholders (a relative of Maurice was stadtholder in Groningen and Frisia provinces) was highly puzzling to the tsar, his advisors and their officials, who saw the world as consisting of monarchies.

In fact, the Russian delegation's main goal had been to visit the Holy Roman Emperor rather than the government of the United Provinces, but after being brushed off in Vienna, the diplomats regrouped in Hamburg and decided to request a meeting with the Dutch, who were thought to be likely more inclined to pay the new regime in Moscow proper respect. A letter of inquiry about a possible vist, addressed by Tsar Mikhail to the stadtholder Maurice—and conveyed by Dutch merchants from Hamburg to The Hague— was read in the Estates-General in January 1614.[3]

The Russians arrived in the subsequent May. The Dutch rejected the Russian request to sell them arms, but offered to mediate in the war between Sweden and Muscovy. In search of blanket trading privileges resembling those of the English Muscovy Company, Dutch Russia traders exerted pressure on the Dutch Estates-General to dispatch a reciprocal mission to

Moscow. Even if the Russia lobby was becoming a significant pressure group, the Dutch legislature took a cautious approach in granting this request: At a low rank, it appointed Isaac Massa as government agent to accompany the two Muscovite diplomats back home. The trio took the searoute to Arkhangel'sk in the late spring of 1614.[4] After their return to Moscow in the late summer of 1614, Ushakov and Zaborovskii were reprimanded by Tsar Mikhail's bureaucrats for a number of irregularities, but the new Russian government was nonetheless fairly pleased with the hospitable reception of its envoys in the Netherlands.[5] As we will see below, Massa, meanwhile, was to accomplish little on behalf of the Dutch trade lobby.

Wijnroks suggests that after 1613 the Estates-General explored the pros-and-cons of closer diplomatic ties while pondering whether Russia might become a viable partner in the Dutch struggle with the burgeoning forces of the European Counter (or Catholic) Reformation.[6] Certainly, after 1618 Dutch subsidies for the Protestant side in the Thirty Years' War were to be significant in keeping its forces in the field, and this was a time when Poland-Lithuania, an erstwhile haven of religious tolerance, drifted more and more into the fanatical Catholic orbit. To enlist Russia in an international anti-Catholic coalition, especially to keep the Poles in check, might be strategically useful.

More than any religious crusade, however, Dutch seventeenth-century policy toward Russia was driven by the priorities of business, as Massa's brief in 1614 indicates. Merchants determined most of the agenda of the Dutch government toward Russia. This outsized influence of the trading interest was not unusual for the United Provinces: In its starkest form this can be seen in the Dutch East India Company, a mercantile organization to which the Estates-General in effect transferred any decision-making regarding political and military affairs east of Africa's Cape. Undeniably, too, the Republic sustained meddling in the affairs of Sweden and Denmark was largely spurred on by economic motives, because violent conflict between the two Scandinavian rivals might disturb the Dutch "mother trade" of shipping grain from the Baltic to the Netherlands. In theory, allying with Muscovy might tip the scale toward either of the two, which might be useful for Dutch designs if it led to the permanent bridling Denmark, which commanded the Sound linking the Baltic Sea to the North Sea and raised irksome tolls on the vast amount of Dutch ships passing through it. More often than not the Dutch therefore favored Sweden over Denmark, until Denmark was definitively forced to give up its stranglehold on the Sound by the 1660 Treaty of Copenhagen.

Denmark and Muscovy had few disputes, however, so Dutch incitement of the Russians against the Danes was a fool's errand, especially because the two states did not share any borders. Russia and Sweden, meanwhile, continually quarreled over the control over the north-eastern Baltic shores. The first true opportunity for a military pact between the tsar and the Republic's government therefore only arose in the mid-1670s, when for a short while both Muscovy and the Republic were hostile to Sweden. In 1676, Russia and the Republic seemed on the verge of an alliance, because the Dutch had fallen out with Sweden, then an ally of Louis XIV, the Dutch mortal enemy.[7] But the Dutch desire to fight Sweden proved short-lived, even if at the time substantial military aid was rendered to Denmark, Sweden's main opponent. In their turn, the Russians were ever more distracted by growing unrest on their south-western borders, where the Turks and Crimean Tatars were on the move. In early 1676, Tsar Aleksei died before any meaningful discussions with Ambassador Van Klenck started about Russia joining the anti-Swedish (and anti-French) coalition, and the boyars that stepped in as regents for the 14-year-old Fyodor III were unwilling to take any great risks given the southern threat.

Beset by problems nearer to home, Russia ultimately proved too remote even for the stadtholder and other leading politicians at The Hague to establish a full-fledged legation until Johan Willem van Keller received his credentials in 1677. It never became a viable candidate to join a coalition against various nearby enemies of the Dutch, such as Spain, France, some of the German principalities, or Britain. None of those countries threatened Muscovy, of course.

Conversely, the Dutch Republic did not factor into Russian political calculations before 1697, unless it was as provider of desperately needed military hardware and expertise. Even after the Grand Embassy, Muscovy remained preoccupied with its immediate neighbors throughout our period, all the way until 1725. The Russian emissaries that did visit The Hague before 1697 were mainly looking for arms (as the Ushakov mission did), or other scarce military expertise (as the Miloslavskii mission of 1646–1647 did, although it, too, sought arms) of which Russia was in urgent need. Peter the Great's mission in 1697 did have the overt aim of persuading the Dutch to join a military alliance against the Ottoman Turks, but the Dutch had always been on good terms with Istanbul, and were just at that very time extracting themselves out of a war with France. And a military alliance was only part of Peter's agenda on his lengthy visit.

Before in 1677 Van Keller became permanent Dutch envoy to the tsar's court, and with the exception of the failed Brederode-Bas-Joachimi embassy of 1615–1616 (which never reached Moscow), the four main Dutch "extraordinary" embassies (led, respectively, by Albert Burgh, Koenraad Burgh, Jacob Boreel, and Koenraad van Klenck) therefore largely concentrated on trade issues once they reached Moscow. The limited mission of Nicolaas Heins in 1670–1671 was more politically oriented and resembled the Brederode embassy in its efforts to mediate between Sweden and Russia.

But in both cases the Russians suspected (not without ground[8]) that Dutch sympathies were on the Swedish side and both ended as a comprehensive failure. The four other embassies accomplished more, but only in terms of commercial issues. Whatever immediate political goal they had (as was most emphatically the case with van Klenck's embassy of 1675–1676) was not met.

Before the 1630s, the Russians meanwhile professed to refrain from sending a full-fledged embassy to Holland in honor of a(n invented?) tradition that had foreign Powers first send an embassy to Moscow before they reciprocated.[9] In fact, almost all of the Russian emissaries that subsequently did visit The Hague before 1697 ranked as envoys rather than full-fledged ambassadors.[10] This reflected the continued Russian discomfort with the international status of a republic founded by people who had overthrown their God-given monarch.[11] Still, the Muscovite attitude toward the Dutch was also contingent on the strength of the Russian need both for the affirmation of their own diplomatic status and for Dutch-shipped goods. Thus, during the first years of Tsar Mikhail's reign, they expressed a strong desire to welcome a full-fledged Dutch embassy.

NOTES

1. On this point, see Kordt, "Ocherk," cvii.

2. This political construction is difficult to frame in the terminology of any current political system; the stadtholders of the various Dutch provinces had originally been the governor in the name of the lord who officially ruled the province. After Philip II had been abjured by the United Provinces, he was more or less pro forma replaced by his advisory council (*Raad van State*). But the legislature in which representatives of all seven provincial legislatures met, the Estates-General, absorbed ever more executive powers from the Council of State. The stadtholder, formally, was an appointee of those two bodies, and operated as a sort of prime minister, a role he combined with that of supreme commander of the navy and land forces. But there were traditional sentiments about the noble class as born to rule in play as well in the Republic. This usually led to an almost automatic succession to the stadtholderate of the next in line of the house of Orange-Nassau upon the death of whomever carried the princely title in its senior line. To complicate matters further, there were usually two stadtholders, with a scion from the cadet branch of the Nassau family ruling in the northern provinces. When tensions rose between prince and Estates-General, the prince could rely on a far greater popularity than the parliament, although both sides preferred leaving the general population out of politics. The regents, who controlled the Estates-General, were never very popular after an all too brief early spell of solidarity of rich and poor in the first years of the revolt; a smoldering class antagonism made most towndwellers fonder of the Oranges than of their local councillors. In the countryside, traditional deference to the bluebloods informed an even stronger support for the Oranges.

3. Kordt, "Ocherk," cv–cvi.
4. Wijnroks, *Handel*, 230; Kordt, "Ocherk," cvi–cviii.
5. Kordt, "Ocherk," cix–cx.
6. Wijnroks, *Handel*, 218.
7. See Boterbloem, "Russia and Europe."
8. The Dutch signed a treaty of alliance with Sweden in August 1614 (Kordt, "Ocherk," cxxvi–cxxvii); Heinsius (see below) was a Swedophile who was dispatched to Moscow from a post at Stockholm.
9. Kordt, "Ocherk," cx–cxi. This was all the more desirable with the election of a new tsar, as was underlined in a letter in 1615 to the Estates-General (ibid., cxxvii–cxxviii).
10. The only exception may have been the mission led by Bogdan Ordin-Nashchokin in 1663.
11. A good comprehensive overview of Russian diplomatic practice is Jan Hennings, *Russia and Courtly Europe: Ritual and the Culture of Diplomacy, 1648–1725*, Cambridge: Cambridge UP, 2016.

Chapter 7

Isaac Massa

Isaac Massa (1587–1643) had traded with Russia since the early 1600s and spent lengthy periods there. In 1614 and 1615, the Estates-General retained him briefly as its *chargé-d'affaires* in the vain hope of gaining blanket trading privileges for all Dutch merchants in Muscovy.[1] Massa is one of the most remarkable figures in the history of Dutch-Russian relations, not in the least because he penned a revealing account of what he witnessed and heard during the Time of Troubles (which was only printed long after his death).[2] His family hailed from the southern Netherlands, while he considered his native town of Haarlem as his place of residence, perhaps reflective of a period when Amsterdam was not yet dominating the trade on Muscovy (Karel du Moulin lived nearby on the Elswout estate). As a teenager, he started as a sort of trainee for one of the Dutch trading houses (it is not quite clear which) in Russia, after which he set up shop himself, and proceeded to trade with the tsar's empire for most of his subsequent life.

In Massa's brief of 1614, the Estates-General instructed him to demand free trade throughout Russia for Dutch subjects, a privilege similar to that made in 1612 by the Turkish sultan regarding Dutch merchants active within the Ottoman Empire.[3] Additionally, on the personal urging of Stadtholder Maurice, Massa was to request the tsar for free passage across Muscovy into Asia for a company of Amsterdam merchants, who included Reinier Pauw and his son Adriaan, and three members of the Witsen family. They wanted to explore the trade routes to Bukhara, Iran, and Armenia. The silk route's significance was waning, but the lengthy and risky sailing journey between the United Provinces and East Asia had to prove itself yet as a more effective and profitable route to transport commodities than the caravan routes over land. Trading with Inner Asia by carrying goods across Muscovy and loading them at Arkhangel'sk, for an equally risky but shorter trip (about six weeks was the norm) from there to the Dutch ports, was ultimately never an attractive enough option for Dutch traders to pursue in a sustained fashion. But the trade with Iran and the Caucasus seemed more feasible and not just the Dutch repeatedly brought up the matter of permits to travel down the Volga and across the Caspian Sea in search of raw silk and other prized commodities with the tsar's officials in the course of the seventeenth century.[4] Eventually, the tsar himself sponsored this trading link's intensification, but preferred Armenian-Iranian merchants conducting this trade instead of Western Europeans.

After the four-month journey from Arkhangel'sk to Moscow, Massa finally met Tsar Mikhail in early 1615. Massa informed his Russian interlocutors of the Dutch intentions to dispatch an embassy to the Baltic region to broker a peace between Sweden and Russia, ending a war that had erupted in the darkest days of the Time of Troubles. Massa, prone to boasting, met a rather skeptical reception from the Russians, who considered him more of a minor figure, messenger rather than true envoy (which was not far from the truth).[5] From some of his discussions with officials of the Muscovite foreign office (*posol'skii prikaz*), it appears evident that Massa expressed a willingness to represent the Russians as their agent at The Hague, both evidence of a less than firm loyalty to his native country and of his desire to find another diplomatic job after his merely temporary employment as a low-level messenger by the Estates-General and Prince Maurice.[6] Massa made no headway toward earning the Dutch major gains regarding the conditions by which they were allowed to trade in Muscovy; given this failure, it is probably not coincidental that the Estates-General afterward showed little interest in hiring Massa on permanently as its agent in Russia.[7] Likewise, the Russians had no interest in the Amsterdam venture of Pauw and his companions.

In October 1615, Massa was back in the United Provinces, this time accompanied by the Russian envoys Ivan Kondyrev and Mikhail Neverov, who in addition to calling in at The Hague had been ordered to visit Paris.[8] Besides expressing the Russian wish for a more formal diplomatic visit by the Dutch, the Russian emissaries now informed the Estates-General that the tsar urged it to recall any Dutch subjects fighting in the Polish and Swedish military forces then deployed against Muscovy. Additionally, Tsar Mikhail requested large-scale arms' deliveries and subsidies. In response, the Estates-General quite disingenuously claimed that it had always prohibited Dutch subjects from serving foreign Powers.[9] No military aid was offered to Russia. The Dutch rulers, whose subjects traditionally conducted a heavy trade with the *Rzeczpospolita* and were pro-Swedish as well, had no intention to arm Russia in its fight with its Polish-Lithuanian or Swedish foes in any formal fashion.[10] In practice, though, they looked the other way when Dutch merchants did ship arms to Russia.[11]

Meanwhile, the Estates-General happily fulfilled the Muscovite request to supply Kondyrev and Neverov with a French translator to accompany them on their visit to Paris. After several weeks in France (to which they had traveled on Dutch ships), the envoys returned in early January 1616 to The Hague. Awaiting the opening of the sailing season to Arkhangel'sk in late spring, the Russian envoys spent several months engaged in leisurely discussions with the Dutch traders and officials, causing offence to their Dutch hosts through their debauchery.[12] On the key points of arms deliveries and a full-scale embassy the Estates-General refused to budge.

By the time that the Estates-General had responded to the queries conveyed to them by the Russian envoys, the Dutch mission under Van Brederode had departed for the Baltic to help the Russo-Swedish peace negotiations.[13] In what is today's Estonia, the Russian-Swedish peace negotiations proceeded for a while in the presence of those Dutch emissaries, the nobleman Reinoud van Brederode (1567–1633), the Amsterdam merchant and regent Dirck Bas (1569–1637), and the Zeeland city regent Aelbrecht Joachimi (1560–1654). Whereas it is moot how much the Dutch envoys made a difference, the discussions led to the acceptance of a brief armistice between both warring sides in March 1616.[14] The English agent John Merrick proved more tenacious in bringing both sides together. It was his mediation that persuaded both sides to conclude a more permanent treaty in February 1617, almost a year after the Dutch emissaries had left the Russian-Swedish frontier in the Baltic.

For the Dutch authorities, the elaborate Brederode mission was an expensive affair without much of a yield. The Dutch envoys, ultimately, lacked sufficient patience and flexibility necessary to broker a viable peace, both a sign of a country whose diplomatic experience was limited yet, as well as of its pro-Swedish inclinations: From the Russian point of view, the Dutch diplomats' partisanship was confirmed when they returned home via Stockholm, where King Gustavus Adolphus showered them with honors, which was not unreasonably taken as proof of their pro-Swedish bias.[15] Still, a lesson seems to have been learned: The Dutch authorities did seem to have understood from this rather dismal experience that in the future it would be better to dispatch diplomats to Moscow who were more au courant with Russian affairs and less hostile to Muscovy.

For a short while, the somewhat amateurish behavior and anti-Russian sentiment of the Brederode mission rubbed the Russians the wrong way.[16] After being appointed once more Dutch agent, Massa (together with Kondyrev and Neverov) returned to Moscow in the summer of 1616, but met with a hostile reception as a consequence of the diplomatic bungling in the Baltic. After his arrival in Moscow in September, his miffed hosts made him wait for an audience with the tsar for more than half a year, until April 1617.[17] Massa then delivered a spirited address trying to restore Russian respect for the

Dutch.[18] After congratulating Mikhail on the conclusion of the recent Peace of Stolbovo with Sweden, he explained that the United Provinces needed all the resources they had to field a 50,000-strong army and a navy to defend themselves against pope, emperor, and Spanish king, and thus could not supply the Russians with arms or funds. He also somewhat disingenuously suggested that, whereas the Brederode mission had intended to travel to Moscow the previous year, illness and old age had crippled the envoys during their deep-winter sojourn at the Swedish-Muscovite border and forced them to return home rather than traveling further eastward. As usual, he asked for far-reaching trading privileges and dispensation from taxes on commerce for his compatriots.

That autumn, however, Massa returned to the Netherlands having once more accomplished little, although he came equipped with a bevy of arguments to explain to the Estates-General the Russian dismay with the failings of Dutch diplomacy, the ongoing Russian suspicion about the service of Dutch military in the armies of the Poles and Swedes, and the Russian wrath at the rejection of their demands for arms and subsidies.[19] As before, blanket trade privileges had been rejected, he reported; this situation might change if the Dutch rendered the Russians support against the Poles and dispatched envoys to mediate a peace between Poland and Muscovy. At The Hague, Massa continued to lobby for the appointment of a permanent Dutch trade agent and the mounting of a full embassy to Moscow, depicting such a move as the best expression of the Dutch desire for a close friendship with the tsar.[20] The Dutch Estates-General, however, was increasingly distracted by the developments in Prague that proved to be the beginning of the Thirty Years' War, as well as the Calvinist Synod of Dordt and subsequent domestic turmoil between Arminians and Gomarists that culminated in the public execution of Reinoud van Brederode's father-in-law Johan van Oldebarnevelt in 1619.

While Massa tried to persuade the Estates-General to establish closer ties with Muscovy (and to reimburse him personally for all the costs he had incurred on his recent trip to Russia), the Russians dispatched another emissary, Ivan Baklanovskii, to Sweden, Denmark, and the Netherlands to seek help in the ongoing war against the *Rzeczpospolita*.[21] He arrived on June 7, 1618, at The Hague, surprising the Estates-General with his sudden appearance. It transpired that he solely sought subsidies and arms for the struggle with Poland. After listening to Baklanovskii, the Estates-General asked the provincial estates of Holland and Zeeland whether they could not to some degree provide the Russians with such aid.[22] Holland (led by Amsterdam) proved amenable to the Russian request, while the Estates-General itself decided to aid the Muscovites with a mere small subvention and shipment of arms, after Baklanovskii stubbornly refused to accept his recredentials.

Baklanovskii then, accompanied by Massa, and brought to Den Helder by the Amsterdam regent Gerrit Witsen, sailed for Russia in July 1618.

When Massa and Baklanovskii arrived at Arkhangel'sk in late August of that year, they witnessed the bizarre departure of the English envoy Dudley Diggs, who had refused to travel to Moscow after arriving at the port earlier that summer to offer the tsar a modest English subsidy.[23] The Dutch, despite the lukewarm support for the tsar expressed at The Hague, stepped into the breach. Thus, they recovered from the damage done by their lackluster performance in mediating between Sweden and Russia, and regained Tsar Mikhail's favor. The hegemony of Dutch trading at Arkhangel'sk was confirmed in subsequent years and remained in place until St. Petersburg began to overtake Arkhangel'sk as Russia's main port of call almost a century later. Different from the English, though, Dutch merchants received merely individual dispensation from certain fees and tolls, rather than as a company or trading "nation." Usually, such privileges lasted for a limited term, at most the duration of a tsar's reign.[24] And rights came with certain duties, such as the delivery of news to the court, or the obligation to facilitate the tsar's demands for specific commodities, and most of all in helping the shipment of arms to Russia.

Massa was to spend most of 1619 in Moscow, where the Truce of Deulino with Poland and the return from Polish captivity of the patriarch, the tsar's father Filaret, were celebrated.[25] In his meetings with the tsar and patriarch, senior officials, as well the tsar's uncle Ivan Nikitich Romanov, the issue of Dutch trading with Iran was raised, but the Russian attitude was somewhat evasive by deferring any resolution in this regard to the return of a Russian embassy to Shah Abbas (1571–1629). Massa returned to Holland with the last ships that left Arkhangel'sk in that year, not long after a large fire had destroyed the goods he had stocked at the port for his private trade, which represented a substantial loss to his business.

NOTES

1. Kordt, "Ocherk," cxii; Wijnroks, *Handel*, 230–1, 361–3.
2. Massa, *Short History*, ed. Orchard; G.W. van der Meiden, "Isaac Massa and the beginnings of Dutch-Russian Relations," available as pdf file at https://commons.wikimedia.org/wiki/File:Isaac_Massa.pdf, accessed September 9, 2016; Johannes Keuning, "Isaac Massa, 1586–1643," *Imago Mundi* 10, 1953, 65–79; *Skazaniia inostrannykh pisatelei o Rossii*, vol. 2; John Michael Montias, *Art at Auction in Seventeenth-Century Amsterdam*, Amsterdam: Amsterdam UP, 2002, 132–3; and Isaak Massa, *Kratkoe izvestie o Moskovii v nachale xvii v.*, Moscow: Gos. sots-ekon. Izdatel'stvo, 1936, available at: http://www.vostlit.info/Texts/rus11/Massa/pred.phtml?id=906, accessed September 17, 2019; see Kordt, "Ocherk," cxv.

3. Kordt, "Ocherk," cxvii; Wijnroks, *Handel*, 230–1.

4. Already in the 1570s, the Van de Walle group had been alerted to the silk arriving in Moscow from Iran (Wijnroks, *Handel*, 115).

5. Kordt, "Ocherk," cxxvii–cxviii.

6. Ibid., cxxv–cxviii.

7. See as well ibid., cxxxiv–cxxxv.

8. Ibid., cxxix.

9. Various Dutch military units fought for the Swedes in the 1600s and Venice in the 1610s (see Boterbloem, *Dirty Secret*, 30, 96, 149).

10. Kordt, "Ocherk," cxxx–cxxxi.

11. See Boterbloem, *Dirty Secret*, 171–2.

12. Kordt, "Ocherk," cxxxii–cxxxiii; Wijnroks, *Handel*, 232.

13. For the sequence of events leading to the negotiations near Narva, see Kordt, "Ocherk," cxxxvi–cxxxviii. The author of the first authentic Dutch account on Russia, Johan Danckaert, had served in the Swedish army for several years (see Blom and Bas-Backer, *Op reis voor vrede*, 21–2; Danckaert, *Beschrijvinghe*). Danckaert proceeded to join the Brederode embassy as a sort of area expert.

14. Kordt, "Ocherk," cxxxv–cxlviii; F. Blom and P. Bas-Backer, *Op reis voor vrede*, Zutphen: Walburg, 2014; J. Driessen, "Het Gezantschap van Reinoud van Brederode in 1615 en 1616 naar Rusland," in *Rusland in Nederlandse ogen*, eds J. Driessen, W. Roobol, and Marc Jansen, Amsterdam: Van Oorschot, 1986, 51–73; Phipps, *Sir John Merrick*, 74–118; *Otchet Niderlandskikh' poslannikov'*.

15. It is quite possible that the hostility of the Dutch diplomats toward Merrick was not merely because they suspected him to be overly pro-Russian, since Massa had previously denounced him as well to the Estates-General as an anti-Dutch intriguer (Phipps, *Sir John Merrick*, 85–6). Joachimi had previously been successful in negotiating a compromise with the English regarding fishing rights and was to depart on several more diplomatic missions after this fiasco. Bas, too, had prior diplomatic experience.

16. Kordt, "Ocherk," cxlviii–cl, cliii; Wijnroks, *Handel*, 126.

17. Kordt, "Ocherk," clii.

18. Ibid., clii–cliii.

19. Ibid., cliv; Wijnroks, *Handel*, 233–4.

20. Kordt, "Ocherk," clv–clixi; Wijnroks, *Handel*, 233–4.

21. Kordt, "Ocherk," clxi–clxiii.

22. Ibid., clxiii–clxvi; a sort of gift of some gunpowder and lead was awarded (Wijnroks, *Handel*, 235).

23. Kordt, "Ocherk," clxviii; Wijnroks, *Handel*, 235.

24. Wijnroks, *Handel*, 285–7.

25. Kordt, "Ocherk," clxxi–clxxvi.

Chapter 8

Business Opportunities

The Persian trade (especially in raw silk, which was cultivated in the northern Iranian provinces near the Caspian Sea) via Russia continued to interest members of the United Provinces' mercantile community long after Massa raised it with the Russians in the 1610s. After the lobbying by one group of powerful Amsterdam merchants for a high-level mission to convince the tsar of its benefits in 1615, however, little was undertaken to renew such pleading before the Muscovites until the late 1620s.[1] But, as we mentioned, the subsequent high-level pleading even by full-fledged ambassadors proved fruitless: Whenever in the next decades Dutch envoys did raise the issue of the trade on Persia, the Russians remained firm in their refusal to concede to Dutch traders the right to ship raw silk up the Volga to Moscow and beyond. The tsars were jealous of their sovereignty and protective of the native Muscovite merchant estates, who belonged to the key stakeholders in the Romanov monarchy. The Armenian trading diaspora, unsteadily supported by the Iranian shah, ultimately seemed harmless enough to be given some trade rights in 1667, as they had no designs of challenging Muscovite traders' privileges.[2]

Each Dutch plea to convince the tsar to allow Dutch merchants to carry silk across the Caspian up the Volga and on to Arkhangel'sk, then, was rebuffed. Attempts in this regard met with "domestic" opposition, too, for the *VOC* shipped Iranian silk to the Republic via the Persian Gulf port of Bandar-e-Abbas, while some Iranian silk was loaded on to Dutch ships in the Levantine harbors of Aleppo and Smyrna-Izmir as well, transported by overland caravans to these ports from Iran.[3] A sign of a sometimes clear absence of national solidarity among the Dutch merchants, this probably weakened the Dutch authorities' resolve to pursue the matter stringently.

Throughout the seventeenth century, meanwhile, not merely the Dutch, but the English (whose first attempts in exploring a trade route from Asia to

Western Europe via Russia went back to Anthony Jenkinson's travels in the 1560s), Holsteiners, and Swedes (especially through the persistent efforts of the erstwhile Netherlander Ludvig Fabritius/Lodewijk Fabricius in the early 1680s) sought permission to ship raw silk across the Caspian Sea to Arkhangel'sk or Riga. Ultimately, the Russians declined to accede to these requests (except to the Holsteiner proposal, which failed in practice), with one key exception: From the spring of 1667, the tsar's government allowed Armenian merchants, subjects of the Iranian shah, to regularly deliver raw silk across the Caspian to Moscow and onward.[4]

It seems, on the one hand, that Russian merchants doggedly refused to allow any foreign competitors a share of their domestic trade.[5] On the other hand, as with other Dutch requests to be allowed to trade within Russia without any restriction of movement, or being subject to the residential segregation of expatriates in Russia, fear of contamination with heresy stopped the tsars from granting foreigners the right to freely traverse their country. Finally, perhaps, Russian merchants (whose estate was differentiated into four ranks, all with their own rights and duties) rendered a great number of services to the tsar in exchange for the privilege of being allowed to trade: Among the more important ones were collecting tolls and the obligation to aid with the vast trade that was conducted on behalf of the tsar personally. Most Dutch petitions for a lessening of excises or sales taxes did not—and probably could not, as they did not sufficiently know the intricacies of the Russian state's operation—offer such services in exchange for greater trading privileges.[6] In other words, the tsar was not offered any significant gain from allowing Dutch merchants greater freedom of trade beyond the possibly greater return of sales and excise fees on a higher turnover of goods. Only rarely, then, and usually only for a limited timespan, did certain Dutch firms receive substantial privileges, as De Vogelaer and Van Klenck did in 1614 (a concession which lapsed in the 1640s). These were usually only granted as a reward for exceptional services rendered to the Russian crown, and limited to a reduction of tariffs on the import-and-export trade.

Thus, Andries Winius (in the 1640s), Peter Marselis (in the 1640s and again in the 1660s), and Jan van Sweeden (in the 1660s) seem to have realized that they might gain higher profits if they wholly committed themselves to become the tsar's servitors, even if this came with shouldering a significant burden of obligations exacted by the tsar's government.[7] Marselis and Van Sweeden legally became "*Moskovskie inozemtsy*," that is, tsarist subjects of foreign extraction enjoying substantial privileges, while acquitting themselves of various duties on behalf of their sovereign; they remained loyal to the churches in which they had been baptized, however.[8] Winius wholly Russified by becoming an Orthodox believer, for which the Dutch expatriates in Moscow vilified him even after his death, as Nicolaas Witsen witnessed.[9]

But he did formally join the highest merchant rank of the *gosti*, a rare feat for anyone not born-and-raised Russian Orthodox.[10]

Whereas any intensification of diplomatic relations between the United Provinces and Muscovy had failed to materialize in the 1610s, while very little was accomplished before the end of the 1620s to develop any closer collaboration, the Dutch import-and-export trade with Russia thrived. In both decades, no fewer than 20–30 ships were annually loaded in the Dutch ports with destination Arkhangel'sk.[11] Among the goods shipped to the White Sea port was occasionally even grain, as in 1621.[12] This may have ended when grain prices on the Dutch market began to rise, a development at least in part caused by the wars that engulfed the Low Countries and the Holy Roman Empire from 1618 onward. A reversal occurred because of this scarcity: The Dutch government began to try to import grain from Russia. This was difficult to realize, as the tsar maintained a monopoly over the grain export. The Russian monarch was reluctant to part with this staple of the Russian diet, as any sensible protection of his country against harvest failure meant storing most of any surplus corn yield.[13] But for several years the Dutch stubbornly attempted to purchase Russian grain in bulk. The first sign of their wish to buy the crop can be traced to 1624; once again, it was Isaac Massa who parlayed the Dutch wishes in this regard to the tsar.[14] Some grain was indeed shipped to the United Provinces in 1625, but nowhere near a volume to make it a feasible alternative to the grain shipped to the Republic from eastern Baltic ports.

In early 1626, then, the Estates-General commissioned Isaac Massa to develop a plan for regular import of Russian grain to the United Provinces.[15] But once drafted, the plan was rejected, possibly because Massa faced a phalanx of hostile competitors who were opposed to Massa's proposal to give him a monopoly on the trade. The Vogelaers and Karel du Moulin were among those who joined forces in opposition to Massa's design (Du Moulin shared a house with Jurriaan van Klenck in Iaroslavl' in the 1620s).[16]

Faced with such formidable competitors, Massa, it appears, switched the basis of his Dutch business operations to Sweden, pledging allegiance to the Swedish crown (in some ways foreshadowing the later moves in Russia by Winius or van Sweeden).[17] In this period, Massa sent the tsar several newsletters from the United Provinces about developments in Europe, underlining the somewhat opportunistic nature of his loyalty, even if he was far from unique in providing the tsar with intelligence: A good number of his Dutch compatriots were interrogated or asked to write memoranda regarding the outside world by high Russian officials when visiting Moscow, a debriefing Massa himself participated in as well.[18]

These were the beginnings of the composition of the *kuranty* for the tsar, the composition of summaries of the most important news from Europe and the world, eventually extracted from the growing number of newspapers that were printed in Central and Western Europe and in the course of the seventeenth century began to arrive more regularly in Moscow.[19] While merchants such as Massa, Du Moulin, or Van Klenck were interrogated about developments in Europe and elsewhere, they were equally willing to serve as the tsar's agents in purchasing scarce commodities (including arms, jewelry, and gemstones), or hiring experts who wielded rare skill in Western Europe.[20] Among those experts were brick-makers, fortress builders (one of whom was Cosmo de Moucheron, a son of either Balthasar or Melchior de Moucheron), gunsmiths, doctors, textile workers (drapers, fullers, tailors), and mercenary officers.[21] Already in the 1620s, one can identify some manufacturing enterprises founded in Russia by the Dutch, among which were ropeworks set up by Karel du Moulin near Arkhangel'sk.[22] Du Moulin later expanded into tar production. Soon after, it seems, Julius Coyett arrived and began a glass-blowing enterprise, while Andries Winius started his iron- and arms works near Tula in 1632.[23]

NOTES

1. For its broader context (and the economic potential that might derive from a revived trade along the silk route), see Naarden, "Nicolaas Witsen," 5.

2. See Boterbloem, *Fiction and Reality*, 60–1.

3. See Boterbloem, *Fiction*, 61.

4. Raw silk had reached Arkhangel'sk sporadically earlier in the seventeenth century (Kotilaine, "When the Twain," 75–6).

5. Wijnroks, *Handel*, 287.

6. Paul Bushkovitch, *The Merchants of Moscow, 1580–1650*, Cambridge: Cambridge UP, 1980.

7. In Winius's case this seems most obvious, for he switched from running his iron- and armaments works (after a long drawn-out conflict with his erstwhile partners) to arms' importation on the tsar's behalf, the latter likely being a far more lucrative endeavor. For Marselis, apart from Amburger, *Die Familie Marselis*, see also Wijnroks, *Handel*, 265–6.

8. On this status and its origins, see Kotilaine, "When the Twain," 111; Wijnroks, *Handel*, 287. Contrary to Wijnroks's suggestion, *Moskovskie inozemtsy* were not necessarily Orthodox Christians (see ibid., 300).

9. Witsen, *Moscovische Reyse*, vol. 3, 411 and 411n1. For others, see Wijnroks, *Handel*, 299–300, as well as N. Novombergskii, *Materialy po istorii meditsiny v Rossii*, vol. 3, part 1, St. Petersburg: Stasiulivich, 1906, 66–7 (a Dutch employee of the Apothecary Office, Kadam [?], converting to Orthodoxy).

10. Other Dutch traders, such as in 1660 Jan and Daniel Bernards, scions of a long established family of Russia traders were honored with this title, but did not formally

join the Russian merchants' estate (Lahana, "Novaia Nemetskaia Sloboda," 102; Wijnroks, *Handel*, 256–7).

11. "Notariele Akten"; Wijnroks, *Handel*, 303–6, 308, and ibid., 304, Table 3. See for the 30 ships in 1618, Harry Donga, *Christoffel van Brants en zijn hofje. De geschiedenis van het Van Brants Hofje vanaf 1733*, Hilversum: Verloren, 2008, 28; and Kordt, "Ocherk," cccxxvi (which shows that the number is found in a Massa petition to the Estates-General). The surviving notary documents attesting to shipments to Arkhangel'sk may represent an undercount, especially as these sources only list notary acts made up in Amsterdam; some ships may have sailed without such a contract; and some contracts were made up before or after the sailing season, which makes it difficult to assess when a ship actually sailed for Russia. Wijnroks suggests that the Amsterdam records probably represent about two-thirds to three-quarters of the number of ships departing for Russia in the early decades of the seventeenth century (Wijnroks, *Handel*, 304–6).

12. Kordt, "Ocherk," clxxx.
13. Ibid., clxxx.
14. Ibid., clxxxii–clxxxvi.
15. Ibid., clxxxix–cxci.
16. Wijnroks, *Handel*, 271, 364–8. It is interesting that such cutthroat competition was also common among the contemporary Muscovy Company's merchants (see Arel, *English Trade*, 8–9).
17. Massa was ennobled by King Gustavus Adolphus in 1625, as he apparently had rendered the Swedes invaluable help (Kordt, "Ocherk," clxxxvii–clxxxviii).
18. See further, too, Montias, *Art at Auction*, 133–4; it seems his brothers (possibly without him) may have continued his business with Russia until the early 1640s.
19. Kordt, "Ocherk," cxci–cxcii.
20. Ibid., cclxvii–cclxix, ccc; Wijnroks, *Handel*, 91–5, 106. As Wijnroks suggests, the Van de Walle consortium had ties to the diamond trade (see Wijnroks, *Handel*, 115–16).
21. Kordt, "Ocherk," ccxcv–ccciii; Wijnroks, *Handel*, 291.
22. Kordt, "Ocherk," cccii–cccv; Wijnroks, *Handel*, 349–52.
23. Boterbloem, *Dirty Secret*, 174; Boterbloem, *Fiction*, 46.

Chapter 9

Guns and Grain

In the later 1620s, Isaac Massa was denounced as a self-serving turncoat by his Dutch competitors, not least by Jurriaan van Klenck; in his turn, Massa described Van Klenck in a letter to the Tsar Mikhail as a "dishonest, two-faced" character.[1] Massa's denunciations found their way to the Estates-General, however, damaging his reputation in Holland further.[2] This sort of vicious mutual slander, which would recur with the conflict between Winius and his former partners at Tula in the 1640s, or Jan van Sweeden and his rivals in the 1660s, shows how high the stakes were in the occasional cut-throat nature of the Dutch business world of the day.[3] It is probably not coincidental that Massa around 1630, Winius around 1648, and Van Sweeden in the mid-1660s switched their allegiance from the United Provinces to serving the Swedish or Russian monarchs, thus outflanking their Dutch competitors.[4]

While Massa's star was eclipsed in his fatherland, attempts to establish a regular trade of grain from Russia to the Netherlands proceeded.[5] By March 1629, on the urging of several Amsterdam tycoons, including Guillelmo Bartolotti (Willem van den Heuvel, 1602–1658) and Elias Trip (1570–1636), who proposed the creation of a trading company dealing with the matter, the Estates-General decided that an embassy to Russia should be dispatched.[6] It was given the specific aim of investigating the possibilities of shipping grain regularly from Russia to the Republic, to supplement, or substitute for, grain loaded along the Baltic shores. A key advantage was the cheap price of Russian compared to Polish grain, but this was offset by a significant and ultimately insurmountable problem: ensuring a regular supply.[7] The remoteness of Arkhangel'sk within Muscovy, located itself in an Arctic region that did not produce a grain surplus, was one obstacle. Grain from faraway areas needed to be transported to the White Sea port. Even if that proved possible, the town lacked sufficient warehouses to store grain. Significant investment, then, was needed and this was the main reason Trip and the others suggested the creation of a company monopolizing the Russian grain trade. But the Estates-General rejected the idea of creating a monopoly company for this purpose, probably because it wanted to explore the possible scope of Russian grain exports first. The Dutch authorities did agree around the same time to support Trip and Gommert Spranger in acquiring vast amounts of saltpeter in Russia in exchange for substantial arms purchases, as saltpeter was produced not far from Arkhangel'sk. This constituted the first wholehearted official Dutch support for the arms trade with Russia, which would take further flight.[8]

It took some time to select an ambassador, as the Dutch maritime provinces quarreled about preeminence; only in the spring of 1630 it was decided that the embassy was to be led by Albert Burgh (1593–1647) of Amsterdam and Johan van Veltdriel of the Frisian port of Dokkum; both men were members of the Estates-General for their provinces, besides being magistrates of their cities.[9] The mission was to travel via Arkhangel'sk, rather than through Narva or Riga. The party sailed from Texel on July 12, swiftly making progress and arriving at Arkhangel'sk after slightly more than five weeks on the water, an unusually fast trip.[10] Moscow was reached in mid-December 1630, the slow journey overland—which was however not especially long[11]—rather contrasting with the speed of the seaborne travel. In January 1631, after the ceremonial welcoming audience in which the envoys greeted the tsar, discussions began between the ambassadors and the tsarist officials, who were led by one of the most influential court nobles, Prince Ivan Borisovich Cherkasskii (c. 1580–1642), who was assisted by the boyar Mikhail Borisovich Shein (c.1580–1634), and several clerical assistants (*d'iaki*).[12] The Dutch were looking for lower tariffs for all of their compatriots, fewer restrictions in trading with the Russians otherwise, and a steady supply of grain; they dangled elaborate arms' sales before the Russians in exchange for this grain. In addition, they suggested the permanent installation of a diplomatic resident in Moscow.[13] As Burgh and Van Veltdriel pointed out to the Russians, permanent envoys represented the United Provinces in only a handful of countries (respectively, France, Britain, Venice, Sweden, and the Ottoman Empire). This proposal, then, was aimed to reflect the special fondness and high regard of the Dutch for Muscovy. A somewhat eccentric additional request sought to allow Dutch grain farmers to come to Russia to break new ground on which to cultivate their crops in Muscovy. More prosaically, the embassy was loaded with a bevy of expensive gifts, among which a variety of state-of-the-art weapons figured prominently, specimens displaying Dutch technological ingenuity.[14]

In response, the Russians expressed their puzzlement with what they understood to be the existence of a Turkish-Dutch alliance (which was in fact a mere trade treaty), while asking whether their own officials might be allowed to hire mercenaries in the United Provinces.[15] Further Muscovite bewilderment seems to have been generated by the lack of any Dutch interest in anything but commerce. The official Russian reply of March 1631 rejected the Dutch request to be allowed to trade freely throughout Russia. And the Russians could not promise any regular export of grain, even if they were willing to dispatch occasional shipments from Arkhangel'sk; a Dutch monopoly on this trade was out of the question. The relocation of Dutch farmers to Russia was rejected, since the Russians feared the outbreak of quarrels with Russian agriculturalists.

The Dutch authorities had grown anxious about grain deliveries, meanwhile, as granaries in the country had been depleting in the autumn of 1630 and winter of 1630–1631; several lower-ranked emissaries were dispatched to Moscow to urge the ambassadors to request the Russians for a substantial immediate grain export in spring 1631.[16] Once the rather disappointing negotiations with the Russians were over, Van Veltdriel left Moscow before Burgh, who stayed a bit longer to iron out some further details; when Burgh was on his way back, he crossed with another Dutch messenger at Vologda in the spring of 1631.[17] There, Burgh was apprised of the even more acute need for grain that had arisen in the United Provinces. To redouble his efforts to get as much grain as he could get from the Russians, the Estates-General implored him to return to Moscow, while it also ordered him to lobby for trading rights for a Dutch consortium that wanted to import Iranian silk across the Caspian and along the Volga to Moscow and onward to Arkhangel'sk.

Burgh was permitted to go back to the Russian capital by the Russians to reopen discussions with the tsar's officials. The silk-transit proposal was rejected, but the tsar proved willing to deliver more grain to Arkhangel'sk that year, even if not to the amount desired by the Dutch; nor were the Russians willing to guarantee grain supplies for a three-year period at a fixed price suggested by the Dutch. As Kordt wrote, the Burgh-Van Veltdriel embassy made evident that Russian grain could not replace the Baltic supply that fed the United Provinces.[18] And for the Russians, as Wijnroks adds, the Dutch proved overly reluctant about supplying arms to Russia to aid its preparations for another war with Poland.[19] Nonetheless, in effect little was placed in the way of Russian efforts to acquire weapons in United Provinces, or hire mercenary soldiers there, in the early 1630s.[20]

The embassy, then, while aimed at shoring up economic ties, did not meet with any substantial success: Wijnroks deems it a fiasco.[21] Perhaps such a judgment is too harsh, even when it had been a rather expensive venture that, from the Dutch government's perspective, yielded little immediate return. Still, the mission certainly did not harm private trade and Dutch business with Russia flourished for the rest of Mikhail's reign and beyond. From the

Russian perspective, meanwhile, the prospect of an outright military alliance with the Dutch (which might be shepherded through a permanent envoy) seemed hardly useful because of the United Provinces' remoteness.

In addition, before Peter the Great's rule the Russian elite (from whose ranks the Romanovs had only recently been elevated to the tsarship) was uncomfortable dealing with a country of rebellious upstarts who lacked a monarch (this discomfort is evident as well in the Russian response to the beheading of the English monarch Charles I in 1649, when they broke off all diplomatic relations). Indeed, in 1630 and 1631 the Dutch had yet to be officially recognized as independent from Habsburg rule by all European Powers (this would only happen at Münster in 1648). Republics were an anomaly in early modern Europe, and the tsar and his entourage may have feared that any overly close ties with the Dutch political rebels might jeopardize the international prestige craved by the still novel and somewhat shaky Romanov monarchy. Tsar Mikhail had been enthroned toward the conclusion of a devastating political rebellion in Russia itself, and his rule was still to be formally acknowledged by some important players on the European scene, such as the Polish king.

The enormous potential of maritime trade and the utility of a navy or a merchant marine had yet to dawn upon the Russian leadership; Muscovy had been a landlocked country for most of its existence, with foreign ships or carts bringing goods to its border ports. No need was felt to explore any possibilities in this direction for more intensive relations with the Dutch in a quest to strengthen the Russian state by opening new avenues for economic gain.

Apart from the Dutch interest in grain and silk and the Russian interest in arms, a number of other goods were in significant amounts traded between the two countries by this time. Wijnroks and Kotilaine both note how in the early decades bullion formed a considerable part of Russian imports shipped by the Dutch.[22] Gemstones (including pearls) and textiles, too, were initially of some importance as well.[23] Because only three to four dozen ships departed Arkhangel'sk for Western Europe every year, the capacity for shipping bulk goods from Russia was limited.[24] Thus, pelts, silk, leather, tar, wax, hemp, rope, or potash were loaded at Arkhangel'sk, rather than great amounts of lumber or grain, but shipping volume did increase in the course of the century, allowing for the increased transport of heavier products such as lumber.

As a final relevant point regarding the Russia trade, Wijnroks, even if unable to render a wholly comprehensive calculation through the inadequacy of the sources, argues that the Dutch export to Muscovy was significant in value for the Dutch.[25] Like the trade on the East Indies, it was not particularly large in *volume* as compared to the trade on the Baltic. But it did amount to more than 500,000 rubles per year for much of the seventeenth century, or more than 10 percent of the total *value* of Dutch exports, as he suggests in in his inconclusive computation.²⁶ What seems certainly true is that the value of the Dutch trade with Russia has been underestimated in much of the historiography on the Republic.

Despite the failure of the Van Veltdriel-Burgh mission to shore up relations between Moscow and The Hague, Russian agents in the United Provinces were allowed to recruit mercenaries and enable arms' shipments to Russia in the early 1630s. The tsar and his father, Patriarch Filaret, sought revenge for the humiliation (Filaret had spent almost a decade in Polish captivity) they had suffered at the hand of the Poles and the loss of territory as confirmed by the 1618 Truce of Deulino. The Scottish officer Alexander Leslie (1582–1661), who would become a renowned commander in the British civil wars, visited the United Provinces in the early 1630s and met with few obstacles in recruiting hundreds of soldiers in a country itself still entangled in a military conflict with Spain.²⁷ Leslie was helped by several Dutch assistants, such as the officer Hendrik van Dam and the entrepreneur Lus T(h)ieleman A(c)kema, soon to become a successful industrialist in Russia, who particularly aided in the acquisition of vast amounts of weapons.²⁸ A(c)kema was a Frisian Mennonite; finding employment in the arms trade-and-manufacturing branch constituted a rather unusual career path for an adherent of this pacifist religion.

NOTES

1. Kordt, "Ocherk," cxciv–cxcv; Wijnroks, *Handel*, 366–70. Apparently (at least according to Massa), Van Klenck's acquisition of the monopoly on caviar export had made him as rich as his former De Vogelaer bosses (Kordt, "Ocherk," cxcv). Meanwhile, Massa counted Elias Trip and Guillermo Bartolotti as being in his camp; given Massa's popularity in Stockholm (where De Geer and Trip were towering figures), this seems to fit the evidence (ibid., cxcv). For De Geer and Trip, see Jonker and Sluyterman, *At Home*, 58–9.

2. Kordt, "Ocherk," cic–cc. As previously noted, he switched wholly to the Swedish side.

3. See as well Wijnroks, *Handel*, 354, 358.

4. Note as well the divided loyalty of the Marselis or De Geer families (see Boterbloem, *Dirty Secret*, 153–8).

5. For a fairly detailed contemporary account including a rendition of some of the instructions and official exchanges between the Dutch and Russian governments, see Lieuwe van Aitzema, *Saken van Staet en Oorlogh . . .*, vol. 1, 's-Gravenhaghe: J. Veely, J. Tongerloo, and J. Doll, 1669, 1041–52.

6. Kordt, "Ocherk," ccvii–ccviii.

7. Kotilaine, "When the Twain," 124.

8. Kordt, "Ocherk," ccix–ccx; Wijnroks, *Handel*, 236, 323–5. On Spranger, see Wijnroks, *Handel*, 260–1, 263–5. He died in 1637 in Amsterdam (see Montias, *Art at Auction*, 23, 25, 99, 118).

9. Kordt, "Ocherk," ccxvi; Wijnroks, *Handel*, 236–7. Dokkum, at the time, was a key port housing the Frisian Admiralty (it moved to Harlingen in 1645; see Thea Roodhuyzen, *De Admiraliteit van Friesland*, Franeker: Van Wijnen, 2003, 8–9). See also the recent T.S. Minaeva, "Deiatel'nost' perevodchikov pri prieme gollandskikh posol'stv' na Russkom Severe v xvii veke," *Vestnik Severnoi Federal'nogo Universiteta, Seriia: Gumanitarnye i sotsial'nye nauki* 6, 2019, 23–33.

10. Kordt, "Ocherk," ccxxxvi–ccxxxvii.

11. Some of the slow pace resulted from the changing weather in the autumn, which forced travelers to switch from traversing waterways by boat to snow by sleigh-ride, usually after a pause for some days when water was beginning to freeze but roads were not yet frozen hard. The distance between the two cities is about 1000 kilometers as the crow flies, but amounted in effect to about 1,500 kilometers.

12. Shein was to be executed in 1634, seen as the main culprit for the Russian defeat in the Smolensk War.

13. Kordt, "Ocherk," ccxl.

14. Wijnroks, *Handel*, 237; Aitzema, *Saken*, 1049–50. About the key importance of the arms trade, see also Boterbloem, *Dirty Secret*.

15. Kordt, "Ocherk," ccxli–ccxliv.

16. Ibid., ccxlv–ccxlvi; Aitzema, *Saken*, 1041.

17. Kordt, "Ocherk," ccli–ccliv.

18. Kordt, "Ocherk," cclvii–cclviii.

19. Wijnroks, *Handel*, 237.

20. Boterbloem, *Dirty Secret*, 172–3.

21. Wijnroks, *Handel*, 237–8.

22. Ibid., 315–21; Kotilaine, "When the Twain," 36–7.

23. Wijnroks, *Handel*, 315–17.

24. Ibid., 329–31.

25. Ibid., 312–13.

26. See especially ibid., 313n22, 314.

27. Ibid., 286, 323n45. Leslie was given funds to pay for his transactions by the Marselises, Klenck, Margaretha van Valckenburg, Karel du Moulin and Jean and Daniël Bernarts. I doubt the Estates-General put a halt to Leslie's and Van Dam's recruitment, even if they formally prohibited it (see ibid., 286).

28. Ibid., 256–7. See K. Boterbloem, *Moderniser of Russia: Andrei Vinius, 1641–1716*, Houndmills, Basingstoke: Palgrave, 2013, 37–8; Boterbloem, *Dirty Secret*, 176, 198; Posselt, *Franz Lefort*, vol. 1, 153.

Chapter 10

Medicine

During the era covered in this study, the Russian government employed a number of Dutch doctors and other medical personnel.[1] Indeed, from the late years of Ivan the Terrible to Peter's reign at least one Dutch native served the tsar as a member of the highest medical staff in the country. The first of this long-lasting sequence appears to have been Johan Eyloff, like Akema an anabaptist, who was personal physician of Ivan IV in his later years; some suggest that he fled Moscow after the tsar's death in 1584, because he was suspected of having murdered Ivan.[2] Eyloff's descendants seem to have settled in Russia, which might indicate that the story of his flight is a myth, and his departure merely due to some staff changes after Ivan's death.[3] Indeed, Eyloff's story may have been confused with that of a likely compatriot, who is best known to history as Elias van Bommel. Van Bommel, after a stint at the English court of Queen Elizabeth I (r. 1558–1603), was hired by Ivan IV in the early 1570s; once in Moscow, he became notorious as a poison-monger, astrologer, and alchemist, advising an ever more deranged tsar.[4] He ultimately seems to have tried to flee Russia, but was apprehended; accused of plotting against Ivan, he was tortured and executed in 1579.

In the wake of Eyloff followed the Frisian Arent Claeszoon van Stellingwerff, who served a sequence of tsars as apothecary from the mid-1570s until his death in 1621.[5] His son Jacob Arentszoon traveled in the company of Isaac Massa from Moscow to Amsterdam in 1616 to begin his advanced studies there, while a grandson of Arent Claesz left Russia for Amsterdam in the 1640s to learn about trade, with Jurriaan van Klenck facilitating this apprenticeship.[6] Similar to Eyloff, the Dutch medical experts often let down roots in Russia, too, and may have done so more often than compatriots specialized in other trades.[7]

An odd character at the tsar's court was Boudewijn (Beaudoin/Baldwin) Hamey, sr (1568–1641), a physician born in Bruges whose parents had fled to the northern Netherlands to escape Catholic persecution of Protestants.[8] Hamey studied medicine at the new university at Leyden, where he received his degree in 1592.[9] Not finding a position that suited him, he was invited to become the tsar's doctor in 1594—on the recommendation of his mentor at Leyden, the then famous Johannes Heurnius—arriving in Russia in the summer of that same year.[10] Eventually to Hamey's relief, his contract was for a limited term, and he departed Russian service after a mere three years, in 1597, not long before Tsar Fyodor I died.[11] While he had earned a considerable sum, the money had evidently not been good enough to persuade him to prolong his stay, even when his future Dutch wife joined him at Arkhangel'sk (he had made up his mind by then and they returned together to Holland, rather than proceed to Moscow). It is not exactly clear what caused him to dislike his job, but the paranoid atmosphere at the court and the suspicion many Russians harbored about foreigners appear to have worn him out. After Fyodor I's death in 1598, Tsar Boris Godunov invited Hamey to return, but the doctor preferred an uncertain future in London above a much more lucrative job in Moscow.[12] Thus, he avoided the Time of Troubles.

In Boudewijn Hamey's case, one detects the strong sense of alienation that befalls many a person even today when confronted with a very different culture, and still now engulfs many Westerners when visiting the Russian Federation. Some other evidence about this alienation already survives from Hamey's days, such as Dutchmen complaining about the Russian penchant for bacchanalian abandon.[13] The inebriation and open promiscuity practiced by some of the Russians at times offended the Dutch, although it might be asked in how far they behaved differently when celebrating. Indeed, others joyfully immersed themselves in Russian culture: Some of the Dutch expatriates happily joined Russian revelries.

It is interesting to ponder the relatively small proportion of Dutch speakers among the various Western-born and Western-educated medical specialists who were active in Muscovy from the mid-sixteenth to the early eighteenth century, given the marked Dutch presence among Western experts in Russian life otherwise.[14] It is true that usually one Dutchman at least served as physician, pharmacist, or surgeon, but each was surrounded by greater numbers of Englishmen, Scots, and Germans. The reign of Tsar Mikhail was a bit of an anomaly, when a higher than usual number of Dutchmen part of the Kremlin's medical staff: Successively, Valentijn Biels Bijls sr (arriving in 1615, dying in Russia in 1633), Hiob (Job) Paludanus, and Reinier Rooclaes Pauw were hired to serve as the monarch's personal physician, while Hendrick Hassen (Haasen/Hasenius) was hired as a pharmacist in this same period (and Stellingwerff only died in 1621).[15]

A hiatus followed after Pauw, who had not been very successful in treating some of his patients, returned to the Republic in 1643.[16] It may be that Tsar Aleksei, who succeeded in 1645, was initially less fond of Dutch physicians than his father had been, perhaps because of Pauw's poor record. Soon after Aleksei's death, in 1677, Andrei Vinius took the helm of the key medical office in Muscovy, the *Aptekarskii prikaz*, and Dutch surgeons and doctors reappear, such as Jan (van) Termundt (c. 1640–1704) and Zacharias (Arnoldus) van der Hulst (d. 1694).[17]

Job, or Jacob, Paludanus had two stints in Russia, from 1616 to 1621 and again from 1627 until his death about a decade later. With permission granted by the Dutch Estates-General to serve the tsar, he arrived at Arkhangel'sk in 1616 together with the Massa and the pharmacist Hasenius.[18] A translator was assigned to him, one Elisei Pavlov, and Paludanus was well provided for on his descent down from Arkhangel'sk to Moscow, a sign of the great respect for the doctor's learning at the court in Moscow. Despite the great appreciation he received from the Russians, Paludanus was homesick, and with the help of a letter of Stadtholder Maurice of May 1621 given leave to go home by Tsar Mikhail.[19] Paludanus returned in 1627, however, and seems to have died in Russia in 1636 or 1637.[20]

It is noteworthy that Paludanus was probably a protégé (and possibly a relative) of Bernhard (Berent) Paludanus (ten Broecke, 1550–1633), a well-known doctor who resided in Enkhuizen (where he was friend with the Dutch pioneering explorer and travel writer Jan Huyghen van Linschoten). This Bernhard Paludanus was one of the first people ever to have a curiosity chamber, which was sold to the patron of Adam Olearius, Friedrich III of Holstein-Gottorf (1597–1659); Olearius would inventorize the Paludanus collection for the duke.[21] Olearius subsequently acquired everlasting fame for the account of his travels to Muscovy and Iran as part of a 1630s Holsteiner embassy, a book popular as well in Dutch translation, as we saw.[22] An agreement was struck to establish a Holstein-based trading company transporting raw Iranian silk across Russia to Europe, but the plan faltered. This was due in part because the crossing of the Caspian Sea proved treacherous for deep-lying ships; on one such ship, partially built by Dutch shipwrights and crewed by Dutch sailors, Olearius's party was shipwrecked.[23]

It seems relevant as well that Bernard Paludanus was asked to take on the organization of Leyden University's *Hortus Botanicus* in 1591 (which offer he declined); a link with the seventeenth-century development of a herb garden of the Apothecary Office in Moscow may be suspected, particularly because Heurnius, Hamey's patron, will have known Bernard Paludanus.[24] Meanwhile, Bernard Paludanus had visited Poland-Lithuania in the 1570s, which may explain the willingness with which his protégé departed for

Moscow, for whom Russia was likely not as wholly mysterious a land as it may have been for others.[25]

Valentijn Biels (Bijls) earned more than 4,000 guilders annually, plus a bonus of considerable amounts of valuable goods such as furs, when he was in the Tsar Mikhail's service.[26] In other words, remuneration was good, for Biels's salary alone translates into 20 times the annual income of the average Dutch craftsman.[27] As we saw already with Jacob Arentszoon van Stellingwerff, travel prohibitions that applied to most foreigners were waived for medical personnel: Biels's son, who went by the same name as his father, was allowed to leave Russia to study medicine in Holland. While the money and perquisites were good, physicians' responsibilities, meanwhile, were onerous, given the delicate nature of human health before the discovery of inoculation, antibiotics, and so on. For, as Unkovskaya writes, "all royal physicians [treated] large numbers of nobles, as well as the royal family and courtiers."[28]

At the height of the 1620s Dutch frenzy to capture the Russian market and explore the opportunities for enrichment that Muscovy seemed to offer, a number of veritable adventurers tried to enter the country, among whom was Quirijn Breemburch, a quack who dabbled in the gray zone between magic and medicine.[29] At other times as well, opportunists of all hue knocked on the Russian gate, with mixed results. Thus, the soldier of fortune François Lefort, as we will see, was lucky to be allowed to stay after he had arrived from the Netherlands at Arkhangel'sk in 1675.[30]

A different sort of adventurer, albeit not Dutch by birth (nor was his sponsor Konrad Nordermann), was Quirinus Kuhlmann. Kuhlmann resided for a significant period of his life in the Republic, which was a relative sanctuary for people with unorthodox ideas.[31] Kuhlmann appeared in Moscow in 1689 where he began to preach in the *sloboda* about the Day of Judgment being at hand; he said he had been overcome by visions in which the tsar (presumably Peter, even if Ivan V was still around as well) was to lead the forces of the good in their ultimate battle with evil. He was denounced to the Russian authorities, who burned both Kuhlmann and Nordermann at the stake on Red Square, an utterly rare occasion in Russian history of the public execution of a heretic.

The young Peter the Great became friends with the Frisian surgeon Jan (van) Termund (Termundt/Termond), who served the tsars for almost four decades.[32] In this age, surgeons were not considered as academically accomplished as doctors, for they were skilled practitioners rather than university-trained. They probably saved more lives than doctors, however, as they regularly healed soldiers and sailors wounded in battle with crude but effective methods, especially in preventing gangrene from developing. Termund, meanwhile, served in capacities other than that of surgeon; when he fell into

Cossack captivity in 1670, he was on a trip to Iran to gather herbs, plants, and potions for the tsarist pharmacy and botanical garden.

Termund was in 1678 employed as a surgeon in Moscow's Apothecary Department (then headed by A.A. Vinius); as such he was performing the role of an army doctor, as is evident from the fact that in the course of that year he was dispatched to Sevsk to treat the wounded mercenary officer Andrew Hamilton.[33] Sabine Dumschat suggests that he became Peter's "*Leibartz*" (personal physician), despite, as a mere surgeon, lacking academic medical training.[34] What seems evident is that Termund instructed Peter in the art of medicine and allowed the tsar to accompany him on visits to his patients. Besides training Peter, he taught several other Russian apprentices.[35] Being a brawler and a drunk might have Termund further recommended to Peter, who was utterly fond of carousing himself.[36] As a clear sign of the tsar's affection for Termund, the latter participated in the 1697–1698 Grand Embassy to Western Europe, overseeing the ambassadorial suite's medical staff.[37] Concomitantly, his salary grew exponentially, from 1,800 guilders (360 rubles) for the year in 1692—about half of Arnoud van der Hulst's—to 3,200 guilders in 1697.[38] To place this in perspective, the average skilled worker in the Dutch Republic annually earned approximately 200 guilders.[39]

When he was a teenager, Peter's personal physician was Arnoud (Zacharias) van der Hulst, who died in 1694. It is difficult to assess the intimacy of the doctor–patient relationship in Muscovy.[40] Before Aleksei's rule doctors had to literally keep their distance from their patients, who remained dressed. Diagnoses were cast long-distance, so to say. Physicians were not even allowed to be in the presence of women of the royal family. In the course of the seventeenth century things gradually loosened up a bit, but it is not quite clear in how far true confidentiality existed between Van der Hulst and Peter. Van der Hulst, though, did seem to have alerted Peter to Frans Timmerman's ability in being able to explain the workings of the astrolabe and the scientific principles of seafaring.

Finally, the Mennonite Nicolaas Bidloo (c. 1670–1735) deserves mention, a figure who played a larger role in Russia than that of a medical expert alone. Near the Western suburb, he founded a (military) training hospital (especially intended to educate surgeons) after several years of serving as Peter's personal physician on military campaigns.[41] His estate and gardens became one of the most admired properties in the foreigners' suburb in its final decades. Because he sketched his manor himself with great technical skill, we, too, can admire its effigy still today.[42]

The strong admiration for Western medicine at the Muscovite court, meanwhile, is puzzling; as Roy Porter and others have shown, the greater success of "modern" Western academic and nonacademic healing methods over traditional remedies was marginal at most, both in Western countries themselves and in countries in which Western doctors practiced, such as Russia.[43] The lives of the Romanov tsars were remarkably brief, with Mikhail, Aleksei, and Peter all dying around the age of 50. Ivan IV, likewise fond of Western physicians, was 53 when he died. Perhaps it was a genetic defect, perhaps it was poor or one-sided nutrition, but Western doctors proved incapable of prolonging the tsars' lives into their 60s (Elizabeth I was almost 70 and Louis XIV neared 80 when they passed away, after all). And the doctors were likewise unable to stop the spread of epidemic diseases, as in the case of the 1654–1655 scourge (which may have killed three-quarters of the population in some Russian settlements).[44] Such illnesses ran their course, with survivors saved by luck rather than through medical procedures (even if quarantine was applied in Russia, too).

NOTES

1. For an exhaustive overview, see Sabine Dumschat, *Ausländische Mediziner in Moskauer Rußland*, Stuttgart: Franz Steiner Verlag, 2006. She counted 294 medical doctors from abroad (primarily Christian Europe) who can be linked to Russia between the late fifteenth century and 1696; 240 of them indeed worked at the tsar's court (ibid., 16). After Peter's Grand Embassy, a veritable invasion of foreign doctors commenced, while from that point onward the Russians themselves in ever greater numbers studied medicine (ibid., 16–17).

2. I. van Esso, "Hollandsche artsen in Russischen hof- en staatsdienst in de 16e, 17e en 18e eeuw," *Bijdragen tot de Geschiedenis der Geneeskunde* 18, 1938, 1102–12: 1105; Dumschat, *Ausländische Mediziner*, 443–4, 605–6. Esso identifies as well as Dutch medical experts Valentijn Bijls—father and son—, Job Paludanus, Reinhardt Pauw, the charlatan Quirinus Bremburg, Jacob Arensen, Russified son of the Moscow-residing pharmacist Zacharias Arensen [van Stellingwerff]—who absconded once he began studying in seventeenth-century Amsterdam—, Matthias Damius, who like Bremburg did not get beyond Arkhangel'sk in the 1620s, Henricus Dominicus Koopman/Kaufman (sent back from Arkhangel'sk in 1620s), and Zacharias van der Hulst; as well, under Peter, Verstegen, Huyson, Van Haghen, Hovy and Termont (ibid., 1105–12). Specifically accompanying Cornelis Cruys in 1697 were, besides Van Haghen, the surgeons Haskus, Plaatman, Nuyts, Schiot, Van Wessem, Van Huysum, Van der Weer, Diederik van der Hulst, van Eych, Van der Noot, and Ravesteyn (ibid., 1112). Termu(o)n(d)t, a protagonist of Struys, *Drie aanmerkelijke Reysen*, may have been in Russian service from 1660 until his death in 1704; he was likely known previously in his native Frisia as Jan van Kollum (see Eekhoff, "Friezen," 33).

3. Dumschat, *Ausländische Mediziner*, 470; Johan Eyloff and his son Joris seem to have dabbled in trade, chartering ships carrying goods to Russia in the early 1580s (Wijnroks, *Handel*, 119, 121).

4. Dumschat, *Ausländische Mediziner*, 121, 133, 248, 574–5.

5. Ibid., 441–2, 679.
6. Ibid., 414, 679–80.
7. Thus also the Stellingwerff-Hassen clan, and the Biels and the Van der Hulst families, see ibid., 471, 474–6.
8. See John J. Keevil, *Hamey the Stranger*, London: Geoffrey Bles, 1952, 9.
9. Ibid., 13, 20.
10. Ibid., 23–5, 39–40.
11. Ibid., 59–63.
12. It seems his son (identified as the "Englishman Baldvinus Hamaeus") was acquainted with the Muiden Circle of artists, see Montias, *Art at Auction*, 216.
13. Wijnroks, *Handel*, 292–3.
14. See Dumschat, *Ausländische Mediziner*, 101.
15. Ibid., 566–7, 629–30, 654–6; and several others tried to get hired, such as Quirinus Bremburg, ultimately expelled from Moscow as a quack (ibid., 197–8, 265, 576–7). Hassen stayed to work as pharmacist in Moscow, until his death in 1656 (ibid., 251).
16. Ibid., 154–5, 268–9, 655. This Reinier Pauw was probably the same as the son of the Amsterdam regent and notorious Contra-Remonstrant (strict Calvinist) of the same name, who was interested in the trade on Central Asia; the elder Pauw attempted to have the famous writer Joost van den Vondel tried for a play that praised the beheaded Johan van Oldenbarnevelt; Vondel seems to have received the support of both Albert Burgh (the Muscovy ambassador of 1630–1631) and of Dirck Bas (the ambassador of 1616) in the matter, both of whom were of a more liberal Calvinist inclination (see Montias, *Art at Auction*, 81).
17. See Boterbloem, *Moderniser*, 102–12; Dumschatz, *Ausländische Mediziner*, 85–9, 165, 289, 323–4, 370, 632–3, 684–5. Van der Hulst's son, known as Zakharii Zakhar'evich von der Gulst, studied in Leyden and was a key figure in the fledgling medical community of St. Petersburg (ibid., 633).
18. Richter, *Geschichte*, vol. 2, 25–6. Much more recent is Dumschat, *Ausländische Mediziner*. As she points out, Richter germanized every name, including those of Netherlandic doctors (see Dumschat, *Ausländische Mediziner*, 37; see as well Van Esso, "Hollandsche artsen," 1104). For Paludanus, see ibid., 654. For Hassen/Hasenius, see Wijnroks, *Handel*, 291–2n27.
19. Richter, *Geschichte*, vol. 2, 27–9. Asked in the *posol'skii prikaz* for further clarification about his desire to leave, Paludanus apparently pleaded for his release by noting that he wanted to care for his elderly parents. Dumschat suggests that he sailed back to Holland in the company of Jan Marcuszoon de Vogelaer in 1622 (Dumschat, *Ausländische*, 654).
20. Richter, *Geschichte*, vol. 2, 29. Pauw arrived in 1638 (see Dumschat, *Ausländische*, 655). His family was accompanied by Peter Marselis on their trip to Russia (via Riga, while Pauw himself went by way of Arkhangel'sk).
21. See F.W.T. Hunger, *Bernardus Paludanus (Berent ten Broecke) (1550–1633)*, Leiden: Brill, 1928 [special issue of *Janus* 32, 1928], 8–10, 12.
22. Olearius, *Beschrijvingh*.
23. Phillips, *Founding*.

24. Hunger, *Bernardus*, 5–6.
25. Ibid., 2. Paludanus appears to have been a convert to Calvinism (ibid., 5)
26. Richter, *Geschichte*, vol. 2, 22–4; his son was helped out by Karel du Moulin to complete his studies at Leyden after his Biels sr's death in 1633 (Dumschat, *Ausländische Mediziner*, 249–50). It took years for Biels jr to complete his studies, which cost Du Moulin and the Russian government hundreds of rubles before Biels finally returned to settle in Moscow in 1643. Surprisingly, Biels jr was dismissed in 1644, but, as the tsar's subject, could not leave the country (Dumschat, *Ausländische Mediziner*, 273).
27. Van Deursen, *Plain Lives*, 7.
28. M. Unkovskaya, "Samuel Collins," *Oxford Dictionary of National Biography*, available at: https://doi-org.ezproxy.lib.usf.edu/10.1093/ref:odnb/5951, accessed October 2, 2019.
29. Wijnroks, *Handel*, 293.
30. A.Z. Myshlaevskii, "Vyezd v Rosiiu Frantsa Leforta (Sovremennaia perepiska)," *Russkaia starina* 3, 1898: 635–49.
31. Boterbloem, *Moderniser*, 124–5 and 132n18, 133n21, 133n22, and 133n23. Van der Hulst and Vinius seem to have been interested in Kuhlmann's preaching.
32. Boterbloem, *Fiction and Reality*, 93, 113, 178.
33. Richter, *Geschichte*, vol. 2, 14. See as well John Appleby, "Ivan the Terrible to Peter the Great: British Formative Influence on Russia's Medico-Apothecary System," *Medical History* 27, 1983, 289–304.
34. Dumschat, *Ausländische*, 165.
35. Ibid., 358.
36. Ibid., 458; Bogoslovskii, *Petr Velikii*, vol. 1, 140.
37. Bogoslovskii, *Petr Velikii*, vol. 1, 379.
38. Posselt, *Franz Lefort*, vol. 2, 109note.
39. Van Deursen, *Plain Lives*, 7.
40. Lahana, "Novaia Nemetskaia Sloboda," 166.
41. Driessen, *Tsaar Peter de Grote*, 63; Alla Vein, "Nicolaas Bidloo, the Dutch Director of the First Hospital in Russia: A 300-Year Anniversary," *Nederlands Tijdschrift voor Geneeskunde*, January 2008, 2909–12; Van Zuiden, *Bijdrage*, 22–3. Leo de Boer made a documentary film about him, "Paradijs in Moskou," broadcasted by *NTR* on February 9, 2014, available at: https://www.npostart.nl/het-uur-van-de-wolf/09-02-2014/NPS_1242425, accessed November 22, 2019.
42. See Erik de Jong, "Virgilian Paradise: A Dutch Garden near Moscow in the Early Eighteenth Century," *Journal of Garden History* 4, 1981, 305–44. See for them the documentary "Paradijs in Moskou."
43. For example, see Roy Porter, *The Greatest Benefit to Mankind: A Medical History of Humanity*, New York: Norton, 1997, 231.
44. Lahana, "Novaia Nemetskaia Sloboda," 96.

Chapter 11

Dutch Entrepreneurs

Much has been written (especially by the American scholar Joseph Fuhrmann) about the activities of Andries Denijszoon Winius (and his initial partners Lus Tieleman Akema and Peter Marselis) as a pioneer industrialist in 1630s Muscovy.[1] Fuhrmann established that the great majority of manufacturing and mining entrepreneurs in seventeenth-century Muscovy were Dutch natives. Almost invariably, male relatives (fathers, sons, brothers, nephews) got eventually involved in the business, and at least in the case of Jan van Sweeden, his widow (who was a daughter of the formidable Ruts family[2]). Most entrepreneurial families of Dutch stock operated for several decades in Russia. Although a superficial glance might lead one to conclude that few of these businesses were truly successful, since almost all of them were taken over toward 1700, or even entirely disappeared, one can actually argue the opposite, as we already saw in the case of the Vogelaer firm (even if this was a trading house, not a manufacturing enterprise). Business history suggests that companies rarely survive for more than a few decades (with most start-ups collapsing within a handful of years); in Muscovy, however, an enterprise such as Coyett's glass-blowing plant survived from the 1630s into the 1670s and beyond, while in one form or other the Tula iron- and weapons plants founded by Winius outlasted the entire Romanov dynasty.[3] A high proportion of Dutch-led enterprises were therefore rather robust ventures, although, of course, there were rather few of them—several dozen at most by Fuhrmann's count—in this preindustrial (or proto-industrial) age, in a country where capital (or credit) was in short supply. And, of course, some businesses did fail quickly, such as the textile mills Zakhar (Arendt) Paulsen and Egidius Tabbert ran in the 1680s.[4]

Meanwhile, like Karsten Brandt teaching Peter about sailing in the late 1680s, Dutch manufacturers taught numerous Russians the tricks of their trade, often enough a stipulation imposed on the entrepreneurs by the tsarist authorities. Although this was not always a smooth process—there were complaints about the transfer of knowledge and expertise occurring at the Tula works and other similar plants—it worked on the whole and likely gained further momentum once the "second generation" joined the family business. These children of the pioneering businessmen or craftsmen tended to be fluent in Russian: Instruction of Russian speakers in their trade was less of an ordeal for them. As with the Russian army and navy, the constant objective of the Russian government was to have Westerners train Russians in their expertise. In this manner, Russians would eventually replace the Westerners. It proved both a successful method in the manufacturing branch and in the armed forces. Like the military, the burgeoning manufacturing sector aided Muscovy in its attempts to best its long-standing foes Sweden, the *Rzeczpospolita*, and, eventually, the Crimean Tatars and their patrons, the Ottoman Turks after 1650.[5]

An outstanding example of a mentor transferring highly prized knowledge and expertise was the interpreter on the Russian side of the Boreel, Heins, and Van Klenck missions, Andrei Andreevich Vinius.[6] This son of Andries Winius was instrumental in presenting strategic information about Europe and the world through the *kuranty*, or in the account of his own ambassadorial mission of 1672–1673, as well as guiding communications with the West during his long spell as head of the post office (begun by Van Sweeden). He led the government's apothecary office in Moscow, and made it into a fledgling health department with a broader mission in the 1670s and 1680s, in which Western doctors, surgeons, and pharmacists taught Russian apprentices. What is most germane here is that, accompanied by native Russians, he prospected for copper, iron, and gold in the region where the Kama joins the Volga during the 1670s, and actively encouraged the search for ore in Siberia when he headed the Siberian office in the 1690s and 1700s.[7]

Jan van Sweeden's name has already been mentioned several times in the previous pages. He seems to have started out as a *factor* (after arriving in Russia no later than 1646), a company agent, after which he set out on his own in the later 1650s. At that time, he moved from commodity trade to other areas, possibly inspired by the example of people such as Andries Winius.[8] Van Sweeden stood at the forefront of "Russian" entrepreneurship in the 1660s (until his sudden death in 1668).[9] A dispute erupted between him and the Amsterdam-based Russia traders Octavio Tensini and Govert van der Raeck in the mid-1660s. Van Sweeden persuaded the Russian authorities that these merchants owed him a large sum of money for goods delivered in Amsterdam. In Arkhangel'sk, their *factors* Philips Verpoorten and Daniel Hartman had been roughly interrogated by the Russians in response to Van Sweeden's request to investigate.[10] The Dutch ambassador

Jacob Boreel came to the defense of the Hartman-Verpoorten side on his visit to Moscow in 1665. Bizarrely, while Boreel angrily complained about Van Sweeden's heinous misdeeds to his tsarist interlocutors, Nicolaas Witsen, one of the high-level retainers (*"edelen"*) of the ambassador, seems to have happily sought out Van Sweeden to interview him about some finer details of the geography of the Russian empire and its adjacent parts.[11] Neither Van Sweeden nor Witsen seems to have cared much about the fact that Van Sweeden might have to stand trial for malpractice and intimidation in Holland, if he chose to return there. Perhaps Witsen saw the accusations against Van Sweeden as a tad frivolous (the Russian authorities firmly dismissed them). But perhaps Boreel's bark was louder than his bite: The bickering reminds of the sharp hostility (on behalf of Akema and Marselis) the Dutch Estates-General expressed toward Andries Winius in 1647 and 1648, which was then followed by an apparently unproblematic return of Winius as Russian agent to the Republic in 1653. Of course, Witsen himself did not have any grievances against Van Sweeden. From Witsen's meeting with the exiled Patriarch Nikon as well, it appears evident that this young Amsterdam patrician was quite willing to insubordinate his ambassadorial superior (as Naarden suggests), for he declined to notify Boreel of this clandestine visit to the tsar's strongest domestic political enemy, who would be deposed as head of the Russian church the next year.[12] If the tsar had found out about the encounter of one of the Dutchmen with Nikon, the embassy would likely have found a sudden ignominious end.

Van Sweeden became the first Russian postmaster-general in 1665 (around the time of the departure of the Boreel embassy for Holland), and soon was occupied as well with establishing a papermill and a textile manufactory near Moscow. By 1667, he was the key manager of the naval project that saw his agent David Butler (his relative by marriage) hire a number of Dutch shipwrights and sailors in Amsterdam.[13] The majority of the crew arrived in Moscow (from Riga) in late 1668, only to hear the news of Van Sweeden's recent death. They were allowed to stay at Van Sweeden's house in Moscow, where Maria Ruts-Van Sweeden, daughter of two famous Dutch families of Russia traders (her mother was a Maria de Moucheron, a daughter of the fortress builder Cosmo), hosted them until their ill-fated journey began that led them to Astrakhan and beyond.[14]

NOTES

1. See Fuhrmann, *Origins*; I.N. Iurkin, *Andrei Andreevich Vinius, 1641-1716*, Moscow: Nauka, 2007; Boterbloem, *Moderniser*; Lahana, "Novaia Nemetskaia Sloboda," 103–4; Jonker and Sluyterman, *At Home*, 59.

2. Wijnroks, *Handel*, 272. The Ruts family seems to have hailed from Cologne. David Nicolaasz. Ruts, who was married to a De Moucheron, was the junior partner of Du Moulin in the 1620s; in those days, Du Moulin frequently joined forces with both Jurriaan van Klenck and Thomas de Swaen, and was in business with Elias Trip shipping arms to the tsar. Based on one particular incident in the early 1640s, Arel suggests Peter Marselis was "German," which is odd, as his cause was championed by the Dutch Estates-General against Winius a few years later; it is true that one branch of the Marselis family worked out of Hamburg, but that does not make them necessarily "German"; it does show the difficulty (and anachronistic nature) of assigning people fixed national identities in this age, especially if hailing from the cosmopolitan merchant stratum (see Arel, *English Trade*, 209). Even Dutch diplomats (such as Jacob Boreel) sometimes proved willing to defend the cause of the Hamburgers and Bremeners, in part since many of their merchants who were active in Russia hailed from Netherlandic refugee communities.

3. See the graphics provided by JP Morgan, Chase and Company mentioned earlier in the notes in the section regarding De Vogelaer and Van Klenck's firm.

4. Lahana, "Novaia Nemetskaia Sloboda," 142, 149. Paulsen's residence is described in ibid., 206–7. More clothmakers seem to have arrived in Peter's reign (see ibid., 215–16).

5. Ibid., 105, 127, 142.

6. Iurkin, *Andrei Andreevich Vinius*; idem, *O pervoprestol'nogo grada Moskvy. A.A. Vinius v Moskve i Podmoskov'e*, Moscow: Moskva iazik, 2009; S.G. Miliukov, "Dumnyi d'iak Andrei Andreevich Vinius," unpubl. *Kandidat* dissertation, Moscow, 2000; Boterbloem, *Moderniser*.

7. See Boterbloem, *Moderniser*, 160–82.

8. Bruno Naarden suggests that Van Sweeden became Andrei Vinius's patron or guardian after Andries Winius's death, but his source is unclear (Naarden, "Nicolaas Witsen," 14).

9. Boterbloem, *Fiction*, 42–8; Boterbloem, *Moderniser*, 43–4, 54–5.

10. Witsen, *Moscovische Reyse*, vol. 1, xxxvi. See also *Nationaal Archief*, Archief der Staten-Generaal, 8523 (Boreel *Verbael*), 399–403, where Boreel argued that the money for Van Sweeden had been deposited on an account in Amsterdam, but that he now would be merely entitled to what would be left after restitution and damages were paid to Verpoorten, Hartman, Tensini, and Van der Raeck. The Russian reply appears to show intimidation of Van Sweeden by Tensini when Van Sweeden tried to collect his money in Amsterdam (Boreel *Verbael*, 674–89). One gets a whiff of old friends or partners falling out, each miffed by the breach of the mutual trust they once enjoyed (cf. Arel, *English Trade*, 8–9).

11. Witsen, *Moscovische Reyse*, vol. 1, xxxv–xxxvii; vol. 3, 373–88.

12. Naarden, "Nicolaas Witsen," 14.

13. Boterbloem, *Fiction*, 66–7.

14. Maria's grandfather (Nicolaas) was portrayed in 1631 by Rembrandt.

Chapter 12

Pivot: Boreel's Embassy

The Boreel Embassy departed from the Republic at a turning point for both Dutch and Russian history. While this seems evident in hindsight, its sponsors, participants, or hosts remained unaware of traversing a crossroads in history. In 1664, the Dutch were on top of the world. Their political chief Johan de Witt, the *raadspensionaris* of Holland, posturing as a sort of conductor of the European orchestra, carefully brokered its conflicts to maintain peace among its musicians. This proved an impossible task. Certainly, it seemed promising that the former eternal foes Spain and France finally concluded a lasting peace in 1659, the Treaty of the Pyrenees. But while their long-term conflict (which in some ways went all the way back to the Burgundian-Valois enmity of fifteenth-century France) had now ended, a peaceful Europe remained elusive. France soon replaced Spain as the aggressive Catholic Power in Western Europe. Since 1661 personally governed by the ambitious young Louis XIV, France was bristling to teach the arrogant Dutch *parvenus* a lesson and establish hegemony in Western Europe.

Not long before, the Dutch had for the first time gone to battle with the English (in a war from 1652 to 1654 which had concluded with a qualified English victory) and (in defense of Denmark) had also clashed with Sweden in the late 1650s. In Germany, the Thirty Years' War had led to an unsettled outcome, with the Habsburgs ultimately unable to truly dominate the affairs of the Holy Roman Empire, not least since they were set upon by the Ottoman Empire (with whom they fought another short war in 1663 and 1664). The Turks further underlined their continued expansionist designs by their victory in the Candian War with Venice in 1665, concluding 25 years of armed conflict. They clearly had their sights set on further conquests, particularly at the expense of a weakening Poland-Lithuania, which was not only still slugging it out with Russia in the Thirteen Years' War, but was enfeebled by the crisis to which it had almost succumbed during the mid-1650s. This "Deluge" (*Potop*) had seen it overwhelmed by Sweden, Russia, and the Transylvanian prince György Rakoczi: It was especially Austrian-Habsburg aid that saved the day for the Poles. In Germany proper, meanwhile, the Habsburgs faced a number of independent-minded princes who at most paid token homage to Emperor Leopold I (r. 1658–1705). Among them, especially the ruler of Brandenburg-Prussia (Frederick William, nicknamed the Great Elector, r. 1640–1688)—who was related by marriage to the Orange-Nassau family—was poised to increase his power.

Further abroad, the Dutch concluded a peace with Portugal in 1661, which confirmed the Dutch loss of Brazil. Their East India Company continued to wrest Sri Lanka from Portuguese control, nonetheless, while their West India Company increased its involvement in the slave trade from Africa to the Americas. The Second Anglo-Dutch War unofficially began around the time of Boreel's departure for Moscow, with major fighting between Dutch and British fleets off the West-African coast. The English wanted a share of the booming slave trade, and to cut the Dutch further down to size by reducing the Dutch share of global trading. The loss of Brazil to Portugal and the contest in the Atlantic (which would also involve Surinam and New York) with Britain shows the impossible challenge De Witt faced. Overextended everywhere, the Dutch could hardly enforce an all-European peace that would allow the Republic to maintain its economic lead. Although the war with Britain ended in a qualified Dutch victory, the end of Dutch preeminence neared. De Witt's balancing act collapsed within a few years after Boreel had returned from Moscow in 1665.

The Dutch were by the 1660s well established in Asia (and had a bridgehead at Africa's southernmost point as well), but they were unable to impose their will on the great potentates of the continent: The Ottoman sultan, the Iranian shah, the Mogul emperor of India, the Qing emperor of China, or the shogun of Japan who ruled in name of the Mikado (and a host of rulers of lesser stature in south-east Asia and elsewhere). They were tolerated for the assortment of commodities they bought and sold and the ease with which they shipped them in and out, but they were kept at arm's length, usually only permitted to occupy coastal fortresses, or maintain offices at the benevolent discretion of these sovereign rulers.

The Boreel embassy, then, came at the very moment that the Dutch economic fortune crested. The decline that followed was initially slow, and at first displayed itself more as a political (and military) enfeeblement than a prolonged economic downturn. This weakening coincided with a cultural waning, which may, or may not, have been coincidental: the successors of Rembrandt and Hals, who died in the 1660s and Vermeer, who died in 1675, did not match their talent, and in Dutch literature, too, an age of epigones commenced after about 1670. But the Dutch did not resign themselves to their fall without a fight (literally). Only after the 1713 Peace of Utrecht, which definitively ended 40 years of almost incessant wars with Louis XIV's France, the Dutch resigned themselves to their diminished status. Within the following decades, the Republic's control over its own fate slipped ever more from its hands.

Second, the Boreel embassy occurred at the moment Russia began to find its bearings, arriving as a significant player on the forefront of the European scene at the very moment that saw the Dutch beginning to fade into its background. While the Dutch were by 1665 ever more desperately trying to hold on to their brief spell as Europe's foremost nation, Russia was leaving behind its outsider status and on the verge of joining Europe's leading core of states. The war with Poland that had begun in 1654 had not been an unmitigated military success, but it had neither been a disaster of the sort suffered in the previous wars with the *Rzeczpospolita*, while Polish resolve was crumbling because of internal strife. As a result, the Treaty of Andrusovo of early 1667 was a clear defeat for the Poles and a clear victory for the Russians. This triumph was accompanied by further assertive moves by Tsar Aleksei Mikhailovich (1629–1676), who affirmed his control of the Russian Orthodox Church at the synod of 1666–1667 that saw the previously powerful Patriarch Nikon deposed. Within months of Andrusovo, the New Commercial Code was introduced, which was at a minimum an attempt to guarantee a greater flow of revenue into the treasury (more about it below). Around the same time, the treaty with Armenian merchants was concluded that aimed at redirecting the transport of the raw silk produced in Iran through Russia. This initiative triggered a Russian project to build a small naval flotilla to protect the trading vessels traversing the Caspian Sea from northern Iran to Astrakhan on the Volga, which had a pronounced Dutch flavor.

By 1667, the Romanov tsars' rule in Muscovy was firmly anchored: Any serious challenge to their legitimacy had withered away, while their territory in Europe was now larger than that ruled by Ivan IV, and all of Siberia fell under their authority as well. Russia's rise as a European and eventually global power had taken off. By the time of the Treaty of Utrecht, Sweden had been bested, Poland was becoming a Russian protectorate, and the Russian navy celebrated its first victory in battle in 1714.

In other words, the Boreel Embassy arrived in Moscow at a critical juncture: Forty years earlier, the United Provinces had only just begun to emerge as a sovereign polity, and the Romanov tsars' throne was utterly shaky. The Dutch first rose to great prominence in Europe and beyond it, but their momentum slowed down precipitously by 1665; Russia's rise was less spectacular and slower, but after 1665 it gradually caught up, and eventually clearly bypassed, the Republic in terms of international significance. This development became ever more clear in the course of Peter the Great's reign, especially after 1700.

***

As Wijnroks points out, while most Antwerp merchants fleeing the Spaniards went to Holland and Zealand in the 1580s, some settled elsewhere, such as in the German North-Sea ports of Bremen, Emden, and Hamburg.[1] Culturally, these traders and their families remained often half-Dutch (by remaining Calvinists, like the Marselises did, or using the Dutch language) for some time, an identity frequently reinforced through strong economic ties with the northern Netherlands.[2] Most lost their ancestral link to the Low Countries only after a couple of generations of residence in these Imperial cities, a transformatory process which might be accelerated when a family branch in the Republic became extinct.

People and goods often traveled with ease across the Republic's borders back and forth to Germany (i.e., the Holy Roman Empire). An incessant stream of Germans moved to the Republic, in far greater numbers than Dutch people moving to Germany, in the seventeenth (and eighteenth) centuries. The borders, while legally determined, were literally liminal: In people's sense of identity, regional allegiance, shared dialects or religion, and the community of one's profession were at least as important as any "national" allegiance. We will see further down a good example of this in Christoffel Brants, a son of immigrants from the area near Emden in East-Frisia, who became a veritable tycoon of the Amsterdam-based Dutch trade with Russia toward 1700.

Quite tellingly, when Jacob Willemszoon Boreel (1630–1697) served as Dutch ambassador to the tsar in Moscow in 1665, he submitted not only Dutch but also Hamburg traders' grievances, and was received in Moscow both by Dutch and northern Germans as the champion of the foreign merchant community in Russia.[3] It reflected how, in the context of the Russia trade the cities of Hamburg and Bremen operated as a sort of satellites for Dutch merchants, many of whom had offices in either of those German cities as well as in the Republic before the end of the seventeenth century.[4] National allegiance was (and perhaps is) often fickle: Boreel spent much of his time trying to persuade the Russian authorities that his fellow Dutch native Jan van Sweeden was a crook.[5]

The grounds for the dispatch of the Boreel embassy are murky, although a key reason may have been a desire to match the English, who had sent the Carlisle embassy to Russia in 1663.[6] That mission had been a response to the Prozorovskii embassy that had been sent by Tsar Aleksei to pay its respects to the newly enthroned Charles II.[7] A Russian mission had visited the Republic in 1663, too, but it had been headed by the *dvor'ianin* Bogdan Ordin-Nashchokin (accompanied by the *d'iak* Abram Kashcheev and a retinue of some 60 people), a noble of far lower rank than Prince Pyotr Prozorovskii (1621–1670), a sort of peer of the realm who traced his ancestry back to the earliest days of Russian history in the first millennium CE.[8]

During the 1660s, the Republic was more than usually self-conscious about its international stature, after five of the seven provinces had declined to appoint the young prince William of Orange-Nassau as his father's successor as stadtholder (Frisia's and Groningen's stadtholderates were occupied by a member of the Nassau-Dietz cadet branch). Therefore, it no longer had a blue-blooded prince administering the country's government and heading its armed forces, who could be displayed as a sort of monarch to those, such as Russians, to whom a republic equaled the rule of the rabble, or a rogue state. In addition, the 1660 Restoration of the Stuarts on the other side of the North Sea made Britain once more a—for the Muscovites much more palatable—monarchy (the tsar had banned English merchants from trading with his subjects after Charles I's beheading in 1649[9]). The low tsarist regard for the Dutch state as a third-rate polity run by and for merchants bereft of a monarch was reinforced. It may be that the Estates-General decided that they needed to ensure that their country's merchants maintained their preeminent status in Muscovy and mounted toward this goal an opulent mission, rivaling or even outshining Carlisle's.[10] But, as we will see, the ambassador himself lacked tact, and precious little was accomplished in terms of currying Russian favor. Indeed, soon after Boreel's party left Russia, the tsar imposed new duties on foreign trade that at least on paper seemed more onerous than those previously in force in Muscovy.

Formally, Boreel arrived with a brief that had to do with trade issues and nothing more. The Estates-General at The Hague seems to have been blind to the key priority for the Russian ruler, which was politics, not economics. Peace with the *Rzeczpospolita* seemed far off yet, despite some diplomatic parlaying between the two sides. The Dutch would have ingratiated themselves with the tsar if they had offered to mediate in this conflict, and even more so if they would have suggested that ending the war between Muscovy and Poland-Lithuania was their mission's main aim. This clearly becomes obvious from an episode in the middle of March 1665, when the Russian negotiators suddenly called a special session with their Dutch interlocutors and (through the tsar's main advisor Afanasii Ordin-Nashchokin) probed Boreel about the Dutch willingness to serve as mediators in this conflict.[11] Boreel was taken aback by this sudden turn of events and did not grasp the opportunity offered on that occasion. The Dutch might have gained the tsar's deep gratitude if Boreel had undertaken to broker a peace; indeed, the chances that a peace beneficial to Russia might be concluded were fairly decent, as the *Rzeczpospolita* was subsumed by domestic strife around this time. Boreel remained noncommittal, however, disinclined to move beyond his brief, and thus disappointed the Russians.[12]

No evidence has been brought to light, meanwhile, explaining why the Russians suddenly thought that Boreel might serve as a mediator to end the war. They may have remembered the clumsy Brederode mission dispatched to end the Russo-Swedish War, but since it had dismally failed, this hardly could have been an important consideration in soliciting Dutch services. Perhaps it was known at the court that the Dutch leading politician Johan de Witt was pursuing a peace policy, attempting to avoid war by establishing a balance of power in Europe, and might thus be interested in ending the Eastern European war. Certainly, it puzzled them that such an expensive embassy had been sent merely to discuss such trifles as matters of trade.

The embassy was at best an exercise in projecting power, and at worst an expensive failure. Its greatest flaw was its lack of purpose. Perhaps the mission could have been steered toward a more fruitful direction by the Hague regents once it had arrived (after all, letters regularly went back and forth between The Hague and Moscow by then, even if they took four-to-six weeks to arrive at their destination), but, soon after Boreel set sail for Riga in 1664, the Estates-General became preoccupied by the war with England that had broken out and was soon fought at locations closer to home than in the Atlantic Ocean.

To some degree, Boreel's attitude in Moscow clinched the embassy's failure; it was not his mission's success that made Jacob Boreel into a leading regent in the Republic in the years subsequent to his return from Moscow in 1665. When he embarked in 1664, he had yet to make his mark as a politician in the Republic. His appointment, it seems, was a consequence of his father Willem's role as a leading diplomat.[13] Willem Boreel had liaised with the embattled Charles I in the midst of the British civil wars, and was from 1649 to 1668 the Dutch permanent ambassador at Louis XIV's court in Paris. It was likely thought that Jacob, who had a law degree, had become a skillful diplomat at his father's side, but he proved to be a rather querulous sort in Russia, afflicted by a good measure of hubris. He often failed to interpret Russian moves correctly and showed in general great cultural insensitivity, and besides tact lacked flexibility. In other words, he was a rather poor diplomat.

As Kurland points out, Jacob Boreel was well positioned within the Dutch oligarchy, and smartly married into the (infinitely wealthy) arms and slave traders' family of the Trips and Cooymanses in 1667, ensuring a life of comfort.[14] Subsequently, Boreel was to fill a number of other short diplomatic roles for the Republic, but, if he is remembered at all today, it is as the rotund Amsterdam *schout* (a sort of sheriff in the English style) and mayor, whose house was plundered by an enraged mob in a tax revolt just before his death.[15]

After an exceedingly long journey, because, both before disembarking at Riga and in Russia, the embassy was forced to wait out of fear that its members might be infected by the plague that had engulfed Western Europe, Boreel spent much of his time in Moscow harping on the evergreen issue of the proper title with which the Dutch Estates-General were to be addressed by the Russians, about which The Hague had not long before complained to Bogdan Ordin-Nashchokin in 1663.[16] Likewise, Boreel reiterated complaints regarding the expulsion from Moscow of the Dutch merchants in 1652, the demolition of their church there, and the prohibition to hire Russians as their servants, which had hitherto fallen on deaf ears.[17] He additionally demanded punishment of those who had abused their power when collecting custom duties, or by mistreating Dutch merchants, and he advocated free access for the Dutch to the Russian market. Few of the wrongs he decried were righted afterward.[18]

What truly draws the historian's attention to this embassy is the presence among Boreel's retinue of someone destined to be one of the great figures of the Dutch seventeenth century, the politician and scientist Nicolaas Witsen. Thanks to Witsen's copious notes and diary, we have a detailed snapshot of mid-seventeenth century Muscovy, which rivals Olearius's account in its richness.[19] While his text remained in manuscript for 300 years, it did lay the basis for Witsen's description of "North- and East Tartary," the first fulsome description of Siberia and regions nearby ever printed in any Western language, as well as the first detailed Western-style cartographic map of Siberia that Witsen drafted.[20] Both would not just be of interest to scientists and scholars in the Republic of Letters, but to Tsar Peter the Great himself, and in his wake to Russian-based bureaucrats and to scholars everywhere interested in this part of the world.

NOTES

1. Wijnroks, *Handel*, 220–1.
2. Amburger, *Die Famile Marselis*, 21–9.
3. Still, Boreel's loyalty was first and foremost with the Dutch, as is evident from his note to the Amsterdam mayors in March 1665, where he suggests that the Anglo-Dutch war that has just broken out might hinder the trade on Arkhangel'sk, and that this, as in the previous war with the English, would leave the door open to the "Hamburgers, Lubeckers, and Bremers" (Boreel *Verbael*, 505; and ibid., 505–7). Clearly, then, while he championed someone like the Hamburger Verpoorten, this may have had more to do with Verpoorten's role as factor of Dutch traders than with a full-blooded representation of Hamburg's interest before the tsar's government.

In championing the German-speaking Danish subject David Bacheracht (d. 1671), Boreel pointed out to the Russian authorities who noted that Bacheracht was not Dutch, but that he advocated on Bacheracht's behalf because of a business deal the latter had concluded with the Dutchmen Daniel and Jan Bernaerts (Boreel *Verbael*, 753–4). This, though, sounds especially strained, even when the Bernaerts (Bernards) brothers had indeed employed Bacheracht (Amburger, *Die Familie*, 128).

4. Wijnroks, *Handel*, 307.

5. See Boterbloem, *Dirty Secret*, 88–97.

6. The instructions given by the Estates-General to Boreel seem to focus on soliciting greater respect for the Republic from the side of the Russians and on improving trading conditions (Boreel *Verbael*), 3–72.

7. He was accompanied by the *d'iak* I.A. Zheliabuzhskii (1638–1709). See, for the English embassy under the earl of Carlisle, Charles Howard, Guy Miege, *A Relation of Three Embassies from His Sacred Majestie Charles II . . .*, London: John Starkey, 1669. King Charles, certainly, was grateful for the unflinching Russian support for the Stuart cause, if that meant rather little in practice.

8. Jordan Kurland transcribed some of the details that can be found in the Dutch National Archives regarding Ordin-Nashchokin's visit on note cards (the original is in the "Lias Moscoviën" for the year 1663 in the *Nationaal Archief*, Archief der Staten-Generaal).

9. See I. Lubimenko, "Anglo-Russian Relations during the First English Revolution," *Transactions of the Royal Historical Society* 11, 1928, 39–59: 48. Note as well envoy Gerasim Dokhturov's dismissive response, and subsequent hostile attitude, with respect to the merits of the Parliamentary cause in 1645 and 1646, as suggested by Lubimenko (ibid., 40–2).

10. On this sort of display, see Hennings, *Russia and Courtly Europe*. The leading Dutch politician, Johan de Witt, was married into one of the leading Amsterdam families, that of the Bickers, whose rise was in no small measure due to their involvement in the Russia trade.

11. Boreel *Verbael*, 483–5. It seems significant that, not long before the Russians turned to Boreel with their request, Peter Marselis had been dispatched by Tsar Aleksei to Berlin, Vienna, and Copenhagen to inquire whether any of their governments were willing to mediate in the conflict (ibid., 458–9). Marselis rivaled Van Sweeden as the tsar's favorite foreigner in those days.

12. Ibid., 486–7.

13. Scheltema suggests that Dirk Tulp (son of the famous anatomist and regent Nicolaas Tulp) declined the honor, after which Boreel was asked (Scheltema, *Rusland en de Nederlanden*, vol. 1, 267). For his and his father's career, see especially J.E. Elias, *De vroedschap van Amsterdam*, vol. 1, Amsterdam: Israel, 1963, 537–41.

14. Draft of Kurland dissertation (typescript), 2; Elias, *De vroedschap*, vol. 1, 537–41.

15. See P.C. Molhuysen and P.J. Blok, eds, *Nieuw Nederlandsch Biografisch Woordenboek*, Leiden: Sijthoff, c. 1911, vol. 7, 177.

16. *Nationaal Archief*, Archief der Staten-Generaal, Lias Moskoviën, 1663, 4.

17. In Boreel's list of complaints about Russian injustices committed against Dutch residents in Moscow, the date of the expulsion from Moscow is given as January 28, 1654, more than a year later than the *ukaz* of October 1652 that banished Westerners from the capital had been issued: this discrepancy seems to have been the result of the issue of the decree and its actual enforcement on the ground (see Boreel, *Verbael*, 20, 373).

18. One last time, in early May 1665, after his official visit had already come to an end, he tried in a "*Replique*" (rebuttal), to press his points again, but it was all in vain, see Boreel *Verbael*, 733–54.

19. Witsen, *Moscovische reyse*.

20. Witsen, *Noord en Oost Tartarye*; for a fine overview of their making and significance, see Naarden, "Nicolaas Witsen en Tartarye."

Chapter 13

Dutch Mercenaries in the Tsar's Service

In a 1665 memorandum to Tsar Aleksei, Ambassador Boreel sketched the significance of Dutch military aid to Russia:

> Since many years ago and through numerous and various important incidents, your Tsarist Majesty has evidently found that They, the Highmightinesses, my Gracious Lords, more than any other potentates in Christendom have tried through signs of friendship to show your Tsarist Majesty that They, the Highmightinesses, have been especially inclined to render on every occasion pleasing favours to Your Tsarist Majesty, such as to consent to the purchase and exportation of arms and great quantities of ammunition for warfare, even at times when they refused this to other crowns in Europe; and such as to supply Your Tsarist Majesty with experienced and skilled officers of war, and with artisan masters, and further anything that Your Tsarist Majesty needed.[1]

Boreel's depiction of his compatriots' strategic importance was not wholly free of hyperbole, as he was in search of trading and other concessions from Aleksei, but he was right in hinting that the Russians had embarked on a military modernization that saw Dutch merchants and mercenaries lend an important hand.[2] Indeed, among the Dutch ambassador's numerous complaints that he brought to the Kremlin was one that Erdman Swellengrebel (1615–1675) had not been properly remunerated for weapons (muskets, carbines, and pistols) delivered to the Russians in 1661, which was valued at a whopping 13,000 rubles.[3] Thirteen-thousand rubles was the equivalent of 65,000 guilders, the approximate equivalent of the combined annual wage of 300 skilled Dutch workers.[4]

One of the American historian Richard Hellie's major works outlined how crucial Western European influence was for Russia's military reform, something which both Reger (for the land forces) and Phillips (for the navy) in their outstanding dissertations further explored and underlined.[5] Other scholars such as Brian Davies, Robert Frost, Michael Paul, V. M. Malov, and Carol Belkin Stevens further highlight how Muscovy adapted to the far-going changes that affected the European art of war in the seventeenth century.[6] Mercenaries were of crucial importance in helping the Russians adapt to this modernization, even if the transfer of their skill to Muscovy's military did not occur without some setbacks. We do not have a very clear idea how the tsar and his advisors exactly decided on the recruitment of foreign experts, the importation of foreign weapons, the introduction of advanced military technology, or the training of the army in a "Westernish" style. But we can infer the reasons behind these innovations fairly well.

Firstly, Moscow suffered a series of humiliating military defeats at the hands of both Polish-Lithuanians and Swedes during the later phase of the Livonian Wars (1558–1583), the foreign intervention in the Time of Troubles (1605–1618), and the Smolensk War (1632–1634). In the latter war, a first, ham-fisted, Russian attempt was made to use a large number of mercenary warriors during a military campaign. Mercenaries were all the rage at this time: They were doing most of the fighting on the battlefields of the Holy Roman Empire and the Low Countries. This first Russian try proved a failure, but it did involve for the first time Dutch mercenaries in numbers—and non-Dutch mercenaries contracted in the Republic and dispatched from there—as well as massive Dutch arms' shipments, brokered by Karel du Moulin, Hendrick van Ringen, Gommert Spranger, Elias Trip, Paul de Willem, Thomas de Swaen, David Ruts, and others.[7]

Even earlier, Dutch fortification experts (Cosmo de Moucheron, Jan Corneliszoon van Rodenburgh, Cornelis Claeszoon) and cannon casters (Hans Falck) had joined the tsar's service.[8] Those engineers were hired in response to the incessant incursions by Tatar raiders from the south into Muscovy, rather than to satisfy a desire to thwart Russia's foes to the west. Dutch renown regarding fortress-building made the Russians turn to specialists from the United Provinces in shoring up the ever longer fortified border they constructed south of Moscow for many decades.[9] Later, under Peter, the Russians turned to the exposés written by another, rather famous, fortification-and-siege master, Menno van Coehoorn (1641–1704), one of whose key works was translated from Dutch into Russian.[10]

Meanwhile, some of the crucial changes affecting Western European field battles or sieges had little significance for Eastern European warfare.[11] In this less populated part of the world, heavily walled citadels were fewer and distances far greater. As a consequence, sieges were fewer, even if the epic struggle regarding the capture of Moscow itself (1610–1612), or the sieges of Smolensk (1610, 1632–1634, 1654), Chyhyryn (1677 and 1678), and Azov (1637–1642, 1695–1696) cannot be ignored. But war on horseback—in which significant changes occurred as well through the increasing deployment of fast-moving and more mobile lighter cavalry that made more frequent use of firearms—remained of greater significance than in combat further west.[12] A sign of the particularly high level of Polish military skill in this regard was the presence of a number of Polish military officers in the Dutch armies fighting Spain during the first half of the seventeenth century.[13] Beginning in 1600, the Russians needed half a century to catch up and match Polish-Lithuanian military expertise not just in this, but in other respects.

Having learned from the Smolensk fiasco of the 1630s (or so it appears), Aleksei Mikhailovich and his retainers used a more subtle approach in reforming their armed forces, combining Western advances in some respects but adapting them to Eastern European conditions. They attempted to avoid ruffling too many Russian feathers by imposing far-reaching reforms too bluntly or indiscriminately, and allowed Russian nobles to have the senior command of the regiments. Such caution became all the more imperative when, in the early years of Aleksei's rule, rebellions broke out in Moscow and elsewhere in which resentment of foreigners was an element.

But this unrest did not stop Tsar Aleksei from hiring mercenaries and ordering his armies to drill in Western style and Western European battlefield deployment. At that point, Dutch influence on Russian warfare on land reached its brief acme. In 1647, the tsar's future father-in-law, I. D. Miloslavskii, recruited during a mission to the United Provinces a number of veteran officers who had been schooled by the battlefields of the countries along the North-Sea shore. Among them were Scotsmen, such as William Bruce (the father of Iakov Brius [1669–1735]), but the most important recruits were four of the members of the Van Bockhoven family, Catholics likely hailing from the eternal Spanish-Dutch battleground that had been northern Brabant.[14] When they arrived, Moscow printing presses were busy churning out the first secular book ever printed in Russian, a translation of Wallhausen's version of Jacob de Gheyn's drill book.[15] This was likely more than a mere coincidence. For a short while, the senior member of the family, Isaac van Bockhoven, appears as head of Aleksei's personal guard to have held a post not unlike Glissenberch under Ivan IV. He then trained infantry and cavalry Russian troops in Western combat methods, as laid out in de Gheyn's illustrations. While his sons (or nephews) and son-in-law would serve the tsar until the late 1670s, Isaac disappears from the record at the time of the outbreak of war with Poland in 1654; he either died in battle, or disease took his life (plague was rampant in Moscow in 1654 and 1655).

In Reger's dissertation several other Dutchmen who served the tsar in the Thirteen Years' War are listed, but it is likewise clear that they were heavily outnumbered by Scots and to a somewhat lesser extent "Germans" (people hailing from the Holy Roman Empire) among the officer corps.[16] Even if that was perhaps only marginally due to a better Russian performance in battles or sieges thanks to Western-style military training or Western mercenary guile, at the end of this conflict, as we saw, Russia finally got the better of Poland.

After 1667, Dutch officers continued to serve in the tsar's land armies, although their number gradually declined. In part this was because some of the mercenary officers' offspring Russified (as happened with the Van Bockhoven's descendants), and in part because Dutch officers found ample employment in Western Europe, at least until 1713. But their influence remained undeniably significant for quite some time. Thus, the Genevan François Lefort, a later favorite of Peter the Great, arrived in Arkhangel'sk in 1675, fresh from a stint in the Dutch armies then employed against France; he married into the Van Bockhoven clan, as did Peter's other favorite foreigner, Patrick Gordon, a Scottish mercenary officer.

While the Dutch significance for Russian land warfare was receding in the last third of the seventeenth century, their importance for Muscovy's fledgling navy increased. As recorded by Olearius, some Dutch shipwrights had already been involved in the ill-fated attempt under Mikhail to launch a Western-type sailship (named the *Friedrich*) on the Caspian Sea, even if that initiative was rather driven by the briefly ambitious Holsteiners than by the Muscovites. The northern Germans were interested in capturing the trade that saw raw silk transported via Russia from Iran to Western Europe.[17] But the true origins of the modern Russian navy belong to Aleksei's reign. For it was then that, fresh from their victory over Poland-Lithuania, the Russians themselves decided to build a small naval detachment to patrol the Caspian Sea's waters and convoy merchant ships traversing it from the Volga mouth to northern Iran. Its flagship was to be the *Eagle* (*Oryol*), a vessel built under the lead of a team of Dutch shipwrights; its crew was largely made up out of experienced Dutch sailors.[18] Both Peter Marselis (who also involved himself in those years in the rebuilding of Arkhangel'sk, after another devastating fire had laid this port in ashes again[19]) and Andrei Vinius were drawn into this project, but its key organizer was Jan van Sweeden, the pivotal Russian-based Dutch entrepreneur of the 1660s.

The *Oryol* project, however, proved an expensive fiasco.[20] The construction of the ship, yacht, and a couple of smaller boats was slow, and the flotilla (built at Dedinovo in central Russia, and then hauled down the Oka and Volga rivers) only reached Astrakhan in the Volga delta well-nigh two years after the venture had started. The vessels arrived there in the late summer of 1669, upon which the crew was told to pause before entering the Caspian Sea, possibly because of the presence in the river-delta region of a growing number of Cossack marauders, led by Stenka Razin. After an armed truce between Razin and the tsar's local officials that held for several months, the Cossacks and their allies took up arms again in the spring of 1670 and eventually besieged, stormed, and took Astrakhan.

Most of the Dutch sailors managed to escape capture by the Cossacks, although a few fell in defending the city. But their ships were abandoned and never set sail on the Caspian. Three of those Dutchmen who survived the Razin siege at Astrakhan wrote an account of their travails: The captain David Butler and the sailmaker Jan Struys, as well as the mercenary soldier Lodewijk Fabricius, who fortuitously escaped being slaughtered by the Cossacks.

The crew had failed to train any Russian to sail (and the Russian contribution to the building of the ship seems to have been limited to purely menial tasks). In declining to oblige the foreigners to train Russians in their skill, the Russian authorities may appear to have repeated the same mistake made as when they hired mercenaries to best the Poles in 1632. But at least one of the *Oryol*'s sailors (like some of the mercenaries who stayed behind in Russia after the Smolensk War) returned to Moscow and would belatedly train one particularly crucial Russian how to sail. In 1688, Karsten Brandt was responsible for refitting a little boat (*botik*) found abandoned in a warehouse as a small sailing vessel. On the *botik*, Tsar Peter I learned how to sail on the lakes near Moscow. Brandt thus triggered the young tsar's obsession with seafaring, and Russia's belated entry into the Age of Sail.[21]

In the course of the 1690s, and especially during the 1697–1698 Grand Embassy, numerous Dutch shipwrights and sailors were hired by Peter and his courtiers. But, whereas Dutch-imported arms still sustained the Russian army throughout most of the first decade of the eighteenth century, few of these seamen saw battle in this same period (while, as said, very few Dutch soldiers served in the Russian land forces, as they predominantly fought in the Low Countries). The Russian victory over a Swedish flotilla at Gangut in 1714 was a bit of a farce, as overwhelming Russian naval superiority made this outcome a foregone conclusion. Dutchmen continued to serve in the Russian fleet for much of the century, as is evident from the *Zeevaartreglement* (*Morskoi ustav*) issued in 1720, the basic set of regulations that were to be observed within the Russian navy, which was reissued in its bilingual iteration until the last decades of the 1700s.[22] But the Russian navy after Peter's death was mostly idle, whiling away at port until the Russo-Turkish war of 1768–1774.

NOTES

1. Boreel *Verbael*, 432–3; on another occasion, he also used the argument that the Republic had even exported arms when it was itself at war and could have used them at home, therefore (ibid., 512).

2. See Boterbloem, *Dirty Secret*, 164–215.

3. Boreel, *Verbael*, 418–21. The *Oryol*'s building in the late 1660s would cost slightly more than 9,000 rubles.

4. See Van Deursen, *Plain Lives*, 7.

5. See Hellie, *Enserfment*; Reger, "In the Service"; Phillips, *Founding*; see also Lahana, "Novaia Nemetskaia Sloboda," 99–101.

6. Davies, *Warfare*; Malov, *Moskovskie vybornye polki*; Stevens, *Russia's Wars*; Paul, "Military Revolution"; Frost, *Northern Wars*.

7. Wijnroks, *Handel*, 323–5, 351–2.

8. Boterbloem, *Dirty Secret*, 174, 178. Hans Falck was a native of Nuremberg, but had worked for decades in the Netherlands; indeed, before him Karsten Middeldorp had been employed by Ivan IV in the 1550s and likely had some Dutch roots (his name, for one, is more Dutch than German, in which it would have been rendered Mitteldorf), as did in turn his Lübeck mentor, who hailed from Overijssel (see S. Bogatyrev, "Bronze Tsars: Ivan the Terrible and Fyodor Ivanovich in the Décor of Early Modern Guns," in *Personality and Place in Russian Culture; Essays in Memory of Lyndsey Hughes*, ed. Simon Dixon, London: MHRA, UCL, 2010, 48–72: 50–61). Bogatyrev's discussion here hints at the earlier Hanseatic link between towns such as Kampen, Zwolle, or Deventer via Lübeck and other German ports with Riga, Narva, and Novgorod (see ibid., 53). Falck became the father-in-law of the German-speaking Glückstadt entrepreneur and merchant David Bacheracht (see Marselis, *Die Familie*, 214). Marriage linked Bacheracht and the Swellengrebels as well.

9. It is worthwhile to note that Dutch skill in these matters was appreciated elsewhere: The British kings Charles I's and Charles II's greatest military engineer was a Dutchman from Zeeland, Bernard de Gomme (1620–1685).

10. Boterbloem, *Dirty Secret*, 206.

11. Reger, "In the Service," 24; Boterbloem, *Dirty Secret*, 148.

12. Even if the Swedish cavalry of Gustavus Adolphus was renowned for its swash-buckling feats in the Thirty Years' War as well.

13. Boterbloem, *Dirty Secret*, 159n9.

14. Boterbloem, "Dutch Mercenaries"; and Boterbloem, *Dirty Secret*, 112–13, 173, 197–9. They received permission from the Dutch Estates-General to embark for Arkhangel'sk, which makes them likely soldiers serving in the northern Netherlandic armies, but it is not impossible that they had served Spain, for in 1647 any fighting had almost wholly ceased when peace negotiations at Münster were making steady progress. Bo(c)khoven was a settlement near 's-Hertogenbosch. Posselt suggests that they may have had a stint in Britain fighting for Charles I as well in the civil wars there (see Posselt, *Franz Lefort*, vol. 1, 269n2).

15. [Johann Jacobi von Wallhausen,] *Uchenie i khitrost' ratnogo stroeniia pekhotnykh liudei*, Moscow: Moskovskii pechatnyi dvor, 1647; J. de Gheyn, *Wapenhandelinghe van roers, musquetten ende spiessen*, 's Gravenhage: n.p., 1607; see as well https://www.kb.nl/en/themes/book-history/more-special-books/exercise-of-arms; Boterbloem, "Dutch Mercenaries."

16. Reger, "In the Service," 208–9.

17. On the Russian-Holsteiner project of the *Frederick*, see Phillips, *Founding*, 14–18; Viskovatov, *Kratkii istoricheskii obzor morskikh pokhodov russkikh i*

morekhodstva ikh voobshche do iskhoda XVII stoletiia. Sankt Peterburg: Morskoi istoricheskii sbornik, 1994, 79–84, 168–9n48, 169–72n49, 172–5n51, 176–8n52; A. Olearius, *The Travels of Olearius in Seventeenth-Century Russia*, trans. and ed. S.H. Baron, Stanford, CA: Stanford UP, 1967, 74n24, 78. Tushin suggests that its builders had not properly taken into account the short but extraordinarily high waves of the Caspian Sea which rendered the *Frederick*'s high masts vulnerable and caused the ship to break (Iu.P. Tushin, *Russkoe moreplavanie na Kaspiiskom, Azovskom i Chernom Moriakh*, Moskva: Nauka, 1978, 44).

18. The Russians like to call it a *fregat* (frigate); even though they use the Dutch word, the ship was more of a fluteship (*fluit*) furnished with (22) cannon.

19. Kotilaine, "When the Twain," 19.

20. Boterbloem, *Fiction and Reality.*

21. Bogoslovskii, *Petr Velikii*, vol. 1, 56–7.

22. *Kniga ustav' morskoi*; Boterbloem, *Fiction and Reality*, 62.

Chapter 14

The Western *Sloboda*

In seventeenth-century Russia, Dutch expatriate communities did not merely exist in Moscow, but also in settlements along the road to Arkhangel'sk and in Arkhangel'sk itself.[1] Many of their members have disappeared in the mist of time, hardly a trace surviving that these communities once existed. The records of private Dutch businesses have long vanished, while any Dutch presence in Russian documents is often masked by the custom to Russify names. Even the word *"nemets"* in Russian is akin in meaning to the now obsolete Dutch word *"diets"* ("Dutch," a Dutch iteration of the High-German *"deutsch"*) in that it does not distinguish *"Hochdeutsch"* from *"Plattdeutsch," "Niederdeutsch,"* or *"Nederlands,"* in other words, German from "Netherlandic." Thus, as we saw, when Muscovite texts speak of *"nemtsy"* (plural of *nemets*), we are unsure if they mean Germans from the empire, or Netherlanders from the Low Countries. In addition, *"nemtsy"* was used more broadly to connote all speakers of Germanic tongues, including English, Scots, or (Anglo-)Irish, and sometimes Danes or Swedes who resided in Muscovy. The noun *"galantsy"* is used in written Russian sources for *"Hollanders"* as well, meanwhile, likely a synecdoche for all natives from the Low Countries. In how far the word was used in contemporary spoken Russian before Peter's reign is impossible to assess.

All of this means that we can merely approximate the numbers of Dutch people who resided in Russia, even if Demkin has at least tried to come up with quite specific numbers for Moscow.[2] Given his calculation and other evidence, we can reasonably assume that at the time of the Boreel embassy the number of those who spoke Dutch or considered themselves "Netherlander," and temporarily or permanently resided in Russia, amounted to about 1,500 Dutch men and women.[3] Extrapolating from Demkin's numbers and using other pieces of evidence, such as the estimates about the Dutch staff working for the larger private merchants' companies, the number of artisans and mercenaries, and so on, as well as calculating their various dependents, one might suggest that throughout the seventeenth century (from approximately 1613 to 1697) this total may have occasionally peaked at approximately 3,000 denizens from the Low Countries residing in Russia for a considerable length of time (rather than merely visiting).[4] This was the population of a small town in those days, and its size was not unlike that of Dutch enclaves elsewhere (such as New Amsterdam), while it even grew further after 1697.

After 1652, when Western foreigners were banned from living within the confines of the Russian capital, the largest Dutch community resided near rather than inside of Moscow.[5] This residential segregation applied to those considered full foreigners (there were different slobodas for other non-Orthodox communities as well).[6] *Moskovskie inozemtsy* such as Jan van Sweeden, even if they had not become Orthodox Christians, were allowed to continue to reside within the city. The *nemetskaia sloboda* ("Western foreigners' suburb") existed for about half a century: Starting from the much more benevolent reception of Westerners after 1697 it began to vanish, while the move of the capital to St. Petersburg in 1713 caused it to disappear altogether.[7]

The establishment of a residentially segregated Western enclave outside of Moscow proper in the early 1650s satisfied a worried Muscovite clergy and laity about the growing "contamination" by this impertinent alien group, but it did not save Orthodox purity. The attempt to purify the Russian Orthodox flock had been steered by Patriarch Nikon (elevated to his office in 1652, the same year the decree was issued banishing Westerners from residing in Moscow). He relinquished his zeal once he fell from favor in 1658, after which he allowed his portrait to be painted in the Western style and received Nicolaas Witsen while in exile in the 1660s. That later move was doubly iconoclastic, since he did not only welcome a Western heretic on to the premises of an Orthodox monastery, but foreign-embassy retainers were officially not allowed—both for state-security reasons and to halt them from corrupting Russian souls—to wander off on their own adventures.[8] Nikon's behavior after he left office makes one ponder the true depth of his religious fervor.

Martha Lahana notes the irony that "the isolation of the Europeans allowed them to construct a 'little Western town,' where interested Russians eventually would observe and adapt foreign customs for themselves."[9] At least for those ardent admirers of Western ways such as Peter the Great, the suburb almost resembled an ideal future Russian society.[10] The banishment caused initial hardship, as—once the *ukaz* took effect—the foreigners were allotted a very brief period to move from Moscow to the *sloboda*, where houses had to be built from the ground up (even if Russian craftsmen could erect wooden houses in a day).[11] The greatest sorrow was caused by the obligation to sell one's real estate inside Moscow within a month, which allowed Russian purchasers to acquire Western-owned property at rock-bottom prices.

The new residential restrictions partially applied to towns besides Moscow as well.[12] In practical terms, though, foreign businessmen, artisans, or military officers who were henceforth assigned to live in the various segregated neighborhoods to which they had been conscripted interacted with Russians no different than before.[13] The "social-distancing" laws were not as harsh as they may appear from a superficial reading, while their application was lax. Martha Lahana's dissertation in some ways is a debunking of the entire concept of incessant Russian xenophobia that appears to inform the slew of measures that curtailed foreigners' mobility and activity in Muscovy in this era.[14] Certainly, the *sloboda*'s foundation meshes with Western observers' recording of Russian distrust, or even fear, of foreigners in a number of travel accounts.[15] But this was not much different from the general or usual all-human response to others to whom one has not been accustomed.[16] Common conservative inclinations made the Russians across Muscovite society wary of dangers that might corrode the purity of their religion and culture. Pragmatism made clerical and lay leaders among them nevertheless willing to overlook the strangeness of these others, however, as they brought goods, services, and skills (not in the least as military officers) that Russia needed. And, as can be seen from their severe craving for tobacco, even those outside of the elite appreciated certain foreign delights.[17] By 1672 at the latest, the worst of the antiforeigner sentiment had markedly ebbed away.[18]

Although we know that Western Europeans were banished to those *slobodas*, we do not know exactly who these Western Europeans were.[19] As we already saw, Dutch people were numerous among merchants, clerks, and artisans, while their proportion was somewhat lower among the mercenaries in Russian service. Located within the perimeter of Moscow itself, a Calvinist (Dutch) church existed since at least the 1620s, meanwhile, which had been dismantled in response to the 1652 decree, but the *sloboda* seems to have harbored a new place of worship soon after.[20] As a probable sign of appreciation for the Dutch, around 1685 the first stone-and-brick Protestant church (the Russian word used for them at the time was *kirk*, which may have derived from either Dutch or Scottish) to arise in the suburb was the Calvinist house of worship.[21] Its building thus predated Peter's takeover as ruler of Russia. This church was in part financed by contributions from the Republic, not in the least by Nicolaas Witsen. Beginning in earnest during Peter's reign as supreme ruler that commenced in 1689, meanwhile, Western European building styles and "Dutch" gardens spread beyond the *sloboda*.[22]

The greatest significance of the *sloboda* is how it caught Peter the Great's attention, first indirectly—when he began to meet its residents in the 1680s—and then directly, when he began to frequent the suburb soon after becoming full-fledged tsar in September 1689. One crucial thing that delighted the young monarch was foregrounded by Moritz Posselt, even if it may no less be reflective of Posselt's own industrious and industrial epoch that was the German mid-nineteenth century: "A fundamental constant [*Grundton*] was found in all families [of the *sloboda*], in everyone of its households: It was the law that one had to work [*Es war der Gesetz der Arbeit*]."[23]

Peter was himself a restless character, playing hard but working even harder (to borrow the cliché), and recognized something here that was one essential part underscoring the economic boom of first the Dutch Republic and then Great Britain. The importance of this work ethic on the march to modernity has only recently been highlighted again—even if now stripped from its Weberian corollary of Protestantism—by historians.[24] Without falling into a simplistic dichotomy of the lazy Slav Oblomov versus the industrious Germanic Stoltz, Peter himself at least seems to have become convinced that the sort of sustained hard work as demonstrated by the *sloboda*'s busy bees was key on the road to his country's military power and economic prosperity.[25]

NOTES

1. Wijnroks, *Handel*, 299–300. Especially in Arkhangel'sk many foreigners stayed only for part of the year, even if they returned there annually.

2. Demkin counts a total of 664 Dutch merchants and factors residing in Muscovy at some point during the seventeenth century (see Demkin, *Zapadnoevropeiskoe kupechestvo*, vol. 1, 26). But a great many others should be added to that number: The staff of merchant houses was often large (as we noted with the Du Moulin and van Klenck-De Vogelaer companies earlier). Mercenary officers such as the Van Bockhovens were also accompanied by servants, especially needed when for considerable periods Westerners could not employ Orthodox Slavs among their household staff. Peter Marselis even retained a Calvinist minister.

3. Of interest is the following list, even if it remains more often than not a guessing game who on this list might be hailing from the United Provinces, and is heavily weighted toward Peter's era; as completely as possible, it endeavors to list all foreigners (and sometimes Russians) registered by the Russian government who entered Muscovy in the seventeenth and early eighteenth century (before Peter ended the *prikazy* [offices] and replaced them by "colleges"), available at https://forum.vgd.ru/252/82368/0.htm, accessed June 26, 2020. I have estimated here a presence in all of Muscovy of 100 Dutch merchants and factors and others involved in trade, about 60 army officers, and about 50 artisans and specialists employed by the manufactories of Marselis, Ackema, Coyett, van Sweeden, the tsar's armament shop in Moscow as well as shopkeepers, tavern owners and innkeepers, apothecaries and doctors, and all of their wives and children. There were additionally a fair number of Dutch servants, since Orthodox believers were not permitted to work for heretics (the complication

here is that some of these servants were Tatars and so on, who sometimes converted to Reformed Christianity, such as the *Oryol* sailor's Cornelis Brak's wife Maria). Of course, as elsewhere, several Dutch residents of Russia married exogamously and may have begun to be counted as Muscovite by the authorities, or considered themselves as such. Muscovy had no significant settlement by Dutch farmers, although there were several such settlements in northern Germany, Poland, Denmark, and elsewhere in Europe (see P. de la Court, *The True Interest and Political Maxims of the Republic of Holland*, New York, 1972 [1662, 1669, English translation: 1746], 130). I am not counting some of the sailors who wintered at Arkhangel'sk, if failing to depart in time before the ice buildup.

4. Among the artisans were also experts in gemstone-crafting, gold- and silver-smiths (see Van Zuiden, *Bijdrage*, 13–14, 17).

5. There had been earlier, during the sixteenth century, foreign enclaves largely made up of Western Europeans (see Lahana, "Novaia Nemetskaia Sloboda," 52–5, 65–72). At least in one of them Dutch mercenaries (and a Protestant church) have been identified, which is unsurprising given Glissenberch's prominent role at Ivan IV's court. But either Ivan himself or the various marauders pillaging the Moscow region after 1600 seem to have destroyed these settlements (ibid., 55).

6. Ibid., viii–ix.

7. See ibid., viii. It was located in what is now the middle of Moscow (in Basmannyi *raion*).

8. Ibid., 98–9; Witsen, *Moscovische Reyse*, vol. 2, 267–89. Nikon, after a quarrel with the tsar about the division of power between Aleksei and him, went into self-imposed exile in 1658; he was deposed in 1666.

9. Lahana, "Novaia Nemetskaia Sloboda," 73; see as well ibid., 95.

10. See further ibid., 299.

11. Ibid., 86–91. From Kurland's research it appears that often foreign mercenaries took those banished into their homes (see *Nationaal Archief*, Archief der Staten-Generaal, Lias Moskoviën, 1663, 5 [Kurland note-card numbering]).

12. Lahana, "Novaia Nemetskaia Sloboda," 87–9.

13. Ibid., 92–4.

14. Ibid.

15. For other antiforeigner measures during the 1650s, see as well Lahana, "Novaia Nemetskaia Sloboda," 97.

16. See, for example, Elias, *Civilizing Process*, 62, 419–20.

17. Struys, *Rampspoedige reizen*, ed. Boterbloem, 61.

18. Lahana, "Novaia Nemetskaia Sloboda," 124.

19. Ibid., 248–9. Not that there are no lists with names in Russian documents, but the names are usually Russified and their Western version cannot be easily identified.

20. Ibid., 256–7. In the 1660s, both Patrick Gordon's wedding was celebrated in it as well as the wedding of one of Jan Struys's companions, Cornelis Brak (see Boterbloem, *Fiction and Reality*, 77–8).

21. Lahana, "Novaia Nemetskaia Sloboda," 209.

22. Ibid., 215; Van Zuiden, *Bijdrage*, 21, 27–8.

23. See Posselt, *Franz Lefort*, vol. 2, 31.

24. Jan de Vries, *The Industrious Revolution: Consumer Behavior and the Household Economy, 1650 to the Present*, Cambridge: Cambridge UP, 2008. See Max Weber, "Die Protestantische Ethik und der Geist des Kapitalismus," in M. Weber, *Gesammelte Aufsätze zur Religionssoziologie*, vol. 1, Tübingen: J.C.B. Mohr, 1922, 17–206.

25. See I.A. Goncharov, *Oblomov*, trans. Stephen Pearl, New York: Bunimand Bannigan, 2006. The layabout protagonist became a detested type among progressive Russians in the nineteenth century thanks to Dobroliubov's essay ("What is Oblomovism?"), see [N.-bov], "Chto takoe oblomovshchina?," *Sovremennik* 5, 1859, 59–98.

Chapter 15

The New Commercial Statute of 1667

Although occasionally foreign merchants' competition might slightly lessen Dutch profits, internal Russian opposition to foreigners encroaching onto Russian mercantile territory was more detrimental to those yields. In the first decades after the Time of Troubles, Russian merchants tolerated the presence of foreigners competing with them inside Muscovy (especially its northern parts) without much complaint, but once Mikhail and Filaret had become more firmly established as rulers of Russia and domestic tranquility had been restored, mercantile grumbling became louder.[1] Eventually, such disaffection found its expression in the 1649 *Ulozhenie*, a codification of many key Muscovite laws: Its rules underlined Russian merchants' rights and duties, and restricted foreign economic activity; further limitations were added to this activity in 1653.[2] Perhaps, too, the decree that forbade Western foreigners to reside within the confines of Moscow of 1652 was informed by mercantile demands (even if, as with the *Ulozhenie*, religiously driven xenophobia played its role as well).[3]

At the same time, on good ground did Russian government officials (not least those stationed at Arkhangel'sk) lament the evasion of import duties by Dutch merchants, which seems to have been widespread during Mikhail's reign.[4] Likewise, several Dutch traders bought crops directly from their producers rather than through Russian middlemen, another violation of the tsar's regulations.[5] Smuggling never truly disappeared, despite the occasional penalizing of those engaged in the practice. No doubt, bribery of officials allowed merchants to bring in or take out contraband. The Dutch were wont to accuse Russian merchants of not playing fair, but the Russians may have had as much justification in distrusting Dutch trading practices.

It is worth pondering whether a link might have existed between the long list of rather specific (and, even from a neutral perspective, somewhat petty) grievances delivered by Boreel in 1665 to the tsar's court and Russia's New Commercial Statute (*Novotorgovyi Ustav*) of 1667, which aimed to streamline the parameters of foreign trade and its tariffs and fees within one uniform system.[6] Although this regulation hardly amounted to the imposition of a rigorous mercantilist protection seeking to end foreign trade with Russia altogether, it did reiterate the tsarist government's desire to privilege domestic merchants (who pressured their government in this regard) over foreign competitors.[7] But besides imposing a tariff wall to protect domestic economic actors, its other prime aim may have been to create some clarity regarding trading conditions, to lessen the incidence of disputes between tsarist officials and merchants on the one hand and Dutch and other foreign traders on the other. While the 1667 statute was issued as a gesture toward Russian merchants' complaints about foreign competition and interference, it fundamentally constituted a move that was to replenish the depleted coffers of the treasury by charging foreign traders twice as much in terms of taxes and import duties as previously (which had been imposed in a 1653 decree).[8] It appears to have been intended, then, to ensure a more regular and greater flow of revenue into the tsarist coffers. The decree was not the consequence of a mercantilist policy, in which tariffs intended to curb the import–export trade altogether. In Russia, "European merchants were so busy and prosperous in the 1660s, . . . that the government could . . . increase their taxes and restrictions without endangering the health of [its] international trade."[9]

The volume of Dutch trade on Arkhangel'sk was significant throughout the seventeenth century, with the capacity of Dutch ships' loads peaking at a volume of just above 20 million kilograms in the exact middle of the century.[10] From 1600 to the late 1620s, the secular trend had held steady at one-fifth of that volume, then rose sharply by 1630, followed by a lull stretching from the middle of the 1630s to the late 1640s. A significant upturn began in 1649, and for the rest of the century the total of ship-hold capacity was at least twice as high as in the century's first two decades.[11] Significant *hausses* (three times the volume of the early seventeenth-century decades) can be seen in the second half of the 1670s and 1690s, respectively. The lack of decline in trading volume after its promulgation clearly supports the idea that the 1667 New Commercial Statute did little harm to the Dutch trade with Russia.

In 1663, when the Estates-General complained to the Russians in a letter about various injustices suffered by Dutch merchants in terms of their trade and privileges, another eloquent and undoubtedly self-serving summary can be found of the Dutch importance to mid-seventeenth century Muscovy, which was almost literally repeated by Boreel when he was in Moscow two years later:

> through their High Mightinesses' subjects' great trade, to which no other nation's can even remotely be compared, markedly enriching Your Tsarist

Majesty's countries and treasury by the uninterrupted supply of silver and other [commodities], . . . it has always been shown, not merely through words but deeds as well, that we are good and upstanding close friends of His Tsarist Majesty, having among other things always permitted as well the free exportation of great quantities of ordnance and the hiring of many experienced officers to join His Tsarist Majesty's service, which we High Mightinesses have often refused to other potentates.[12]

In other words, certainly in the eyes of the Dutch government, the Dutch were indispensable to the Russians, as Boreel reiterated a few years later. While they exaggerated their own importance in such bouts of rhetorical flourish, they were not altogether wrong, and their crucial role as arms traders only diminished after 1710. But the (lack of) any critical Dutch response to the New Commercial Statute shows as well that the Dutch could hardly dispense with the Russian market.

The New Commercial Statute may have clarified the trade conditions for the Dutch to some degree in Russia. In 1675, Ambassador Koenraad van Klenck was less encumbered than Boreel by a long list of complaints to submit to the tsar, even if trade was not the main focus of Van Klenck's agenda. Van Klenck launched another fruitless attempt to persuade Russia to allow greater foreign mercantile activity (particularly in handling the silk trade) within Russia. Van Klenck did not insist too much on this point, which indicates that he did not expect to make very much headway in this direction. Van Klenck was a different sort of diplomat from Boreel, much more flexible and far better versed in Russian affairs, and aware of the stubborn quality of the Russian negotiation style, or their inclination not to concede certain points.

The mid-century Dutch dominance over Russian foreign trade with the West is reflected in the memoirs of Tsar Aleksei's former personal physician, the Englishman Samuel Collins (c. 1619–1670), published in the early 1670s.[13] The rancor of his remarks reflected the envious hostility many English people felt across the globe for the Dutch at the time when Collins wrote his remarks; this jealousy played a large factor in causing three wars between the two North-Sea countries within a mere two decades. The embittered doctor condemned the Russians as "false, Truce-breakers, subtile Foxes, and ravenous Wolves," but their innate duplicitous nature had much worsened from "their traffick with the Hollander, by whom they have much improv'd themselves in villany and deceit."[14] Collins further likened the Dutch to "Locusts," who slandered the English by distributing "lying pictures, and libelling pamphlets [making] the Russian think us a ruined Nation," bribing "the Nobility with gifts," and "eat[ing the] bread out of the English-mens mouths."[15]

Beyond Collins's palpable frustration, the omnipresence and strong influence of the Dutch in Moscow can be detected in his words. Obviously,

Collins, who seems to have known little Russian, mainly moved among the highest circles of Russian society and primarily communicated with fellow Western Europeans, so his remarks mainly reflect the Dutch impact on those communities and should not be mistaken for a towering Dutch effect throughout Russia. Still, Collins's description of this context, on the eve of Peter the Great's birth in 1672, makes the subsequent fascination of Aleksei's youngest son with the Dutch more intelligible.

The assortment of goods exchanged between Russia and the Republic had changed by the 1660s. No longer were furs in high demand among Western European clients, despite the Russians' continued adherence to their custom to award diplomatic visitors with sable and other precious pelts upon departure from Muscovy.[16] Perhaps this drop was as much caused by a fall in supply as in demand, a result of the rather ruthless trapping methods the Russians practiced, which quickly depleted the number of fur-bearing animals in Siberia.[17] We already saw efforts around 1630 to ship grain to the Republic. Kotilaine charts several other episodes of grain exports, but it never became a staple among the commodities the Dutch shipped westward, after its brief peak around 1630.[18] After the midcentury point, other bulk goods were increasingly shipped back from the White Sea port to the Republic, however, such as naval stores (tar, hemp, or masts—the latter especially after 1670–), potash, and hides of domesticated animals (*iufti*), the processing of which became a veritable cottage industry in northern Russia.

Peter the Great's Russia proved rather more welcoming to foreign entrepreneurs and tradesmen than the Muscovy of his predecessors, even though it continued to enforce regulations that mandated Western artisans or entrepreneurs to have Russians apprentice with them with a view of eventually being able to replace the foreign experts. After 1690 many Russians went abroad to learn the Western ways as well, of course, again to foster expertise that could be applied at home. The different strategy in such matters pursued by Peter nevertheless confirms a substantial continuity in Russian dealings with foreigners. Long before his supremacy, rather than being blinded by unrestrained xenophobia, the Russians were masters at keeping foreign influence at arm's length. Thus, they staved off the danger of being colonized, at least in economic terms.

Despite the imposition of fees and restrictions on business activities (not least in terms of handling goods beyond Arkhangel'sk) throughout the entire era from 1575 to 1725, vast profits were made by Dutch merchants and entrepreneurs in Russia.[19] For Russia was neither capable of developing its own substantial merchant marine nor of establishing a manufacturing sector that could produce sufficient commodities (both quantitatively and qualitatively) to substitute for highly desired imported goods.

Restrictive Russian policies regarding Dutch trade did not just generate individual merchants' complaints or those levied by Dutch diplomatic representatives. The merchants, who had always tried to collaborate if it was in their interest, began to coordinate ever more closely. In what seems an echo of the bundling of forces in Dutch politics in the course of the seventeenth century, the Russia trade fell gradually into fewer hands. Initially, during the takeoff period between about 1585 and 1620, many had tried to make their fortune in trading on Arkhangel'sk. Fairly soon, however, the spoils were divided between a fairly small number of groups who began to monopolize the trade. These groups almost resemble clans, family networks in which a significant degree of marriage alliances were typically struck to shore up solidarity and trust.[20] Wijnroks suggests that "the marriage negotiations that preceded the wedding passed through the same stage as company mergers [, of which e]ven the terminology was often similar."[21]

By the late seventeenth century, these groups began to regulate the Russia trade even in a more formal fashion in order to establish full control over it. Thus, in 1693, a Directorate of Muscovite Trade was founded in the Republic, although the immediate cause for its organization was a desire to provide merchantmen better protection; it raised money for convoying by the Dutch navy against raids by corsairs and other ships in the Nine Years' War (1688–1697).[22] Its secondary purpose was to be able to face the Russian authorities and Russian traders in a more resolutely united fashion. But the Dutch merchants failed to set aside their customary internecine jealousies and envy, which caused this effort to fail. In part, though, this failure was the result of Peter's successful policy of drawing the Dutch merchants in, making them part of his efforts to create a new Russia, rather than approaching with the guarded hostility that had marked his predecessors' attitude to Westerners of which the *sloboda*'s segregation was the most evident expression. The Dutch no longer needed to protect each other against an unreliable and occasionally hostile customer. Russia after 1697 was literally open for business.

NOTES

1. Wijnroks, *Handel*, 287.
2. For a full translation into English, see R. Hellie, ed., *The Muscovite Law Code (Ulozhenie) of 1649*, vol. 1 (text and translation), Irvine, CA: Charles Schlacks jr, 1988; Lahana, "Novaia Nemetskaia Sloboda," 90–1. Lahana charts the growing mercantile and clerical resentment (see ibid., 65–73).
3. Ibid., 69–73.
4. Wijnroks, *Handel*, 288–9, 312, 333.
5. Ibid., 290.

6. See Kotilaine, "When the Twain," 44–5.
7. Ibid., 44.
8. Ibid., 103. For a slightly different (and more negative) take of this code's effect, see Kotilaine, "When the Twain," 47.
9. Lahana, "Novaia Nemetskaia Sloboda," 102.
10. Kotilaine, "When the Twain," 83, figure 2.3.
11. Note that even after 1650 at times ships departed the Republic in partial ballast.
12. *Nationaal Archief*, Archief der Staten-Generaal, Lias Moskoviën, 1663, 18 [Kurland cue-card numbering].
13. For more on Collins, see Unkovskaya, "Samuel Collins," and Dumschat, *Ausländische Mediziner*, 175, 389–404, 586–8. Collins had studied at Leyden. He arrived in Russia in 1660, persuaded to do so by John Hebdon sr, almost the sole English competitor of the Dutch in the 1660s (who nonetheless had traded in Amsterdam as a Russian factor before 1660; Hebdon seems to have been a Stuart royalist). Collins definitively left Russia in 1667.
14. S. Collins, *The Present State of Russia*, ed. Marshall Poe, London: Dorman Newman, 1671, 128–9.
15. Ibid. For more on the publication history and editions of *The Present State*, see I. Osipov, *Obzor svedenii ob izdaniiakh i perevodakh v xvii stoletii sochineniia Semiuelia Kollinsa "The Present State of Russia,"* Komi, Russian Federation: n.p., 2007.
16. Kotilaine, "When the Twain," 53–69, 81–2.
17. It is probably germane to mention here that in 1665 Jacob Boreel complained when on his departure he and his retainers received significantly fewer furs than Coenraad Burgh had been given in 1648; his Russian hosts suggested that, whereas he had indeed been given fewer pelts, they were each worth far more than in the late 1640s; one suspects that the tsar's stocks had depleted (see Boreel, *Verbael*, 724–5, 729–31).
18. Kotilaine, "When the Twain," 71–5.
19. See, for example, Lahana, "Novaia Nemetskaia Sloboda," 103.
20. Wijnroks analyzes the sixteenth-century Antwerp and Amsterdam family networks in detail, see Wijnroks, *Handel*, 179–209, 239–79.
21. Ibid., 188.
22. Knoppers, "Eighteenth Century Dutch Trade," 1.

Chapter 16

Envoys

Before in 1677 Van Keller in Moscow and in 1699 Andrei Artamonovich Matveev (1666–1728) at The Hague were formally installed as permanent residents for their respective governments, senior Russian diplomats (Bogdan Ordin-Nashchokin, Il'ia Danilovich Miloslavskii) repeatedly visited The Hague and Dutch envoys (the two Burghs, Boreel, Van Klenck) Moscow. In addition, as we saw, smaller missions were dispatched with some regularity, including of diplomatic messengers announcing the arrival of full-fledged (extraordinary) embassies.[1]

Little needs to be said about the (second) embassy of Albert Coenraadszoon Burgh who fell ill and died in Novgorod before he had reached the capital; his son Coenraad (1623–1669) who accompanied him on this trip took over at the helm of this mission, which arrived in Moscow in 1648. It was probably the most futile of all embassies, accomplishing little of substance in terms of its request for better trading conditions for Dutch merchants, although it coincided with the formal international recognition of the Dutch Republic as an independent sovereign nation as part of the 1648 Westphalian Peace, which was duly conveyed to the Russian hosts after Burgh received news about it. In this, it can be considered the counterpart to the 1614 Russian mission that announced the coronation of a new tsar.[2] When the Burghs left their country for Russia in 1647, though, they may have expected the imminent formal granting of Dutch independence, but its proclamation at Münster occurred during Burgh's sojourn in Moscow in January 1648. In other words, this mission was not primarily dispatched for ceremonial purpose, for otherwise its dispatch would have waited until 1648. Otherwise, the mission of the two Burghs accomplished little: Coenraad Burgh's endeavors were not helped by the social and political unrest that engulfed Moscow, eventually leading to rioting in June 1648 that killed hundreds of people. Politically, none of these "extraordinary embassies" accomplished much, as we saw; economically, though, they may have had some more significance, in that they ensured that the two countries, important commercial partners, remained on speaking terms.

The tsars, in their discussion with Dutch envoys such as Boreel or Van Klenck, needed to perform a balancing act in which they needed to marry Dutch with Russian mercantile interests. It is moot whether or not they truly were as unreceptive to meet Dutch demands or to requests to investigate grievances as the Dutch ambassadorial records appear to indicate if looked at in isolation. Certainly, the tsar and his advisors may have counted on the fact that, even without satisfying their Dutch ambassadorial interlocutors, Dutch traders would be coming to their northern port, because the economic opportunity (or the ability to make a profit) in trading with Russia remained too good to ignore. So the tsars could afford to be rude (as they had been, perhaps, regarding the Winius–Marselis–Ackema conflict in the late 1640s, and certainly were in supporting Jan van Sweeden unconditionally in 1665). At the same time, though, perhaps the Dutch complaints about wrongs they wanted to be righted were actually comparatively few in number: The amount of ships anchoring before Arkhangel'sk every summer remained invariably high, usually 30 or more in the second half of the seventeenth century.[3]

Even if Jacob Boreel appears to have brought a long list of grievances to Moscow in 1665, they were a compilation of problems that had arisen over a period of a number of years prior to his arrival (including the forced relocation of 1652, which by 1665 might still have stung for those who had been subjected to it, but was too long ago for anyone to expect restitution for the damage suffered in it). He hardly presented profoundly substantive matters to the tsar's counselors (indeed, that is why I called them petty above). Boreel's list evidently did not stop the promulgation of the New Commercial Statute in 1667, which shows that the Russians had been rather unfazed by the Dutch ambassador's lamentations of a couple of years earlier.

Conversely, the question is in how far in dispatching its embassies the Dutch government expected true progress in bettering relations with the tsar and his entourage. Were they mainly intended as pageantry, with the missions, tacitly or not, largely intended to display Dutch might to a domestic audience and foreign foe (as the English were in 1664–1665[4]), in an exercise of projecting power?

Their display, before Van Keller became the permanent Dutch diplomatic resident, periodically reminded the Russians of the considerable clout of this upstart republic; it cannot be entirely coincidental that the Dutch designated astoundingly rich men as their envoys. They knew they could not impress the Russians with their aristocratic pedigree, but they could convey the opulence of their country by sending some of their wealthiest, aware of the Russian weakness for such sumptuousness (the Dutch embassies continually handed out presents to all and sundry during their sojourns to grease the wheels, from what must have seemed a horn of plenty). The expeditions' display seems to try to suggest that this was a country, despite its dubious provenance, that had some heft, not in the least as the native land of so many traders who provided the Russians with the scarce and strategic goods deemed essential for Muscovy's survival. While their economic power will have generated respect for the Dutch among the Russian elite, this was probably somewhat negated by the Dutch utter inability to accomplish anything diplomatically, whether it was in brokering a Swedish (in 1616–1617), or Polish (in 1665) peace.

This is the context in which the three Dutch embassies (and the more limited Heinsius mission) dispatched to Russia in the reign of Aleksei Mikhailovich should be read. Much more significant to the Russians may have been some of the diplomatic or trade missions to the Republic initiated by the Muscovites across those three decades. For example, the visit of the *okol'nichii* Ivan Danilovich Miloslavskii and the *d'iak* Ivan Baibakov to the Republic in 1646 and 1647, as well as the subsequent trip by Andries Winius in 1653, both dispatched first and foremost for military purposes, prepared Russia for a war that (despite middling military successes) allowed it to claim Great-Power status after 1667.

Equally important were the arms purchases on behalf of the tsar made by the English merchant John Hebdon (1612–1670) in the Republic in 1658 and 1659.[5] They were essential in rekindling the Russian war with Poland, the outcome of which hung in abeyance; in this instance, the facilitators and suppliers of crucial military aid in the Republic were the redoubtable firm of De Vogelaer and Van Klenck. Although appearing a rather trivial event at the time, of great historical consequence would be the recruitment of a number of Dutch shipwrights and sailors to set up a Russian navy to sail the Caspian Sea, for among them was one Karsten Brandt, organized by Jan van Sweeden and David Butler for the tsar.

In between the large embassies led by Boreel (1664–1665) and Van Klenck (1675–1676), a smaller mission to Moscow on Dutch behalf was executed by Nicolaas Heinsius (1620–1681) in 1669 and 1670. Heins(ius) was a member of a prosperous family of Flemish refugees, the son of the well-known humanist Daniël Heinsius (1580–1656), a classical scholar and professor at Leyden University.[6] But Nicolaas, who was a poet of Latin verse, and had served as the Swedish queen Christina's librarian not long before her abdication in 1654, was in his day possibly even better known than his father. This was mainly for a negative reason: Heinsius's marriage woes became a public scandal in the 1660s. He briefly was Dutch resident in Stockholm, after which he executed several diplomatic missions on behalf of the Estates-General. Toward the end of his life he was appointed personal physician of the Swedish ex-queen in Rome, but died at The Hague soon after this prestigious appointment. Altogether, while a bit of a misfit, he managed to collect a vast library, of some 13,000 volumes, a sign of great wealth. He was a known Swedophile, and probably for that reason not the smartest choice to represent the Republic in Moscow.

Perhaps chastened by the failure to offer mediation in the Polish-Russian conflict in 1665, the main purpose of Heinsius's visit was to prevent a Swedish-Russian war from breaking out, although he made a spirited attempt as well to decrease the tariffs on foreign trade that had been raised by the New Commercial Code.[7] Much of Heinsius's time was spent addressing trade disputes as well as matters of diplomatic protocol, including how the Russian government was to address its Dutch counterpart and how the tsar should be called in Dutch printed works ("tsar" rather than "grand prince").[8] Indeed, the visit had started on the wrong foot, when an ill Heinsius violated protocol by refusing to sit on a horse for his ceremonial entry into the Russian capital.[9] He stubbornly demanded the use of a carriage, claiming that the Russians had neither nourished nor housed him properly on his progress from the border to Moscow. This had caused him to fall sick. Further delay followed when *tsarevich* Aleksei Alekseevich died in early 1670. It took more than three months after his arrival near Moscow before, in March, Heinsius finally saw the tsar; and the length of Heinsius's sojourn in Russia eventually stretched out to a year.[10] Despite its length, the trip proved a failure, as the Russians did not believe that any serious conflict had arisen between them and the Swedes regarding the terms of the 1661 Peace Treaty of Kardis (and were somewhat puzzled by Heinsius's brief in this regard).[11]

Meanwhile, Heinsius had probably not been starved on purpose on his progress from the border to Moscow. Whereas the Russians could be petty or evasive in their diplomatic ways, they were usually generous in entertaining their guests; their treatment of Heinsius was likely due to the fact that they had not been notified about his impending arrival:

> [After accepting my recredentials], one of the tsar's servants in the very same chamber brought a large bag with gifts for virtually all my servants, and opened it and proceeded to pull out numerous . . . sable pelts, while . . . Translator [Andrei V]inius spoke on behalf of the [*d'iak* Vasilii] Bobinin, that His Majesty had agreed to honour the extraordinary representative [Heinsius] and his retinue with a few presents, according to His country's custom.[12]

Heinsius, who had signaled numerous times earlier that he did not want any gifts, since his mission had been a failure (and he had initially not been treated properly as a diplomatic guest), refused this token of appreciation. The

Russians did not know how to take no for an answer, and Peter Marselis, the then Muscovite postmaster, dispatched the pelts through the mail to Riga.[13]

Heinsius, then, did little to improve the relationship between the two countries. The Russians were probably rather distracted by more pressing matters, such as the Razin rebellion that reached its height in the summer of 1670 (and about which Heinsius reported in some detail), or Afanasii Ordin-Nashchokin's fall as the tsar's most influential advisor, which occurred in the course of Heinsius's visit, creating uncertainty about the direction of Muscovy's foreign policy.[14] But the Dutch envoy was exceedingly petulant, and never seems to have been able to disabuse the Muscovites of the idea that not just he himself, but his masters favored Sweden over Russia. In that the Russians were probably right, as the Dutch were ever more desperately clinging to the 1668 Triple Alliance with Britain and Sweden. In effect, this alliance fell apart through the secret Treaty of Dover between Charles II and Louis XIV of June 1670, when Heinsius was in Moscow. Sweden was to choose the (Anglo-)French side in the war that broke out in 1672.

Despite Heinsius's fiasco, the tsar sent in his wake two envoys to The Hague, the merchants (they were explicitly identified as "*kuptsy*") Thomas Kelderman (sometimes Kellerman) and Vladimir Voronin.[15] They were received in The Hague in December of 1671, negotiating for a 1.5 million guilder loan in bullion.[16] The tsar promised to pay the loan off in two installments in August 1671 and August 1672 at Arkhangel'sk; it was to be paid in kind with potash, tallow, tar, hemp, flaxseed, and fur, among other things. It shows how the Russian government still lacked sufficient cash; given the restlessness through lack of pay of a number of *strel'tsy* and other troops in the tsar's service (as reported by Heinsius), causing the defection of some to Razin, the need for cash was quite acute.[17] But since the Dutch themselves were cornered, the sum was not granted.

The trifecta of the missions by Paul Menzies (Menesius; 1637–1694), Andrei Andreevich Vinius, and Emel'ian Ukraintsev (1641–1708) to Europe in 1672–1673 seems to mirror the Dutch exercises to boost their state's status by dispatching well-endowed embassies.[18] Travelling across Europe, these three envoys alerted Western Europe's leading monarchs to the new status of Russia as a Great Power (even if this reflected more Russian ambition than reality). But there was a more concrete reason for this diplomatic offensive: Tsar Aleksei Mikhailovich decided to dispatch this trio of ad hoc diplomats to Europe to persuade various Powers to come to the aid of Poland-Lithuania, which had been attacked by the Ottoman and Crimean-Tatar armies, and had lost the important fortified city of Kamenets-Podol'skii. This was an unprecedented initiative on the part of the Russians: Whereas they had dispatched diplomats to various courts for bilateral discussions since the fifteenth century, a multilateral diplomatic *démarche* was a first.[19] It showed that those reigning in Muscovy began to see their country as part of a European community of states. And while the Russian diplomatic efforts hopelessly failed in a Europe preoccupied by Louis XIV's moves, the 1683 Ottoman siege of Vienna forced the Holy Roman Emperor Leopold I a decade later to forge an alliance against the Turks not unlike what Aleksei's messengers had advocated in 1672 and 1673. Their quest was not as quixotic as it appeared.

This trio of diplomats was well trained and intrepid, and would go on to reach even higher rank in Russia in subsequent decades. A rising star in the tsarist foreign office, Emel'ian Ukraintsev was sent to Sweden, Denmark, and the Republic. Paul Menzies, a longtime Scottish mercenary in Russian service, was dispatched to Berlin, Dresden, Vienna, Venice, and Rome.[20] Andrei Andreevich Vinius was sent to England, France, and Spain. Vinius reached England in 1673 by sailing from the small Dutch port of Hellevoetsluis on a small vessel designated for the transport of mailed letters and packages (this service continued even while England and the Republic were at war). Why Ukraintsev was sent to The Hague rather than Vinius (whose command of Dutch was undoubtedly superior) is curious, although it may have had to do with a certain distrust regarding Vinius's loyalty to the Russian cause.[21] On his way from Denmark to Amsterdam, French sailors paid Ukraintsev's ship a visit, but he successfully hid the tsar's missives from their search of the vessel.[22] In the letter Ukraintsev brought to the Estates-General in the spring of 1673, the tsar expressed the hope that the war between the Dutch and the Anglo-French alliance might end and all would turn together against the sultan and his Crimean ally (as well as their Cossack support, as Cossack communities had abandoned their alliance with the tsar and the Polish king) instead.[23]

At The Hague, Ukraintsev was told how the war with Britain and France stopped the Republic from offering the embattled Poles a helping hand, but was complimented in the Estates-General's response to Aleksei Mikhailovich for his exemplary behavior as Russian envoy.[24] Ukraintsev, then, for once defied the expectation of boorish misbehavior for which Russians were notorious in this age.[25]

One should not exaggerate the extent of Russian diplomatic sophistication, though, for the reports Andrei Vinius wrote for the tsar about the countries he had visited are not exactly an impressive feat of political economy, despite some insightful flashes.[26] He also dedicated a few words to the country of his ancestors through which he had traveled. His description of the Dutch Republic as having become a sort of absolute monarchy under stadtholder William III was a distortion of its political system. No doubt did William III enjoy a great amount of power in the Republic in 1673, but it was not unchecked.[27] Despite its inaccuracy and brevity, this was the first Russian political economy of the Republic ever composed. It is moot whether or not

Vinius "dumbed down" his description for his audience, or if he was truly as naïve about the three kingdoms that he visited (he was, after all, a master at summarizing Western newspapers for the tsar[28]). Regardless, the mindset of the Russian court clearly opened up around 1670, and the Russians were quick learners, of which there is no better proof than the life of Peter, the *tsarevich* who was born in 1672, mere months before Vinius and company set out on their journey.

Certainly, Russian diplomatic adroitness was entering a new phase in the final years of Tsar Aleksei's rule, which was fostered by a coterie of worldly characters at the highest levels of the tsarist bureaucracy who took a lively interest in the world outside Muscovy and influenced Russia's worldview. They cultivated close relationships with Westerners both in Moscow and abroad, and Vinius was a pivotal figure not just through his translation of newspapers, his interpreting for the tsar during diplomatic visits, or his diplomatic reports: In 1675, he regained control over the incoming and outgoing mail between Moscow and Europe, a job he would keep for a quarter century.[29] He seems to have been on good terms with many high-ranking Russians and with many of the foreign contingent residing in Moscow, while he regularly corresponded with several foreign acquaintances. It seems no coincidence that this was a man of Dutch ancestry, fluent in its language.

NOTES

1. Such a messenger was usually called a "*gonets*" in Russian, or "*renbode*" in Dutch. John Hebdon (see below) seems to have held the status of Russian resident at the Hague in the early 1660s (*Nationaal Archief*, Archief der Staten-Generaal, Lias Moscoviën 1645–1673, October 2, 1660 and *Nationaal Archief*, Archief der Staten-Generaal, Lias Moscoviën, December 8, 1660); I.Ia. Gurliand, *Ivan Gebdon, komissarius i rezident*, Iaroslavl': Tipografiia gubernskogo pravleniia, 1903, 19–20. Subsequently, Hebdon switched his loyalties back to the restored British royal house and became its agent in Moscow. He eventually teamed up with Patrick Gordon.

2. Loviagin, ed., *Posol'stvo*, xvii; Uhlenbeck, "Rusland," 81.

3. See "Notariele akten," which listing may be an undercount, and are based merely on notary acts found in Amsterdam's archives. There may have also been journeys that never entered any notary book. See as well the shipping volume cited in a previous segment.

4. Just prior to Boreel's embassy, King Charles II had sent the Carlisle embassy to Russia in 1663–1664.

5. Van Zuiden, *Bijdrage*, 12–16; Gurliand, *Ivan Gebdon*, 21. For more on Hebdon, see Gurliand, *Ivan Gebdon*. Hebdon was portrayed by Ferdinand Bol on this trip to the Republic in 1659.

6. See "Heinsius, Nicolaas," in A.J. van der Aa, *Biographisch Woordenboek der Nederlanden*, vol. 8 part 1, Haarlem: Van Brederode, 1867, 439–49.

7. *Nationaal Archief*, Archief der Staten-Generaal, Lias Moskoviën (*Verbael* by Heinsius *Verbael*), 43–5; 66–121.

8. *Nationaal Archief*, Archief der Staten-Generaal, Lias Moskoviën, 1669 and 1670. See as well *RGADA* 50/7 (1669), ll. 44–8, 132–4.

9. On such quarrels, see Hennings, *Russia and Courtly Europe*, 15–16.

10. See as well *RGADA* 50/3 (1669), ll. 8–12, 48–55. Having returned from negotiations with Polish representatives at the border, Afanasii Ordin-Nashchokin, Aleksei's favorite in the later 1660s, was Heinsius's interlocutor, joining the *dumnye d'iaki* Gerasim Dokhturov and Lukian Golosov and the *d'iak* Efim Iur'ev, who soon were denounced by Ordin-Nashchokin as his enemies who had undermined his policies (he took the tonsure after resigning, see ibid., l.12; see as well *Nationaal Archief*, Archief der Staten-Generaal, Lias Moskoviën, Heinsius letter of March 26, 1670 and letter of August 7, 1670). All four earlier had been involved with the *Oryol* project. Andrei Vinius served again as the tsar's Dutch translator for the Heinsius visit.

11. Heinsius *Verbael*, 66–98; see *Nationaal Archief*, Archief der Staten-Generaal, Lias Moskoviën, Heinsius letter of July 31, 1670.

12. Heinsius, *Verbael*, 122.

13. Ibid., 134.

14. *Nationaal Archief*, Archief der Staten-Generaal, Lias Moskoviën, Letter from Heinsius to Staten-Generaal, July 3, 1670 [New Style]; Letter from Heinsius to Staten-Generaal, July 31, 1670 [New Style]; Letter from Heinsius to Staten-Generaal, August 7, 1670 [New Style]; Letter from Heinsius to Staten-Generaal, August 14, 1670 [New Style]; and Letter from Heinsius to Staten-Generaal, August 18, 1670 [New Style].

15. *Nationaal Archief*, Archief der Staten-Generaal, Lias Moskoviën, August 14, 1670.

16. *Nationaal Archief*, Archief der Staten-Generaal, Lias Moskoviën, December 13, 1670. Koenraad van Klenck helped out in furnishing some of the money needed in exchange for some of the goods the Russians offered (see A.V. Demkin, "Dlia popolneniia ego velikogo gosudar'a kazny," *Istochnik* 4, 1999, 3–9).

17. See also Kotilaine, "When the Twain," 110.

18. *Pamiatniki diplomaticheskikh'*, vol. 4, 803–946. For more on these visits, see below in the next section.

19. For more on this, see Boterbloem, "Russia and Europe."

20. See Paul Dukes, "Paul Menzies and His Mission from Muscovy to Rome, 1672–1674," *Innes Review* 2, 1984, 88–95.

21. See Boterbloem, *Moderniser*, 79. In a curious turn, Ukraintsev later became Andrei Vinius's brother-in-law.

22. *Nationaal Archief*, Archief der Staten-Generaal, Lias Moskoviën, June 7, 1673 [Note from Ukraintsev, October 1672].

23. *Nationaal Archief*, Archief der Staten-Generaal, Lias Moskoviën, May 1673 [Letter from tsar, October 1672].

24. *Nationaal Archief*, Archief der Staten-Generaal, Lias Moskoviën, May 1673 [Letter to tsar, May 29, 1673]. During negotiations conducted by the Russian envoys of the Grand Embassy at The Hague in October 1697, the Dutch were reminded that they had promised Ukraintsev their wholehearted support if the Russians would go to war with the "infidels," that is, the Ottoman Turks, but had never lived up to that promise (N.I. Pavlenko, *Lefort*, Moscow: Molodaia Gvardiia, 2009, 174).

25. Especially the visit of Il'ia Miloslavskii in 1646 and 1647 had left a bitter taste in Dutch mouths (see C.C. Uhlenbeck, "Rusland omtrent het midden der zeventiende eeuw," *De Gids* 55, 1891, 38–81: 45).

26. Boterbloem, *Moderniser*, 83–6.

27. See as well N.A. Kazakova, "A.A. Vinius i stateinyi spisok ego posol'stva v Angliiu, Frantsiiu i Ispaniiu v 1672–1674 gg.," *Trudy otdela drevnerusskoi literatury* 39, 1985, 348–64: 363; and *Pamiatniki diplomaticheskikh' snoshenii*, vol. 4, 803–946.

28. See Boterbloem, *Moderniser*, 55–6.

29. See ibid., 98–9. He had briefly held the job in 1672 (ibid., 66–8).

Chapter 17

The *Oryol*

A certain Hollander, named Botteler [David Butler] who had been appointed commander at Astrakhan on a certain newly invented [*van een nieuwe inventie*] ship with which sail the Caspian Sea, is said to have, together with his Hollander crew, defended himself well [against Stepan Razin], but ultimately they have been killed [*nedergemaeckt*], too.[1]

Thus reported Nicolaas Heinsius in a letter to the Dutch Estates-General from Moscow in August 1670. The message about Butler's demise was premature (he did fall into Cossack captivity, and faked his identity before getting away), while most of his sailors had in fact escaped the Cossacks altogether.[2] Those sailors, among whom Jan Struys and Karsten Brandt acquired lasting fame, were lucky, for the Cossacks, as Heinsius suggested in the same letter, showed otherwise no mercy toward captured Russian nobles or foreign mercenary officers.[3] From that latter group, only one was deliberately spared, the gunner Lodewijk Fabricius, another Dutchman, whose fluency in Russian and skill as artillerist may have saved his life.[4] From a memorandum by the Dutch resident Johan Willem van Keller to Ivan V and Peter I of May 1687, even 17 years after the fall of Astrakhan to Stepan Razin some of the *Oryol*'s crew remained in Tatar captivity in the Caucasus.[5] Whether a(nother) letter pleading for their release was ever sent to the *shamkal*, the ruler of the Caucasian region (in Dagestan) in which the surviving Dutch were thought to be held captive, is unclear.

While a few Dutch sailors were killed in the Cossack storming of Astrakhan in the summer of 1670, at various stages, Struys, Brandt, a number of other sailors from the *Oryol*, their captain Butler, and their compatriots Fabricius and Termund all fled the city more or less unscathed. Their travails were far from over, even if they are not the topic of this book. As noted previously, what is relevant here, though, is that Struys and Fabricius left us with writings that are important sources to give us some idea of the Dutch view of Russia in the final years of Tsar Aleksei, and that Brandt, after returning to Russia, mentored the young tsar Peter in his efforts to start a Russian navy. Termund, already in the tsar's service as a surgeon, eventually returned to Moscow and became another influential friend of Peter the Great.

The story of the building of the *Oryol* and its descent toward Astrakhan may be the moment that best exemplifies the "Dutch moment" in Russian history. Dutch craftsmen, merchants, entrepreneurs, and mercenaries all left their mark on the *Oryol* venture: Almost everything comes together in this undertaking, which began in 1667 and came to an ignominious end in 1670, even if it would have a long afterlife thanks to the publication of its sailmaker Jan Struys's *Drie aanmerkelijke en seer rampspoedige Reysen* in 1676. The plan to build a ship was probably inspired by Jan van Sweeden, who launched a multitude of initiatives in mid-1660s Russia.

Earlier, Van Sweeden had likely been a patron of the young Andrei Vinius after the death of the latter's father in 1663 (or thereabouts). Vinius, working in the *posol'skii prikaz* as an interpreter and translator (by 1668 he had begun to regularly supply the court with abbreviated translations of Western newspapers), suggested to the tsar and his key advisors to build a galley fleet to complement the *Oryol*. He argued in a 1667 memorandum to his supervisors—Afanasii Ordin-Nashchokin headed the foreign office and oversaw the *Oryol* project, assisted by the *d'iaks* Gerasim Dokhturov, Luk'ian Golosov and Efim Iur'ev—that building a seafaring sailship squadron seemed perhaps attractive, but was impractical: Galley ships ("*katorgi*")—rowed by convicts—might be more efficient in the shallow waters of the Caspian Sea.[6] Even when oars-driven ships were not built then, Vinius thus coined the word "*katorga*" in Russian as a synonym for hard labor performed by convicts.

While Van Sweeden and Vinius were likely allies, they were not especially fond of Peter Marselis, who also played a role in the *Oryol* project. In 1667, Peter Marselis seems to have advised the tsar about the terms of the New Commercial Statute, which, however limited its aim and ineffective as an instrument, did stimulate Russian domestic enterprise and increase the Russian share in the country's export trade, an effort of which the *Oryol* project was part.[7] At the same time, Marselis developed plans for a rebuilding of the Arkhangel'sk warehouses, after another devastating fire had laid waste to the port; sensibly, he suggested a rebuilding with brick and stone of the *gostinnyi dvor'*, the main warehouse.[8] More germane for the *Oryol* project, however, was that Marselis's iron forges and arms manufactory supplied the ship with cannon and some other metalware.[9] By then a veteran of 20 years' service in the tsar's military, Colonel Cornelis van Bockhoven meanwhile was appointed to supervise the building of the ship and its auxiliary vessels.

Van Sweeden, Marselis, and Vinius all three alternated as Russian postmaster between 1664 and 1675, an apparently highly coveted job. Whether the elderly Peter Marselis disliked Andrei Vinius as much as he had detested the latter's father is unclear, but traces of a lingering competition between the two families may be seen both with regards to the mail operation and in a subsequent search for precious metals. In 1676, Andrei Vinius and a son of Peter Marselis prospected separately in efforts to discover gold, silver, and gemstones, only to find copper ore.[10]

Similar to the utter debacle of hiring great numbers of mercenary soldiers without properly integrating them in to the Russian army (or paying them adequately) in the Smolensk War of 1632–1634, the *Oryol* project seems at first sight an utter fiasco, given its end. The ship was to decay on the shores of the Volga estuary long after the Razin rebellion was suppressed. But in both cases, as we saw, the outcome was perhaps not as negative as it appears. Lessons were (to be) learned: After the Smolensk War, Western mercenaries were much more effectively used in modernizing the Russian army, while without his boarding of the *Oryol*, Karsten Brandt would likely have never settled in the *nemetskaia sloboda*, where he was eventually found by Peter the Great, and was to build the cradle of the Russian navy.

NOTES

1. Letter of Heinsius to Staten-Generaal, August 14, 1670, 122. It is interesting that Heinsius here and elsewhere suggests that Razin's rebellion had been provoked by the hanging of Razin's brother on the order of a drunken Prince Iurii A. Dolgorukii. This particular cause of the rebellion has been dismissed in recent historiography, as there is no evidence in Russian records about it, but this is one of the earliest references to this story.
2. See Boterbloem, *Fiction and Reality*.
3. Struys, *Drie aanmerkelijke en seer rampspoedige reysen*.
4. Brandt passed himself off as a "Persian," and Butler pretended to be a servant of Termund, who was spared because he was a doctor whose services were cherished by the Cossacks.
5. *RGADA* 50, 1687, May 11 [21], 1687 (Van Keller to Tsars Ivan and Peter).
6. Arkheograficheskaia kommissiia, *Dopolneniia k aktam' istoricheskim'*, Sanktpeterburg': Eduard Prats, 1865, vol. 5, 404–5.
7. Boterbloem, *Fiction*, 63; Kotilaine, "When the Twain," 46–7.
8. Veluwenkamp, *Archangel*, 117–18.
9. Boterbloem, *Fiction*, 69–70.
10. Arkheograficheskaia kommissiia, *Dopelnenniia k aktam istoricheskim*, Sanktpeterburg': Eduard Prats, 1859, vol. 7, 53–7; Boterbloem, *Moderniser*, 88–9.

Chapter 18

Becoming Russian?

Andrei Andreevich Vinius was basically considered Russian, while Peter Marselis and Jan van Sweeden, who lived much of their adult lives in Muscovy, thereby acquired a sort of honorary status as *"moskovskie inozemtsy."* All three distanced themselves from the transient Dutch mercantile community in Russia and switched sides to the tsar's camp, even if their unwavering loyalty to Muscovy is doubtful. Their allegiance was before anything to their own purse or well-being. For a fee (in money or kind), Vinius clearly was willing to divulge information, but remained more of a venal Russian official rather than becoming a wholesale mercenary selling his services to anyone as long as the price was right.

Peter Marselis's overarching loyalty was to his family firm (although he had no qualms about enlisting the Dutch Estates-General to plead his cause in the conflict with Andries Winius). He is an especially good example of someone who placed kin (and possibly religion, as he retained a Calvinist minister in Muscovy) before country: He was part of a clan that operated as a sort of modern multinational company, with offices in Amsterdam, Hamburg, Copenhagen, and Moscow.[1] Perhaps "supranational" might be a better term for this firm, as the overarching loyalty of Peter and his brothers Selio, Leonard, and Gabriël was to the firm their father had founded (and to each other, it seems), and only then to whichever polity in which territory they happened to reside. They were perhaps strikingly modern in running their business: It is these days a long-established entrepreneurial strategy to circumvent tariffs and import regulations by opening company branches within the countries' whose governments follow such protectionist policies, as is done, for example, by car manufacturers.

Jan van Sweeden least wavered in his commitment to the Russian cause, but that appears to have been based on a calculation that Muscovy and the tsar offered him the most gain during the decade that he was a pivotal figure among expatriates in Russia. More money could be made by identifying with the tsar's realm and thus avoid the various antiforeigner policies and discriminatory acts such as the 1652 ouster from Moscow, or the restrictions of the various trade regulations imposed upon foreigners, as in 1667.

Mercenary soldiers' loyalty, of course, was literally up for sale. In his diary, Patrick Gordon occasionally mopes about the forced prolongation of his stay in Russia, but, somewhat exceptionally, he was allowed to travel to Scotland on a few occasions and then did not decide to remain in remote Aberdeenshire.[2] In Russia, the pay was excellent and Gordon was a big fish in a small pond within the community near Moscow in which he resided. Russian commanders and courtiers displayed a rather flattering amount of appreciation for his military expertise and bravery in battle. The thrill of being close to the absolute summit of power in Russia in his last decade alleviated any homesickness, while the choice to stay in Russia was made easier for him, a staunch supporter of the Stuart cause and a Catholic to boot, after the Catholic James II was deposed as British monarch in 1688.

While Russia's munificence is more important than anything in explaining Western mercenary faithfulness to the tsar, it is tempting to ponder the role of ostracization that some foreign officers had experienced in their homeland, where they had been religious outcasts. This goes for Gordon and Menzies, but also for the Van Bockhovens, who were all Catholics. In the Republic, some Catholics can be identified in high positions—even if more in private business than in public office, from which they were formally excluded—but the options for Catholics to join its elite were severely restricted.

But François Lefort was a Calvinist, and many other Western officers in Muscovite service were Lutheran or Calvinist as well: religious dissent was not a game-changer for most in declaring for Russia. Among the entrepreneurs even a Mennonite such as Tieleman Lus Akema can be found (and the sixteenth-century physician Eylof was a Mennonite as well). The evidence about religious dissenters coming to Muscovy as refugees from the hegemonic religion of their native country is too anecdotal to truly make a case for overachieving foreigners becoming a success in their new surroundings in a sort of Weberian fashion. While the Western immigrants in Russia were an enterprising lot, no convincing correlation can be argued between religious conviction and a business *nous*, or an exceptional skill in matters military.

In the Ottoman Empire, the ultimate test of passing as a loyal subject of the sultan was to convert to Islam, as not a few Dutchmen did in the sixteenth and seventeenth centuries.[3] In Muscovy, too, conversion to Orthodoxy was the final step toward becoming a true Muscovite. Very few Dutchmen or women did so, however: Andries Winius (and his wife, likely against her will[4]) is the most famous case, while Filips Albrecht van Bockhoven is another of a leading Dutch expatriate choosing Russian Orthodoxy (he converted not long before his death). From Peter's reign onward, however, conversion to Orthodoxy no longer was a precondition to be wholly included in the Russian community. This may have made it easier for many Dutch immigrants to "go native" and definitively settle in Russia.

While the country in which they settle changes immigrants, they have in their turn an influence on the countries in which they settle, of course. Some of these are ephemeral: New Yorkers are called Yankees, because they were once, in the seventeenth century, known as Dutch "Jan-Kezen."[5] Otherwise, the Dutch influence on American culture was rather ephemeral, even if Roosevelts and Van Burens became president, Breukelen Brooklyn and Haarlem Harlem, while the Vanderbilts were famous as the richest people alive in the nineteenth-century United States. Surely, this slightest of imprints was due to both the small numbers of Dutch settlers in seventeenth-century North America and the brevity of the Dutch colony's existence there. But Dutch-style projects and plans developed by people such as Van Sweeden, Marselis, or Vinius had somewhat deeper impact on Muscovy: They transferred to Russia concepts, or organizational and technological skills, that bore fruit. This transmission of expertise and know-how constitutes another important aspect of Dutch-Russian relations in this period.

Some of the Dutch immigrants settled in Russia, others returned. Decisions to remain or leave were dependent on a great variety of circumstances, and the immigrants' attitudes and actions seem remarkably modern—or perhaps they are of all times—in making these decisions. For most, however, economic reasons trumped everything.[6]

NOTES

1. See Amburger, *Die Familie Marselis*.
2. See Gordon, *Diary*.
3. Boterbloem, *Fiction*, 25. A rather odd double conversion happened in the case of the notorious traitor Jacob Janszoon (Janssen), a Dutch native who first had converted to Russian Orthodoxy and then switched sides at the first siege of Azov in 1695; *Jakushka* was on explicit Russian request handed over by the Turks after the 1696 capture of the town, and broken at the wheel in Moscow (see Wittram, *Peter I*, vol. 1, 127).
4. Witsen, *Moscovische reyse*, vol. 3, 411.
5. See Boterbloem, *Dirty Secret*, 121–3; and for a more detailed and well-measured discussion, see Wim Klooster, *The Dutch Moment: War, Trade and Settlement in the Seventeenth-Century Atlantic World*, Ithaca, NY: Cornell UP, 2016.
6. Boterbloem, *Dirty Secret*, viii.

Chapter 19

Koenraad van Klenck's Embassy

As we saw, the four first extraordinary embassies (if we include the Brederode mission) the Dutch dispatched to Russia did not appear to accomplish much of substance; neither did Heinsius's mission. They were mounted at considerable cost and had little to show for their efforts upon their return to the Netherlands. It might be argued, though, too, that they did soften up the Russians, making them aware of the High Mightinesses' might, and alerting them that the Dutch merchants hailed from a country of great economic clout and exceptional technological, not least military, advancements. But the two polities were located too far away from each other to foster more than a passing interest in each other's political fate. In addition, before the 1670s, the Dutch were frequently allied to Sweden and key trading partners of the Polish Commonwealth, two of Muscovy's age-old foes. In the eyes of the Dutch regents, any quarrel with those two empires would hardly be compensated by any closer political tie with Russia. The Russians, not without reason, were suspicious as well of the cordial relationship the Republic maintained with the Sublime Porte, another long-standing Muscovite enemy.

But a reversal of alliances occurred in the 1670s: The Dutch were confronted by an aggressive France, which struck an alliance with Sweden. The Republic, meanwhile, found an ally in Sweden's age-old rivals Denmark, a country often in league with Muscovy against Sweden. Poland-Lithuania, meanwhile, was engulfed by domestic conflict, which was aggravated by a war with the Turks (and their Crimean-Tatar allies), as we saw earlier. Even if King Jan III Sobieski (r. 1674–1696) was not fond of Muscovy, the *Rzeczpospolita* and Russia would not go to war with each other again.

The Dutch, too, allied with their old Habsburg adversaries both in Madrid and in Vienna, inveterate foes of the Ottoman sultans. The Republic maintained its friendship with another fast-rising newcomer, Brandenburg-Prussia, keen to diminish Swedish power in the Baltic area. Its ruler, Frederick William of Hohenzollern, had married into the Dutch stadtholder family of Orange-Nassau in the 1640s; Louise Henriette, his (first) wife, who died in 1667, had given him a son and heir (Frederick III, after 1701 King Frederick I) who could still speak enough Dutch to hold a conversation in the language with Peter the Great in 1697. Seemingly, the road to a Russian-Dutch pact lay open.

This new international constellation caused the dispatch of the Koenraad van Klenck embassy to Russia in 1675. Its overt immediate goal, to strike a military alliance with Russia against Sweden, was not met. But of all five seventeenth-century Dutch embassies, Van Klenck's mission did probably most impress the Russians and accomplished most in terms of softening up the Russians toward the Dutch. Van Klenck, who read and spoke Russian with ease,[1] was the best prepared of all ambassadors. He was easily accepted as the de facto chief of the Dutch mercantile interest during his stay in Russia, while, like Boreel, he also represented the Hamburg and Bremen traders, still being seen—and thinking of themselves—as satellites within the Dutch mercantile orbit (or perhaps "lower German North-Sea trading community").

Besides parlaying with these Western European traders in Moscow and representing their interest before the tsar, Van Klenck met with a host of Asian merchants as well, once more carefully exploring the possibilities of a wholesale rerouting of the Iranian silk trade across Russia to Arkhangel'sk. Mainly for domestic consumption, Van Klenck's splendid visit was eternalized by a visually impressive brochure illustrated by the greatest Dutch etcher of his generation, Romeyn de Hooghe (1645–1708).[2] This glittering pamphlet projected to a Dutch audience their country's awesome (and restored) power, while its subtext may have been to display a show of the Republic's unity, at a time when its elite was still divided because of the bloody denouement of the De Witt administration in 1672.

The choice for Koenraad van Klenck as extraordinary ambassador was a wise one for a number of reasons. Extremely wealthy, he was the head of a firm that had been trading on Russia for a century and had previously lived himself for extended stints in Muscovy. He was thus finely attuned to its culture. He had furthermore helped to supply the tsar with crucial arms deliveries in his hour of need in the Thirteen Years' War, for which he was fondly remembered at the court. From the Dutch perspective, too, it was a happy coincidence that he was not only a powerful Amsterdam merchant and a member of its city council, but also a (Holy-Roman-Imperial) nobleman, the head of a family who had been retainers of the Nassaus since the middle of the sixteenth century. Thus, Koenraad van Klenck represented at least in some measure both sides in the Orange-regent (or Orange-Amsterdam) conflict that since the Dordt Synod and the Twelve Years' Truce was simmering in the Republic, and sometimes burst into flames, as it had in 1672. And he was not a commoner, which will have pleased the Muscovites.

The careful organization of Van Klenck's embassy appears to show how the Dutch had learned their lessons from their previous diplomatic interactions with the Russians. This astuteness can be illustrated in a number of ways, a sample of which will be outlined here. Firstly, there was the shrewd choice of the ambassador himself. Van Klenck, of course, was a formidable character; unlike him, none of his predecessors had known Russian, had lived in Russia, or had been part of a firm that had traded on Russia since before Mikhail Romanov became tsar (and he was a nobleman). Secondly, the embassy's official translator, Abraham van Asperen, had played the same role for Boreel (and he had previously been involved in the Russia trade). Thirdly, Balthasar Coyett, one of the four "nobles" in the retinue, had relatives in Russia who had worked there since the 1630s as glassblowers; his book bespeaks that he was rather well informed about Russia.[3] Fourthly, the mission's second-in-command, Johan Willem van Keller, had earlier visited Russia as an aide to Heinsius. It is not clear how many further "area specialists" (as they now are known today in the US State Department) could be counted among the many retainers Van Klenck brought along, but there was undeniably one more: This was the "palfreyman and constable" Jan Janszoon Struys, then not yet known as the author of the travel account that was soon to bring him fame.[4]

Already then almost 40 years old, Struys had been the sailmaker for the *Oryol* flotilla, his four-year contract with the tsar voided after a year-and-a-half when he had been forced to flee from Astrakhan across the Caspian Sea to avoid the grim fate of most foreigners who faced Stenka Razin. Many of his fellow refugees had succumbed during their effort to make it back to safe ground, but Struys had survived brutal violence and Caucasian enslavement to return to his homeland in 1673. His strong desire to go back to Moscow seems evident from notary documents drawn up in Amsterdam: He planned to ask for himself and several of his comrades (or their dependents) the arrears the tsar's government owned them (it is not clear whether he expected payment of the full four-year term for which he was hired in 1668, but he had not been paid after the fall of 1669, so he may have at least felt justified in asking for a minimum of the three-quarters of a year before he fled Astrakhan that had not been remunerated).[5]

What is equally intriguing is why Van Klenck brought Struys along. He was awarded the title of "constable and palfreyman," a bit of an unusual combination. What was a "constable" supposed to do on a diplomatic mission: Prepare the salute shots at Arkhangel'sk? And Struys was not by trade a groomer of horses, so the role of palfrey did not suit him very well either.

It is moot how much Russian Struys knew by then, but one suspects that he may have been able to understand a decent amount of it after more than two years in Muscovy (and as a half- or illiterate person he was probably capable of picking up spoken language relatively quickly[6]). Several of his fellow refugees had made it back to Moscow by 1675, including Lodewijk Fabricius (then still an officer in the tsar's army), Jan Termund, and Karsten Brandt (the former assistant constable of the *Oryol*).[7] They would have been easy to find, as they resided with other Western expatriates in Moscow's *nemetskaia sloboda*. In other words, even if Struys might not be especially fluent in Russian, he might have been a useful agent, acquiring intelligence for Van Klenck after reacquainting himself with his old fellow travelers. All of this hints at something not very evident from the sources: The Dutch knew the value of intelligence and were poised to gather as much information as possible. Knowledge was power, as an astute businessman like Van Klenck had learned all too well.[8]

And they may have gathered intelligence from agents who were employed in the tsarist bureaucracy: We already met the Dutch-immigrant son Andrei Andreevich Vinius, the translator on behalf of the tsar assigned to the Boreel embassy, at several moments; he now again was appointed as tsarist interpreter for the Van Klenck embassy, as he had translated for the Russian camp during the Boreel and Heinsius missions.[9] From the Russian perspective this made sense: Both Vinius's language skill and his diplomatic experience—he had after all recently visited the Western European monarchies—would facilitate proceedings.

Vinius, it appears from ample evidence, however, was willing to divulge Russian state secrets, for money and other favors.[10] He proved again a pivotal figure in liaising with the Van Klenck embassy (while the highly talented Ukraintsev, too, was one of Van Klenck's interlocutors[11]). Although in his habits hewing to Orthodox custom, Vinius did receive Dutch retainers at home, even introducing them to his wife and one of his daughters.[12] He thus deviated from the rule that prohibited Russian-Orthodox women to have any contact with foreigners, to avoid being exposed to heresy and other assorted temptations.

This custom of female seclusion among the Russian elite originated in the late Byzantine Empire. Vinius may have chafed at these stuffy traditions, not just because he had only converted on his father's orders—and against his stepmother's will—to Orthodoxy as a teenager, but also because he was very much a connoisseur of Western culture. This affinity was rooted in his sustained reading of Western newspapers and reinforced because of his own recent trip to the courts of Spain, France, and England, which had seen him visit the Republic as well. While we are unsure about how much he had remained in regular contact with the young Amsterdam regent Nicolaas

Witsen since both had met in 1665, it is nonetheless likely that the two maintained at least a sporadic correspondence.[13] If this contact indeed was as intensive as some have proposed, the exchange of letters had to be kept carefully secret, as no one at the tsar's court would have looked kindly at the leaking of information to foreigners.[14] Because Vinius oversaw for years the handling of the mail with Europe, and because not many would be able to decipher even the addresses of the missives in which he conveyed information to the Amsterdam politician and scientist, Vinius's opportunity of communicating with Witsen (or indeed others) was indeed fairly good. Vinius also was a sort of cat with nine lives, a master dissembler who managed to recover every time from what would have doomed others, as he did in 1676, 1689, and 1708.[15] So the Van Klenck Embassy was not only expertly led, arriving with lavish gifts and numbering several Russianists among its staff, but it could also count on a valuable back channel in Vinius, it appears.

The Russian record of the visit lists the most important representatives of the Western European community residing in or near Moscow who welcomed Van Klenck when he officially entered Moscow on January 21, 1676 (New Style):

[noted as their head—*golova*) Frants Karp's son lCarlo's son?] Guasconi, Andrei [Heinrich] Butenant, Kondratei [Konrad] Norderman[n], Danilo [Daniël] Hartman, Ivan Far'ium, Vakhromei [Werner] Meller [Muller], Kornilo [Cornelis] Bogart [Bogaert], Adolf Gutman [Houtman], Eremei [Jeroen?] Fantroin [van Troyen], Kondratei [Coenraet] Kanegiter [Cannegieter], Andrei Kenkel', Elisei [Gillis] Gliuk [Cloeck], Andrei [Heinrich] Svellengrebel' [Swellengrebel], Petr' [Pieter or Peter] Gasenius [Hasenius], Ivan [Jan or Isaac?] Gutman [Houtman], Matvei [Matthias] Rozvinkel' [Romswinckel], Ivan [Jan] Fankerin [van Keeren?], Stepan Elal [Stephen Euell or Jewell?], Boris Gein, Zakharei Gerdin [possibly Patrick Gordon].[16]

This is a good cross-section of the leading figures of the leading Western expatriates residing in the Russian capital of 1676. Most, albeit not all, of these people can be identified; whereas the first three, or the last one, are not "Dutch," they were all strongly linked to each other in a Dutch-dominated network. The Florentine Francesco Guasconi (b. 1640) and his family worked in part out of Amsterdam, and usually with Dutch partners, as a shipper and trader; Butenant was a Hamburger who took over Marselis's iron forgeries but also continued to work as a merchant (and partnered with Hartman), while the German-born Nordermann, originally a merchant when he began to work in 1660s Muscovy, subsequently became a prospector and entrepreneur involved in mining operations (and was executed as a heretic with Quirinus Kuhlmann on Red Square in 1689), in which he partnered with Andrei

Vinius.[17] Patrick Gordon (if this is him) had married into the Van Bockhoven clan in the 1660s. Altogether, it is not too far-fetched to recognize in this welcoming party the major figures within the Dutch expatriate community in 1670s Muscovy. They paid their respect to someone who had been once one of them and become the most successful one of them all in entering the highest echelons of Dutch society, the Amsterdam regent Koenraad van Klenck.

I have argued elsewhere that, while Van Klenck returned home in the spring of 1676 with ostentatiously little to show for his efforts, this might not have mattered much to him or to many of his fellow regents in Amsterdam, who at this time were relieved to witness the Dutch war with France whittling down, and had little appetite for a flaring up of this war by its escalation into an all-out European conflict.[18] He may have hoped to improve the trading conditions for his compatriots (and himself), but, based on the previous fruitless attempts, could not count on very much progress in this respect, or on receiving any Russian permission to establish direct trade routes for Dutch merchants between the Republic and Iran or China, an issue on which he spent some effort during his negotiations with the Russians. Privately, though, he was able to shore up his business relations, both with his fellow Dutchmen, with several of whom he had partnered, and with the Russians, Armenians, and others, on this, what was to be his last, trip to Muscovy. And the visit was unexpectedly useful as well. Tsar Aleksei's suddenly died in early February, which led to the succession of a minor (Fyodor III). A regency was duly installed, which further added to Russian inertia toward accepting any sweeping Dutch political or economic proposals. But Van Klenck could witness firsthand that no major changes would ensue Aleksei's demise.[19]

On his return in the fall of 1676, Van Klenck resumed his duties as a leading politician in Amsterdam, even if he would never be elected mayor. He played a role in organizing the Surinam Society in the mid-1680s, which restructured this slave-plantation colony. But he had by then left most of his Russian business to others, among whom Adolf Houtman seems to have been preeminent.

The Republic extricated itself out of the French war in the 1678 Treaty of Nijmegen. It awaited with bated breath further aggressive moves by Louis XIV, idly standing by between when the French king's troops occupied William III's ancestral principality of Orange (1682) and witnessing the subsequent War of the Reunions between France and the Habsburgs of both Madrid and Vienna (1683 and 1684). In 1685, a double blow was landed on the Dutch by the accession of the openly Catholic James II to the British thrones and Louis's Edict of Fontainebleau. But the Dutch weathered the storm: Calvinist refugees from France decamped in their thousands to the Republic and elsewhere (with Nicolaas Witsen playing a leading role in the effort to help them) during the 1680s, which seems to have steeled Dutch resolve against the French king and may have contributed to an economic upsurge. And the Dutch stadtholder William III was proclaimed king of England in early 1689 in London.

This latter development was to be of consequence for Russian-Dutch affairs, for in 1698 Tsar Peter I crossed the North Sea from Holland to England on the invitation of King William III, whom he much admired. There Peter found confirmation that it was England that had taken over from the Republic as the leading maritime country, having developed shipbuilding techniques that had surpassed those of the Dutch.[20] Meanwhile, William's invasion of England combined with Louis's invasion of the Rhineland to lead to another war between the Republic (this time allied with Britain and several other countries) and France, known as the Nine Years' War or the War of the League of Augsburg. In the very last days of that war, Peter's Grand Embassy departed for Western Europe. The Treaty of Ryswyck (1697) and the Treaty of Karlowitz that ended the Austrian-Ottoman War (1699) put paid to Peter's dreams of an all-out Christian offensive against the Turks. In this respect, the tsar's timing turned out to be all wrong. But that Russian mission bore fruit in other significant ways.

NOTES

1. When Ukraintsev visited in 1673, the Estates-General tried to find Van Klenck because of his command of Russian to improve communications with the Russian envoy, but he was inspecting the Frisian sea defenses (see Scheltema, *Rusland en de Nederlanden*, 306). Already in the 1650s, he had been asked to translate documents from Russian into Dutch (see Boterbloem, "Koenraad," 200n46).

2. *Relaes van't gepasseerde*. De Hooghe made other engravings about the embassy that were published in Coyett's anonymously published account (see [Coyett], *Historisch Verhael of Beschryving*).

3. See also O. Schutte, ed., *Repertorium der Nederlandse vertegenwoordigers, residerende in het buitenland*, 1584–1810, Den Haag: M. Nijhoff, 1976, 285–6; [Coyett], *Historisch Verhael of Beschryving*.

4. A palfreyman is someone who takes care of the horses, and usually stands on the back of a horse-drawn coach when travelling with his master.

5. *Stadsarchief Amsterdam*, Notarieel Archief 4304 (Notary Nicolaes Hemminck), 227–227 verso, 247.

6. On this issue, see Boterbloem, *Fiction*, 27, 74–5, 158.

7. A number did not, as we noticed previously: In late 1680, Van Keller requested Tsar Fyodor III for help in ransoming some of the crew, who had been missing since the Tatars had captured them in the Caucasus in 1670 (see *RGADA* 1680 book 1, December 12, 1680 [Van Keller to Tsar]). And we saw how Van Keller was even trying to obtain the release of them at the end of that decade.

8. For more on this see, for example, M. Klebusek, "The Business of News," *Scandinavian Journal of History* 3–4, 2003, 205–13.

9. See Boterbloem, *Moderniser*.

10. He willingly told Van Keller in late 1676 how often he handled—that is read—letters by the Danish and Brandenburg residents as postmaster (*Nationaal Archief*, Archief der Staten-Generaal, Lias Moskoviën, Secrete Brieven [Letter by Van Keller, December 2, 1676]). See also his correspondence with Florence: Ingeborg van Vugt, "Giovacchino Guasconi as Book Agent between the Dutch Republic and the Grand Duchy of Tuscany," unpubl. MA Thesis, Leiden University, 2014, 15–16, and 15n44, 16n48; he is somewhat confusingly identified here as "Andreas Winius," possibly in agreement with the Italian transcription of his name. He certainly was not the Dutch diplomatic resident in Moscow, of course, contrary to Van Vugt's suggestion.

11. The main negotiators appointed by the tsar were *kniaz* Mikhail Iur'evich Dolgorukii, the boyar Artemon Sergeevich Matveev, the *dumnyi d'iak* G.K. Bogdanov, and the *d'iak*s Vasilii Bobynin and Emel'ian Ukraintsev (see Loviagin, ed., *Posol'stvo*, 89bis). Negotiations were also attended by the translators Van Asperen, Vinius, and Adam Bessels (Van Klenck's secretary), as well as a number of lower-level secretaries and scribes on both sides. Matveev and Dol'gorukii (together with his famous father Iurii) were murdered in the 1682 revolt.

12. Loviagin, ed., *Posol'stvo*, 124.

13. See Wladimiroff, *De kaart*, 131–2; Peters, *De wijze koopman*, 106–8.

14. See Wladimiroff, *De kaart*.

15. Boterbloem, *Moderniser*, 101–2, 103, 123, 139–43, 191–6.

16. *RGADA* 50, 9/1675, 11 [21 New Style] January 1667.

17. On Guasconi, see M. Di Salvo, *Italia, Russia e mondo slavo: studi filologici e letterari*, Florence: Firenze UP, 2011; and Van Vugt, "Giovacchino Guasconi," 15–17.

18. See Boterbloem, "Russia and Europe." Indeed, the Russians slowly dispatched an army to the Baltic border with Sweden in 1676, without ever intending to give battle; this allowed them at the time of the Grand Embassy in 1697 to claim before their Dutch interlocutors that they had checked Sweden from unleashing its forces against the Dutch Republic in coalition with the French (see Pavlenko, *Lefort*, 172).

19. The major consequence that resulted from the tsar's passing away was the fall of his last favorite, Artamon Matveev, in the summer of 1676; Matveev was strongly pro-Western, but his banishment seems to have changed little in terms of the direction of Russian foreign or domestic policy.

20. For some of the British-Russian relationship after 1697, see M.P. Romaniello, *Enterprising Empires: Russia and Britain in Eighteenth-Century Eurasia*, Cambridge: Cambridge UP, 2019.

Chapter 20

The Interregnum, 1676–1689

After Aleksei's death in early 1676, Russia saw a fairly quick succession of regimes: A regency held the reins for five years until Fyodor III briefly took the helm in 1681; another regency lasting mere weeks followed in 1682 on behalf of Peter I alone, which was terminated in a bloody coup; from the summer of 1682 until 1689, ruling in the name of Ivan V and his half-brother Peter I, the Miloslavskii family dominated, of which eventually Ivan's sister Sofiia, supported by her favorite Vasily Golitsyn, became the leader; and, finally, the ousting of Sofiia and Golitsyn by Peter and his backers in the late summer of 1689. Despite the recurrent unrest in Moscow, Russia maintained itself as an empire: Siberia had been gradually reduced to Russian rule between 1583 and the 1680s, and the country's landmass had thereby become larger than that of any other polity in the world.

A war with the Turks did rage in the late 1670s, which cost Cornelis van Bockhoven his life at the siege of Chyhyryn in Ukraine in 1678, but it unfolded in the empire's borderlands and ended in 1681.[1] Subsequently, Russia was likely fortuitous that its neighbors' attention was distracted by the Ottoman offensive that began with the siege of Vienna in 1683. It led to a prolonged war that saw Austria (backed by some of the German principalities), Poland, and others, all formally united as a Holy League under the pope's auspices, pitted against the Ottoman Empire, allied as ever with the Crimean Tatars. The latter, as was their wont, raided Muscovite territory, but never invaded Russia with a view of occupying significant territory. Sweden, another long-time competitor of Muscovy, remained tranquil after its clear military defeats in the Scanian War (1675–1679) against Denmark and Brandenburg-Prussia, about which business Van Klenck had visited Moscow in 1676.

That Sofiia Alekseevna, a daughter of Tsar Aleksei from his first marriage, gained prominence after 1682, was a startling reversal from the custom to keep women away from public life, even if, rather paradoxically, she still could not show herself publicly.[2] Her downfall would be the two futile campaigns against the Crimean Tatars of 1687 and 1689. On paper, these seemed a good idea, in that they aimed to destroy once and for all this thorn in the Russian side, but they proved overambitious in practice, the Russian capacity to take on the Tatars and their Turkish backers being too weak yet. In 1686, Sofiia did oversee the signing of a permanent peace with the *Rzeczpospolita*, which recognized the Russian territorial acquisition of the 1667 Truce of Andrusovo as permanent, and thus definitively yielded Muscovy Kyiv and eastern Ukraine.

But with it all the empire's heartland remained largely unperturbed by the unrest on its outskirts, and Russian rule in Siberia was firmed up, even if the Chinese Qing dynasty halted any further Russian descent along the Pacific shore southward through the 1689 Treaty of Nerchinsk. The exact border between Europe(an Russia) and Asia(n Siberia), meanwhile, was only established with some precision as running north–south from the Arctic Ocean along the Ural mountains and Iaik (Ural) river draining into the Caspian Sea, long after Russian explorers had laid claim to northern Asia. This was done at the suggestion of a Swedish prisoner of war, Philip Johann von Strahlenberg (1676–1747), who had fallen in Russian captivity during the Great Northern War (1700–1721).[3] Previously, in 1687, Nicolaas Witsen had for the first time produced an at least in part accurate rendition of Siberia following the rules of Western cartography.[4] Young Tsar Peter's curiosity about the world was just awakening in earnest when Witsen's map was presented to him.

And trade with the Dutch, who from 1677 onward had a permanent envoy at the tsarist court in Johan Willem van Keller, flourished, despite the frequent changing of the guard in the Kremlin. In his dissertation, Kotilaine calculates that still "in 1679 and 1680, the Dutch accounted for 46.2 and 43.6 percent, respectively, of the duties collected from foreign merchants."[5] While relatively few Westerners were allowed to trade in the Russian interior, two-thirds of those who could were Dutch merchants; this pronounced presence was not affected by any political unrest.[6]

Below, six of the greatest representatives are presented whose activities illustrate the latter stages of this age of great Dutch influence in Russia: the merchants Houtman and Timmerman, the diplomat Van Keller, the bureaucrat and entrepreneur Vinius (again), the sailor and shipwright Brandt, and the scientist and regent Witsen (again). Several of the Dutch doctors and surgeons that remained prominent in this age have been earlier sufficiently discussed: They may serve as additional good examples of the significant role of the Dutch in this transitional age for a rising Russia and a declining Dutch Republic.

Adolf Houtman (c. 1627–1710), whom we met earlier when he greeted Koenraad van Klenck on his entrance into Moscow, was a key player among the Dutch mercantile contingent in this period.⁷ Houtman was likely born on a small manor near Delden in Overijssel province. Although the exact year is unclear, he was fairly young when in the early years of Aleksei's reign he moved to Vologda, an important city on the route from Arkhangel'sk to Moscow. An utterly driven man, he spent long years in Muscovy. Initially, he worked at least in part on the side as one of Van Klenck's factors. Still in 1678 performing in this role, for example, he took care of a delivery of grain to the Republic for Van Klenck.⁸ Houtman's own firm, like so many others, was in essence run like a family business. Several of Houtman's brothers and children assisted him in his activities.

The last generation of major Dutch Russia traders, who included Houtman, the brothers Thesingh, Jan Lups, Christoffel Brants, and Abraham Kintsius, all met Tsar Peter at Arkhangel'sk during the Russian monarch's second trip there in the summer of 1694.⁹ In 1697 and 1698, it was Houtman who, with the Thesinghs, helped the tsar and his entourage to purchase strategic goods in the Republic, not least weaponry.¹⁰ Only when he was already in his 70s, Houtman moved definitively back to the Republic, leaving behind in Moscow one son, likely Isaak (1667–c. 1703). Isaak Houtman had married Suzanna van Sweeden (c. 1675–1719)—a daughter of Jan van Sweeden—in the *sloboda* in 1695.¹¹ Houtman spent his dotage in Amsterdam, accompanied by several of his children, on the magnificent (and utterly pricey) manor he had acquired that was located just outside of Amsterdam, at its Maliebaan, which he had called *Vrijheid, Blijheid* (*Freedom, Merriment*). He also owned a townhouse in the city on the prestigious Keizersgracht. He was buried, like his patron Koenraad van Klenck, in the city's Westerkerk, burial ground of Amsterdam's wealthiest citizens.

A very well educated Utrecht nobleman who had mastered a number of languages, Baron Johan Willem van Keller first spent some time in Stockholm, before he joined Heins as aide on his tortured diplomatic mission to Moscow in 1670.¹² He then accompanied Koenraad van Klenck's embassy as its "marshal," which meant that he officially served as the ambassadorial company's manager (or *major domus*). On what may have been Van Klenck's initiative, Van Keller then remained behind in Moscow. In response to an ensuing formal request of the Estates-General, the Russian government accredited him as (the first) permanent Dutch resident to the tsar's court in 1677. In this position, which he occupied until his death in 1698, he soon became a senior figure among the Western European expatriate community of the Russian capital. His lengthy letters have proved a fine source for the history of Muscovy in the period of Van Keller's residence.¹³

Van Keller shows in his letters to the Estates-General an acute awareness about the political constellation of the Muscovy of his day, even if, as we saw above in his dismissive description of the Russian *mardi-gras* (*maslennitsa*) celebrations, some Russian customs repelled him. Both his advanced age and his aristocratic sensibility may have informed this response to Russian debauchery, which appears to have included that of Peter the Great's "All Drunken Assembly" that began to gather in the 1690s.[14] Confirmation for his puritanical convictions might be discerned in Van Keller's zealous reporting to The Hague of any Catholic, and especially Jesuit, machinations in Russia (which were hardly worrisome). Obviously, he was born (somewhere in the 1630s, one surmises) in an age that Europeans lustily slaughtered each other in the name of religion, so his fear of the "papists" may have been informed by the experience of his youth. In addition, the Edict of Fontainebleau and James II's succession to the British throne in 1685 were a shock to much of Protestant Europe, and will have rekindled Van Keller's old anxieties.

Van Keller subtly played the diplomatic game, meanwhile, closely watching the various moves by both permanent and visiting envoys. To quote Jan Hennings, he used "[f]avouritism, personal networks, mixed cross-border loyalties, patronage relationships, and a high degree of professionalism in representing both personal status and sovereign dignity in various roles."[15] Van Keller deserves his place among the outstanding permanent residents who skillfully served the Republic in its Golden Age, such as Cornelis Haga (1578–1654) in Istanbul, or Christiaan Rumpf (1633–1706) in Stockholm.

Despite his name, which means carpenter, Frans Timmerman was a merchant who in his early years had started out as a factor of Dutch trading firms. He had been arrested in Arkhangel'sk and jailed in nearby Kholmogory for malfeasance in 1663, after which he had languished for eight months in a Moscow prison cell, but was absolved of his crimes through Jacob Boreel's pleading on his behalf during the latter's visit to Russia.[16] In the midst of a severe falling out regarding matters of protocol between Boreel and the Russians (in particular, the title with which the tsar was to address the Estates-General), Timmerman was rearrested, but quickly released when Boreel protested.[17] Boreel's persistent support for him shows that Timmerman was already by then a person of some prominence within the Dutch community.

Oddly, his stint in Muscovy's cells did not turn Timmerman off of Russia. Different from people such as Jurriaan or Koenraad van Klenck or, later, Christoffel Brants, who preferred to have their headquarters in Amsterdam, Timmerman seems to have sunk down roots in Russia, mainly residing in Moscow's *sloboda*, while frequenting Arkhangel'sk. Timmerman must have been a man of versatile skill: Fluent in Russian and steeped in the art of trade, he was knowledgeable about mathematics, ballistics, and other fields of science, areas in which he was to teach the youngest of the two tsars during the 1680s. In 1688, he came to Tsar Peter's attention because he could explain how an astrolabe worked.[18] Peter was then a teenager unencumbered by the affairs of state, from which he had been excluded since 1682 by the relatives of his half-sister Sofia and his half-brother Ivan V.[19] Without much of a care in the world, Peter was free to roam; equipped with a voracious curiosity, he began to frequent the *sloboda*. Not only someone like Timmerman resided there, but people like Karsten Brandt as well, in addition to numerous Western military experts such as Patrick Gordon and François Lefort. With all of them as his mentors, the young tsar began to investigate the increasingly complex ways of modern warfare, the use of cannon, siege warfare, the deployment and training of infantry and cavalry, and the sailing of ships. Timmerman remained close to Peter until the Dutchman's death in the early 1700s, and served a key supervisor of the shipbuilding effort undertaken in preparation for Peter's Azov campaigns of the mid-1690s.[20]

The pivotal role within—and outside of—the tsarist bureaucracy played for almost half a century by Andrei Andreevich Vinius has already been highlighted; recent literature on him has become quite substantial.[21] Entrepreneur, diplomat, prospector, merchant, translator, postmaster, healthcare chief, bibliophile, spy, correspondent, teacher, and scientist, Vinius wore many hats throughout his life. He became another confidant of Peter the Great, and even survived the tsar's wrath after a strange self-imposed exile in the Republic in the 1700s. But long before he met Peter, Vinius had provided invaluable services to Aleksei, Fyodor, and Sofiia. His very activity is evidence how the difference between the policies of Peter and his predecessors was perhaps less pronounced than conventional wisdom in Russia and elsewhere ever since Peter's Grand Embassy has suggested.[22] Despite his ancestry, Vinius was more Russian than Dutchman because of his Orthodox religion, while Russian seems to have been his first language. There is no doubt, however, that from the moment of the arrival of the Boreel embassy in 1665 he liaised intensively with all manner of Dutchmen and women, among which his ties with Nicolaas Witsen were particularly crucial.[23] He arranged for the printing of an etched portrait of Sofiia in Amsterdam to salvage her power in a last-ditch effort in 1689, as well as for the building of a modern sailship for Peter in the Dutch capital some years later, not long before the tsar visited the Republic in person.[24] Although the effort to spread Sofiia's countenance to bump her popularity was ill-timed (and Vinius barely managed to extricate himself largely unharmed from his overly close association with Sofiia's party), it may have further sparked Peter's interest in printing and Western art. The tsar hired the painter and etcher Adriaan Schoonebeeck (1661–1705), a pupil of De Hooghe, to train Russian apprentices; the tsar was to have Russian-language works printed in Amsterdam through Jan Thesingh (1659–1701) before the Russian presses could be updated and increased to a sufficient capacity to spread printed work across Peter's empire to the tsar's satisfaction.[25]

With Brandt and Timmerman (and to a lesser degree Peter's physician Dr. Arnoud Van der Hulst and Van Keller), it was Vinius who was most influential in making Peter a Dutchophile. And it seems (before Vinius was demoted for corruption in 1703) that Vinius was in many ways the sort of model-subject Peter desired, a feverishly busy and utterly versatile man who acquitted himself with aplomb of every task which he was given. Vinius showed how a Russian could don all the quintessentially industrious characteristics Peter admired in Dutch men. The spread of this go-getter attitude among his subjects could transform his country into an invulnerable and prosperous Great Power.

Nicolaas Witsen (1641–1717) was possibly the most influential booster of Russo-Dutch ties in the Republic.[26] He wrote a revealing ego-document about his own travels to Russia as a young man, drafted and published the first modern map of Siberia, wrote the first Western description of Northern Asia (or Inner Eurasia), oversaw the building of Russia's first naval ship in Amsterdam, and was host to Peter the Great when he visited the Republic in 1697 and 1698. Witsen wrote a study about shipbuilding through the ages as well, and was six times mayor of Amsterdam, as well as *VOC* director as one of the *Gentlemen XVII*.[27]

Witsen, too, prepared the travel account of Everhard IJsbrant Ides for publication.[28] In 1691, Ides was dispatched by Peter the Great on an embassy to China, from which he returned to Moscow in 1695. Ides's account aided Witsen in his lifelong investigation of Siberia. It was written in a curious hybrid language of northern German and Dutch—possibly reflective of the *lingua franca* of the Baltic-North Sea region mentioned earlier—which Witsen translated into a Dutch that was more standard for the age. Peter returned to Holland and may have been on time to say goodbye to Witsen, who lay on his deathbed in 1717.[29]

In Witsen and Vinius (who were distantly related) we see two pivotal figures who had been involved as young men in the Boreel embassy; with them, one can connect almost every aspect of the genesis, flourishing, and decline of the Russo-Dutch relationship in the Early Modern era. Witsen's grandfather and other relatives made their fortune in part from the trade with Russia in the late sixteenth and early seventeenth century, which yielded them not just vast wealth but also political power as mayors of Amsterdam, an annual appointment repeatedly occupied by Witsen's father Cornelis Janszoon Witsen as well. The Witsen family's ties to Russia thus stretched out over 125 years, almost the entire period with which this book is concerned.

Likewise, the pivotal role of father Andries Winius and son Andrei Vinius lasted a long time, for well-nigh a century. Of Frisian ancestry, Andries Denijszoon Winius clearly was an upstart (as the Witsens had once, somewhere in the 1570s, been) in 1620s Amsterdam, for whom the possibilities in Russia seemed better than in an Amsterdam where, already then, the ranks of the political elite were closing to outsiders.[30] The regents concomitantly began to monopolize the economic spoils. Thus, Winius eventually made Russia his home, antagonizing its Dutch expatriate community by what was seen as his self-serving or even cynical opportunism, which saw him in the middle of the 1650s make the final Russifying step by converting to Orthodoxy. This choice allowed his son to reach the pinnacle for those of common birth within the Muscovite bureaucracy (before Peter's Table of Ranks that was introduced in 1718), becoming a *dumnyi d'iak*, that is, a chancellor of the *duma*, the tsar's council.

Karsten Brandt, finally, is a most intriguing character, because he was a latter-day version of those sixteenth-century ancestors of Witsen or Deni(j)s Tjerkszoon, Andries Winius's Frisian father.[31] In other words, he was part of a new (perhaps third consecutive) generation of Dutch men equipped with a similar sort of enterprising spirit as those who had brought the Republic its vast prosperity in the previous three-quarter century. This adventurous mindset had first led him to Russia as part of the *Oryol* crowd during the late 1660s. Unfazed by the Razin rebellion, he returned from the Caspian littoral to work as a carpenter in Moscow. That Timmerman identified Brandt as the person to refurbish the small *botik* that Peter had found in a warehouse in dilapidated state shows that he enjoyed a fine reputation as a craftsman (and was associated with shipbuilding, as stories about the demise of the *Oryol* and its crew must have been diffused throughout the *sloboda*). Brandt himself did not leave any testimony about his life, as far as we can tell. Nevertheless, by his actions he does show how among those of lower birth who remain largely anonymous in pre-1700 Dutch history, Russia must have been a land of opportunity for a number of years. That he was far from unique in believing in this chance for economic betterment is evident from the hundreds of Dutch people who made their way to Russia to seek their luck in the 1690s and 1700s. Locher suggests that in Amsterdam alone more than 1,000 Dutch experts embarked to serve Tsar Peter in Russia in the late seventeenth and early eighteenth century.[32]

The pluck of these men should not blind us to the other side of the coin: Jozien Driessen makes a good point in suggesting that many a Dutchman (perhaps after conversation with his wife, as was the case with Boudewijn Hamey) opted *not* to enlist in Russian service, even in the days of Peter.[33] Despite often quite attractive terms, Russia remained a faraway destination from which one could not return overnight. Only a minority of those who left the Republic for the East Indies ever came home, and before Peter's takeover in 1689 it had often been exceedingly difficult to leave Russia, so that many Dutch people never returned from Muscovy either. Such a step was for a good number of people too radical to contemplate.

NOTES

1. The war formally lasted from 1676 to 1681, ending with the Treaty of Bakhchisarai.
2. See Hughes, *Sophia*.
3. He conveyed his findings after his release in a printed German-language treatise of 1730, see Philip Johann von Strahlenberg, *Das nord und ostliche Theil von . . . das ganze Rußische Reich mit Siberien . . .*, Stockholm: By the author, 1730.
4. The Russians did have their own kind of maps which remained in use until 1700 or so (see Kivelson, *Cartographies of Tsardom*). See Naarden, "Nicolaas Witsen."
5. Kotilaine, "Where the Twain," 134.
6. Ibid., 134, 135 Table 2.4, and 136.
7. His family tree is available at: http://www.pietheres.nl/Parenteel%20Houtman.htm, accessed October 6, 2019. Arel for some reason spells his name as "Hautman" (see Arel, *English Trade*, 261). I doubt Houtman led a company "modeled on the Muscovy Company" (ibid.) in the 1680s; as successor in the De Vogelaer-Van Klenck firm to Koenraad van Klenck, he did not need any such models, while his business, too, seems to have been much more of the sort of clannish Dutch variety, with a significant number of members of his extended family involved.
8. See *RGADA* 1678, book 50, 1, February [OS] 18, 1678.
9. Donga, *Christoffel*, 28.
10. Ibid., 30.
11. *Diary of Gordon*, vol. 5, 343.
12. *Nationaal Archief*, Archief der Staten-Generaal, Lias Moskoviën, November 13, 1671 [Memorie van Heinsius].
13. See Eekman, "Muscovy's International Relations"; and, for an especially good example Bushkovitch, *Peter*. See *Nationaal Archief*, Archief der Staten-Generaal, Lias Moskoviën, Secrete Brieven van Johan Willem van Keller, nos 7365 and 7366.
14. Zitser, *Transfigured Kingdom*.
15. Hennings, *Russia and Courtly Europe*, 28–9.
16. Boreel *Verbael*, 413–17.
17. Ibid., 526–7.
18. Bogoslovskii, *Petr Velikii*, vol. 1, 54–6.
19. Lahana, "Novaia Nemetskaia Sloboda," 164.
20. Ibid., 165–6, 172–3.
21. Iurkin, *Andrei Andreevich*; idem, *O pervoprestol'nogo*; Kozlovskii, *Andrei Vinius'*; Boterbloem, *Moderniser*.
22. For some further recently published new evidence of Vinius's linguistic skills, see his translations and summaries of Haarlem, Hague, and Amsterdam newspapers in 1671, in V.B. Krys'ko and I. Maier, *Vesti-Kuranty 1671–1672gg.*, Moskva: Azbukovnik, 2017, 207, 213, 226 (and signs of his diplomatic trip, see ibid., 336); for his rise to renewed prominence as the key summarizer of foreign news (and Russian postmaster) for the young Peter in the early 1690s, see S.M. Shamin, "Formirovanie vneshnepoliticheskikh predstavlenii Petra I i vypiski iz kurantov 1690–1693 godov,"

Rossiiskaia istoriia 4, 2012: 111–20. He had been in trouble previously for his association with Sofia Alekseevna's faction in 1689 (he was interrogated in connection with the Shaklovityi case); see also E.A. Saveleva, "Andrei Andreevich Vinius, ego biblioteka i albom," in *Rossiia-Gollandiia: Knizhnye sviazy xv-xx vv.*, ed. N.P. Kopanev, St. Petersburg: Evropeiskii Dom, 2000, 103–23; Boterbloem, *Moderniser*.

23. See in particular I. Wladimiroff, *De kaart van een verzwegen vriendschap: Nicolaes Witsen en Andrej Winius en de Nederlandse cartografie van Rusland*, Groningen: Instituut voor Noord- en Oost-Europese Studies, 2008; as well, Naarden, "Nicolaas Witsen," 14.

24. Bogoslovskii, *Petr Velikii*, vol. 1, 174–7.

25. Shamin, *Kuranty*; J.W. Veluwenkamp, "'N huis op Archangel'," 132–3.

26. See Witsen, *Noord en Oost Tartarye*; see Naarden, "Nicolaas Witsen en Tartarye"; Peters, *wijze koopman*; and Wladimiroff, *De kaart*.

27. N. Witsen, *Aeloude en hedendaegsche scheeps-bouw en bestier: waer in wijtloopigh wert verhandelt, de wijze van scheeps-timmeren, ...* Amsterdam: Casparus Commelijn, 1671; and idem, *Architectura navalis et Regimen Nauticum. Ofte Aaloude en Hedendaagsche Scheeps-Bouw en Bestier . . . .* Amsterdam: Pieter and Joan Blaeu, 1690.

28. See Boterbloem, *Fiction*, 159; Ides, *Drie-Jaarige Reize*.

29. Peters has found no evidence that Peter visited Witsen in his last days; the tsar was on a formal visit, which may have limited his ability to visit people outside of the protocol (M. Peters, "'Mercator Sapiens' (De wijze koopman). Het wereldwijde onderzoek van Nicolaes Witsen (1641–1717), burgemeester en VOC-bewindhebber van Amsterdam," unpubl. Ph.D. diss. RU Groningen, 2008, 58).

30. Again, an interesting parallel may be drawn with the Muscovy Company, in which at exactly the same moment "new merchants" came to the fore, who, more than the established "merchant aristocracy" that was royalist, were to be Pro-Parliament in the 1640s (Arel, *English Trade*, 10). Arel thus finesses Brenner's analysis of the London merchant community of this era (see Robert Brenner, *Merchants and Revolution: Commercial Change, Political Conflict and London's Overseas Traders, 1550–1653*, Princeton, NJ: Princeton UP, 1993).

31. For more on him, see Boterbloem, *Fiction*, 67, 79, 84, 99, 102–3, 123–4, 128–9, 169–78.

32. Th.J.G. Locher, *Peter de Grote*, Amsterdam: Ploegsma, 1947, 213.

33. Driessen, *Tsaar Peter*, 19.

Chapter 21

Peter the Great

In the second half of 1687, the regency ruling on behalf of Tsars Ivan V and Peter I bypassed the Dutch Estates-General, always reluctant to part with its funds, in search of a loan from Dutch lenders to help finance a second military campaign toward the Crimea.[1] Long-serving bureaucrats like the top foreign-office clerk (*dumnyi d'iak*) Ukraintsev and his brother-in-law, the specialist *par excellence* in Dutch affairs Andrei Vinius, likely prevailed in convincing the regent Sofiia and her favorite V.V. Golitsyn that any direct Russian requests to the Dutch government for aid might have little chance in succeeding. After the 1679 peace with Sweden, the Dutch had returned to their traditional pro-Swedish inclinations. They may have been unwilling as well to offend the Sublime Porte with a Russian arms' deal. Throughout the seventeenth century, the Dutch authorities maintained reasonably cordial relations with the Ottoman Turks, which were all the more important given the frequent attempts necessary to ransom Dutch sailors captured by Barbary corsairs. The North-African potentates were nominally subordinate to the Ottoman sultan.

Clearly aware that Amsterdam was the center of Dutch finances, the Russian agents therefore turned directly to the city of Amsterdam requesting a loan for no less than 10 million guilders (two million rubles), an astronomical sum. The sum was not furnished, however, after the city's council discussed the matter specifically with Jacob Boreel, Koenraad van Klenck, and Daniel Bernard, all Amsterdam regents of great wealth who were intimately familiar with Muscovy for decades. At the time, the city council was husbanding a great amount of funds in expectation of a renewal of the military conflict with Louis XIV. It seemed imprudent to furnish the pile of money requested by the Russians.

This rejection may have doomed the 1689 Muscovite campaign, which, like its predecessor in 1687, never witnessed any serious military engagement of the Muscovite army with the old Russian bugbears, the Crimean Tatars; the expedition ran out of time and, indeed, means before it even reached the Crimea.[2] This wasteful effort, the second of its kind, proved fatal to the regency of Sofiia Alekseevna; her desperate attempt to rid herself of her half-brother failed and made Peter I the uncontested ruler of Russia in the late summer of 1689.[3]

Meanwhile, soon after Amsterdam decided not to aid the Russians in 1687, the city had deeply immersed itself in the preparations for the military expedition to England that landed the Dutch-led army at Torbay in the late autumn of 1688. Meeting no resistance of significance, it occupied London, from which King James II fled. His nephew and son-in-law, stadtholder William III of Orange-Nassau, was thereby poised to succeed to the throne (in condominium with his wife Mary). This news, as Johan Willem van Keller wrote the Estates-General in late 1688, was welcomed in Moscow, where Sofiia and Vasily Golitsyn were then still at the helm.[4] By May 1689, with permission of the Estates-General, Van Keller threw a party to celebrate William's formal coronation.[5]

The landing at Torbay (and undoubtedly spurred on by his newfound Dutch acquaintances such as Brandt or Timmerman, as well as Vinius) made Peter I an even greater admirer of William III. Peter was to meet his hero several times on his Grand Embassy in the Republic and England during 1697 and 1698.[6] His admiration in part reflected the general reputation of bravery William had acquired in Protestant Europe, which in anti-Polish and anti-Catholic Muscovy had some resonance. In addition, William's archenemy was the French King Louis XIV, who was seen in Russia as a duplicitous character—as well as an odious Catholic—colluding with the Ottoman Turks, another long-standing enemy of Russia. But, faced with the conclusion of the treaties of Ryswyck and Karlowitz, Peter instead shifted his focus to the fight with another of the trio of old Russian foes, Sweden. Even though William and Peter had personally gotten along well when they met, this shift precluded any sustained close official relationship between the Republic and Peter's Russia, as the Dutch remained partial to Sweden, their frequent ally in the seventeenth century. William died in 1702. Soon a parting of the ways between Russia and the Republic became observable that resonated in the cooling of the diplomatic ties between the two countries.

After Peter fended off the feeble attempt by his half-sister to shore up her power and he ousted her in a successful countermove (which saw most of the higher nobles and significant parts of the army switch sides) in the late summer of 1689, it was not immediately clear which political course would be followed by the new regime. Peter had been supported by the conservative clergy (including the patriarch) in his resistance against his half-sister's attempts at usurping more (of his) power. Speculation about the new regime's political directions did not cease when Peter initially showed little inclination to truly occupy himself with governmental affairs, leaving the state's business to various trusted boyars, among whom were some of his mother's relatives. Peter, evidently, had been surprised by the turn of events in the summer of 1689; having just begun to learn how to sail and staging mock battles with his so-called play regiments (*poteshnye polki*), he was still in the middle of his preparation, or education, for the role of tsar as he had begun to envision it. In the next few years Peter was to take the reins in earnest reluctantly and slowly, a process that may be said to have been only completed after his mother passed away in 1694.

Instead of ruling his country, to quote Jozien Driessen, "Peter . . . was personally [finding] out about the latest developments in science and technology, shipbuilding and artillery use, propaganda campaigns and information gathering, fortification and waterworks, medicine and religion" in the early 1690s.[7] In addition, "[h]e learned how to make watches, coffins, and ships, drawing, etching, pulling teeth, dissecting bodies, and manufacturing paper and silk."[8]

Once he did take full command, Peter proved both a restless and cruel ruler, a do-er rather than a thinker, even if he pursued certain *idée-fixes* in a dogged or obsessed manner, such as the creation of a Russian navy.[9] His *leitmotiv* seems to have been to make Russia into a Great Power, part of Europe's Concert.[10] He appears to have concluded early on (somewhere in the late 1680s) that this could only be accomplished by making Muscovy at least in part a maritime Power, as increased overseas trade (backed up by a navy) might sustain a mighty military machine that could definitively overcome Swedes, Turks and Tatars, and Poles. Intensive contact with Western Europe, too, would assure that Russia would be on top of the latest developments in science and technology and thus remain at the forefront of innovation. In addition to a navy that held its own while providing cover for a merchant marine, Peter's program encompassed the creation of a domestic manufacturing branch that would rival its Western counterparts, backed up by a scientific infrastructure of which the Academy of Sciences would serve as the pinnacle. In all these areas, foreigners would at first lead the way, who would be eventually replaced by Russians whom they had taught their expertise.

Clearly, Peter was not as original as his legend (created both at home and abroad, and already being consciously forged in his lifetime) was to make him out to be. His program had—albeit in part, haltingly, and less coherently—been followed by his predecessors as tsar. Peter saw with rather greater clarity than they did how the program could be tied together as a more fulsome plan for Russia's modernization (and a guarantee for its long-term survival as an independent, powerful state). What was different in Peter's manner of rule as well was his relentless pursuit of his goals, once he had decided that technological modernization was the path toward Russia's future.

While he chased his goal of making Russia into a modern and formidable military Power, meanwhile, he shifted somewhat with regards to the model he tried to emulate. Or, perhaps, he was eclectic, copying some crucial elements now from one country, then from another, seeking the best aspects of each of them. One could argue that he was captivated by the Dutch Republic and the accomplishments of its denizens for about a decade (1688–1698), after which he abandoned this infatuation and sought his inspiration in a variety of countries, such as England, parts of Germany, Sweden, and eventually France.[11] He never lost his love for the Dutch (and Dutch arms' merchants, printing presses, or curiosity cabinets continued to comprise crucial elements of his modernization project), but he did increasingly recognize how the Republic was far from the only country from which Russia could learn valuable lessons.

The height of Peter's enthusiasm for the Dutch occurred in the mid-1690s, perhaps from the death of his mother (who had been less fond than her son of the ways of the non-Orthodox) in 1694 to his first visit to England in early 1698 (or even the final months of 1697, when the reality of the Dutch Republic that he visited proved less compelling to him that he had anticipated[12]). It was during this brief three- or four-year period that he began to write his name in Dutch, and that he conceived of his plan to visit the Republic.[13] It was then that the tsar enthusiastically addressed correspondents with Dutch titles, while those of his intimates who wrote letters to him as *"Min her Bombardir,"* or "Mr. Gunner."[14] According to *kniaz* B.I. Kurakin (1676–1727),

> And because of his majesty's then fondness for everything foreign he began to study all sort of expertise and the Dutch [*golanskago*] tongue. And his master for that language was the d'iak of the *Posol'skii prikaz*, by birth a Hollander, Andrei Vinius, a wise man and of good character.[15]

Boris Ivanovich Kurakin was in his youth a *spal'nik* (a gentleman of the bedchamber, or page) and an early recruit to the play regiments of Peter, so his testimony should not easily be dismissed, but we know that Peter was not particularly academically gifted (his handwriting might indicate a form of dyslexia). In other words, his Dutch will have not been especially fluent. Still, as Cornelis de Bruin noted when meeting Peter in 1702, the tsar's knowledge of spoken Dutch was remarkable:

> The Prince said this all in Dutch, and desired that I would continue to speak this language with him, stating that he understood me very well. He gave solid

evidence of this, since he translated all what I said with such precision to the Russian lords who were in his company that the [Dutch resident Nicolaas van der Hulst] and other Dutch gentlemen present there marvelled at it.[16]

The very last decade of the seventeenth century, then, may have been the height of Dutch influence on Russia, but its precipitous decline followed swiftly. Within a mere few decades, outside of the Dutch continuing to convey their aptitude at seafaring to the Russians, few people anywhere remembered much about the Dutch significance as the harbingers of Russia's future. The tsar would visit the Republic again in 1716, but was then rather more keen on seeing France for the first time for himself than staying for long in Holland. Not unlike how in his eyes many of his own Russians had fallen behind the times during the tsar's younger years, so did the Dutch fall behind the times during Peter's later years.

NOTES

1. A.M. Loviagin, *Iz gollanskikh bibliotek i arkhivov*, Sanktpeterburg: N.p., 1902, 9–13.
2. Already by late April 1689 Van Keller predicted that if the campaign failed a "general rebellion" might break out in the country (*Nationaal Archief*, Archief der Staten-Generaal, Lias Moskoviën, Letter from van Keller, April 29, 1689).
3. *Nationaal Archief*, Archief der Staten-Generaal, Secrete Brieven, Letter from van Keller, October 11, 1689. For more, see Bushkovich, *Peter*; and Hughes, *Peter*.
4. *Nationaal Archief*, Archief der Staten-Generaal, Lias Moskoviën, Letter from van Keller, January 28, 1689.
5. *Nationaal Archief*, Archief der Staten-Generaal, Lias Moskoviën, Letter from van Keller, May 20, 1689.
6. See Leo Loewenson, "The First Interviews Between Peter I and William III in 1697: Some Neglected Material," *Slavonic and East European Review* 87, June 1958, 308–16; Idem, "Some Details Of Peter the Great's Stay in England in 1698: Neglected English Material," *Slavonic and East European Review* 95, June 1962, 431–43: 438; Vladimir Matveev, "Summit Diplomacy of the Seventeenth Century: William III and Peter I in Utrecht and London, 1697–98," *Diplomacy and Statecraft* 3, 2000, 29–48: 33–7.
7. Driessen, *Tsaar Peter*, 7.
8. Ibid., 8.
9. Locher, *Peter*, 193.
10. None of the European Powers with whom he parlayed in 1697 and 1698 to urge a vigorous continuation (and even expansion) of the war with Ottoman Turkey waged by a European coalition paid more than token attention to his proposals; this may have strengthened his conviction that Russia was not yet seen as a Power itself (see Locher, *Peter*, 86).

11. Venice was another early favorite, but less so than the United Provinces.

12. It is likely that his enthusiasm cooled off when the official discussions between the Russian Grand Embassy and the Estates-General at The Hague in September and October 1697 bore no fruit whatsoever from the Russian perspective, even if they were conducted in a friendly atmosphere (see Pavlenko, *Lefort*, 171–5).

13. Locher, *Peter*, 75–6. The suspicion is that Andrei Vinius, with whom Peter was particularly close in these years, may have tutored him in the language, but the evidence for this is meager.

14. As Posselt writes, the grenadiers (*Bombardiere*) of his play regiments were Peter's "closest" or "dearest" companions (Posselt, *Franz Lefort*, vol. 2, 70).

15. See B.I. Kurakin, "Gistoriia o Petre I i blizhnikh k nemu liudakh. 1682–1695 gg.," *Russkaia starina* 10, 1890, 238–60: 253.

16. De Bruyn, *Reizen*, ed. Hannema, 42 [my translation].

Chapter 22

Patrick Gordon and François Lefort

Despite his then great fondness for the Dutch, Peter the Great's favorite Westerners in the 1690s were a Scotsman, Patrick Gordon (1635–1699) and a "Swiss" man, François Lefort (1656–1699).[1] While it is an impossible task to precisely assess the strength of the national identity of people who have lived for decades away from their native country—where they had been surrounded by those who speak their mother tongue—both Gordon's diary and correspondence (in English, often to Scotland) and Lefort's correspondence (in French, mostly to Geneva) indubitably show a continued allegiance to the land of their youth and its culture.[2] Still, their loyalty was divided: Gordon and Lefort were both mercenaries by profession, which informed their faithful service to the tsar (as their military commander), if it did not make them into avid patriots of Russia. Indeed, they seem to have identified more with the community of expatriates that was the *sloboda* than with the country in which it was located. Additionally, both were strong devotees of their churches, Catholic for the Scot, Calvinist for the Genevan. In sum, for this couple, as much as this was the case for the Dutch people in Russia with whom they interacted, the sort of sentimental nationalism that became widespread in Europe during the nineteenth century would have been alien.

In this duo as well we can trace a rather strong Dutch influence, meanwhile. Or perhaps the word affinity is more appropriate: Both married into the Van Bockhoven clan. Philips Albrecht van Bockhoven languished in Polish captivity when his teenage daughter Katerina (1650–1671) was courted by Gordon; the Scotsman was so keen to marry her that he persuaded her guardian, Cornelis van Bockhoven, to grant permission for the wedding, since she was underage; meanwhile, the wedding was conducted by the then Dutch *Calvinist* minister Joannes Krawinckel (c. 1620–1677) in Moscow.[3] This is not a little odd, because Gordon otherwise was a zealous Catholic partisan (and so was his betrothed!), who proved instrumental in building the first Catholic church near Moscow later, in the 1680s. Clearly, Gordon was smitten with Katerina and was willing to park for her his religious principles at the door of the Calvinist house of worship.

After the early death of his first wife Katerina, Patrick Gordon married another Dutch girl, this time a daughter of a family which both traded on Russia and served as mercenaries.[4] This Roonaer family hailed from southern Holland; already in the early 1650s, the brothers Anthony Goriszoon (b. 1631) and Jacobus Goriszoon (b. 1626) Roonaer lived in Moscow.[5] One of them at least was a mercenary officer, apparently, for a Colonel "Ronart" greeted Boreel on his ceremonial entry into Moscow in early 1665.[6]

François Lefort married in 1678 Elisabeth Souhay, the daughter of the recently deceased Colonel Franz (François) Souhay, mortally wounded (like his in-law Cornelis van Bockhoven) in the war against the Tatars in 1677 or 1678.[7] At that point, the only one alive of the second generation of the Van Bockhovens (who had arrived with the *pater familias* Isaac van Bockhoven and Il'ia Danilovich Miloslavskii in Russia in 1647) was her uncle Philips Albrecht (albeit quite old), who had reached the rank of major-general.[8] He, too, would die of natural causes soon after.

In Patrick Gordon we find the person who has left us with the most detailed ego-document of anyone who lived for a longer period in seventeenth-century Russia, his diary.[9] While it has not survived in full, a good amount has come down to us and has been finally published (and annotated) in English in recent times. But in his day he was known for his military skill, not for his diary, which remained in manuscript. Although Gordon could not prevent the loss of the fortress of Chyhyryn to the Turks in 1678, he played a key role in capturing Azov in the mid-1690s. Most importantly, though, he became Peter the Great's mentor in military affairs in the late 1680s, guiding the young tsar's through the maneuvers of the play regiments, and explaining the intricacies of modern warfare to the tsar. On Peter's ultimately successful campaigns to Azov in the mid-1690s, Gordon was pivotal as a commander leading the siege to a successful conclusion on the second try.

François Lefort's merits for the Russian cause are less evident. Lefort had earned his military stripes as a young man in the Dutch armies fighting those of Louis XIV in the 1670s.[10] Likely travelling with the fleet that brought Van Klenck to Arkhangel'sk, he arrived in Russia in 1675. Since he and most of his group, a motley crew of soldiers of fortune, had not been recruited by any of the tsar's agents, his fate hung in the balance for many months; he was almost sent back to Western Europe, but managed to persuade enough people who mattered—including the above mentioned Francesco Guasconi and eventually the Russian authorities—that he had something to offer of use if given a chance.[11] He found support as well in the family network of the

Van Bockhovens, given the marriage he concluded with Elizabeth Souhay a mere two years after his arrival in Moscow.[12] By 1679, he travelled as an army officer in Russian service to Kyiv to join the regiment stationed there, led by its new commander, his cousin (by marriage), Patrick Gordon.[13] He was now well on his way to reach the very pinnacle of Russian society, which he managed by 1690: In September of that year the tsar personally visited his house in the *sloboda* for the first time.[14] From then on, Lefort was an intimate of Peter, almost his bosom buddy. He was the official chief of the Grand Embassy to Holland in 1697, the tsar preferring to keep a low profile.

No historian appears to have made the case that Lefort, even if he posed as a consummate officer, was indeed a sophisticated military talent, even if the Genevan attained both the rank of army general and of naval admiral in the Russian armed forces. He must have had great personal charm, as is evident from his success in ingratiating himself both with Guasconi, the Van Bockhoven clan, and, subsequently, Peter. It remains a bit opaque, nonetheless, why people were so easily drawn to him. One surmises that he impressed with his flair and sophistication, behaving like a true "man of the world." He seemed to command several languages and threw a good party, happy to participate in the tsar's prolific drinking bouts; Kurakin suggests that he died of alcoholism.[15] He did of course appeal to the tsar's hankering after things Dutch; indeed, the eulogy read at the burial of "General and Admiral" François Lefort was in Dutch, as the tsar understood this language better than German.[16] Both Gordon, who had reached a fairly advanced age, and Lefort, still young at 43, died in 1699. At that moment, Peter stood on the threshold of the Great Northern War that was to truly make Russia a Great Power in Europe and earned the tsar himself the epithet of "Great."[17]

After the death of his two foreign friends, Peter continued to socialize with men and women of foreign extraction, and relied on them for advice. One such person was Iakov Viliminovich Brius (1669–1735). Brius's Scottish father William, a mercenary officer, had arrived together with the Van Bockhovens in 1647 in Arkhangel'sk. One therefore surmises that Iakov Brius was well acquainted with the Dutch community in Russia as well. Other friends of Peter were the Scottish doctor Robert Erskine (Areskine, 1677–1718) and the scholar-librarian Johann Daniel Schumacher (1690–1761), who was instrumental, together with I. L. Bliumentrost (1676–1756, a medical doctor of German descent), in establishing the Russian Academy of Sciences. Cornelis Cruys (about whom more below) proved important in the buildup of the Russian navy. But none of them became quite as close companions of Peter's as Gordon and especially Lefort had been.

After 1699, Peter consciously drew his own plan, mainly surrounded by *Russian* friends and advisors, among whom Aleksandr Menshikov was by far the most influential.[18] The tsar's favor protected Menshikov from any hostile court intrigues, and from his invulnerable position Menshikov caused formerly close confidants of the tsar such as Ukraintsev and Vinius to be disgraced.[19] But what appears most crucial for our purposes here is that after 1699 the tsar's veneration of the Dutch vanished. The foreigners' role in Russian affairs became far more measured. It was particularly reduced in the economy and military, while even the transfer of Western technology to Russia declined. Culturally, of course, Western influence remained significant (at times almost dominant) in Russia until Pyotr Chaadaev's *Philosophical Letter* of the 1830s bemoaned how Russia had ever failed to contribute anything of significance to the course of human history. Ironically, this thesis was belied exactly at the moment when Chaadaev conjured it up, through such timeless and quintessentially Russian creations as Pushkin's poems and Glinka's compositions made in that decade.[20]

NOTES

1. Apart from the diary, see as well on Gordon, [*The World of Patrick Gordon*], *Special Issue* of the *Journal of Irish and Scottish Studies*, ed. Paul Dukes, 2, 2014; for Lefort, Myshlaevskii, "Vyezd v Rosiiu"; Pavlenko, *Lefort*; and Posselt, *Franz Lefort*. The Swiss state did not include Geneva yet.
2. See as well Arel, *English Trade*, 9–10.
3. See Boterbloem, "Dutch Mercenaries."
4. Ibid.
5. See for this information genealogical research, available at: http://www.uwstamboomonline.nl/passie/sites/index.php?mid=201966&kid=2147&pagina=tekstpagina, accessed October 8, 2019.
6. See Boreel *Verbael*, 264.
7. Posselt, *Franz Lefort*, vol. 1, 262–3, 268. Souhay was promoted from the rank of lieutenant-colonel to colonel when he lay on his deathbed.
8. Ibid., 263.
9. See *Diary of Gordon*.
10. Posselt, *Franz Lefort*; Myshlaevskii, "Vyezd v Rosiiu." He fought in the regiment of Friedrich Casimir, the prince of Kurland, participating in the 1674 siege of Grave, among other things (see Pavlenko, *Lefort*, 13–14). Seeking his luck in Nijmegen, where peace negotiations were conducted between the Dutch and French, he met the Dutch colonel Jakob van Frosten who asked Lefort to accompany him to Russia in the summer of 1675 (ibid., 15).
11. Posselt, *Franz Lefort*, vol. 1, 191–205.
12. Another influential early acquaintance made was with Paul Menzies in the *sloboda*, who was good friends with fellow Catholic Guasconi (and Patrick Gordon), see ibid., vol. 1, 220–1. Menzies married in 1677 Peter Marselis's wealthy widow, see ibid., 248n2.

13. Ibid., vol. 1, 280–1; Bushkovitch, *Peter*, 177–8. Around this time Van Keller became godfather to Lefort's first child as well (ibid., 283–4).

14. Posselt, *Franz Lefort*, vol. 2, 11.

15. Kurakin, "Gistoriia," 249.

16. T. Ilyushechkina, "'Opisanie Sibiri' v kruge interesov rossiiskoi i evropeiskoi diplomaticheskoi eliti kontsa xvii-nachala xviii v.," *Quaestio Rossica* 1, 2015, 83–108: 100; Posselt, *Franz Lefort*, vol. 2, 523note.

17. This title was perhaps undeserved, since it was mainly awarded for his military victories, which were actually rather few in the war of attrition that was the (second) Great Northern War.

18. Whereas this is not the topic of this book, it is of course worthwhile to ponder in how far they were (had become) *Westernized* Russians; evidently, the chasm between *narod* (people) and elite that became characteristic for Imperial Russia begins in Peter's reign (even if the Schism of 1667 may have been a prelude), as the nineteenth-century Slavophiles most emphatically pointed out.

19. Boterbloem, *Moderniser*, 191–3.

20. See K. Boterbloem, *A History of Russia and Its Empire: From Mikhail Romanov to Vladimir Putin*, second ed., Lanham, MD: Rowman and Littlefield, 2018, 79–80.

Chapter 23

Russians in the Republic

The Russian Embassy of 1697 and 1698 to Western Europe was true to its name a *grand* affair.[1] Wary of his compatriots' distrust of foreign contamination, the tsar decided that it would be unwise to publicly announce his upcoming absence and left for Western Europe under the pseudonym of Pyotr Mikhailov. Formally, the embassy was led by Lefort, together with the boyar Fyodor Golovin (1650–1706)—who eventually, like Lefort earlier, was to become both admiral and general in the Russian armed forces, a clear sign of Peter's fondness for him—and the *dumnyi d'iak* Prokofii Voznitsyn (d. 1702), who wielded considerable prior diplomatic experience. The embassy's itinerary was to lead via the Baltic and Prussia to Holland, on to England, and back to Holland, from which subsequently Vienna, Venice, and Rome were to be visited. Ultimately, however, the tour was aborted at Vienna, where in the summer of 1698 news of unrest in Moscow reached the tsar, who then hastily departed Austria for his capital.

Still, this was an astonishing long period of time to be away, since the tsar left Moscow in March 1697 and would not return there until one-and-a-half years later. It was an especially risky venture for a head of a monarchy in which the person of the ruler played such a significant role. Peter relied on Patrick Gordon's loyal support, who stayed behind (as did Vinius), as well as several boyars, such as Fyodor Romodanovskii (c. 1640–1717), Ivan Buturlin (1661–1739), Boris Kurakin, Boris Golitsyn (1654–1715), and Fyodor Apraksin (1661–1728), in all of whom he placed great trust. This trust was rewarded: Even before the tsar's return, Gordon managed to suppress the *strel'tsy* riot about which Peter had gotten word in Vienna. Were it not for Gordon's resolute actions, Peter might have easily lost his throne.

The Grand Embassy was both a triumph and a failure. While it failed to conclude any military alliance against the Turks, it confirmed Peter's conviction that much of what he saw in terms of technology and culture was key to Russia's modernization. Peter explored Dutch culture with avid enthusiasm and studied its technological accomplishments. He developed his own ship-building skills to his heart's content and pursued his scientific interests with abandon. Nicolaas Witsen, who was the main liaison between the Dutch (both at The Hague and Amsterdam) and the Russian party, pulled out all the stops to please his Muscovite guests, including the staging of a mock seabattle on a lake west of Amsterdam on one occasion and a gigantic fireworks on another.

It proved impossible to oblige the tsar in his desire to remain anonymous among the Russian group: People soon realized the true identity of the giant that was Peter, six-and-half-feet tall in an age where most men were at least a foot shorter than that. The tsar also suffered from a pronounced tic. Consequentially, Peter was found out within days in Zaandam, after which he transferred to Amsterdam, where he could be more sheltered from the public eye. It was a particular relief to him, particularly, when Witsen managed to have Peter apprentice on the closed-off shipyards of the *VOC*. In an apparent further effort to please the tsar (even if the venture was lucrative for him personally as well), Witsen, somewhat out of step for someone who had by then primarily become a city regent and gentleman-scientist, took on the guise of arms trader, arranging for a delivery of 10,000 fire-arm muzzles to Russia during Peter's sojourn in Amsterdam.[2]

Equally significant was the embassy's relentless hiring spree of Western experts who were to participate in Russia's accelerated modernization, of which innovations in the land army and the establishment of a navy were to be the most pivotal elements. Whereas the majority of men hired in Europe by the embassy hailed from the Republic, Peter's sojourn in the London area (December 1697–April 1698) convinced him that the Dutch were falling behind the English in terms of their technology's state (as in shipbuilding), and he grew increasingly fond of hiring British over Dutch experts.[3]

Conversely, dozens of Russians were, like the tsar himself, assigned to take on the study of various trades in the Republic (and elsewhere). Whereas many Dutchmen (and a few women) had worked in the tsar's realm previously, only a few isolated Russian individuals had sojourned for any length of time in the Netherlands before 1690. The few attempts by Russians to travel to the United Provinces to conduct trade stood no chance: It proved impossible for them to familiarize themselves with its alien language and culture, while the lack of any basic knowledge about long-distance seafaring stood in their way, too. Apart from the few diplomats who spent considerable time in the Republic, such as Ushakov, Miloslavskii, or Ukraintsev, other Russian agents who had visited such as Andries Winius or Jan van Sweeden should hardly be counted as Russians, since they had spent their formative years in the Low

Countries, despite Muscovy being their place of residence in their adult life.[4] And neither should John Hebdon sr be thought of as a Muscovite, of course.

Even before Peter visited Western Europe in 1697, though, the tsar had begun to send a trickle of young Russian men to Europe (not just Britain and Holland, but Venice as well, for example) to study Western science and technology. A veritable stream of Russian apprentices headed westward from the time of the Grand Embassy onward. Not all, of course, dedicated themselves earnestly to their studies in the Republic, as the temptations were many.[5] But much was learned by many, and on a rather greater scale than had been the case before the 1690s. For a few decades, a steady flow of born-and-bred Russians decamped to the Dutch Republic for extended periods of time. Among them was the first Russian ambassador-in-residence at The Hague, Andrei Artamonovich Matveev.

By the time Peter took the reins, Andrei Matveev had experienced quite a few harrowing moments in his life, such as the fall from grace and banishment from Moscow of his father, Artamon Sergeevich Matveev (1625–1682). Artamon Matveev was an erstwhile *strel'tsy* commander who had become Tsar Aleksei's favorite after Ordin-Nashchokin's demise in 1671, and had succeeded Ordin-Nashchokin in running the *posol'ski prikaz* before he was dismissed in 1676.[6] An upstart likely resented for his rise to prominence, Matveev had been exiled to the inhospitable and remote settlement of Pustozer'sk by some of the ranking boyars with whom he had been feuding before Aleksei's death.[7] Once he decided to do without overbearing boyar interference in ruling his country, Tsar Fyodor III, apparently impressed with what he heard about him, called Matveev back. Tragically, Matveev only reached Moscow after Fyodor's untimely death in early 1682; he was then, possibly mistakenly, murdered by the rabid mob of *strel'tsy* who had been coaxed into rebelling against the Naryshkin faction. Andrei Matveev himself survived the episode, though, and put to good use what for his day was a splendid education for a Russian. It prepared him well for the lengthy diplomatic service on which he embarked under Peter the Great. While the first resident ambassador at The Hague, he was also one of only two truly senior Russian government officials (and nobles) to lead this mission before 1917.

After Matveev's definitive transfer to the Vienna in 1712 (he had sojourned for considerable lengthy stints in France and Britain in the 1700s), his successor was Boris Kurakin, Peter's brother-in-law from the tsar's first marriage (they were married to the sisters Lopukhina), and one of the first Russians to leave behind a fascinating ego-document.[8] Kurakin served only briefly in The Hague, where his main task was to attend the negotiations that led to the 1713 Treaty of Utrecht ending the War of the Spanish Succession. After several short-lived forays at various smaller European courts, he became ambassador to France by 1716. After Kurakin's departure from The Hague, the Russians proceeded to appoint second-rate diplomats to their Dutch embassy, indicative of the rapid decline of the Republic's international status that became evident around this time.

It is meanwhile not without interest that both Matveev and Kurakin are among the first Russians to leave us with autobiographical notes.[9] Such memoirs were rare before 1700; one wonders whether their prolonged exposure to Western European culture triggered an interiority hitherto unknown in Russia (Avvakum's autobiography may have been an exception to this, if it is authentic[10]). Kurakin, at least, was very much aware that he was a pioneer in composing this sort of Western style of ego-document.[11] Perhaps, then, we may see in this evidence of a significant cross-cultural influence as well, although linking Matveev or Kurakin to Dostoyevsky might be overly far-fetched.

In one important respect the Grand Embassy failed comprehensively, as we already noted. Peter sought an alliance to once-and-for-all destroy the Turks, shoring up the flagging enthusiasm of the surviving members of the Holy League and hoping to join the maritime Powers to this pact. Britain and the Republic, however, were happy to extricate themselves from the Nine Years' War with France by way of the Treaty of Ryswyck, while the tsar found in Vienna in 1698 that the aging Holy Roman Emperor Leopold I was in the process of halting the conflict with the Porte that had begun with Vienna's second siege by the Ottomans in 1683. As a result, Peter appears to have concluded that, for the time being, it was more realistic to focus on what seemed to be a more limited conflict and to try to settle the old scores with Sweden first. He could not know that this war would take up most of the remainder of his life.

NOTES

1. The most comprehensive recent overview in Russian is Irina Guzevich and Dmitrii Guzevich, *Velikoe posol'stvo: Rubezh epok, ili nachalo puti, 1697–1698*, second ed., St. Petersburg: Dimitrii Bulanin, 2008.
2. Driessen, *Tsaar Peter*, 29.
3. See, for example, Hughes, *Peter*, 52.
4. One interesting visit that is hard to categorize—part diplomatic, part private trade, and part state-ordained trade—is that by Thomas Kel(d)erman and Vladimir Voronin to the Republic in 1670 and 1671, mentioned earlier in the text; they visited as tsarist trade agents, with the key aim of trying to improve the liquidity of the tsar's government, which was short of bullion (silver), see the transcribed documents about this trip, available at: http://www.vostlit.info/Texts/Dokumenty/Niederlande/XVII/1660-1680/Russ_Handelsreise_1670/text.phtml?id=4765), accessed March 14, 2020; and (in slightly different version) available at: http://www.vostlit.info/T

exts/Dokumenty/Niederlande/XVII/1660-1680/Russ_Handelsreise_1670/text2.htm, accessed March 14, 2020. Kelderman addressed the Estates-General in Dutch, but, although a *moskovskii inozemets*, he was not necessarily of Dutch heritage (Dutch being the trade *lingua franca* of the Baltic-Northern Europe zone, of course).

5. Driessen, *Tsaar Peter*, 112–14.
6. On Ordin-Nashchokin's fall, see Bushkovitch, *Peter*, 54–5.
7. Bushkovitch, *Peter*, 55–79.
8. On him, see especially Ernest A. Zitser, "The Vita of Prince Boris Ivanovich 'Korybut'-Kurakin: Personal Life-Writing and Aristocratic Self-Fashioning at the Cort of Peter the Great," *Jahrbücher für Geschichte Osteuropas* 2, 2011, 163–94; Kurakin, "Gistoriia."
9. See Zitser, "Vita," 168–9.
10. See Brostrom, ed. *Archpriest Avvakum*.
11. Zitser, "Vita," 169.

Chapter 24

A Final Blaze of Business: Lups and Brants

In the summer of 1686, 21-year-old Christoffel Brants (1664–1732) loaded for the first time a ship in Holland with commodities destined for sale at Arkhangel'sk.[1] Brants was the child of Lutheran German immigrants who had moved to Amsterdam some years before the boy's birth. His father was wealthy enough to become a taxpaying citizen (*poorter*) in 1659, soon after his marriage to a native from his birth village in East Frisia.[2] But Enno Brants had not arrived as a man of great means, as he identified himself as a cooper (*kuiper*) on his wedding license. In other words, he made vats to transport goods, essential packaging for commodities transported on ships, but as such a modest handicraft. Enno seems to have been the typical immigrant of modern times, a hard worker who was trying to get ahead in life, lured away from his East-Frisian village by Amsterdam's opportunities. Eventually, he traded in Russian naval stores as part of a company set up by Hendrik Thesingh, whose own son was subsequently involved in organizing the printing of Russian works in Amsterdam at Peter the Great's behest.[3]

Christoffel Brants may have been drawing on both his father's assets and been additionally financed by relatives in north-west Germany in chartering his first vessel, but he appears to have personally travelled to Russia (on a later ship) to oversee the transactions; this makes it likely that the senior partner, Matthijs Barts, who loaded the rest of the *Graaf Floris*, offered him payment for services to be rendered in Russia through offering Brants a share of the space in the hold.[4] However the exact business deal was struck, this young man's appearance as a Russia trader seems sudden; his biographer surely is correct in suggesting that he must have apprenticed in the trade prior to 1686, perhaps already travelling to Russia (and learning the language) before then. This is all the more likely given the fact that he settled by about 1690 in Arkhangel'sk as an agent (for the Thesinghs and possibly others), while he concomitantly loaded ships for his own private account.[5] But Brants's sudden appearance as a significant merchant, too, may confirm how business opportunities in Russia may have remained promising and more easily explored by newcomers for far longer than the much more closed world of the *VOC* or West India Company.

Brants met Peter the Great in Arkhangel'sk during the tsar's first visit to his northern port in the summer of 1693. Spending most of the 1690s there, by 1698 Brants, in partnership with Jan Thesingh, had branched out into the importation of arms, shipping 5,000 muskets from Amsterdam to Russia at the moment when Peter's Grand Embassy came to its abrupt close.[6] When the Great Northern War began in 1700, Brants still spent most of his time in Russia, both in Moscow's foreigners' suburb and at Arkhangel'sk. Although the Estates-General placed an embargo on the export of arms to Russia (as Sweden was officially a Dutch ally), Brants and his partners encountered few problems in shipping vast amounts of arms to Russia, in exchange for the usual assortment of Russian export goods such as potash, tar, grain, and other goods.[7] His sister Helena married in 1705 Jacob Lups, a union which strengthened the ties further between Brants and Jacob's brother Jan Lups, his key business partner after 1700; such marriage politics, as we saw previously, were customary among the Dutch communities at home and abroad.[8]

In Moscow, Brants eventually bought the house in which Peter's tutor Frans Timmerman had lived earlier, which suggests that it was Timmerman who may have introduced Brants to Russia's highest circles, and possibly to the tsar himself.[9] Wielding significant means in the 1700s, Brants and Lups even financed Russian troops directly.[10] The partners were also highly valued by Peter the Great, as can be seen from Cornelis de Bruin's remarks:

> They [the tsar and his retainers] began with their Epiphany celebrations on January 3, 1702 (Old Style). The first reception was at Mr. Brants's, where at nine in the morning no fewer than 300 people arrived, in part by sleigh, in part on horseback. The tables had been properly prepared, and covered with many delicacies, starting with cold dishes that were soon followed by warm dishes. People were merry and drank heartily. Then His Majesty departed with his company at 2 PM, and went to Mr. Lups's house, where the welcome was no less opulent, and that same night they went to visit several other gentlemen [in the *sloboda*].[11]

Brants did so well that from 1705 onward a magnificent estate with formal garden was built for him not far from Amsterdam, which he fittingly dubbed *Petersburg*. In Pomerania in 1712, Peter the Great knighted Brants, which was a bit of an odd move, as such a ritual was not part of Russian customs.[12] Meanwhile, Brants fell out with Jan Lups in 1710, never to make up.[13]

It had been Brants and Lups, too, who hosted the skillful artist Cornelis de Bruin in Moscow after he had arrived at Arkhangel'sk in 1701; De Bruin stood at the beginning of a long journey that would lead him to the Persian Gulf.[14] During it, he kept a diary and made a large number of lifelike sketches that were to be engraved in the printed version of his travels.[15] In 1702, De Bruin painted in Moscow portraits of the tsar's nieces as well.[16] He was to stay in the Russian capital altogether for more than a year.

Christoffel Brants was Peter's Dutch host on the tsar's second trip to Western Europe in 1716 and 1717, in many ways taking on the role Witsen had played in 1697 and 1698.[17] The tsar showed his approval of Brants by then raising him to the hereditary Russian nobility (he was therefore allowed to call himself "van" Brants, in another strange Germanesque gesture on Peter's part) and making him Russia's official Amsterdam agent in 1717. In this latter capacity, Brants was to hire a great number of Dutch artisans to work in Russia, from all sorts of smiths to millers, weavers, papermakers, and turners.[18] But already before he had involved himself in hiring workers for the tsar, like so many of his compatriots, such as Hendrik van Dam (the associate of Alexander Leslie in 1631), Andries Winius, or Jan van Sweeden, had done for three generations. Brants, too, was a key organizer in shipping the curiosity cabinets of the Dutch collectors Frederick Ruysch and Albert Seba to St. Petersburg.[19]

Brants and Lups were not the only ones profiting from the Dutch trade with Russia, during which what appears in hindsight to be its Indian summer.[20] The almost permanent state of war in Europe after 1688 seems to have triggered the foundation of the Directorate of Muscovy Trade, which was loosely affiliated with the *Gecommitteerden voor de Oostersche Handel* that was primarily geared to the Baltic trade.[21] Those sending merchantmen to Arkhangel'sk regularly paid a contribution to cover the costs of the warships convoying the fleet. Whether the Directorate did much else is not clear; it seems that it was usually the Dutch diplomatic resident who represented the merchants at the tsarist court rather than its agents.[22] Eventually, of course, the Russia trade became a Baltic trade, when Arkhangel'sk was overtaken by the rise of St. Petersburg and the Russian acquisition of Riga (and Narva, although Riga was a much busier port).[23]

The Dutch shippers on Arkhangel'sk may have fallen victim to the complacent inertia that success often breeds. Locher suggests that even if a Dutch ship was the first to ever unload at St. Petersburg, Dutch merchants remained overwhelmingly faithful to their trusted White-Sea port for many years afterward; Arkhangel'sk could be reached along a route that was less dangerous, despite the rough seas of the north Atlantic. Convoys were hardly necessary (which explains the earlier mentioned reluctance to pay convoy money) and Arkhangel'sk was a less expensive port.[24] But after 1750, St. Petersburg (with Riga) became the key Russian port for trade with Europe, replacing Arkhangel'sk. While far from ice-free, St. Petersburg and Riga were reachable for a much longer period of the year, while the incessant military conflicts that had plagued the Baltic region in the sixteenth and seventeenth century vanished after 1721. This made it worthwhile for ships to traverse the shorter distance to the Russian capital or Riga rather than sail the long way by way of the North Cape and the Kola peninsula to Arkhangel'sk.

NOTES

1. Donga, *Christoffel*, 18–19.
2. Ibid., 13–15.
3. Ibid., 19–20; Veluwenkamp, "'N huis," 129–30.
4. Donga, *Christoffel*, 18–19; "Notariele Akten."
5. If he shipped from Amsterdam (and he may not have), before the mid-1690s his shipping from the Republic was sporadic; in 1695, he loaded ships together with his father ("Notariele Akten").
6. Donga, *Christoffel*, 31.
7. Ibid., 21, 31, 33–5.
8. Ibid., 22, 28.
9. Ibid., 33.
10. Ibid., 35–6.
11. De Bruyn, *Reizen*, ed. Hannema, 41 [my translation].
12. Donga, *Christoffel*, 38.
13. Ibid., 37.
14. Ibid., 32.
15. Cornelis de Bruin, *Reizen over Moskovie*.
16. Donga, *Christoffel*, 33.
17. Ibid., 22–3, 38–9.
18. Ibid., 41–2.
19. Ibid., 43.
20. For a more fulsome overview, see J.W. Veluwenkamp, "Dutch Merchants in St. Petersburg in the Eighteenth Century," *Tijdschrift voor Skandinavistiek* 2, 1995, 236–331.
21. Knoppers, "Eighteenth Century Dutch Trade," 2–3; Werner Scheltjens, *De invloed van ruimtelijke verandering op operationele strategieën in de vroeg-moderne Nederalndse scheepvaart*, Eelde: Barkhuis, 2009, 74. See the introduction to the Dutch guide to archival documents regarding Russia for support for this suggestion "Geschiedenis archiefvormer," *Ruslandgids Nationaal Archief*, available at: https://www.nationaalarchief.nl/onderzoeken/index/nt00429?searchTerm=Moscovie, accessed December 6, 2019.
22. Lups, Brants, and others refused to pay any convoy fees anymore toward 1710, which leads one to conclude that it was not a particularly well-oiled machine (see "Geschiedenis archiefvormer").

23. H. van Koningsbrugge, "Der Niedergang des niederländischen Handels mit Rußland und dem Baltikum in den Jahren 1710–1721," in *Around Peter the Great*, eds C. Horstmeier et al., Groningen: NOS, 1997, 87–91.

24. Locher, *Peter*, 216–17; Knoppers, "Eighteenth Century Dutch Trade," 221; Veluwenkamp, "Dutch Merchants in St. Petersburg," 247–9.

Chapter 25

Cornelis Cruys and the Russian Exchange Students

There are grounds to consider the Norwegian-born Niels Olufsen Creutz (1655–1727) as partially Dutch, even if the Norwegians may have better claims on him.[1] This renowned sailor is better known to history under his Dutchified name, Cornelis Cruys; he served as the highest non-Russian navy flag officer under Peter the Great. While he served Peter for two decades, he was ultimately buried in Amsterdam (after dying in St. Petersburg), perhaps indicative of his loyalties (he had concluded his first marriage in Amsterdam as well).

Danish-Dutch relations were often prickly in the sixteenth and seventeenth century, as the Dutch chafed at the tolls collected by the Danish king's agents at the *Sont* (Sound) that links the North with the Baltic Sea (Sweden only acquired Skaneland, the western shoreline of which is the Sont's eastern shore, in 1658). It explains partly why the Dutch more often supported Sweden than Denmark in the numerous conflicts between the two Scandinavian monarchies in this age. Still, the ties between Denmark (which included Norway) and the United Provinces were frequently close, while a steady stream of immigrants from all three Scandinavian lands (Norway, Denmark, and Sweden) moved to the Republic in search of employment in the seventeenth century. The men among them often ended up as sailors on Dutch naval vessels, *VOC* ships, or other merchant ships. Before Cruys, another Danish-Norwegian naval commander, Cort Sivertsen Adler (Adelaer in Dutch, 1622–1675), had already acquired great fame in Dutch service (and Koenraad Van Klenck had been in business with him).[2] Vice versa, Cornelis Maartensz. Tromp (1629–1691) had taken command of the Danish navy in the war with Sweden of the 1670s.[3] The ties with Denmark are otherwise also evident: While Peter Marselis mainly lived in Russia, he regularly visited Denmark on various political missions, but he went there even more frequently to meet his brother Gabriel, who split his time between the Republic and Denmark, and was an immensely important financier and businessman in this northern monarchy.[4]

Cruys may serve both as the epitome of a successful Danish-Norwegian immigrant in the Republic, and as the most outstanding Dutch(-ish) recruit of Peter's drive to find experts to help him modernize his country. At the time of the Grand Embassy, Cruys enrolled in Russian service to aid the establishment of a modern navy, Peter's greatest obsession.[5] But his relationship with Peter was far from smooth: In 1714, he was convicted of dereliction of duty (he received the death penalty which was commuted to banishment to Kazan): During a naval expedition, he had lost several ships under his command in the Finnish Gulf.[6] Like Vinius, he was pardoned after a few years and restored to some of his offices, but never fully rehabilitated. It makes his desire to be buried in the Republic more understandable.

Cruys not only commanded naval detachments (indeed, such service was among the least significant of his work in Russia), but mapped various territories (such as the Donbas), reinforced defensive works at Arkhangel'sk, and helped to draw up plans for the naval base at Kronshtadt.[7] Not long after his own hiring in 1698, he was back in Amsterdam to purchase weapons and hire sailors for Peter. Arms were readily available (Witsen again helped out on this occasion), but sailors much less, because most served on the Dutch naval squadrons that set to sea in the early stages of the Spanish Succession War (1702–1713). To reach his numerical recruitment goal, Cruys turned instead to hiring additional Danes and Norwegians, who routinely flocked to Amsterdam in search of work; as a result, among those arriving in 1703 and 1704 in Russia was the Dane Vitus Bering (1681–1741), who in the service of the tsar was to discover the straits that still bear his name today. Indeed, even the Grand Embassy's hiring spree itself had led to more Scandinavian than Dutch sailors to be recruited, even when Dutchmen were preponderant among ships' officers.[8]

Meanwhile, Cruys tried to drop off a new contingent of young Russians to begin to learn the art of seafaring on the Republic's fleet. This proved difficult as well, because he had arrived in the fall of 1702, that is, during a season when few ships left port in Holland. In the end, rather than apprenticing as seamen, several of the young Russians became apprentices to various craftsmen around Amsterdam.

The "study abroad program" of young Russians, as chaperoned in this instance by Cruys, came to an end with Peter's death. Although this was to some degree due to a resurgence of the old-fashioned distrust of foreign things in Russia after 1725, the genie was out of the bottle: The Russians had acquired enough skills and know-how to maintain the momentum themselves and educate their own in their own country, without the need for expensive study trips abroad. Enough Russians and immigrants in Russia had become versed in the recent development of Western science and technology to instruct other Russians in a sustained fashion in these areas.

Peter had laid the foundation of the Academy of Sciences that opened its doors a mere few months after the tsar's death, while the *Kunstkammer*, a large curiosity cabinet consisting of a variety of especially Dutch collections that had been bought, served as a public museum, keeping the interest in science and nature alive. Dutch artists such as Adriaan Schoonebeeck had taught Russian apprentices the intricacies of Western European painting and etching, which made school. And after a brief phase in which many printed books in Peter's new alphabet were printed in Amsterdam, Russian printing presses increased their production using the new type. As Driessen notes, the Dutch influenced the first Russian gardens that appeared after 1700, and influenced Russian sculpting as well.[9]

NOTES

1. See Hans Van Koningsbrugge et al., eds, *Life and Deeds of Admiral Cornelius Cruys*, Groningen: Nederlands-Russisch Archiefcentrum, 2009; and Eelko Hooijmaaijers, "Cornelis Cruys, a Dutch Rear-Admiral in Russian Service," in Carel Horstmeier et al., eds, *Around Peter the Great*, Groningen: NOS, 1997, 29–34.

2. See Boterbloem, *Fiction*, 22, 46.

3. Ibid., 168, 268n23.

4. Boterbloem, *Dirty Secret*, 153.

5. He deeply impressed one of the official ambassadors, Fyodor Golovin (Pavlenko, *Lefort*, 180).

6. See "Kriuis, Kornelii Ivanovich," in, *Russkii biograficheskii slovar'*, ed. A.A. Polovtsov, vol. 9, Sankt-Peterburg: Glavnoe upravlenie udelov, 501–7.

7. T. Titlestad, *Tsarskii admiral Kornelis Kriuis na sluzhbe Petra Velikogo*, Sankt-Peterburg: Russko-Baltiiskii informatsionnyi tsentr "Blits", 2003, 36–43.

8. Pavlenko, *Lefort*, 179.

9. Driessen, *Tsaar Peter*, 115–20.

Chapter 26

An Era Closes: The Eighteenth Century

Justifiably, Martha Lahana wrote how Peter the Great did not aim for "a country run by foreigners," but "a modern and [powerful] Russia."[1] She added that,

> After about 1700 Peter used immigrants only in posts that natives could not yet fill, and he urgently trained natives to take over those posts. Although the country very rapidly westernized after this time, the innovative role of foreigners in the process seems to have declined.[2]

Lahana's argument fits the evidence, even if historians might point at the ongoing recruitment of Western scientists, artists, or mercenary officers throughout the eighteenth century. Undeniably, the Russians had come into their own, though, only to have to turn to Europe once again in the second half of the nineteenth century for money and expertise to jumpstart their country's belated industrialization. The Dutch played no role in that process, as they themselves industrialized late—more or less at the same time as Russia—and had no expertise to offer in the matter. The question remains open, it seems to me, in how far the vanishing of the Dutch from the Russian scene after the first decade of the eighteenth century was linked to concomitantly diminishing role of the Dutch everywhere internationally.[3] The Russian empire and the Dutch Republic continued to maintain a cordial relationship until the French Revolution, but its broader significance for the course of history was rather minimal.[4]

In the mid-1970s, Jake Knoppers defended a massive doctoral dissertation at Montréal's McGill University about Dutch-Russian trade during the eighteenth century.[5] In many ways, this remains a useful study, although in the eyes of contemporary publishers the topic was apparently not interesting enough to turn the thesis into a book.⁶ Knoppers, in a sense, produced the follow-up work to Kurland's aborted project: his survey of the eighteenth century might have nicely complemented Kurland's overview of the earlier period, as Kurland's work, too, displayed the strong economic slant common to much of Western postwar historiography. At the same time, it is hard to fathom why in his dissertation Knoppers chose to investigate a topic that has only marginal significance. This should have been obvious to him even when he started his project, even if he may have found a much more plentiful, or easier accessible, source base about it (Dutch eighteenth-century sources are much more abundant and written in a legible handwriting). Indeed, Jarmo Kotilaine conducted an ultimately much more significant study about Russia's early modern trade with the West in the period when Dutch merchants were pivotal actors, that is, the seventeenth century.⁷ In Kotilaine's dissertation and subsequent book, which have often been used as the basis of the narrative in the previous pages, the Dutch play a foremost role, made all the more evident because the Finnish historian compares and contrasts it with that of their seventeenth-century competitors.

Still, Knoppers's work deserves some attention here, as it does address some questions the answer to which might have otherwise remained moot. In the first place, he points out how, despite all of Peter I's efforts, the Russian trade with the West remained "passive," during the eighteenth century.⁸ By this, he means that commodities were mainly carried by Dutch and other European vessels, and that there was yet little sign of a carrying trade conducted by Russian ships. Meanwhile, Arkhangel'sk remained a more important port of call than St. Petersburg for the Dutch throughout the eighteenth century.⁹ And finally, although the Dutch trade in value and volume declined in the second half of the eighteenth century, it flourished (indeed reached an unprecedented height) until the 1740s, more or less coinciding with Jonathan Israel's end-point regarding the "Dutch Primacy" in global trade.¹⁰

NOTES

1. Lahana, "Novaia Nemetskaia Sloboda," 183.
2. Ibid., 183. See also ibid., 184.
3. For some contemplation on this issue, see Hans van Koningsbrugge, *Het verhaal van twee verloren vriendschappen. De Nederlandse Republiek, Zweden en Rusland, 1714–1725*, Groningen: Instituut voor Noord- en Oost-Europese Studies, 2013; Waegemans, *De tsaar*.
4. Of note for this later period as well is the now digitally available publication P.N. Holtrop and Th.J.S. van Staalduine, eds, *De Hollandse Hervormde Kerk in Sint-Petersburg, 1713–1927*, 3 vols, Kampen: Kok, 2003, available at: http://res

ources.huygens.knaw.nl/retroboeken/hollandse_hervormdekerk_petersburg/#page=0&accessor=toc&view=homePane, accessed March 1, 2020.

5. Knoppers, "Eighteenth Century Dutch Trade." Oddly, the dissertation carries another title as well: "Dutch Trade with Russia from the Time of Peter I to Alexander I. A Quantitative Study in Eighteenth Century Shipping," while copyright was established by the author in 1977. See as well his MA thesis: Knoppers, "Visits."

6. It is very much a work of cliometrics, which had begun to lose its appeal by that point (and never was a very readable brand of historiography).

7. See Kotilaine, "When the Twain"; idem, *Russia's Foreign Trade*.

8. Knoppers, "Eighteenth Century Dutch Trade," xxxix; see also ibid., 301, 303.

9. Ibid., 240, 242, 336.

10. Ibid., 271; and see the table in ibid., 266; J. Israel, *Dutch Primacy in the World Trade, 1585–1740*, Oxford: Oxford UP, 1989.

Epilogue

Christoffel "van" Brants and Jan Lups were the last of the Dutch mercantile magnates to have a significant influence on Russian history.[1] Without the reliability of their arms' deliveries, Russia might not have been able to sustain its exhausting war against Sweden until 1721. At the outset of this book, Admiral Van Kinsbergen has been mentioned, but he did not leave a deep imprint on Russia's history, since he was in Russian service only for a short while. Conversely, the Russian influence on Dutch affairs gradually increased after 1725, but became never near as significant as the Dutch role in seventeenth-century Russia.

Indeed, Russians and Russia appear sporadically on the pages of Dutch history after 1725. Together with British troops, thousands of Russian soldiers landed at the northernmost point of Holland province in 1799, when the northern Netherlands were a French-Revolutionary satellite state. Making little headway, the Russian presence in the northern part of Holland lasted a mere few months. More than 15,000 Dutch soldiers were part of the *Grande Armée* that invaded Russia in 1812, their *pontonniers* playing a particularly heroic role in enabling the remnants of Napoléon's forces and the emperor himself to escape the Russians, across hastily engineered bridges crossing the Berezina river in late November that year.

Subsequently, Tsar Nicholas I (1799–1855) was the only significant monarch among Europe's five Great Powers who made an attempt to prevent Belgian independence in the 1830s, breaking up the recently founded Kingdom of the Netherlands. Nicholas's involvement was driven in part by his belief in the "legitimacy" of the monarchical dynasties established, or restored, at the 1814–1815 Congress of Vienna. Their agreed borders needed to be maintained in the name of political and social stability and conservative traditions. But Nicholas had also a more direct interest in the fate of the

Oranges, for his sister was married to the Dutch crown prince, William of Orange-Nassau, the later King William II (r. 1840–1849). His opposition, in the end, was overruled, and Belgium was recognized as an independent state in 1839.

Around 1900, the last tsar, Nicholas II (1868–1918), took the initiative to call international peace conferences in an attempt to prevent war from braking out, which gathered at The Hague, and of which today's International Court of Justice is in some ways an heir. The conferences obviously missed their mark. Nicholas II went on to find notoriety in history for reasons different than being a pacifist. In the last decades of Romanov rule, emigration from Russia swelled, but not many emigrés settled in the Netherlands (they were mainly Ashkenazi Jews). Nor did political exiles settle in the Netherlands, as it was not a hotbed of revolutionary activity such as London, Paris, New York, Vienna, or Zürich.

A few Russians settled in the Netherlands after they fled the 1917 revolution that ended tsardom. Several Russian revolutionary archives were spirited away from the Bolshevik regime and ended up at the International Institute of Social History in Amsterdam. But the Netherlands did not become a major destination for those fleeing Lenin's dictatorship.[2] In the Second World War, a detachment of (Soviet) Georgian auxiliaries became famous for their mutiny against the Germans in the early months of 1945 on the island of Texel, a revolt that was bloodily suppressed. The heroic stand of the Georgians is still commemorated today. Probably more Dutch volunteers fought with the Nazis against the Soviet Red Army, meanwhile, than Georgians served Hitler (and many of the latter had only enlisted to avoid being worked to death as forced laborers by the Nazis, a common fate for Soviet POWs). Besides Georgians, other contingents of Soviet POWs who preferred serving the Nazis over virtual extermination in German POW camps were stationed in the occupied Dutch kingdom, as at Assen.

In a kind of warped parallel, meanwhile, for the Netherlands the age of Russian (Soviet) Communism from 1917 to 1991 appears an oddly parallel period to the early modern era of Dutch capitalism for Russia. It was then, in the twentieth century, that Russia in its Soviet guise was at its most influential in the Low Countries (in Belgium it played a similarly important part), with many joining the Dutch Communist Party or its trade unions and other affiliated organizations, or subscribing to its newspaper (significantly called "The Truth," *De Waarheid*, carrying the same name as the Soviet-Russian paper *Pravda*). This influence was almost as exclusively one-way as that of seventeenth- and eighteenth-century foreign trade had been in the opposite direction, with the Dutch having little to no effect on the Soviet Union's history.[3] There is no denying that Soviet Communism had a significant impact on Dutch politics. For a while the Dutch Communist Party was a factor in Dutch twentieth-century politics, with its most heroic stance coming during the Second World War, when many Communists joined the anti-Nazi resistance, sacrificing their lives in it. During the Cold War, leading members of the Dutch Communist party frequented the Soviet Union. The Dutch Communists, however, had no importance within the international Communist movement. When the *Communistische Partij van Nederland* faded in the 1970s, the Dutch link with Russia became very brittle.

Especially in the Cold War, intensive study of the Soviet phenomenon was the field of expertise of many a Dutch academic, as we saw at the outset of this book. Some Soviet dissidents settled in the Netherlands, while a number of Dutch scholars (Karel van het Reve and Jan-Willem Bezemer foremost) tried to help the regime's political opponents within the Soviet Union as much as they could. Mikhail Gorbachev's *Perestroika* and *Glasnost'* took both Russians and Dutch by surprise, meanwhile, as did the rapid dismantling of the Iron Curtain in 1989 and collapse of the Soviet Union in 1991.

The Dutch tried to aid the former Soviet states in the confusion that followed, but, as with other Western countries, at least their government was not especially helpful. The Cold War proved remarkably soon a faint memory, with other pressing issues taking center stage during the 1990s, such as the European Union's closer ties and further expansion and the Yugoslav tragedy. In a move mainly inspired by the eternal thirst to cut educational budgets (but certainly reflective of the general direction of policy), the University of Amsterdam, my alma mater, abolished its once flourishing Eastern European Institute around 2000. Some of those involved in making this decision seemed to frame the survival of this department as an affront to the myth of the newfound European unity (which then still very much was to include the Russian Federation) and were eager to do away with a relic of the odious days of European disunity during the Cold War.

Despite the efforts made by the investigators of the Witsen Project—the fruits of which have very much informed the previous—Russia became after 1991 once more a remote and exotic place for most Dutch people, rather than the looming threat it had been between 1917 and 1991. And likewise, today in Russia the Netherlands are primarily known for rather trivial pursuits, such as their men's football teams, players, and coaches (some of whom were quite successful in the Russian Premier League). Ultimately then, only a weak echo appears to survive today of the once crucial relationship between Russia-Muscovy and the Netherlands. Oddly, in a parallel with the seventeenth century, those ties are far more more cultural[4] and economic than political.

The economic ties between the Netherlands and the Russian Federation significantly intensified after 1991. Economists specializing in such matters will know that the Netherlands and Russia are extremely important trading partners (the Dutch in recent years have sometimes been the most important Russian export partner!), and that Dutch investments in the Russian Federation amount to tens of billions of euros.[5] So perhaps we are witnessing a kind of return to those long-gone days of Jan van de Walle, Karel du Moulin, Andries Winius, Jan van Sweeden, Koenraad van Klenck, Adolf Houtman, or Christoffel Brants.

***

Jordan Kurland correctly pinpointed the arrival of the Boreel embassy as a highly significant moment in the development of the relationship between Muscovy and the Republic, but he did not establish the exact reason for it. He did not investigate the most important aspect of it, which were the first meetings of Nicolaas Witsen and Andrei Vinius during the Dutch mission's sojourn in Moscow. These ushered in the heyday of Dutch-Russian relations in the early modern age, which went far beyond commerce alone. Without this acquaintance, Witsen would neither have drawn his map nor written his book, nor facilitated the building of Peter's first ship, nor overseen the tsar's trip to Holland. Without it, Vinius might not have caught the eye of Tsar Aleksei as the Russian interpreter assigned to the Boreel mission. Having come to the tsar's attention in this then very much personalized style of government, Vinius rose further in the tsar's estimation because of his composition of the *kuranty*, and reached the highest levels of the tsarist bureaucratic hierarchy, eventually becoming a close advisor to, and language teacher of, Peter the Great. While Jordan Kurland therefore divined how crucial the arrival of the embassy was, from his notes it appears evident that he had not yet truly fathomed the significance of the establishment of the Witsen–Vinius link (which was even kept *sub rosa* in Witsen's handwritten notes[6]), when he broke off his study in the middle of the 1960s. He appears to have stared himself blind on the trading aspect of the age's Dutch-Russian relationship, which may reflect the almost hegemonic position economic history occupied in US historiography among the subfields of the discipline during the middle of the twentieth century; as Kurland wrote in a line that opened one draft of his third chapter, "between the return . . . of Coenraad Burgh and . . . 1664 . . . commercial relationships between the Netherlands and Muscovy were to reach their greatest extent."[7]

In the first place, statistically this was simply not true, as Kotilaine's work shows. When thinking of the various manufactories set up by Vinius, Ackema, or Marselis, for example, Dutch influence undeniably *began* to reach its maximum extent toward 1650. In land warfare, the drill manual that was published in Russian coincided with the arrival of the Van Bockhoven clan to contribute to a much better Russian performance in the Thirteen Years' War, a key conflict on the road to Russia's rise as a Great

Power. But after 1664–1665 the volume of trade between the Republic and Muscovy steadily increased and the contacts between the two countries intensified in all sorts of ways in unprecedented fashion, a trend that lasted until the early eighteenth century. Vinius's fall from grace in the very year during which St. Petersburg was founded, 1703 (and subsequent Dutch exile from 1706 to 1708), coincided with the decline of Nicolaas Witsen's clout as Amsterdam regent. Their mutual fading from the scene coincided with the swift waning of the Dutch influence in Russia, even if trade volume between the two countries remained relatively high for several decades afterward.

Did Kurland, before he abandoned his dissertation, find out about the imminent publication of Witsen's long-lost diary and notes, the most exciting historical source that sprouted from the Boreel embassy? The exhaustive Locher-De Buck edition of Witsen's diary found its way into print in 1966. Thus, we may ponder the question whether Kurland's decision to interrupt his dissertation was in part influenced by the discovery that two Dutch scholars (De Buck and Locher) were on the verge of publishing an exhaustively annotated and edited version of Witsen's journal, a unique account about mid-1660's Russia that was far livelier and fuller of insightful and original content than Boreel's own report to the Estates-General, or the other accompanying materials about the embassy he had consulted.

Besides Witsen and Vinius, a number of other Dutch natives played an outsized role in pointing Russia the way to the future during the mid-to-late 1660s. All of them shared an at least fleeting acquaintance with each other. Vinius's protector Van Sweeden, the subject of Boreel's wrath, was one; Timmerman, who was championed by Boreel, a second; Koenraad van Klenck a third; caught in the cauldron that was Razin's rebellion, Struys and Brandt, Fabricius and Termund all met at Astrakhan in 1670; Cornelis van Bockhoven had supervised the building of the *Oryol* abandoned at Astrakhan.

Van Keller's letters, Heinsius's missives and report, Balthasar Coyett's book, Struys's book, Fabricius's memoirs, and Van Klenck and Boreel's letters and reports all are voluminous sources that allow us to reimagine Muscovy in the days of Tsar Aleksei Mikhailovich. In his last decade of his rule, Russia was poised to don the mantle of a European Great Power. Achieving this status was delayed because of Aleksei's untimely death, but the path toward this status was resumed in 1689; Russia assumed its spot among Europe's mightiest countries in the 1700s. As I said, it appears that Jordan Kurland had caught a whiff of the significance of this aspect of Aleksei's reign's latter period, but he had not quite figured out how all of the strains (or people) came together in that "marvellous decade" (to adopt Isaiah Berlin's words about a different era) when he broke off his dissertation work.

The chain of historical events that began with the Antwerp merchants exploring the trading possibilities at Kola and beyond connects through the scions of Amsterdam merchants on Russia, Nicolaas Witsen and Andrei Vinius, to Peter the Great. One might argue that individual human beings are ephemeral to the historical process, and that others would have substituted for these people with the same outcome of Russia being a global Power. Even if the agency of individual human beings is more often than not imperceptible when looking at the long-term patterns of history, I suggest that they are not, by pointing at the team of Dutchmen I mentioned above, among whom Witsen and Vinius stand out most. I suggest as well that without the Dutch intervention, Muscovy's story might have been one of history's footnotes, like that of the contemporary polities of Dzungaria or the Kalmyk khanate.

One last point: Whereas they proved indispensible mentors of the Russians in placing Muscovy on the rails to modernity, were there any significant benefits the Dutch themselves derived—besides the profits and rewards obtained by a good number of individuals, or the access to some rare strategic goods (saltpeter perhaps most crucial, but even that could be found elsewhere such as Bengal)—from their relationship with the Russians before 1725? Did they learn anything from the Russians? If anything, this yield was not very great, it seems. Indeed, they did not even learn anything truly profound (or correct) about the Russians and their empire before Witsen's eclectic, confusing, and confused study about Siberia, which was in any event read by only very few. In their printed works, it was rather easier, and frankly expected by its readership, to repeat shopworn clichés about Russian superstitions, duplicity, and inebriation, tropes readily believed by a gullible readership (as we saw, we know little about what those who could or did not read thought about Russia, when they became acquainted with it). The true scholarly Dutch study of Russia (Witsen's work on Siberia is a chaotic compilation of disjointed facts and anecdotes) was only to begin in the early nineteenth century, with Scheltema pointing the way in the 1810s. And only in that century the Dutch, like others, fell for the first time under the spell of Russian culture and its lasting accomplishments, such as the works by Pushkin, Gogol', Dostoyevsky, Tolstoi, Turgenev, Tchaikovsky, Chekhov, Stravinsky, Stanislavsky, Prokofiev, the art of Pavlova or Nijinsky, and so on. After that, the Russian influence on the Netherlands reached its height in the middle decades of the twentieth century, when a Dutch Communist Party sang Moscow's praises and even many non-Communists were sympathetic to Russia's attempts to lead humanity to the promised land, that remained, however, forever out of reach. But this influence disappeared as abruptly as the Dutch influence in Russia after 1700.

NOTES

1. Perhaps with the exception of the Dutch bank Hope and Company, which lent significant funds to the Russian government in the last decades of the nineteenth century (Jonker and Sluyterman, *At Home*, 122).
2. Some Russian refugees were actually of Dutch ancestry, whose forebears had settled there as part of the influx of Dutch people in the seventeenth and eighteenth centuries (the Van der Bellen family, another part of which ended up in Austria, were neighbors of my mother in the city of Haarlem's *tuindorp*—garden village—in the twentieth century).
3. Some early twentieth-century Dutch socialists had some significance because of their interactions with the early Soviet leadership, such as Sebald Rutgers, Anton Pannekoek, or Henk Sneevliet.
4. For example, a branch of the Hermitage Museum nowadays exists in Amsterdam.
5. See some of the numbers on the website of the Russian Embassy in the Netherlands, available at: https://netherlands.mid.ru/web/netherlands-en/economic-relations, accessed October 20, 2019. Granted, these are 2014 numbers, before some of the sanctions related to the Crimean and Ukrainian conflicts began to have an effect.
6. Both Vinius and Witsen would have been severely compromised if anything about this relationship would have leaked (for more, see Wladimiroff, *De kaart*).
7. Kurland files in author's possession.

Glossary

boyar	Russian high nobleman
d'iak	government secretary
dumnyi d'iak	government secretary of the court, highest non-noble official
dvor'ianin	"man of the court": Russian nobleman (gentleman)
Estates-General	central Dutch government institution, representing all seven provinces, gathering at The Hague
gost'	highest merchant rank in Russia
kniaz	prince (tracing ancestry to Russia's first prince Riurik)
moskovskie inozemtsy	Muscovite foreigners, privileged non-Russians
narod	Russian people
oprichnina	reign of terror in Russia (1565–1572)
posol'skii prikaz	Muscovy's foreign (ambassadorial) department
raadspensionaris	chief administrator of Holland
Rzeczpospolita	Polish-Lithuanian "Commonwealth"
sloboda	suburb
smutnoe vremya or *smuta*	Time of Troubles in Russia, c. 1598–c.1618
stadhouder (*stadtholder*)	military and civilian governor of Dutch province
staroobriadtsy	Old Believers, split off from Russian Church in 1667
strel'ets pl. *strel'tsy*	musketeer
torgovaia kniga	manual for trade(rs) *Tsentral'nyi Gosudarstvennyi*
Ulozhenie	Muscovite law code (that of 1649 is used below)

velikii kniaz	Grand Duke (or Grand Prince) of Muscovy
VOC	*(Vereenighde Oostindische Compagnie)* Dutch East-India Company
Zeevaartreglement (*morskoi ustav*)	Russian naval regulation of 1720

Bibliography

Adams, Julia. *The Familial State: Ruling Families and Merchant Capitalism in Early Modern Europe*. Ithaca, NY: Cornell UP, 2007.
Aidarova, G., R. Fakhrullin, and K. Boterbloem. "Istoriko-arkhitekturnyi analiz izobrazheniia Kazani gollandskogo mastera Kornelisa de Breina." *Vestnik St. Peterburgskogo Universiteta, Seriia: Istoriia*, 2, 2020: 566–84.
Aitzema, Lieuwe van. *Saken van Staet en Oorlogh . . . .* Vol. 1. 's-Gravenhaghe: J. Veely, J. Tongerloo, and J. Doll, 1669.
[Aleksei Mikhailovich]. Available at: http://www.vostlit.info/Texts/Dokumenty/Russ/XVII/1640-1660/AlexejI/index.htm, accessed September 30, 2019.
Amburger, E. *Die Familie Marselis*. Gießen: Wilhelm Schmitz, 1957.
Anderson, M.S. *Britain's Discovery of Russia, 1553–1815*. New York: St. Martin's Press, 1958.
Anisimov, E. *The Reforms of Peter the Great*. Armonk, NY: M.E. Sharpe, 1993.
Appleby, John H. "Ivan the Terrible to Peter the Great: British Formative Influence on Russia's Medico-Apothecary System." *Medical History* 27, 1983: 289–304.
Archpriest Avvakum: The Life of Archpriest Avvakum Written by Himself. Ed. and trans. K.N. Brostrom. Ann Arbor, MI: Michigan Slavic Publications, 1979.
Arel, M.S. "The Archangelsk Trade." In *Modernizing Muscovy*. Eds J. Kotilaine and M. Poe. London: Routledge, 2004: 175–201.
———. *English Trade and Adventure to Russia in the Early Modern Era: The Muscovy Company, 1603–1649*. Lanham, MD: Lexington Books, 2019.
———. "The Muscovy Company in the First Half of the Seventeenth Century: Trade and Position in the Russian State - A Reassessment." Unpubl. Ph.D dissertation. Yale University, 1995.
Arkheograficheskaia kommissiia. *Dopolneniia k aktam' istoricheskim'*. Vol. 5. Sanktpeterburg': Eduard Prats, 1865.
———. *Dopelnenniia k aktam istoricheskim*. Vol. 7. Sanktpeterburg': Eduard Prats, 1859.

[Avvakum]. "Zhitie Protopoa Avvakuma, im samim napisannoe." Available at: http://old-russian.narod.ru/avvak.htm, accessed September 30, 2019.

Bantysh-Kamenskii, N. *Obzor' vneshnikh' snoshenii Rossii po 1800 god', chast 1*. Moscow: Lissner and Roman, 1894.

Baron, S.H. "Osip Nepea and the Opening of Anglo-Russian Commercial Relations." *Oxford Slavonic Papers*, New Series 11, 1978: 42–63.

Belov, M.I. "Rossiia i Gollandiia v poslednei chetverti XVII v." In *Mezhdunarodnye sviazi Rossii v XVII-XVIII vv.* Ed. L. Beskrovnyi. Moskva: Nauka, 1966: 58–83.

Bespiatikh, Iu.N. "Gollandtsy. 'Nemetskaia sloboda' v Arkhangel'ske v xvii-xviii vv." Available at: http://www.vostlit.info/Texts/Dokumenty/Russ/XVIII/1700-1720/Archangelsk/Archangelsk_inozemcy/text.htm, accessed September 28, 2019.

Bezemer, J.W. and Marc Jansen. *Een geschiedenis van Rusland*. Amsterdam: Van Oorschot, 2014.

"The Bibliography of Edward L. Keenan." *Harvard Ukrainian Studies* 1, 1995: 1–22.

Blom, F., and P. Bas-Backer. *Op reis voor vrede*. Zutphen: Walburg, 2014.

Boeck, Brian. *Imperial Boundaries*. Cambridge: Cambridge UP, 2009.

Boer, Leo de. "Paradijs in Moskou." Documentary film. Broadcasted by *NTR* in series *Het uur van de wolf*. February 9, 2014. Available at: https://www.npostart.nl/het-uur-van-de-wolf/09-02-2014/NPS_1242425, accessed November 22, 2019.

Bogatyrev, S. "Bronze Tsars: Ivan the Terrible and Fyodor Ivanovich in the Décor of Early Modern Guns." In *Personality and Place in Russian Culture; Essays in Memory of Lyndsey Hughes*. Ed. Simon Dixon. London: MHRA, UCL, 2010: 48–72.

Bogoslovskii, M.M. *Petr I. Materialy dlia biografii*. Vols 1 and 2. Moskva: Nauka, 2005 [1941–1942].

Boterbloem, K. *The Dirty Secret of Early Modern Capitalism: The Global Reach of the Dutch Arms Trade, Warfare and Mercenaries in the Seventeenth Century*. London: Routledge, 2019.

———. "Dutch Mercenaries in the Tsar's Service: The Van Bockhoven Clan." *War and Society* 2, 2014: 59–78.

———. *The Fiction and Reality of Jan Struys: A Seventeenth-Century Dutch Globetrotter*. Houndmills, Basingstoke: Palgrave Macmillan, 2008.

———. *A History of Russia and its Empire: From Mikhail Romanov to Vladimir Putin*, second ed. Lanham, MD: Rowman and Littlefield, 2018.

———. *Moderniser Of Russia: Andrei Vinius, 1641–1716*. Houndmills, Basingstoke: Palgrave, 2013.

———. "Russia and Europe: The Koenraad van Klenk Embassy to Moscow (1675–76)." *Journal of Early Modern History* 3, 2010: 187–217.

Brakel, S. van. "Statistische en andere gegevens betreffende onzen handel en scheepvaart op Rusland gedurende de 18de eeuw." *Bijdragen en Mededeelingen van het Historisch Genootschap* 34, 1913: 350–404.

Brandon, Pepijn. *War, Capital and the Dutch State (1588–1795)*. Leiden: Brill, 2015.

Braudel, F. *Civilization and Capitalism: 15th to 18th Centuries*. 3 vols. New York: Harper and Row, 1981–1982.

Brenner, Robert. *Merchants and Revolution: Commercial Change, Political Conflict and London's Overseas Traders, 1550–1653.* Princeton, NJ: Princeton UP, 1993.

Bronnen tot de geschiedenis van het bedrijfsleven en het gildewezen van Amsterdam. Ed. J.G. van Dillen. Vol. 3 (1633–72). Den Haag: Nijhoff, 1974.

Brown, Peter B. "Early Modern Russian Bureaucracy: The Evolution of the Chancellery System from Ivan III to Peter the Great, 1478–1717." Unpubl. Ph.D. diss. Chicago, IL: University of Chicago, 1978.

———. "Tsar Aleksei Mikhailovich: Muscovite Military Command Style and Legacy to Russian Military History." In *Military and Society.* Eds M. Poe and E. Lohr. Leiden: Brill, 2002: 119–46.

Bruin, Cornelis de. *Reizen over Moskovie: door Persie en Indie.* Amsterdam: R. and G. Wetstein et al., 1714 [First ed.: Amsterdam: W. and D. Goeree, 1711].

———. *Reizen over Moskovie. Een Hollandse schilder ontmoet tsaar Peter de Grote.* Ed. Kiki Hannema. Amsterdam: Stichting Terra Incognita, 1996.

Buck, Piet de. "De Amsterdamse handel op Archangel (1600–1725)." In *Amsterdam, haven in de 17de en 18de eeuw.* Eds Judica Krikke, Victor Enthoven, and Kees Mastenbroek. Amsterdam: Orionis, 1990: 28–33.

———. "De Russische uitvoer uit Archangel naar Amsterdam in het begin van de achttiende eeuw (1703 en 1709)" *Economisch- en Sociaal-Historisch Jaarboek* 51, 1988: 126–93.

Bulatov, V.E., et al. *Russia and the Netherlands: The Space of Interaction, from the Sixteenth to the First Third of the Nineteenth Century.* Moscow: Kuchkovo Pole, 2013.

Bushkovitch, Paul. *The Merchants of Moscow, 1580–1650.* Cambridge: Cambridge UP, 1980.

———. *Peter the Great: The Struggle for Power (1671–1725).* Cambridge: Cambridge UP, 2007.

Campense, Alberto, "Lettera d'Alberto Campense intorno le cose di Moscovia. Al Beatissimo Padre Clemente VII Pontifice Massimo." In *Ramusio's Navigationi.* Vol. II. Milano: Eunadi, 1978–1988.

Collins, S. *The Present State of Russia.* Ed. Marshall Poe. London: Dorman Newman, 1671.

[Coyett, Balthasar]. *Historisch Verhael of Beschryving van de Voyagie gedaan onder de Suite van den Heere Koenraad van Klenck.* Amsterdam: Jan Claesz. ten Hoorn, 1677.

Cracraft, J. *The Petrine Revolution in Russian Culture.* Cambridge, MA: Harvard UP, 2004.

———. *The Revolution of Peter the Great.* Cambridge, MA: Harvard UP, 2003.

Croiset van der Kop, A. "K voprosu o gollandskikh terminakh po morskomu delu v russkom jazyke." *Izvestiia otdeleniia Russkogo Iazika i Slovestnosti.* Vol. 15, book 4, 1911: 1–72.

Danckaert, J.P. *Beschrijvinghe van Moscovien ofte Ruslandt.* Amsterdam: Broer Jansz, 1615.

Davies, Brian. *Warfare, State and Society on the Black Sea Steppe, 1500–1700.* London: Routledge, 2007.

Dekker, Rudolf. *Childhood, Memory and Autobiography in Holland*. Basingstoke: Palgrave, 1999.
"Delo tsarevicha Alekseia Petrovicha po izvestiiam gollandskogo rezidenta de-Bie." Ed. P. Bartenev. *Russkii Arkhiv* 7, 1907: 314–39.
Demkin, A.V. "Dlia popolneniia ego velikogo gosudar'a kazny." *Istochnik* 4, 1999: 3–9.
———. "'Rospisi karablem' zapadnoevropeiskikh kuptsov, sostavlennye v Arkhangel'ske v 1658 g." *Issledovaniia po istochnikovedeniiu SSSR dooktiabrskogo perioda*. Moscow: Akademii Nauk, 1987: 89–113.
———. *Zapadnoevropeiskoe kupechestvo v Rossii v xvii v.* 2 vols. Moskva: Institut rossiiskoi istorii RAN, 1994.
Deursen, A.Th. van. *Plain Lives in a Golden Age*. Cambridge: Cambridge UP, 1991.
Dixon, Simon. *The Modernisation of Russia, 1676–1825*. Cambridge: Cambridge UP, 1999.
[Dobroliubov, Nikolai.] N.-bov. "Chto takoe oblomovshchina?." *Sovremennik* 5, 1859: 59–98.
Donga, Harry. *Christoffel van Brants en zijn hofje. De geschiedenis van het Van Brants Hofje vanaf 1733*. Hilversum: Verloren, 2008.
Driessen, J. "Het Gezantschap van Reinoud van Brederode in 1615 en 1616 naar Rusland." In *Rusland in Nederlandse ogen*. Eds J. Driessen, W. Roobol and Marc Jansen. Amsterdam: Van Oorschot, 1986: 51–73.
Driessen-van het Reve, J.J. *De Kunstkamera van Peter de Grote*. Hilversum: Verloren, 2006.
———. *Tsaar Peter de Grote en zijn Amsterdamse vrienden*. Amsterdam: Amsterdams Historisch Museum, 1996.
Dukes, Paul. "Paul Menzies and His Mission from Muscovy to Rome, 1672–1674." *Innes Review* 2, 1984: 88–95.
Dukes, Paul, Graeme Herd and Jarmo Kotilaine. *Stuarts and Romanovs: The Rise and Fall of a Special Relationship*. Dundee: Dundee UP, 2009.
Dumschat, Sabine. *Ausländische Mediziner in Moskauer Rußland*. Stuttgart: Franz Steiner Verlag, 2006.
Dunning, Chester. *Russia's First Civil War*. Philadelphia, PA: Pennsylvania State UP, 2001.
The Dutch and English East India Companies: Diplomacy, Trade and Violence in Early Modern Asia. Eds. Adam Clulow and Tristan Mostert. Amsterdam: Amsterdam UP, 2018.
Eekhoff, W. "Friezen in Rusland vóór en onder Peter den Groote." *Nieuwe Friesche Volksalmanak* 7, 1859: 29–39.
Eekman, Thomas. "Muscovy's International Relations in the Late Seventeenth Century." *California Slavic Studies* 14, 1992: 44–67.
Elias, J.E. *De vroedschap van Amsterdam*. 2 vols. Amsterdam: Israel, 1963 [reprint].
Elias, Norbert. *The Civilizing Process*. Rev. ed. Oxford: Blackwell, 2000.
Esper, Thomas. "Military Self-Sufficiency in Muscovite Russia." *Slavic Review* 2, 1969: 185–208.
Esso, I. van. "Hollandsche artsen in Russischen hof- en staatsdienst in de 16e, 17e en 18e eeuw." *Bijdragen tot de Geschiedenis der Geneeskunde* 18, 1938: 1102–12.

Fehrmann, C.N. "Albert Pigge, een vermaard Kampenaar." *Kampener Almanak*, 1955–1956: 169–213.
Feldbrugge, F.J.M. *A History of Russian Law: From Ancient Times to the Council Code (Ulozhenie) of Tsar Aleksei Mikhailovich of 1649*. Leiden: Brill, 2018.
Fletcher, G. *Of the Russe Commonwealth*. Ed. R. Pipes. Cambridge, MA: Harvard UP, 1966 [London: Thomas Charde, 1591].
Floria, B.N. *Russkoe gosudarstvo i ego zapadnye sosedi (1655–1661 gg.)*. Moskva: Indrik, 2010.
Frost, Robert. *The Northern Wars: War, State and Society in Northeastern Europe, 1558–1721*. Harlow: Longman, 2000.
Fuhrmann, Joseph T. *The Origins of Capitalism in Russia*. Chicago, IL: Quadrangle Books, 1972.
———. *Tsar Alexis: His Reign and His Russia, Gulf Breeze*. FL: Academic International Press, 1981.
Games, Alison. *The Web of Empire: English Cosmopolitans in an Age of Expansion, 1560–1660*. Oxford: Oxford UP, 2008.
Gelderblom, Oscar. *Zuid-Nederlandse kooplieden en de opkomst van de Amsterdamse stapelmarkt (1578–1630)*. Hilversum: Verloren, 2000.
Gerritsz, Hessel. *Beschryvinghe van der Samoyeden landt in Tartarien*. Amsterdam: Hessel Gerritsz, 1612. Available at: https://www.dbnl.org/tekst/gerr049besc01_01/, accessed January 2, 2020.
"Geschiedenis archiefvormer." *Ruslandgids Nationaal Archief*. Available at: https://www.nationaalarchief.nl/onderzoeken/index/nt00429?searchTerm=Moscovie, accessed December 6, 2019.
Gheyn, J. de. *Wapenhandelinghe van roers, musquetten ende spiessen*. 's Gravenhage: N.p., 1607.
Glete, Jan. *War and the State in Early Modern Europe*. New York: Routledge, 2002.
Goeteeris, Anthonis. *Journael der Legatie ghedaen inde Jaren 1615 ende 1616 . . . .* 's-Gravenhage: Aert Meuris, 1619.
Goldgar, Anne. *Tulipmania*. Chicago, IL: U. of Chicago P., 2008.
Goncharov, Ivan. *Oblomov*. Trans. Stephen Pearl. New York: Bunim and Bannigan, 2006.
Gordon, Patrick. *Diary of General Patrick Gordon of Auchleuchries 1635–1699*. 5 vols. Ed. D. Fedosov. Aberdeen: Aberdeen UP, 2009–2014.
Gromyko, M.M. "Russko-Niderlandskaia torgovlia na Murmanskom beregu v xvi v." *Srednie Veka* 1 (17), 1960: 225–58.
Gurliand, I.Ia. *Ivan Gebdon, komissarius i rezident*. Iaroslavl': Tipografiia gubernskogo pravleniia, 1903.
Guzevich, Irina, and Dmitrii Guzevich. *Velikoe posol'stvo: Rubezh epok, ili nachalo puti, 1697–1698*. Second ed. St. Petersburg: Dimitrii Bulanin, 2008.
Hacquebord, Louwrens. *De Noordse Compagnie (1614–1642): Opkomst, Bloei en Ondergang*. Zwolle: Walburg Pers, 2014.
Haks, Donald. *Vaderland en vrede: Publiciteit over de Nederlandse republiek in oorlog, 1672–1713*. Hilversum: Verloren, 2013.
Hart, Simon. *Geschrift en Getal: Een keuze uit de demografisch-, economisch- en sociaal-historische studiën op grond van Amsterdamse en Zaanse archivalia, 1600–1800*. Dordrecht: Historische Vereniging Holland, 1976.

Hart, Marjolein't. *The Dutch Wars of Independence: Warfare and Commerce in the Netherlands, 1570–1680.* London: Routledge, 2014.

Haugh, Alexandra M. "Indigenous Political Culture and Eurasian Empire: Russia in Siberia in the Seventeenth Century." Unpubl. Ph.D. Diss. University of California at Santa Cruz, 2005.

"Heinsius, Nicolaas." In A.J. van der Aa, *Biographisch Woordenboek der Nederlanden.* Vol. 8, part 1. Haarlem: Van Brederode, 1867: 439–49.

Hellie, R. *Enserfment and Military Change in Muscovy.* Chicago, IL: U. of Chicago P. 1971.

Hennings, Jan. *Russia and Courtly Europe: Ritual and the Culture of Diplomacy, 1648–1725.* Cambridge: Cambridge UP, 2016.

Herberstein, S. von. *Rerum moscoviticarum commentarii . . . .* Basel: Oporinus, 1551.

Herckmans, E. "Een Historischen Verhael van de Voornaemste Beroertendes Keyserrycks van Russia, Ontstaan door den Demetrium Ivanowyts, die den Valschen Demetrius t'Onrecht Genoemt Wert." In *Rerum Rossicarum Scriptores*: 129–76. Available at: https://www.prlib.ru/item/445751, accessed November 12, 2019.

———. *Der zee-vaert lof, handelende vande gedenckwaerdighste zee-vaerden met de daeraenklevende op en onderganghen der voornaemste heerschappijen der gantscher wereld . . . .* Amsterdam: Wachter, 1634.

Hinrichs, Jan Paul. "Nicolaas van Wijk [1880–1941]: Slavist, Linguist, Philanthropist." *Studies in Slavic and General Linguistics* 31, 2006: 3 and 5–341.

De Hollandse Hervormde Kerk in Sint-Petersburg, 1713–1927. Eds P.N. Holtrop and Th.J.S. van Staalduine. 3 vols. Kampen: Kok, 2003, available at: http://resources.huygens.knaw.nl/retroboeken/hollandse_hervormdekerk_petersburg/#page=0&accessor=toc&view=homePane, accessed March 1, 2020.

Hooijmaaijers, Eelko. "Cornelis Cruys, a Dutch Rear-Admiral in Russian Service." In *Around Peter the Great.* Eds. Carel Horstmeier et al. Groningen: NOS, 1997: 29–34.

[Houtman family tree] Available at: http://www.pietheres.nl/Parenteel%20Houtman.htm, accessed October 6, 2019.

Hughes, L. *Peter the Great: A Biography.* New Haven, CT: Yale UP, 2002.

———. *Russia in the Age of Peter the Great.* New Haven, CT: Yale UP, 1998.

———. *Sophia, Regent of Russia, 1657–1704.* New Haven, CT: Yale UP, 1990.

Hunger, F.W.T. *Bernardus Paludanus (Berent ten Broecke) (1550–1633).* Leiden: Brill, 1928 [Special issue of *Janus* 32, 1928].

Ides, E. Ysbrants. *Drie-Jaarige Reize naar China.* Amsterdam: F. Halma, 1704.

Ilyushechkina, T. "'Opisanie Sibiri' v kruge interesov rossiiskoi i evropeiskoi diplomaticheskoi eliti kontsa xvii-nachala xviii v." *Quaestio Rossica* 1, 2015: 83—108.

Israel, Jonathan. *Dutch Primacy in the World Trade, 1585–1740*, Oxford: Oxford UP, 1989.

———. *The Dutch Republic.* Oxford: Oxford UP, 1995.

Iurkin, I.N. *Andrei Andreevich Vinius, 1641–1716.* Moskva: Nauka, 2007.

———. *O pervoprestol'nogo grada Moskvy. A.A. Vinius v Moskve i Podmoskov'e.* Moskva: Moskva iazik, 2009.

Izvestiia gollandtsev Isaaka Massy i Il'i Gerkmanna. Sankt-Piterburkh: Tipografiia Akademii Nauk, 1868 [*Skazaniia inostrannykh pisatelei o Rossii. Izdannye Arkheograficehskoi komissieiu* 2].

Jansma, T.S. "Olivier Brunel te Dordrecht." *Tijdschrift voor Geschiedenis* 59, 1946: 337–62.

Jong, Erik de. "Virgilian Paradise: A Dutch Garden near Moscow in the Early Eighteenth Century." *Journal of Garden History* 4, 1981: 305–44.

Jong, Michiel de. "*Staat van Oorlog.*" Hilversum: Verloren, 2005.

Jonker, Joost, and Keetie Sluyterman. *At Home on the World Markets: Dutch International Trading Companies from the Sixteenth Century until the Present*. The Hague: SDU, 2000.

Kazakova, N.A. "A.A. Vinius i stateinyi spisok ego posol'stva v Angliiu, Frantsiiu i Ispaniiu v 1672–1674 gg." *Trudy otdela drevnerusskoi literatury* 39, 1985: 348–64.

Keevil, John J. *Hamey the Stranger*. London: Geoffrey Bles, 1952.

(Kelderman and Voronin trip of 1670–1671:) http://www.vostlit.info/Texts/Dokumenty/Niederlande/XVII/1660-1680/Russ_Handelsreise_1670/text.phtml?id=4765), accessed March 14, 2020; and (http://www.vostlit.info/Texts/Dokumenty/Niederlande/XVII/1660-1680/Russ_Handelsreise_1670/text2.htm, accessed March 14, 2020.

Keuning, Johannes. "Isaac Massa, 1586–1643." *Imago Mundi* 10, 1953: 65–79.

Khodarkovsky, M. *Russia's Steppe Frontier*. Bloomington, IN: Indiana UP, 2002.

Kivelson, V. *Autocracy in the Provinces: The Muscovite Gentry and Political Culture in the Seventeenth-Century*. Stanford, CA: Stanford UP, 1996.

———. *Cartographies of Tsardom*. Ithaca, NY: Cornell UP, 2006.

Klebusek, M. "The Business of News." *Scandinavian Journal of History* 3–4, 2003: 205–13.

Kliuchevskii, V.O. *Skazaniia inostrantsev o Moskvoskom gosudarstve*. Second ed. Petrograd: Pervaia gosudarstvennaia tipografiia, 1918.

Klooster, Wim. *The Dutch Moment: War, Trade and Settlement in the Seventeenth-Century Atlantic World*. Ithaca, NY: Cornell UP, 2016.

Klueting, Harm. *Die niederländische Gesandtschaft nach Moscovien im Jahre 1630–1631: Edition der russischen Protokolle und ihrer niederländischen Übersetzungen. Mit paläographischer und sprachlicher Beschreibung. Ein Beitrag zur russischen Kanzleisprache (Prikaznyj Jazyk) des 17. Jahrhunderts*. Amsterdam: Hakkert, 1976.

Kniga ustav' morskoi o vsem' chto kasaetsia dobromu upravleniiu, v' bytnosti flota na mor'. St. Petersburg: Sankt-Peterburskoi tipografii, 1720.

Knoppers, Jake V. Th. "Eighteenth Century Dutch Trade with Russia." Unpubl. Ph.D. diss. McGill University, 1975.

———. "The visits of Peter the Great to the United Provinces in 1697–98 and 1716–17 as seen in the light of the Dutch sources," Unpubl. MA thesis. McGill University, 1970.

Kolycheva, E.I. "The Economic Crisis in Sixteenth Century Russia." In *Reinterpreting Russian History: Readings, 860–1860s*. Eds. Dan Kaiser and Gary Marker. Oxford: Oxford UP, 1994, 165–70.

Koningsbrugge, Hans van. "Der Niedergang des niederländischen Handels mit Rußland und dem Baltikum in den Jahren 1710–1721." In *Around Peter the Great*. Eds. C. Horstmeier et al. Groningen: NOS, 1997: 87–91.

———. *Het verhaal van twee verloren vriendschappen. De Nederlandse Republiek, Zweden en Rusland, 1714–1725*. Groningen: Instituut voor Noord- en Oost-Europese Studies, 2013.

Kordt, V. [Benjamin Cordt]. *Chuzozemni podorozhi po skhidnii Evropi do 1701*. Kiev: Ukainska akademija nauk, 1926.

———. "Doneseniia poslannikov Respubliki Soedinnenykh Niderlandov." *Sbornik Imperatorskogo Russkogo istoricheskogo obshchestva* 116, 1902.

———. "Ocherk snoshenii moskovskogo gosudarstva s Respublikoi Niderlandov do 1631 god." *Sbornik Imperatorskogo Russkogo istoricheskogo obshchestva* 116, 1902: iii–cccvii.

Kotilaine, J. "In Defense of the Realm: Russian Arms Trade and Production in the Seventeenth and Early Eighteenth Century." In *Military and Society in Russia*. Eds. M. Poe and E. Lohr. Leiden: Brill, 2002: 67–95.

———. Review of *Archangel* by J.W. Veluwenkamp *Kritika* 3, 2002: 715–22.

———. *Russia's Foreign Trade and Economic Expansion in the Seventeenth Century*. Leiden: Brill, 2005.

———. "When the Twain Did Meet: Foreign Merchants and Russia's Economic Expansion in the Seventeenth Century." Unpubl. Ph.D. diss. Harvard University, 2000.

Kotoshikhin, G. "O Rossii v tsarstvovanie Alekseia Mikhailovicha." Available at: http://www.hist.msu.ru/ER/Etext/kotoshih.htm, accessed September 30, 2019.

Kovrigina, V.A. "Inozemnye kuptsy-predprinimateli Moskvy Petrovskogo vremeni." In *Torgovlia i predprinimatel'stvo v feodal'noi Rossii*. Eds. L.A. Timoshina and I.A. Tikhoniuk. Moskva: Arkheograficheskii tsentr, 1994: 190–213.

———. *Nemetskaia sloboda Moskvy i ee zhiteli v kontse xvii-pervoi chetverti xviii vv*. Moskva: Arkheograficheskii tsentr, 1998.

Kozlovskii, I.P. *Andrei Vinius', sotrudnik Petra Velikogo (1641–1717 g.)*. Sankt-Peterburg: N. Ia. Stoikovoi, 1911.

Kreslins, Janis. "Linguistic Landscapes in the Baltic." *Scandinavian Journal of History* 3–4, 2003: 165–74.

Krest'ianskaia voina pod predvoditel'stvom Stepana Razina. 4 vols. Moscow: Institut istorii akademii nauk SSSR, 1954–1976.

"Kriuis, Kornelii Ivanovich." In *Russkii biograficheskii slovar'*. Ed. A.A. Polovtsov. Vol. 9. Sankt-Peterburg: Glavnoe upravlenie udelov: 501–7.

Kronenberg, M.E. "Albertus Pighius, proost van St. Jan te Utrecht, zijn geschriften en zijn bibliotheek." *Het Boek* 28, 1944–1946: 107–58 and 226.

Kurakin, B.I. "Gistoriia o Petre I i blizhnikh k nemu liudakh. 1682–1695 gg." *Russkaia starina* 10, 1890: 238–60.

Kurland, Jordan E. "Leont'ev's View on the Course of Russian Literature." *American Slavic and East European Review* 3, 1957: 260–74.

Lahana, Martha L. "Novaia Nemetskaia Sloboda: Seventeenth Century Moscow's Foreign Suburb." Unpubl. Ph.D. dissertation. University of North Carolina at Chapel Hill, 1983.

"Lannoy, Ghillebert de." In *Biographie Nationale . . . de Belgique*. Vol. 11. Brussels: Bruylant-Christophe, 1890–1891: 308–22.

Lelewel, Joachim. *Guillebert de Lannoy et ses voyages en 1413, 1414 et 1421, commentés en français et en polonais*. Bruxelles: Vandale, 1843.

Lesger, Clé. *The Rise of the Amsterdam Market and Information Exchange*. Aldershot: Ashgate, 2006.

Letiche, J.M. and B. Dmytryshyn. *Russian Statecraft: An Analysis and Translation of Iurii Krizhanich's* "Politika." New York: Blackwell, 1985.

Life and Deeds of Admiral Cornelius Cruys. Eds. Hans Van Koningsbrugge et al. Groningen: Nederlands-Russisch Archiefcentrum, 2009.

Locher, Th.J.G. *Peter de Grote*. Amsterdam: Ploegsma, 1947.

Loewenson, Leo. "The First Interviews Between Peter I and William III in 1697: Some Neglected Material." *Slavonic and East European Review* 87, June 1958: 308–16.

———. "Some Details of Peter the Great's Stay in England in 1698: Neglected English Material." *Slavonic and East European Review* 95, June 1962: 431–43.

Longworth, P. *Alexis: Tsar of All the Russias*. New York: Franklin Watts, 1984.

Loviagin, A.M. *Iz gollanskikh bibliotek i arkhivov*. Sanktpeterburg: N.p., 1902.

Lubimenko, Inna. "Anglo-Russian Relations during the First English Revolution." *Transactions of the Royal Historical Society* 11, 1928: 39–59.

———. "The Correspondence of Queen Elizabeth with the Russian Czars." *American Historical Review* 3, 1914: 525–42.

———. "Letters Illustrating the Relations of England and Russia in the Seventeenth Century." *English Historical Review* 32, January 1917: 92–103.

———. "Project for the Acquisition of Russia by James I." *English Historical Review* 29, April 1914: 246–56.

———. "Struggle of the Dutch with the English for the Russian Market in the Seventeenth Century." *Transactions of the Royal Historical Society*, December 1924: 27–51.

"Ludwig Fabritius's Account of the Razin Rebellion." Ed. S. Kovovalov. *Oxford Slavonic Papers* 6, 1955: 72–101.

Madariaga, Isabel de. *Ivan the Terrible*. New Haven, CT: Yale UP, 2005.

Magnus, Olaus. *A Description of the Northern Peoples, 1555*. Ed. Peter Foote, Burlington, VT: Ashgate, 2010.

Maier, Ingrid. *Vesti-Kuranty 1656 g., 1660–1662 gg., 1664–1670 gg.*, vol. 2: *Inostrannye originaly k russkim tekstam*. Moskva: Iazyki slavianskikh kul'tur, 2008.

———. "Zeventiende-eeuwse Nederlandse couranten vertaald voor de tsaar." *Tijdschrift voor Media Geschiedenis* 1, 2009: 27–49.

Malov, A.V. *Moskovskie vybornye polki soldatskogo stroia v nachal'nyi period svoei istorii 1656–1671 gg*. Moscow: Drevlekhranilishche, 2006.

Massa, Isaac. "Een Cort Verhael van Begin en Oorspronck deser Tegenwoordige Oorloogen en Troeblen in Moscovia, totten Jare 1610 int Cort Overloopen onder Gouvernment van Diverse Vorsten Aldaer." In *Rerum Rossicarum Scriptores*: 1–128. Available at: https://www.prlib.ru/item/445751, accessed November 12, 2019.

———. *A Short History of the Beginnings and Origins of These Present Wars in Moscow*. Ed. G. Edward Orchard. Toronto: U. of Toronto P., 1982.

Massa, Isaak. *Kratkoe izvestie o Moskovii v nachale xvii v*. Moscow: Gos. sots-ekon. izdatel'stvo, 1936. Available at: http://www.vostlit.info/Texts/rus11/Massa/pred.phtml?id=906, accessed September 17, 2019.

Matveev, Vladimir. "Summit Diplomacy of the Seventeenth Century: William III and Peter I in Utrecht and London, 1697–98." *Diplomacy and Statecraft* 3, 2000: 29–48.

Meiden, G.W. van der. "Isaac Massa and the beginnings of Dutch-Russian Relations." Available at: https://commons.wikimedia.org/wiki/File:Isaac_Massa.pdf, accessed September 9, 2016.

Meulen, R. van der. *Nederlandse woorden in het Russisch*. Amsterdam: Noord-Hollandsche Uitgeversmaatschappij, 1959.

———. "Peter de Groote en het Hollandsch." *Onze Eeuw* 13 (3), 1913: 117–38.

Miege, Guy. *A Relation of Three Embassies from His Sacred Majestie Charles II . . . .* London: John Starkey, 1669.

Miliukov, S.G. "Dumnyi d'iak Andrei Andreevich Vinius." Unpubl. *Kandidat* dissertation, Moscow State University, 2000.

Minaeva, T.S. "Deiatel'nost' perevodchikov pri prieme gollandskikh posol'stv' na Russkom Severe v xvii veke." *Vestnik Severnoi Federal'nogo Universiteta. Seriia: Gumanitarnye i sotsial'nye nauki* 6, 2019: 23–33.

Moedernegotie, De. Radio Documentary in Eight Parts. Eds. K. Amsberg and P. de Buck. Hilversum: VPRO, 1999.

Monahan, Erika. *The Merchants of Siberia: Trade in Early Modern Eurasia*. Ithaca, NY: Cornell UP, 2016.

Montias, John Michael. *Art at Auction in Seventeenth-Century Amsterdam*. Amsterdam: Amsterdam UP, 2002.

Muliukin, A.S. *Priezd inostrantsev v Moskovskoe gosudarstvo*. St. Petersburg: Trud, 1909.

Muller, F. *Essai d'une bibliographie Néerlando-Russe . . . .* Amsterdam: F. Muller, 1859.

Muller, S. *Geschiedenis der Noordsche Compagnie*. Utrecht: Van der Post, 1874.

Mund, Stéphane. *Orbis Russiarum: Genèse et développement de la représentation du monde "russe" en Occident à la Renaissance*. Genève: Droz, 2003.

The Muscovite Law Code (Ulozhenie) of 1649. Ed. R. Hellie. Vol. 1 (text and translation). Irvine, CA: Charles Schlacks jr, 1988.

Myshlaevskii, A.Z. "Vyezd v Rosiiu Frantsa Leforta (Sovremennaia perepiska)." *Russkaia starina* 3, 1898: 635–49.

Naarden, Bruno "Nicolaas Witsen en Tartarye." Available at: http://resources.huygens.knaw.nl/retroboeken/witsen/dutch_intro.pdf, accessed November 25, 2019.

Nieuw Nederlandsch Biografisch Woordenboek. Eds P.C. Molhuysen and P.J. Blok. Leiden: Sijthoff, c. 1911.

Nimwegen, O. van. *The Dutch Army and the Military Revolutions, 1588–1688*. London: Boydell Press, 2010.

"Notariele Akten over de Archangelvaart, 1594–1724." Available at: http://resources.huygens.knaw.nl/archangel/app/voyages?language_of_user=nl, accessed September 10, 2019.

Novombergskii, N. *Materialy po istorii meditsiny v Rossii*. Vol. 3. Part 1. St. Petersburg: Stasiulivich, 1906.

Olearius, A. *Beschrijvingh vande nieuwe Parciaensche, ofte orientaelsche reyse, welck door gelegentheyt van een Holsteynsche ambassade, aen den koningh in Persien geschiet is* . . . . Trans. Dirck van Wageninge. Amsterdam: Lambert Roeck, 1651.

———. *Offt begehrte beschreibung der neuen orientalischen Reise* . . . . Schleswig: Zur Glocken, 1647.

———. *The Travels of Olearius in Seventeenth-Century Russia*. Trans. and ed. S.H. Baron. Stanford, CA: Stanford UP, 1967.

———. *Vermehrte Neue Beschreibung der Moskowitischen und Persischen reise* . . . . Schleswig: J. Holwein, 1656.

———. *The Voyages & Travels of the Ambassadors sent by Frederick Duke of Holstein,* . . . . Trans. John Davies. London: Thomas Dring and John Starkey, 1662.

Onnekink, David, and Renger de Bruin. *De vrede van Utrecht (1713)*. Hilversum: Verloren, 2013.

Onnekink, David, and Gijs Rommelse. *The Dutch in the Early Modern World: A History of a Global Power*. Cambridge: Cambridge UP, 2019.

Orlenko, S.P. *Vykhodtsy iz Zapadnoi Evropy v Rossii XVII veka*. Moskva: Drevlekhranilishche, 2004.

Ormrod, David, *The Rise of Commercial Empires: England and the Netherlands in the Age of Mercantilism, 1650–1770*. Cambridge: Cambridge UP, 2003.

Osipov, I. *Obzor svedenii ob izdaniiakh i perevodakh v xvii stoletii sochineniia Semiuelia Kollinsa "The Present State of Russia."* Komi, Russian Federation: n.p., 2007.

Otchet Niderlandskikh' poslannikov' Reinouta fan'-Brederode . . . v' Shvestiiu i Rossiiu v' 1615 i 1616 godakh. Eds A.Kh. Bek and A.A. Polovtsov. Sankt-Peterburg: V.S. Balashev, 1878.

"Overzicht van de betrekkingen van Rusland tot Nederland tot aan het jaar 1800, door N.N. Bantys-Kamenskij. Medegedeeld door Dr. K. Heeringa." *Bijdragen en Mededeelingen van het Historisch Genootschap* 51, 1930: 35–103.

Pamiatniki diplomaticheskikh' snoshenii drevnei Rossii s' derzhavami inostrannymi. Vol. 4. St. Petersburg: V Tip. II Otd-niia Sobstvennoĭ E.I.V. kantseliarii, 1856: 754–1078.

Parker, G. *The Army of Flanders and the Spanish Road*. Cambridge: Cambridge UP, 1972.

———. *The Dutch Revolt*. London: Allen Lane, 1977.

"Patrick Gordon and His Family: Some Additional Letters." Ed. Paul Dukes. *Journal of Irish and Scottish Studies* 2, 2014: 125–51.

Paul, Michael C. "The Military Revolution in Russia." *Journal of Military History* 1, 2004: 9–45.

Pavlenko, N.I. *Lefort*. Moscow: Molodaia Gvardiia, 2009.

Pekarskii, P. *Nauka i literatura v Rossii pri Petre Velikomu*. 2 vols. Saint-Petersburg: Obshchestvennaia pol'za, 1862.

Peters, Marion. "'Mercator Sapiens' (De wijze koopman). Het wereldwijde onderzoek van Nicolaes Witsen (1641–1717), burgemeester en VOC-bewindhebber van Amsterdam." unpubl. Ph.D. diss. RU Groningen, 2008.

———. *De wijze koopman: Het wereldwijde onderzoek van Nicolaes Witsen (1641– 1717), burgemeester en VOC-bewindhebber van Amsterdam*. Amsterdam: Bert Bakker, 2010.

Phillips, E.J. *The Founding of Russia's Navy: Peter the Great and the Azov Fleet*. Westport, CT: Praeger, 1995.

Phipps, Geraldine. "Britons in Seventeenth-Century Russia: A Study in the Origins of Modernization." Unpublished Ph.D. diss. University of Pennsylvania, 1971.

———. *Sir John Merrick, English Merchant-Diplomat in Seventeenth-Century Russia*. Newtonville, MA: Oriental Research Partners, 1983.

Platonov, S.F. *Moscow and the West*. Tr. J. Wieczynski. Hattiesburg, MS: Academic International Press, 1972.

Plokhy, Serhii. *The Origins of the Slavic Nations: Premodern Identities in Russia, Ukraine, and Belarus*. Cambridge: Cambridge UP, 2006.

Poe, M. *Foreign Descriptions of Muscovy: An Analytic Bibliography of Primary and Secondary Sources*. Columbus, OH: Slavica, 1995.

———. *"A People Born to Slavery": Russia in Early Modern European Ethnography, 1476–1748*. Ithaca, NY: Cornell UP, 2000.

Pol, Lotte van der. *The Burgher and the Whore: Prostitution in Early Modern Amsterdam*. Oxford: Oxford UP, 2011.

Porter, Roy. *The Greatest Benefit to Mankind: A Medical History of Humanity*. New York: Norton, 1997.

Posol'stvo Konraada fan Klenka k tsariam Alekseiu Mikhailovichu i Fedoru Alekseevichu. Trans. and ed. A.M. Loviagin. Sankt-Peterburg: Tipografiia Glav. upr. udelov, 1900.

Posselt, Moritz. *Franz Lefort. Sein Leben und seine Zeit*. 2 vols. Frankfurt: Joseph Baer, 1866.

Prud'homme van Reine, R.B. *Jan Hendrik van Kinsbergen, 1735–1819. Admiraal en filantroop*. Amsterdam: De Bataafsche Leeuw, 1990.

Raptschinsky, Boris. "Het Gezantschap van Koenraad van Klenk naar Moskou." *Jaarboek Amstelodamum* 36, 1939: 149–99.

Reger, W.M. "In the Service of the Tsar: European Mercenary Officers and the Reception of Military Reform in Russia, 1654–1667." Unpubl. Ph.D. diss. U. of Illinois at Urbana-Champaign, 1997.

Reizen van Jan Huyghen van Linschoten naar het Noorden (1594–1595). Ed. S.P. L'Honoré-Naber. 's-Gravenhage: Nijhoff, 1914.

Relaes van 't gepasseerde voor ende op de Inkomste ende Receptie van den Heere van Klenck Haer Hoogh. Mog Extraordinaris Ambassadeur binnen der Moscou, geschiet den January 11/12, 1676. 's Gravenhage, 1676 [National Library of the Netherlands, The Hague: Knuttel 7442].

Repertorium der Nederlandse vertegenwoordigers, residerende in het buitenland, 1584–1810. Ed. O. Schutte. Den Haag: M. Nijhoff, 1976.

Rerum Rossicarum Scriptores Exteri a Collegio Archaeographico. Vol. 2: Isaaci Massae et Eliae Herkmanni, Batavorum, Narrationes. Sankt-Peterburg: Typis Academiae Imperialis Scientiarium, 1868. Available at: https://www.prlib.ru/item/445751, accessed November 12, 2019.

Reve, Karel van het. *Geschiedenis van de Russische literatuur*. Amsterdam: Van Oorschot, 1985.
[RGADA inventory]. Available at: https://www.archieven.nl/nl/zoeken?mivast=0 &mizig=210&miadt=467&miaet=1&micode=RGADA&minr=738326&miview=i nv2, accessed October 6, 2019.
Richter, W.M. von. *Geschichte der Medicin in Russland*. Moskva: Wsevolosjky, 1813–1817 [Reprint: Leipzig: Zentral-Antiquariat der Deutschen Demokratischen Republik, 1965].
Roberts, Benjamin. "Marlboro Men of the Early Seventeenth Century: Masculine Role Models for Dutch Youth in the Seventeenth Century?" *Men and Masculinities*, July 2006: 76–94.
Romaniello, M.P. *Enterprising Empires: Russia and Britain in Eighteenth-Century Eurasia*. Cambridge: Cambridge UP, 2019.
Roodhuyzen, Thea. *De Admiraliteit van Friesland*. Franeker: Van Wijnen, 2003.
[Roonaer family genealogy] Available at: http://www.uwstamboomonline.nl/passie/sites /index.php?mid=201966&kid=2147&pagina=tekstpagina, accessed October 8, 2019.
Rubroek [Rubrouck; Rubruk; Ruysbroeck], William of. *The Text and Versions of John de Plano Carpini and William de Rubruquis as Printed for the First Time by Hakluyt in 1598 together with Some Shorter Pieces*. Ed. C. Raymond Beazley. London: Hakluyt Society, 1903.
——— . "Puteshestvie v Vostochnye strany Vil'gel'ma de Rubruk v leto Blagosti 1253." Available at: http://www.hist.msu.ru/ER/Etext/rubruk.htm, accessed September 30, 2019.
Rude and Barbarous Kingdom: Russia in the Accounts of Sixteenth-Century English Voyagers. Eds. L.E. Berry and Robert O. Crummey. Madison, WI: U. of Wisconsin P., 1968.
Russia seu Moskovia itemque Tartaria commentario topographico atque politico illustratae. Leiden: Elzevier, 1630.
[Russian Embassy in the Netherlands on Russian-Dutch economic ties]. Available at: https://netherlands.mid.ru/web/netherlands-en/economic-relations, accessed October 20, 2019.
Salvo, M. Di. *Italia, Russia e mondo slavo: studi filologici e letterari*. Florence: Firenze UP, 2011.
Saveleva, E.A. "Andrei Andreevich Vinius, ego biblioteka i albom." In *Rossiia-Gollandiia: Knizhnye sviazy xv-xx vv*. Ed. N.P. Kopanev. St. Petersburg: Evropeiskii Dom, 2000: 103–23.
Schade, Hans. *Die Niederlande und Russland: Handel und Aufnahme diplomatischer Kontakte zu Anfang des 17. Jahrhunderts*. Frankfurt am Main: Peter Lang, 1992.
Schama, S. *The Embarrassment of Riches*. Berkeley, CA: U. of California P., 1988.
Scheltjens, Werner. *De invloed van ruimtelijke verandering op operationele strategieën in de vroeg-moderne Nederalndse scheepvaart*. Eelde: Barkhuis, 2009.
Scheltema, J. *Peter de Groote, keizer van Rusland in Holland en te Zaandam in 1697 en 1717*. 2 vols. Amsterdam: Hendrik Gartman, 1814.
——— . *Rusland en de Nederlanden*. 4 vols. Amsterdam: Hendrik Gartman, 1817–1819.

Schmidt, Benjamin. *Innocence Abroad.* Cambridge: Cambridge UP, 2001.
Shamin, S.M. "Formirovanie vneshnepoliticheskikh predstavlenii Petra I i vypiski iz kurantov 1690–1693 godov." *Rossiiskaia istoriia* 4, 2012: 111–20.
———. *Kuranty XVII stoletiia: Evropeiskaia pressa v Rossii i voznikovenie russkoi periodicheskoi pechati.* Moscow: Al'ians-Arkheo, 2011.
Shields-Kollmann, N. *Crime and Punishment in Early Modern Russia.* Cambridge: Cambridge UP, 2012.
———. *By Honor Bound.* Ithaca, NY: Cornell UP, 1999.
———. "Law and Society in Early Modern Russia." In *The Cambridge History of Russia.* Vol. 1. Ed. Maureen Perrie. Cambridge: Cambridge UP, 2006: 559–78.
Skazaniia inostrannykh pisatelei o Rossii, izdannye Arkheograficheskoiu komisseiu, vol. 2: *Izvestiia gollandtsev Isaaka Massy i Il'i Gerkmanna* [St. Petersburg], 1868, 129–76. Available at: http://www.vostlit.info/Texts/rus13/Gerkman/text1.phtml?id=337, accessed November 12, 2019; and http://www.vostlit.info/Texts/rus13/Gerkman/text2.phtml?id=338, accessed November 12, 2019.
Skrynnikov, R.G. *Mikhail Romanov*, Moscow: AST, 2005.
———. *Velikii gosudar Ioann Vaislevich Groznyi.* 2 vols. Smolensk: Rusich, 1996.
Solov'eva, T.B. *Dokumenty o sviaziakh Rossii i Niderlandov v fondakh Rossiiskogo Gosudarstvennogo Arkhiva Drevnikh Aktov. Spravochnik.* Moscow: Manufaktura, 1999.
Soloviev, S.M. *History of Russia.* Vol. 26. Ed. and trans. L. Hughes. Gulf Breeze, FL: Academic International Press, 1994.
———. *History of Russia.* Vol. 28. Ed. and trans. L.A.J. Hughes. Gulf Breeze, FL: Academic International Press, 2007.
Spies, Marijke. *Arctic Routes to Fabled Lands: Oliver Brunel and the Passage to China and Cathay in the Sixteenth Century.* Amsterdam: Amsterdam UP, 1996.
———. *Bij noorden om: Olivier Brunel en de doorvaart naar China en Cathay in de zestiende eeuw.* Amsterdam: Amsterdam UP, 1994.
Stevens, Carol Belkin. *Russia's Wars of Emergence, 1460–1730.* New York: Harlow, Pearson, 2007.
Stoppelaar, J.H. de. *Balthasar de Moucheron. Een bladzijde uit de Nederlandse handelsgeschiedenis tijdens den Tachtigjarigen oorlog*, 's-Gravenhage: Nijhoff, 1901.
Strahlenberg, Philip Johann von. *Das nord und ostliche Theil von . . . das ganze Rußische Reich mit Siberien . . . .* Stockholm: By the author, 1730.
Struys, Jan Janszoon. *Drie aanmerkelijke en seer rampspoedige reysen.* Amsterdam: J. van Meurs en J. Van Someren, 1676.
———. *Rampspoedige reizen door Rusland en Perzië in de zeventiende eeuw.* Ed. Kees Boterbloem. Amsterdam: Panchaud, 2014.
Swart, Erik. *Krijgsvolk: Militaire professionalisering en het ontstaan van het Staatse leger, 1568–1590.* Amsterdam: Amsterdam UP, 2006.
Tavernier, Roger. *Russia and the Low Countries: An International Bibliography, 1500–2000.* Groningen: Barkhuis, 2006.
"Terugblik Nederland-Ruslandjaar 2013." Available at: https://www.rijksoverheid.nl/documenten/brochures/2014/06/11/terugblik-nederland-ruslandjaar-2013, accessed January 8, 2020.

Thyret, I. *Between God and Tsar*. DeKalb, IL: Northern Illinois UP, 2001.
Tielhof, Milja van. *The "Mother of All Trades": The Baltic Grain Trade in Amsterdam from the Late Sixteenth to the Early Nineteenth Centuries*. Leiden: Brill, 2002.
Titlestad, T. *Tsarskii admiral Kornelis Kriuis na sluzhbe Petra Velikogo*. Sankt-Peterburg: Russko-Baltiiskii informatsionnyi tsentr "Blits", 2003.
Tolstoi, P. *The Travel Diary of Peter Tolstoi: A Muscovite in Early Modern Europe*. Ed. and trans. M. Okenfuss. DeKalb, IL: Northern Illinois UP, 1987.
Tri puteshestviia Ia.Ia. Streis. Ed. A. Morozov and trans. E. Borodina. Moscow: Sotsgiz, 1935.
Tsvetaev, D. *Protestantstvo i protestanty v Rossii do epokhi preobrazovanii*. Moscow: Universitetskaia tipografiia, 1890.
Tushin, Iu.P. *Russkoe moreplavanie na Kaspiiskom, Azovskom i Chernom Moriakh*. Moskva: Nauka, 1978.
Uhlenbeck, C.C. "Rusland omtrent het midden der zeventiende eeuw." *De Gids* 55, 1891: 38–81.

———. *Verslag aangaande een onderzoek van de archieven van Rusland ten bate der Nederlandsche geschiedenis*. Den Haag: Nijhoff, 1891.
Unkovskaya, M. "Samuel Collins." *Oxford Dictionary of National Biography*. Available at: https://doi-org.ezproxy.lib.usf.edu/10.1093/ref:odnb/5951, accessed October 2, 2019.
Ustrialov, N.G. *Istoriia Tsarstvovaniia Petra Velikogo*. 6 vols. St. Petersburg: Imperial Printing House, 1858–1863.
"Valkenburch, Margaretha van (1565–1650)." [Stefan Kras] *Digitaal Vrouwenlexicon van Nederland*. Available at: http://resources.huygens.knaw.nl/vrouwenlexicon/lemmata/data/Valkenburch, accessed January 14, 2020.
Vein, Alla, "Nicolaas Bidloo, the Dutch Director of the First Hospital in Russia: A 300-Year Anniversary." *Nederlands Tijdschrift voor Geneeskunde*, January 2008: 2909–12.
Veluvenkamp, Ia.V. "Kompaniia 'de Vogelar i Klenk' v gollandsko-russkikh kommercheskikh otnosheniiakh xvii v." In *Niderlandy i Severnaia Rossiia*. Eds Iu. N. Bespiatnikh et al. St. Petersburg: Russko-Baltiiskii informatsionnyi Tsentr, 2003: 37–73.
Veluwenkamp, J.W. *Archangel. Nederlandse ondernemers in Rusland, 1550–1785*. Amsterdam: Balans, 2000.

———. "'N huis op Archangel'. De Amsterdamse koopmansfamilie Thesingh, 1650–1725." *Jaarboek Amstelodamum* 69, 1977: 123–39.

———. "Dutch Merchants in St. Petersburg in the Eighteenth Century." *Tijdschrift voor Skandinavistiek* 2, 1995: 236–331.

———. "Familienetwerken binnen de Nederlandse koopliedengemeenschap van Archangel in de eerste helft van de achttiende eeuw." *Bijdragen en Mededelingen betreffende de Geschiedenis der Nederlanden* 4, 1993: 655–72.

———. "Kaufmännisches Verhalten und Familiennetzwerke im niederländischen Russlandhandel (1590–1750)." In *Praktiken des Handels. Geschäfte und soziale Beziehungen europäischer Kaufleute in Mittelalter und früher Neuzeit*. Eds. M. Häberlein and C. Jeggle. Konstanz: UVK, 2010: 379–405.

———. "De Nederlandse wapenhandel op Rusland in de zeventiende eeuw." *Armamentaria* 31, 1996: 71–6.

Venevitinov, M.A. *Russkie v Gollandii. Velikoe posol'stvo 1697–1698 goda.* Moscow: O.O. Gerben, 1898.

Vesti-Kuranty 1656 g., 1660–1662 gg., 1664–1670 gg. Eds Ingrid Maier et al. Vol. 1: *Russkie teksty.* Moskva: Iazyki slavianskikh kul'tur, 2009.

Vesti-Kuranty 1671–1672 gg. Eds Ingrid Maier and V.B. Krys'ko. Moskva: Azbukovnik, 2017.

Viskovatov, A. *Kratkii istoricheskii obzor morskikh pokhodov russkikh i morekhodstva ikh voobshche do iskhoda XVII stoletiia.* Sankt Peterburg: Morskoi istoricheskii sbornik, 1994 [First ed.: Moscow, 1946].

Vries, Jan de. *The Industrious Revolution: Consumer Behavior and the Household Economy, 1650 to the Present.* Cambridge: Cambridge UP, 2008.

Vries J. de, and A. van der Woude. *The First Modern Economy: Success, Failure and Perseverance of the Dutch Economy, 1500–1815,* Cambridge: Cambridge UP, 1997.

Vugt, Ingeborg van. "Giovacchino Guasconi as Book Agent between the Dutch Republic and the Grand Duchy of Tuscany." Unpubl. MA Thesis. Leiden University, 2014.

Waegemans, Emmanuel. "De taal van Peter de Grote: het Nederlands als wereldtaal——— een gemiste kans?" In *De taal van Peter de Grote.* Ed. E. Waegemans. Leuven: Acco, 2006, 11–15.

———. *De tsaar van Groot Rusland in de Republiek. De tweede reis van Peter de Grote naar Nederland (1716–1717).* Groningen, Antwerpen: Benerus, 2013.

Wallerstein, I. *The Modern World System.* 4 vols. Rev. ed. Berkeley, CA: U. of California P., 2011.

[Wallhausen, Johann Jacobi von], *Uchenie i khitrost' ratnogo stroeniia pekhotnykh liudei.* Moscow: Moskovskii pechatnyi dvor, 1647.

Waugh, Daniel Clarke. "The Publication of Muscovite *Kuranty*." *Kritika: A Review of Current Soviet Books on Russian History* 3, 1973: 104–20.

Weber, Max. "Die Protestantische Ethik und der Geist des Kapitalismus." In *Gesammelte Aufsätze zur Religionssoziologie,* Ed. M. Weber, Vol. 1. Tübingen: J.C.B. Mohr, 1922: 17–206.

Willan, T.S. *The Early History of the Russia Company, 1553–1603.* Manchester: Manchester UP, 1968.

———. *The Muscovy Merchants of 1555.* Manchester: Manchester UP, 1953.

Witsen, Nicolaas. *Aeloude en hedendaegsche scheeps-bouw en bestier: waer in wijtloopigh wert verhandelt, de wijze van scheeps-timmeren, ...* Amsterdam: Casparus Commelijn, 1671.

———. *Architectura navalis et Regimen Nauticum. Ofte Aaloude en Hedendaagsche Scheeps-Bouw en Bestier . . . .* Amsterdam: Pieter and Joan Blaeu, 1690.

———. *Moscovische reyse 1664–5: Journaal en aentekeningen.* 3 vols. Eds. Th. Locher and P. de Buck. Den Haag: Nijhoff, 1966–1967.

———. *Noord en Oost Tartarye, ofte bondig ontwerp van eenige dier landen en volken, welke voormaels bekent zijn geweest . . . .* Amsterdam: N.p., 1692 [Second ed.: Amsterdam: F. Halma, 1705].

Wittram, Reinhard. *Peter I, Czar und Kaiser: Zur Geschichte Peter des Grossen in seiner Zeit*. Göttingen: Vandenhoeck und Ruprecht, 1964.

Wladimiroff, I. *De kaart van een verzwegen vriendschap: Nicolaes Witsen en Andrej Winius en de Nederlandse cartografie van Rusland*. Groningen: Instituut voor Noord- en Oost-Europese Studies, 2008.

[*The World of Patrick Gordon*]. Special Issue of the *Journal of Irish and Scottish Studies* 2, 2014. Ed. Paul Dukes.

Worp, J.A. van. "Elias Herckmans." *Oud Holland* 11, 1893: 162–78.

———. "Herckmans, Elias." In *Nieuw Nederlandsch Biografisch Woordenboek*. Eds P.J. Blok and P.C Mohlhuysen. Leiden: Sijthoff, 1911, vol. 3: 579–80.

Wijnroks, E. *Handel tussen Rusland en de Nederlanden 1560–1640: Een netwerkanalyse van de Antwerpse en Amsterdamse kooplieden, handelend op Rusland*. Hilversum: Verloren, 2003.

Zabelin, I. *Domashnii byt' Russkikh' tsarei*. 2 vols. Second ed.: Moskva: Grachev i kompaniia, 1872.

Zandt, Christiaan. "Nederlanders en Siberië 1665–1725." Unpubl. MA thesis. University of Groningen, 1997.

Zitser, Ernest A. *The Transfigured Kingdom: Sacred Parody and Charismatic Authority at the Court of Peter the Great*. Ithaca, NY: Cornell University Press, 2004.

———. "The Vita of Prince Boris Ivanovich 'Korybut'-Kurakin: Personal Life-Writing and Aristocratic Self-Fashioning at the Cort of Peter the Great." *Jahrbücher für Geschichte Osteuropas* 2, 2011: 163–94.

Zuiden, D.S. van. *Bijdrage tot de kennis der Hollandsch-Russische relaties van de 16e tot de 18e eeuw*. Amsterdam: Gebroeders Binger, 1911.

———. "Nieuwe bijdrage tot de kennis van de Hollandsch-Russische relaties in de 16e-18e eeuw." *Economisch-Historisch Jaarboek* 2, 1916: 258–95.

Index

Aansprekersoproer (1697), 108–109
Abbas I, the Great, shah of Iran, 77
Aberdeenshire, 148
absolutism, 138
Academy of Sciences (Russia), 32, 171, 177, 195
Act of Abjuration (Plakkaat van Verlatinghe), 8
Ad(e)l(a)er, Kurt (Cort) Sivertsen, 193
Aeloude en Hedendaegsche Scheepsbouw (Witsen), 164, 167
Africa, 68, 104, 169
agriculture, 35, 86–87
alchemy, 91
alderman (*schepen*; judge), 57
Aleksei Alekseevich, tsarevich, 136
Aleksei Mikhailovich, tsar of Russia, 6, 18, 28–30, 69, 93, 95–96, 105–106, 110, 113–16, 125, 129–30, 135–40, 144, 156, 159, 161, 163, 183, 204–205
Aleksei Petrovich, tsarevich, 61, 64
Alexander I, tsar of Russia, 3
Akema (Ackema, Akkema), Lus Tieleman, 91, 99, 101, 148
Aleppo, 79
Alexander Nevsky, Eastern Slavonic prince, 37
All Drunken Assembly (Peter the Great), 61, 162

Amburger, Erik, 2, 5–6, 14
American Association of University Professors (AAUP), ix, xi
Americas, 39, 104, 149
Amirev, Ivan, 29
ammunition, 29, 48, 78, 113. *See also* gunpowder
Amsterdam, 4, 8, 26, 29, 39, 41, 43, 46, 57, 59, 73–79, 83, 85–86, 89, 91, 96–97, 100–102, 106, 108–10, 122, 132, 138–39, 147, 152–56, 161–66, 169–70, 182, 187–90, 193–95, 203, 205–7
Amsterdam city council (*vroedschap*), 57, 70, 152, 169
Amsterdam notarial archives, 83, 140
anabaptism, 36, 91. *See also* Mennonites
Anglo-Dutch Wars, 29–30, 104, 109
Anna Pavlovna, queen of the Netherlands, 3
Antwerp (Antwerpen), 8, 25–26, 39, 41–43, 46, 48, 106, 132, 206
apothecary, 82, 91–93, 95–97, 100, 124. *See also Aptekarskii prikaz*
Aptekarskii prikaz, 82, 93, 95–96, 100
apprentices. *See* artisans
Apraksin, Fyodor, 181
Architectura Navalis (Witsen), 164, 167

Index

Archive of Ancient Acts (Moscow; *RGADA--Rossiiskii Gosudartsvennyi Arkhiv Drevnikh Aktov--*), vii–viii, 5
archives, vii–viii, xi, 5, 41, 110, 139, 202. *See also* documents
Arctic Circle, 45, 85
Arctic Ocean (Sea), 160
Areskine (Erskine), Robert, 177
Arkhangel'sk, 3, 9, 14, 15, 21, 24–29, 41–46, 48–49, 55, 62, 68, 73–75, 77, 79–83, 85–88, 92–94, 96–97, 100, 109, 116, 118, 121, 124–25, 127–28, 130–31, 134, 137, 144, 152–53, 161–62, 176–77, 187–90, 194, 198
armed forces. *See* army; cavalry; infantry; military; navy
Armenia, 73
Armenians, 74, 79–80, 105, 156
Arminians, 76
arms dealers. *See* arms traders
arms export, 47–48, 86–89, 113, 117, 129, 188
arms manufacturing, 28, 47, 82, 89, 144
arms trade, 10, 29, 40, 47–48, 57, 67, 69, 74–77, 82, 86–90, 102, 108, 129, 135, 152, 182
arms traders, 29, 57–58, 82, 108, 135, 152, 182. *See also* arms trade
army, 24, 28–31, 37, 76, 78, 95, 100, 114, 117, 124, 145, 154, 158, 170, 177, 182, 202
army size, 76
art, 97, 189, 195. *See also* Bruin; Hals; Hooghe; Rembrandt; Schoonebeeck; Vermeer
artisans, 10, 35–36, 61, 113, 122–25, 130, 189
artillery, 143, 171. *See also* cannon
Artois, province of, 23–24
Ashkenazi Jews, 4
Asia, 3, 25–26, 37, 39, 73, 79–80, 97, 104, 152–53, 160, 164
Asperen, Abraham van, interpreter, 153, 158
Assen, 202

Astrakhan, 30, 101, 105, 116–17, 143–44, 153, 205
astrolabe, 95, 162
astrology, 91
Atlantic Ocean, 104, 108, 189
Austria, 24, 31–32, 104, 157, 159, 181, 207
Austrian Netherlands. *See* southern Netherlands
Avvakum, 7, 184
Azov, 31–32, 114–15, 149, 163, 176

Bacheracht, David, 110, 118
Baibakov, Ivan, *d'iak*, 28, 135
Baklanovskii, Ivan, 76–77
ballast, 41, 132
ballistics, 162
Baltic peoples, 36–37
Baltic Sea (and region), 8, 23, 27, 36–37, 39, 41, 46–47, 60, 62–63, 68, 74–75, 81, 85, 87–88, 152, 158, 164, 181, 185, 189–90, 193
Bandar-e-Abbas, 79
bankruptcy, 48, 56
baptism, 80
Barbary corsairs, 169
barrels. *See* vats
Bartolotti, Guillelmo (Willem van den Heuvel), 85, 89
Barts, Matthijs, 187
Bas, Dirck, 27, 75
Battle of the Downs (Duins), 28
Battle of Gangut (Hangö), 32, 117
Battle of the Ice (Lake Peipus), 37
Battle of Narva (1700), 32
Battle of Poltava, 32
Battle of Quatre-Bras, 3
Battle of the Pruth, 32, 53
Battle of Waterloo, 3
Becker, Bruno, 4, 13
Bek, A. Kh., 2
Belarussians, 37
Belgium, 4, 24, 202. *See also* southern Netherlands; Artois; Brabant; Flanders; Hainault; Liège

Belkin Stevens, Carol, 6, 114
bell founders (casters), 114, 118
Belov, Mikhail Ivanovich, 4
Bengal, 206
Berezina, 201
Bering, Vitus, 194
Berlin, 110, 138
Berlin, Isaiah, 205
Bernard (s, Bernaerts/Bernart), Daniël, 57–58, 82–83, 90, 110, 169
Bernard(s, Bernaerts/Bernart), Jacques, 46, 48, 57–58
Bernard (s, Bernaerts/Bernart), Jan (Jean), 57–58, 82–83, 90, 110
Bezemer, Jan-Willem, xiii, 13–14, 203
Bible, 35, 62
Bicker, Jacob, 43
Bicker family, 43, 46, 110
Bidloo, Nicolaas, 95
Biels (Bijls) Jr, Valentijn, 94, 96–97
Biels (Bijls) Sr, Valentijn, 92, 94, 96–98
Bitter, de, Amsterdam trading family, 43
Bitter, Jan de, 46
Black Death (bubonic plague pandemic), 23, 37
Black Sea. *See* Azov; Crimean Tatars
blacksmiths, 189
blast furnaces, 28
Bliumentrost, I. L., 177
Bobinin, Vasilii, *d'iak*, 136
Bockhoven, Cornelis van, 28, 30, 144, 159, 175–76, 205
Bockhoven, Isaac van, 28, 115–16, 176
Bockhoven, Katerina van, 156, 175
Bockhoven, Philips Albrecht van, 28, 175–76
Bockhoven clan, 7, 28, 115–16, 124, 148, 156, 175–77, 204
Boeck, Brian, 8
Boer, Leo de, 98
Bogaert, Cornelis, 155
Bogoslovskii, Mikhail, 3
Bol, Ferdinand, 139
Bolsheviks, 202. *See also* Communists

bombardir (gunner), 1, 172
Bommel, Elias van, 91
book printing, 1, 8, 28, 36, 115, 163, 172, 187, 195
Boreel, Jacob Willemszoon, vii, ix, xi–xii, 9, 29, 69, 100–11, 113, 117, 121, 127–29, 132–35, 139, 152–54, 162–64, 169, 176, 204–205
Boreel, Willem, 108
Boris Godunov, Russian tsar, 92
Boss, Valentin, xiii
Boston University, viii
botik, 117, 165
boyars (Russian high nobles), 30, 51, 56, 69, 86, 158, 171, 181, 183
Brabant, duchy of, 8, 23–24, 26, 41, 46, 56, 115
Brandenburg. *See* Prussia
Brands, Maarten, xiii
Brandt, Karsten, 1, 3, 30–31, 99, 117, 135, 143–45, 154, 160, 163–65, 170, 205
Brants, Christoffel, 106, 161–62, 187–90, 201, 204
Brants, Enno, 187
Brants, Helena, 188
Braudel, Fernand, 6–7
Brazil, 60, 104
Brederode embassy. *See* Brederode
Brederode, Reinout van, 27, 69, 75–76, 78, 108, 151
Breemburch, Quirijn, 94
Bremen, 102, 106, 152
Breukelen, 149
bribery. *See* corruption
brick, 82, 123, 144
British civil wars, 28, 89, 108, 118
British-Russian landing in Holland (1799), 201
Brius, Iakov Viliminovich, 115, 177
broadsheets (broadsides), 60
Brooklyn, 149
Brown, Peter B., xiii, 8
Bruce, William, 115
Bruges (Brugge), 37, 39, 92

Bruin, Cornelis de, 7, 19, 32, 60, 172, 188–89
Brunel, Olivier, 12, 25–26, 42–44
Brussels, 42
Buck, Piet de, 4, 14, 205
Bukhara, 25, 73
Bulavin rebellion, 32
bulk trade, 41, 47, 81, 88, 130
bullion, 41, 44, 47, 88, 137, 184
Buren, Martin van, 149
Burgh, Albert, 28, 69, 86, 97, 133
Burgh, Coenraad, 28, 132–33, 204
Burgundian Circle (*Burgundischer Kreis*), 24, 35
Burgundian-Valois enmity, 103
Burgundy, duchy of, 23–24, 35, 37–40
Bushkovitch, Paul, 6, 16, 19, 166
business, 42, 46, 48, 55–58, 68, 77, 79–83, 85, 87, 99–100, 102, 110, 121, 123, 130–31, 147–48, 154, 156, 159, 161, 166, 187–91, 193. *See also* arms traders; entrepreneurship; merchants
Butenant (von Rosenbusch), Heinrich (Andrei), 155
Butler, David, 5, 14, 101, 117, 135, 153, 145
Buturlin, Ivan, 181
Byzantine Empire, 23, 38, 154

Calvinism, 25–26, 36, 41, 57, 79, 97–98, 106, 123–24, 147–48, 156, 175–76
Campense, Alberto (Albert Pigge), 39–40
Candian War, 103
Cannegieter, Koenraet, 155
cannon, 114, 119, 144, 163
Cape of Good Hope, 68, 104
capitalism, 10, 57, 99, 202 *See also* business; trade
caravan route, 73
carbines, 113
Carlisle embassy, 106–107, 110, 139
cartels, 44. *See also* monopolies
cartography, 26, 109, 160, 166–67

cash 10, 27, 41–42, 46, 137. *See also* bullion
Caspian Sea, 13, 25, 30, 74, 79–80, 87, 93, 105, 116–17, 119, 135, 143–44, 153, 160, 165
Castile. *See* Spain
Cathay, 26. *See also* China
Catherine I, empress of Russia, 31
Catholic Reformation (Counterreformation), 40, 68. *See also* Catholicism; Jesuits; Council of Trent
Catholicism, 35, 38, 40, 63, 68, 92, 103, 115, 148, 156, 162, 170, 175–76, 178
Cats, Jacob, 56
Caucasus, 74, 143, 153, 157
cavalry, 115, 118, 163
caviar, 41, 89
Central Asia, 25, 73, 97, 164
Ceylon. *See* Sri Lanka
Chaadaev, Pyotr, 178
chancellery script (*skoropis'*), 4
Chancellor, Richard, 25, 39
chargé-d'affaires, 73
Charlemagne, 40
Charles the Bold, duke of Burgundy, 24, 38, 40
Charles I, king of England, 29, 88, 107–108, 118
Charles II, king of England, 106, 110, 118, 137, 139
Charles V, Holy Roman Emperor and king of Spain (as Carlos I), 35
Charles XII, king of Sweden, 32
chartering (of merchant ships), 43, 96, 187
Chekhov, Anton, 206
Cherkasskii, Ivan Borisovich, 86
China, 18, 30, 104, 156, 160, 164
Christianity, 23, 37, 63, 82, 96, 122, 125, 157. *See also* Anabaptism; Calvinism; Catholicism; Lutheranism; Mennonites; Russian Orthodoxy
Christina, queen of Sweden, 135–36

Index

Church Council of 1666-1667 (Russian Orthodox Church), 29, 105, 125
Chyhyryn, 30, 114, 159, 176
civil guard (*schutters*). *See* militia
civilisation process (Norbert Elias), 61–62
Claesz(.), Cornelis, 114
clans. *See* networks
class conflict, 70
clergy (Catholic, Netherlands), 35
clergy (Russian Orthodox), 38, 51, 122, 170–71
climate, 45–46. *See also* weather
Cloeck, Gillis, 155
cloth, 102. *See also* textiles
Coehoorn, Menno van, 10
coffins, 171
Cold War, ix, xi, 4, 203
Collins, Samuel, 129–30, 132
Cologne (Köln, Keulen), 30, 102
collective mindset, 53. *See also* Dutch national identity; nationalism
Columbia University (New York), viii–ix
Columbus (Christobal Colon, explorer), 38
commissary of naval matters (affairs; Amsterdam), 57
commoners, 153
communication networks, 36, 100. *See also* mail; post master
Communism, ix, 14, 202–203, 206
Communistische Partij van Holland/Nederland (CPH/CPN). *See* Dutch Communist Party
Communists (Soviet-Russian), ix, 14, 202–203, 206
Concert of Europe, 103, 108, 171
Congress of Vienna, 201
constable (gunner, artillerist), 143, 153–54, 172
Constantinople, 23, 38
consumer goods, 63
contracts, 49, 83, 92, 114, 153
convoying, 116, 131, 189–90

cooper, 187
Cooymans family, 108
Copenhagen, 29, 68, 110, 147
copper, 29, 100, 145
Copper Riots (Moscow 1662), 29
corruption, 44, 56, 127, 164
corsairs, 131, 169
Cossacks, 15, 26, 29, 96, 116–17, 138, 143, 145
Council of Florence, 23, 38
Council of Trent, 40
Court, Pieter de la, 125
Coyett, Balthasar, 7, 19, 30, 60, 124, 153, 157, 205
Coyett, Julius, 82, 99, 153
Cracraft, James, 6, 16
credit, 10, 99
Crete. *See* Candian War
Crimean campaigns (1687 and 1689), 31, 160, 169–70
Crimean conflict (2014), 207
Crimean Tatars, 39, 69, 100, 137–38, 151, 159, 170. *See also* Tatars
criminality, 59
Croiset van der Kop, A., 6, 12
crop cultivation. *See* agriculture
crusades (in eastern Europe), 36–37
Cruys, Cornelis (Niels Olufsen Creutz), 96, 177, 193–95
curiosity cabinets, 6, 172, 189, 195. *See also Kunstkammer*

Dale, de la, family, 44, 58
Dam, Hendrik van, 89, 189
Danckaert, J.P., 60, 64, 78
Danes. *See* Denmark
Danzig (Gdansk), 41
Dartmouth College, 8
Davies, Brian, 6, 114
Day of Judgment, 94
Dedinovo, 29–30, 116
Delden, 161
Delft, 26
Demkin, A. V., 6, 121, 124
demography. *See* population

Denmark, 18, 29, 62, 68–69, 76, 103, 121, 125, 138, 151, 159, 193–94
dentistry, 171
Deventer, 23, 37, 118
d'iak (secretary, clerk), 28, 67, 86, 107, 110, 135–36, 140, 144, 158, 165, 169, 172, 181
diaries, 4, 7, 9, 109, 148, 175–76, 178, 189, 205
diets, 121
Diggs, Dudley, 77
Dillenburg, 57
diplomacy, 10–11, 24, 44, 67–71, 74–76, 78, 81, 86, 88, 102, 107–108, 129–31, 134–41, 153–54, 158, 160–63, 166, 170, 181–82, 184, 189
Directorate of Muscovite Trade, 131, 189
disease, 45, 96, 115. *See also* Black Death; epidemics
dissection, 171
dissidents (Soviet), 203
Dixon, Simon, 8
Dmitrii, First False. *See* First False Dmitrii
doctors. *See* medical doctors
documents (archival, ego-documents) 2, 5, 7, 11, 15, 18, 83, 121, 125, 153, 157, 164, 176, 183–84, 190
Dokhturov, Gerasim, 110, 140, 144
Dokkum, 86, 90
Donbas, 194
Dordt (Dordrecht), Synod of, 76, 152
Dostoyevsky, F.M., 184, 206
Drie aanmerkelijke en rampspoedige Reysen (Struys), 96, 144
Driessen(-van het Reve), Jozien, 6, 63, 165, 171, 195
drill, 28, 115, 204
dumnyi d'iak, 158, 165, 169, 181
Dumschat, Sabine, 95–96
Dunning, Chester, xiii, 8
Dutch Communist Party (*CPH, CPN*), 202–203, 206

Dutch decline, 9, 47, 104, 173, 178, 184, 197–98
Dutch diplomacy. *See* Brederode; Bas; Boreel; Burgh; diplomacy; Heins(ius); Joachimi; Keller; Klenck; Massa; Veltdriel; Witsen
Dutch East India Company. *See* VOC
Dutch economic boom, 9, 26–27, 39, 41–48, 55–56, 124
Dutch education minister, 12
Dutch government. *See* Estates-General
Dutch (economic) hegemony, 77
Dutch language as *lingua franca*, 6, 62, 164, 185
Dutch national identity, 35–36, 102, 106, 148, 155–56. *See also* Klenck; loyalty; Massa; Sweeden; Winius
Dutch Primacy in World Trade (Israel), 198
Dutch Revolt, 25–26. *See also* Eighty Years' War
Dutch shipping, 1, 10, 26–27, 68, 85, 88, 102, 139, 188–90, 197–98
Dutch trade, volume and value of, 4, 13, 41, 47, 56, 81, 88, 128, 139, 198, 205
Dvina (northern), 25–26, 39, 41–44, 49. *See also* Arkhangel'sk
dvor'ianin, 67, 107
dyslexia, 172
Dzungaria, 206

Eagle (Oryol), 29–30, 116–18, 125, 140, 143–45, 153–54, 165, 205
East Asia, 3, 39, 73, 104, 160
Eastern European studies, 4–5, 8, 203
Eastland Trade. *See* mother trade
economic crisis, 45
economic growth, 9, 46
Edict of Fontainebleau, 31, 156, 162
Edict of Nantes, 26
education, 21, 36, 91–93, 95, 115, 117, 130, 139, 161, 171–72, 183, 187, 194–95, 203, 206

Eekman, Thomas, 3
ego-documents. *See* Avvakum; documents; Gordon; Tolstoi; Witsen
Eighty Years' War, 8, 9, 88, 133
Eisenstein, Sergei, 37
embassies (purpose of), 3, 9–10, 20, 27–31, 60, 69–70, 74–78, 85–87, 93, 95, 101, 103–105, 108–10, 117, 121–22, 131, 133, 135, 139, 151–55, 157–58, 161, 163–64, 170, 174, 177, 181–84, 188, 194, 204–205, 207. *See also* diplomacy
Emden, 106
émigres (Russian), 4, 202
Elias, Norbert, 61–62
Elizabeth I, queen of England, 91, 96
Elsevier publishers, 60
emigration, 46, 202
England, 3, 4, 10, 13, 25–26, 28–30, 39, 41–45, 48–50, 52, 58, 60, 62, 67, 69, 75, 77–79, 86, 88, 91–92, 103–104, 106–10, 118, 121, 124, 129, 132, 134–35, 137–38, 154, 157, 170, 172–73, 181–84
English (people). *See* England
Enkhuizen, 20, 26, 93
entrepreneurs, 6, 25–27, 29, 41–42, 56, 89, 99–102, 116, 118, 130, 144, 147–8, 155, 160, 163
environment. *See* climate
epidemics, 96. *See also* Black Death; disease
Epiphany, 188
Erskine. *See* Areskine
Esper, Thomas, 8
espionage, 81, 154, 163
Estates-General (Burgundian), 23
Estates-General (northern Dutch), 28, 44, 56, 61, 67–68, 70–71, 73–76, 78, 81, 83, 85–87, 90, 93, 101–102, 107–10, 118, 128, 135, 138, 143, 147, 157, 161–62, 169–70, 174, 185, 188, 205
Estonia, 75
etching, 152, 163, 171, 195

Eternal Peace (between Poland and Russia, 1686), 31
ethics, 56, 124
Eurasia, 164
European Union, 203
Eylof, Johan, 42–43, 63, 91, 96, 148
Eylof, Joris, 96

Fabricius (Faber), Ludvig (Ludwig/Lodewijk), 5, 14–15, 80, 117, 143–44, 154, 205
factors (agents), 25, 47, 100, 109, 124, 132, 161–62
factory (*factorij*/station), 26
Falck, Hans, 114, 118
famine, 45
Fankerin, Ivan, 155
Far'ium, Ivan (Jan van Ruim?), 155
favourites, 177–78
Fentzel (Fentsel/Fenzel), Hendrick, 48–50
Fentzel, Herman, 50
Filaret (Fyodor Nikitich Romanov), Russian patriarch, 27, 77, 89, 127
financiers, 46, 123, 169, 187–88
Finland, 198
Finnish Gulf, 194
firearms, 28–29, 115. *See also* artillery; cannon; muskets
fireworks, 182
First False Dmitrii (*Lzhedmitrii*), 27
First World War, 3
fishing, 35, 39, 41, 78
flag, 1, 10
Flanders, 8, 20–21, 23–26, 26, 41–50, 135
Fletcher, Giles, 45, 60
Florence, 23, 38, 158
Floria, B. N., 6
fortification, 114, 171
fortress builders, 114
France, 9–10, 26–27, 30–32, 38, 69, 75, 86
Franche-Comté (Free County of Burgundy), 40

236   *Index*

Franco-Dutch War (French-Dutch War, 1672-1678), 9, 30, 51, 116, 137–38, 152–53
Frederick (Friedrich, ship), 118–19
Frederick I, king of Prussia (previously, Frederick III of Brandenburg-Prussia), 152
Frederick Henry (Frederik Hendrik, van Oranje-Nassau, *de Stedendwinger*), 27
Frederick William of Hohenzollern, the Great Elector, 104
free trade, 73
French Revolution, 197, 201
Friedrich III, Duke of Holstein-Gottorf, 93
Friesland (Frisia, province), 12, 23, 29, 67, 86, 89–91, 94, 96, 106–107, 157, 164–65, 187
Frisian (language), 35
Frost, Robert (historian), 6, 114
Frosten, Jakob van, 116
Fuhrmann, Joseph, 6, 99
furs, 27, 94, 130, 132, 137
Fyodor (Fedor) I, tsar of Muscovy, 26, 45, 92
Fyodor (Fedor) III, tsar of Muscovy, 30, 69, 156–57, 159, 163, 183

galan(t)skaia kniga ("Holland Book"), 62–63, 121
Galen, Bernhard von, bishop of Münster, 30
galley ships, 144
gangrene, 94
gardens, 93, 95, 123, 188, 195, 207
Gecommitteerden voor de Oostersche Handel, 189
Geer, Louis (Louys) de, 89
Gein, Boris, 155
Gelderland. *See* Guelders
gemstones, 82, 88, 125, 145
gender. *See* women
generals (army), 176–77, 181. *See also* Gordon

Geneva (Genève), 116, 175, 177–78
Gentlemen Seventeen (Heeren XVII; VOC directors), 57, 164
geography. *See* Arctic Sea; Atlantic; Caspian Sea; Caucasus; climate; Dvina; North Sea; Urals; Volga; weather
Georgians, 202
Gerdin, Zakharei, 155
German language, 5–6, 28, 35, 60, 97, 110, 121, 152, 164, 177
German occupation of Netherlands (1940-1945), 202
German suburb. *See nemetskaia sloboda*
Germanic languages, 62, 121, 152. *See* as well Danish; Dutch; English; Frisian; German; Swedish
Germany, 2, 37, 46, 57, 92, 102–104, 106, 115–16, 118, 124–25, 152, 155, 172, 187, 189. *See also* Bremen; Emden; Hamburg; Holstein; Holy Roman Empire
Gerritsz(oon), Hessel, 59, 64
Ghent (Gent), 24
Gheyn, Jakob de, 28, 115
Glasnost', 203
glass blowing, 82, 99, 153
Glinka, Mikhail, 178
Glissenberch, Zacharias, 42, 49, 56, 63, 115, 125
Glorious Revolution, 31, 148, 170
Glückstadt, 31, 118
Goeteeris, Anthonis, 7, 60
Gogol', Nikolai, 206
gold, 100, 125, 145
Golden Age (Dutch), 162
Golden Horde. *See* Kipchaq khanate
Golitsyn, Boris, 181
Golitsyn, Vasily V., 30, 159, 169–70
Golosov, Luk'ian, 140, 144
Golovin, Fyodor, 181, 195
Golovin, Russian diplomat (1650s), 29
Gomarists, 76
Gorbachev, Mikhail, 203

Index

Gordon, Patrick, 7, 19, 31, 45, 63, 116, 125, 139, 148, 155–56, 163, 175–79, 181
Gordon, William, 63
gost' (merchant of highest rank), 81
gostinnyi dvor' (merchants' warehouse), 144
government. *See* state
Graaf Floris, ship, 187
grain, 39, 41, 81, 85–89, 130
grain shipping, 39, 41, 46, 47, 68, 81, 85–89, 130, 161, 188
Grand Embassy (of Peter the Great), 3, 10, 31, 69, 95–96, 117, 141, 157–58, 163–64, 170, 174, 177, 181, 183–84, 188, 194
Grande Armée, 201
Great Britain. *See* British Civil Wars; England; Scotland
Great Northern War, 8, 32, 160, 177, 179, 188
Great Powers, 1, 9–10, 52–53, 70, 88, 103, 105, 124, 135, 137, 164, 171–73, 177, 184, 201, 204–206
grenadiers, 174
Griffier. *See* Recorder
Grodno, 32
Groningen (province), 4, 67, 107
Groningen University, 15
Guasconi, Francesco, 155, 158, 176–78
Guelders (province), 28, 32
guilds, 36
gunpowder, 78
gunsmiths, 82
Gustavus Adolphus, king of Sweden, 27, 75, 83, 118
Gutenberg Bible, 35

Haarlem, 73, 149, 166, 207
Habsburgs, 24, 31, 35, 38–39, 49, 88, 103–104, 151, 156
Haga, Cornelis, 162
Hague, The ('s-Gravenhage), viii, 10, 30, 44, 56, 61, 67, 69–70, 74–77, 89, 107–109, 133, 136–39, 141, 162, 166, 174, 182–83, 202
Hague Peace Conferences, 202
Hainault (Henegouwen, province), 23–4
Hakluyt, Richard, 36
Hals, Frans, 104
Hamburg, 67, 102, 106, 109, 147, 152, 155
Hamey, Boudewijn (Beaudoin/Baldwin), 92–93, 165
Hamilton, Andrew, 95
Hanseatic League, 8, 23, 37, 39, 118
Harlem, 149
Harlingen, 26, 90
Hart, Simon, 4
Hartman, Daniël, 100–102, 155
harvest failures, 45, 81
Hasenius, Pieter, 155
Hassen (Haasen/Hasenius), Hendrick, 92–93, 97
healthcare, 94, 100, 163
Hebdon, John, jr, 45
Hebdon, John, sr, 29, 45, 132, 135, 139, 183
Hebdon, Thomas, 45
Heeren XVII. *See* Gentlemen Seventeen.
Heins(ius), Daniël, 135
Heins(ius), Nicolaas, 62, 69, 71, 100, 135–37, 140, 143, 145, 151, 153–54, 161, 205
Hellevoetsluis, 138
Hellie, Richard, 6, 113–14
hemp, 45, 88, 130, 137
Hennings, Jan, 71, 162
Henri IV, king of France, 26–27
Herberstein, Sigismund von, 24, 60, 65
herb garden (of Russian apothecary), 93, 95
Herckmans, Elias, 59–60
heretics, 63, 80, 94, 122, 124, 154–55
heresy. *See* heretics
Hertogenbosch, 's-, 118
Hessel Gerritsz. *See* Gerritsz(oon), Hessel

Heurnius, Johannes, 92–93
Heuvel, Willem van den. *See* Bartolotti
hides (leather, of domesticated cattle), 27, 41, 44, 130
historical materialism, 5. *See also* Communism; Marxism
historiography, 1–21, 41, 89, 145, 198–99, 204
Historisch Verhael (Coyett), 157
Hitler, Adolf, 202
Hoefnagel, Jacques, 42
Holland (province), xi, 1, 8, 10, 21, 23, 26–31, 41–43, 47, 56, 62, 70, 76–77, 85, 92, 94, 101, 103, 106, 121, 157, 164, 172–73, 176–77, 181, 183, 187, 194, 201, 204
Holstein Embassies, 28, 80, 93, 116, 118
Holy League, 159, 184
Holy Roman Empire, 24, 35, 38, 57, 67, 69, 81, 102–104, 106, 114–16, 138, 159, 184
Hooghe, Romeyn de, 152, 157, 163
Hoorn, 26
horses, 115, 153, 157
Horsey, Jerome, 42, 50
Hortus Botanicus, of Leyden University, 93
hospitals, 95
Houtman, Adolf, 55, 57, 155–56, 160–61, 166
Houtman (Jan or Isaac), 155
Hudson, Henry, 46
Hughes, Lyndsey, 6, 16
Huguenots (French Calvinists), 26, 31
Hulst, Nicolaas van der, 173
Hulst, Zacharias (Arnoldus/Arnoud) van der, 93, 95–98, 164
humanism, 38–39, 135
Hundred Years' War, 37

Iaik (Ural) river, 160
Iaroslavl', 81
Ides, Everhard IJsbrandt, 18, 30, 164
illiteracy, 62, 154

immigration, 36, 56, 106, 148–49, 154, 187, 193–95, 197
import substitution, 47, 117, 130
India, 24
industrialisation, 124, 197
industrious revolution (Jan de Vries), 124, 164
industry, 6, 60, 89, 99, 124, 130
infantry, 115, 163
information, 6–7, 57, 59, 61–63, 81, 100, 147, 154–55, 171
Inner Asia. *See* Central Asia
insurance, 56
intelligence (strategic information). *See* information
International Court of Justice, 202
International Institute of Social History, 202
Iran (Persia), 25, 28, 73–74, 77–80, 87, 93, 95, 104–105, 116, 145, 152, 156, 189
Ireland, 121
iron, 82, 87, 99–100, 144, 155
Iron Curtain, 203
Israel, Jonathan, 198
Istanbul, 69, 162
Italy, 46. *See also* Venice
Ivan III, the Great, grand-duke of Muscovy, 24, 38
Ivan IV, the Terrible, tsar of Muscovy, 9, 24–26, 39, 42–43, 48, 56, 91, 96, 105, 115, 118, 125
Ivan V, tsar of Muscovy, 30–31, 94, 143, 159, 163, 169
iuft (*juchtleer*; type of leather), 27, 44, 130
Iur'ev, Efim, 140, 144
Izmir (Smyrna), 79

Jacobites. *See* James II; Stuart Dynasty
Jagiellonian dynasty, 52
James II, king of England and Scotland, 31, 148, 156, 162, 170
Jan III Sobieski, King of Poland-Lithuania, 151

Japan, 104
Jenkinson, Anthony, 25, 80
Jesuits, 162
jewels, 41, 44
Joachimi, Albert, 27, 69, 75, 78
John the Fearless (*Jean Sanspeur*), Burgundian duke, 38

Kalmyk khanate, 206
Kama, 100
Kamchatka, 32
Kamenets-Podol'skii, 137
Kampen, 23, 26, 37, 39, 118
Karakalpakstan, 26
Karakorum, 23, 36
Kashcheev, Ab(v)ram, 107
katorga (pl. *katorgi*), 144
Kazan, 194
Keizersgracht, 161
Keller, Johan Willem van, baron (*domheer van Utrecht*), 7, 19, 61–63, 69, 133–34, 143, 153, 157–58, 160–62, 164, 170, 173, 179, 205
Kell(d)erman, Thomas, 137
Kenkel', Andrei (Hendrik Kenkel?), 155
Keenan, Edward, 8, 20
Kholmogory, 25–26, 43, 55
Khodarkovsky, Mikhail, 8
Kinsbergen, Jan Hendrik van, admiral, 1, 201
Kintsius, Abraham, 161
Kipchaq khanate, 23–24, 37
Kivelson, Valerie, 8
Klenck (Clenk, Clenck, Klenk), van, family, 124, 152
Klenck-Fentzel, Geertruida van, 50
Klenck, Jurriaan (George) van, 26, 45, 47, 50, 55–59, 80–82, 85, 89–91, 102, 124, 162
Klenck (Clenk, Clenck, Klenk), Koenraad (Coenraet) van, 28, 30, 44–45, 60, 69–70, 100, 129, 133–35, 140, 151–62, 166, 169, 176, 193, 204–205
Kliuchevskii, V.O., 1, 3

Kluyting, Cornelis, 28
kniaz, 24, 38, 158, 172
Knoppers, Jake, 13–14, 197–99
Kola peninsula, 25, 42–43, 49, 55, 190, 206
Kondyrev, Ivan, 74–75
Kordt, Veniamin, 2, 5, 21, 44, 49, 55, 87
Kotilaine, Jarmo, 5–6, 13, 16, 88, 130, 160, 198, 204
Kotoshikhin, G. F., 7
Kovrigina, V. A., 6
Kozlovskii, I. P., 2
Krawinckel, Jo(h)annes, 175
Kreslins, Janis, 6, 62
Krizhanich, Juraj, 7
Kronshtadt, 194
Kuhlmann, Quirinius, 31, 94, 98, 155
Kunstkammer, 195
Kurakin, Boris I., 172, 177, 181, 183–84
kuranty, 62, 81, 100, 166, 204. See also newspapers
Kurland, Jordan, v–xiii, 1, 2, 5, 8–9, 108, 110, 125, 198, 204–205
Kyiv (Kiev), 5, 29, 31, 160, 177
Kyiv University, 5

labour, 46, 144, 202
Lahana, Martha Luby, 6, 122–23, 131, 197
Lake Peipus, 37
Lannoy, Gilbert de, 23, 36–38
Latin, 24, 35–36, 59–60, 65, 135
Latvians, 36
law, ix, 29, 56, 80, 106, 123–24, 127
leather. See hides; *iufti*
Lefort, François, 7, 31, 94, 116, 148, 163, 174–79, 181
Lenin (Ul'ianov), Vladimir Il'ich, 202
Leningrad. See Saint Petersburg
Leont'ev (Leontiev), Konstantin, ix
Leopold I, Holy Roman Emperor, 104, 138, 184
Leslie, Alexander, 89–90, 189
Levant, 79

Leyden (Leiden), vii, 4, 12, 60, 92–93, 97–98, 132, 135
Leyden University, 4, 12, 92–93, 97–98, 132, 135
Liège, prince-archbishopric, 35
lingua franca, 164, 185
Linschoten, Jan Huyghen van, 93
literacy, 62, 154. *See also* education; illiteracy
Lithuanians, 36, 47–48, 51, 55. *See also* Polish-Lithuanians
Little Ice Age (c. 1550-1750), 45
Livonia, 25, 45, 114
Livonian Guard (of Ivan IV), 42
Livonian Wars, 25, 45, 114
Locher, Th. J. G., 4, 165, 189, 205
London, 29, 31, 57, 92, 157, 167, 170, 182, 202
Longworth, Philip, xiii, 6
Lopukhina sisters, 183
Lotharius, Holy Roman Emperor, 40
Louis IX, king of France, 23
Louis XIV, king of France, 9, 28, 30–31, 69, 96, 103, 105, 108, 137–38, 156, 169–70, 176
Louise Henriette of Orange-Nassau, 152
Loviagin, A. M., 2
loyalty, 57, 74, 81, 89, 109, 147–48, 175. *See also* Dutch national identity; Russian national identity
Lübeck, 48, 109, 118
Lubimenko, Inna, 3, 11, 110
lumber, 41, 88
Lups, Jacob, 188
Lups, Jan, 161, 187–90, 201
Lus, Sion, 26
Lutheranism, 148, 187

Madrid, 151, 156
magic, 94
Maier, Ingrid, 6
mail, 63, 137–39, 145, 155. *See also* postmaster
Maire, Isaac le, 26, 42, 46
Maliebaan, 161

malnutrition, 45
Malov, V. M., 114
manufacturing, 10, 28, 36, 41, 47, 82, 89, 99–101, 124, 130, 144, 147, 171, 204
maps. *See* cartography
market, 46, 60, 81, 94, 109, 129
Marselis, family, 27, 89–90, 102, 106, 147
Marselis, Gabriël, 27, 147
Marselis, Gabriël Gabriëlszoon, 27, 147, 193–94
Marselis, Leonard Gabriëlszoon, 27, 147
Marselis, Peter Gabriëlszoon, 27, 29, 57, 80, 82, 97, 99, 101–102, 106, 110, 116, 124, 134, 137, 144–45, 147, 149, 155, 179, 193–94, 204
Marselis, Peter Peterszoon, 145
Marselis, Selio (Celio) Gabriëlszoon, 27, 147
Mary (the Rich), duchess of Burgundy, 24
Mary (II) Stuart, queen of England, Scotland and Ireland, 31
mass, 35
Massa, Isaac Abrahamszoon, 7, 19, 45, 56–57, 59, 63–64, 68, 73–79, 81–83, 85, 89, 91, 93
mathematics, 162
Matveev, Andrei Artamonovich, 133, 183–84
Matveev, Artamon Sergeevich, 30, 56, 158, 183
Maurice (Maurits, van Oranje-Nassau), stadtholder, 26, 28, 67, 73–74, 93
Maximilian, archduke of Austria, 24, 35, 40
McGill University, 197
medical doctors, 10, 42, 45, 63, 82, 91–98, 100, 124, 129, 135, 145, 160, 177. *See also* surgeons
medicine, 1, 61, 91–98, 171, 177
Mediterranean Sea, 39, 51, 62

Mennonites (*doopsgezinden*), 30, 89, 95, 148
Menshikov, Aleksandr, 177–78
Menzies (Menezius), Paul, 45, 137–38, 148, 178
mercantilism, 128, 147. *See also* import substitution; New Commercial Code; tariffs
Mercator (Gerhard Kramer), 25
mercenaries, 1, 6, 10, 28, 45, 82, 87, 89, 95, 113–19, 122–25, 138, 144–45, 148, 175–78, 197
merchant ships, 43, 46, 88, 116, 130, 171, 189, 193
merchants (Dutch), *passim*
merchants (English), 3, 12–13, 25–26, 39, 42, 45, 48, 50, 57, 77, 83, 127, 135, 160, 167. *See also* Muscovy Company
merchants (Russian), 21, 24–25, 44, 80–81, 83, 127–28, 137
Merrick, John, 45, 50, 75, 78
Meulen, R. van der, 6
Meyer, De, Dutch merchant, 25
Middle Ages, 13, 36–37
migration. *See* emigrés; immigration
Mikado (Japanese emperor), 104
Mikhail Fyodorovich Romanov, tsar of Russia, 27, 48, 55, 67–68, 70, 74, 76–77, 85, 87–89, 92–94, 96, 116, 127, 153
Mikhailov, Pyotr (Tsar Peter I), 181
military engineers, 118. *See also* fortifications; sieges
military exercises, 28, 52
military expertise, 69, 113–15, 123, 135, 144, 148, 163
military hospitals, 95
military innovation, 6, 113–16, 151, 171–72, 176
Military Revolution, 6–7, 114–16
military theory, 28
militia (*schutters*), 42
Miloslavskaia, Mariia, tsarina of Muscovy, 29–30

Miloslavskaia, Sofiia, regent of Muscovy, 30–31, 159–60, 163, 169–70
Miloslavskii, Il'ia Danilovich, 28, 69, 115, 133, 135, 141, 176, 182
mining, 99, 100, 145, 155, 163
Modern World System (Immanuel Wallerstein), 6, 7
modernisation, 6–7, 113–14, 116, 124, 145, 149, 163–64, 171–72, 176, 182, 194, 197, 206
Moedernegotie. See mother trade
Moguls (Mughals), 104
Monahan, Erika, 7
money (need for, cash), 5, 59, 61, 92, 94, 100, 102, 131, 140, 147–48, 154, 169, 189, 197
Mongolians (Tatars), 23–24, 36–38
monopolies, 25, 27, 44, 81, 86–87, 89, 131, 165
morality. *See* ethics
morskoi ustav (*Zeevaartreglement*), 1, 117
Moscow, vii, xi, 2, 5, 7, 10, 21, 23–25, 27–31, 38–39, 42, 44–45, 51, 55, 57, 59, 62–64, 67–71, 74–82, 86–87, 89, 91–98, 105–11, 114–15, 117, 121–25, 127–29, 133–37, 139, 143–44, 147–49, 152–55, 158–62, 164–65, 170, 175–77, 181, 183, 188–90, 204, 206
Moscow riots (of 1648), 29, 133
Moscow riots (of 1682), 30
Mosely, Philip E., ix
moskovskie inozemtsy, 80, 82, 122
mother trade (*moedernegotie*), 8, 14, 21, 68
Moucheron, Balthasar de, 25–26, 42–44, 46, 48
Moucheron, Cos(i)mo de, 82, 114
Moucheron, Maria de, 101
Moucheron, Melchior de, 25–26, 44
Moucheron, de, family, 25–26, 44, 101–102
Moulin, Karel (Carl) du, 55–57, 73, 81–82, 90, 98, 102, 114, 124, 204

Muliukin, A.S., 2
Muller, Werner, 155
Münster, 29–30, 88, 118, 133
Muscovy Company (English), 3, 12–13, 25–26, 39, 41–45, 49, 57–58, 67–68, 83, 166–67
musketeers. See *strel'tsy*
muskets, 113, 188
Muslims, 148–49
musea, 195, 207
Musch, Cornelis, 56
mutinies, 41, 202

Naarden, Bruno, xiii, 6, 101–102
Napoléon I, Emperor of the French, 1, 3, 205
narod, 179
Narva, 8, 9, 25–26, 30, 41–44, 48, 63, 78, 86, 118, 189
Naryshkin family, 183
Naryshkina, Natal'ia, 30
Nassau, Imperial county, 56–57
nationalism, 172. See also loyalty; Dutch national identity; Russian national identity
natural environment, 45. See also climate
naval stores, 27, 130, 187. See also tar; wood
naval warfare, 101, 105, 116–17, 193–94
navy, 101, 105, 116–17, 164, 177, 193–94
Nazis, 202–203
nemets (pl. *nemtsy*), 62, 121–22
nemetskaia sloboda (foreigners' or German suburb near Moscow), 29, 62, 121–26, 145, 154
nepotism, 56. See also networks; patronage
Netherlands, Kingdom of, vii, 3–6, 201–202
network (communication), 35–36
networks (social), 7, 43, 46, 56–57, 97, 116, 131, 147, 155–56, 162, 166, 175–77, 204

Neverov, Mikhail, 74–75
New Commercial Statute (*Novotorgovyi Ustav*, 1667), 9, 29, 105, 127–32, 134, 136, 144
New York (city), ix, xi, 104, 149, 202
newspapers, 7, 10, 63, 82, 139, 144, 154, 202. See also *kuranty*
Nicholas I, Russian tsar, 201
Nicholas II, Russian tsar, 202
Nieuwe Vestingbouw (Coehoorn), 114
Nijinsky, Vaclav, 206
Nikitin, Afanasii, 24
Nikon (Nikita Minin), Russian patriarch, 9, 29, 101, 105, 122, 125
Nine Years' War (War of the League of Augsburg, 1688-1697), 31, 131, 157, 184
nobility, 28, 32, 35–6, 61–62, 70, 75, 83, 86, 94, 107, 115, 129, 134, 143, 152–53, 161–62, 170, 183, 189
Noordsche Compagnie, 27
Noort, Olivier van, 46
Nordermann, Konrad, 94, 155
North America, 149
North Cape, 39, 190
North and East Tartary (Witsen), 31, 60, 109, 160, 164, 206
north-east passage, 3, 25, 39, 43
North Sea, 63, 68, 106–107, 115, 129, 152, 157, 164, 193
northern searoute (to Indies). See north-east passage
Norway, 26, 193. See also Denmark
notaries, 83, 139, 153
Novgorod, 8, 23–24, 37–39, 43–44, 62–63, 118, 133
Nijmegen, 30, 156, 178

Oblomov (Goncharov), 124, 126
officers (army, navy), 28, 45, 82, 88, 95, 113, 115–16, 123–24, 129, 143, 148, 154, 176–77, 193–94, 197
Oka, 29, 116
Old Believers (*staroobriadtsy*), 29
Oldebarnevelt, Johan van, 76

Olearius (Öhlschlager), Adam, 28, 60, 65, 93, 109, 116
oligarchy, 108
operation theatres, 6
oprichnina, 43
Orange, principality, 156
Orange-Nassau dynasty, 3, 26, 28–29, 56, 67, 70, 104, 107, 152, 170, 201–202
Ordin-Nashchokin, Afanasii, 107, 137, 140, 144, 183, 185
Ordin-Nashchokin, (Nashchokin), Bogdan, 29, 107, 109–10, 133
Orlenko, S. P., 6
Orthodoxy (Russian), 25, 37–38, 63, 80–82, 105, 122, 124, 148–49, 154, 163, 165, 172
Oryol. See Eagle
Os, Dirck van, 26, 43, 46
Ottoman Empire, 1, 23–24, 29–31, 38, 52–53, 69, 73, 86, 100, 103–104, 117, 137–38, 141, 148–49, 151, 157, 159–60, 169–71, 173, 176, 181, 184
Overijssel, 28, 31, 118, 161

Pacific, 9, 160
pacifism, 89, 202
Paludanus (ten Broecke), Bernhard (Berent), 93, 98
Paludanus, Hiob (Job), 92–93, 96–97
paper, 101, 171, 189
Parker, Geoffrey, 7
Parliament (English), 110, 167
Parma, Duke of (Alexander Farnese), 43
patriarch of Constantinople, 38
patriciate (Dutch). *See* regents
patronage, 56, 162. *See also* networks
Paul, Michael, 114
Paulsen, Zakhar (Arendt), 99, 102
Pauw, Reinier, 73–74, 97
Pauw, Reinier Rooclaes, 92–93, 96–97
Pavlov, Elisei, translator, 93
Pavlova, Anna, 206
Pax Mongolica, 37
Peace of Münster, 29, 88, 118, 133

Peace of Nijmegen, 30, 156
Peace of Utrecht, 9, 32, 105, 183
Peace of Westphalia. *See* Peace of Münster
peasants, 37, 45–46
peers, 107
Pekarskii, P., 1
Perestroika, 203
Persian Gulf, 189
Peter I (Alekseevich) the Great, tsar of Russia, xi, 1, 3, 5–6, 9–10, 14–15, 26, 30–32, 52–53, 63, 69, 88, 91, 94–99, 102, 106, 109, 114, 116–17, 121–24, 130–31, 139, 143–45, 149, 152, 155–99, 204–206
Peters, Marion, xiii, 6
pharmacists. *See* apothecary
Philip II, king of Spain (as Philip V, Duke of Burgundy), 25, 70
Philip III (the Good), duke of Burgundy, 23, 36, 38, 40
Philip IV (the Fair), duke of Burgundy, 24
Phillips, E. J., 6, 114
Phipps, Geraldine, 6
photographs, vii
physicians. *See* medical doctors; surgeons
pistols, 113
Plakkaat van Verlatinghe. See Act of Abjuration
Platonov, S. F., 2
play regiments. *See poteshnye voiska/polki*
Plokhy, Serhii, 40
plunder, 48, 50, 109
Poe, Marshall, 16
poison, 91
Poland-Lithuania, 7, 9, 23, 25, 27–30, 37–39, 46–48, 51–52, 55, 68, 74, 76–77, 85, 87–89, 93, 100, 103, 105, 107–108, 114–16, 125, 135, 137–38, 140, 151, 159–60, 170, 175
Polish-Lithuanians. *See* Poland-Lithuania

244

Polivanov, Russian diplomat, 29
Polovtsov, Aleksandr, 2
Pomerania, 188
pontonniers, 201
poorter (tax-paying citizen of Dutch city), 187
pope (Catholic pontiff), 76, 159
Poppen, Amsterdam trading family, 46
population (general, mass), 23–24, 29, 35–36, 45, 53, 70, 96, 122
Porter, Roy, 95
Portugal, 104
posol'skii prikaz (Russian foreign office), 7, 74, 97, 138, 144, 172, 183
Posselt, Moritz, 118, 124, 174
postal service. *See* mail; postmaster
postmaster (-general), 63, 101, 137, 158, 163, 166
potash, 27, 41, 45, 88, 130, 137, 188
poteshnye voiska/polki (Peter I's play regiments), 171–72, 174, 176
Potop ("deluge"), 104
poverty, 70
Prague, 76
Pravda, 202
Premier League (Russian soccer), 203
printing, 1, 7–8, 10, 19, 28, 35–36, 38, 49, 59–61, 73, 82, 109, 115, 136, 163, 166, 172, 187, 189, 195, 205–206
Prokofiev, Sergei, 206
propaganda, 171
prospecting, 100, 145, 155, 163
protectionism. *See* mercantilism
Protestants, 1, 63, 68, 92, 123–25, 162, 170. *See also* Anglicanism; Anabaptists; Calvinists; Lutherans; Mennonites
Prozorovskii, Pyotr, 107
Prozorovskii Embassy, 106–107
Prussia, 52, 104, 151, 158–59, 181
Prussians (extinct Baltic people), 36
Pskov, 23–24, 37–39
puritanical, 162
Purmerend, 26

Pushkin, Aleksandr, 178, 206
Pustozer'sk, 30, 183
Putin, Vladimir, 5, 8

quackery. *See* medicine
quarantine, 96
Qing dynasty, 31, 104, 160

Raeck, Govert van der, 100, 102
Rakoczi, György, 104
Rampjaar ("Year of Disaster", 1672), 9, 30, 51, 152–53
ransoming, 157, 169
Raptschinsky, Boris, 4, 13
Razin, Stenka (Stepan), 4, 30, 116–17, 137, 143, 145, 153, 165, 205
Recorder (*Griffier*), 56
Red Square, 31, 94, 155
regents (Russian), 30-1, 69, 169. *See also* Sofiia
regents (Dutch), 43, 56, 58, 70, 75, 77, 97, 101, 108, 110, 151–56, 160, 165, 182, 205
Reger, William, 6, 114–15
religion (identity, role of), 36, 89, 106, 123, 147–48, 162–63. *See also* Anabaptism; Arminians; Calvinism; Catholicism; Gomarists; Old Believers; Orthodoxy; Muslims; Protestantism
Rembrandt van Rijn, 102, 104
renegades, 149. *See also* Bockhoven (Filips Albrecht van); Winius
Republic of Letters, 109
Reve, Karel van het, 4, 13, 203
RGADA. *See* Archive of Ancient Acts
Rhineland, 157
rich trade, 41
Richter, W.M. von, 1
Riga, 9, 41, 43, 48, 63, 80, 86, 97, 101, 108–109, 118, 137, 189–90
Ringen, Hendrik van, 58, 114
Riurik dynasty, 209
Robinson, Geroid Tanquaray, ix
Rodenburg(h), Jan Cornelis van, 114

Romanov, Ivan Nikitich, 77
Romanov dynasty, xi, 2, 4, 56, 63, 79, 88, 96, 99, 105, 202. *See also* Mikhail; Aleksei; Filaret; Fyodor III; Peter; Ivan V; Alexander I; Nicholas I; Nicholas II
Rome, 136, 138, 181
Romodanovskii, Fyodor, 181
Romswinckel, Matthias, 155
Roonaer, Anthony Goriszoon, 176
Roonaer, Jacobus Goriszoon, 176
Roonaer family, 176
Roosevelt family, 149
ropeworks, 82
Rubroeck (Ruysbroeck), Willem van, 23, 36–37
Rumpf, Christiaan, 162
Rusland en de Nederlanden (Scheltema), 3
Russian Academy of Sciences, 32, 171, 177, 195
Russian Federation, 5, 7–8, 20, 92, 203–204
Russian flag, 1, 10
Russian identity, 62–63, 154–55, 161–62, 164, 177–78. *See also* loyalty
Russian language, 12, 21, 44–45, 139, 152, 154, 163
Russians, in Dutch eyes, 21, 59–63, 161–62
Russo-Swedish War of 1656-1658, 29, 136
Russo-Turkish War of 1676-1681, 30, 69, 114, 137, 159, 166, 176, 229
Russo-Turkish War of 1768-1774, 1
Ruts, David Nicolaeszoon, 102, 114
Ruts family, 57, 99, 101–102. *See also* Sweeden
Ruysch, Frederick, 189
Rzeczpospolita. See Poland-Lithuania

sailing, 13, 28–31, 41, 43, 46, 49, 73, 75, 77, 83, 86, 97, 99, 108, 116–17, 135, 138, 143–44, 163, 171, 190
sailors, 1, 28–31, 39, 93–94, 101, 117, 125, 135, 138, 143, 153, 160, 169, 193–94
Saint Michael the Archangel, 43
Saint Petersburg (Russia), 4, 9, 13, 20, 31, 77, 97, 122, 188–90, 193, 198, 205
Salingen, Simon van, 25, 42
saltpeter (potassium nitrate), 27, 45, 86, 206
Samoyeds, 59
sanctuary, 94
Santa Profetie, 163
Sarai, 36
Scandinavia. *See* Denmark; Norway; Sweden
Scania (territory in south Sweden), 29, 159
Scanian War (1675-1679), 29, 159
Schade, Hans, 5
Scheltema, Jacob, 3, 110, 206
schools. *See* education
Schoonebeeck, Adriaan, 163, 195
Schumacher, Johann Daniel, 177
schutters. See militia
science, 6, 31–32, 95, 109, 155, 160, 162–63, 171, 177, 182–83, 195
Scotland, 52, 148
Scots, 7, 31, 45, 63, 89, 92, 115–16, 121, 123, 138, 175, 177
seafaring regulations. *See Morskoi ustav*
Seba, Albert, 189
seclusion of women, 154
Second World War, 4–5, 202–203
serfs, 46, 53
servants, 53, 63, 109, 124–25, 136, 145
Seville, 39
Sevsk, 95
Shamin, Stepan, 6
shamkal, Caucasian ruler, 143
Shein, Mikhail Borisovich, 86, 90
Shields-Kollmann, Nancy, 8
ship's captains, 44, 49, 117, 143
ship's masts, 119, 130

shipwrights, 28–31, 93, 101, 116–17, 135, 160
shogun, 104
Siberia, 6–7, 9, 25–26, 29, 59–60, 63, 100, 105, 109, 130, 159–60, 164, 206
Siberian Office (*Sibirskii Prikaz*), 100
Siege of Vienna (1683), 31, 138, 159, 184
sieges, 30–31, 41, 49, 114–17, 138, 149, 159, 163, 176, 178, 184
Sigismund III Wasa, king of Poland, grand duke of Lithuania, 51
silk, 73–74, 78–80, 82, 87–88, 93, 105, 116, 129, 152, 171
silver, 39, 125, 129, 145, 184. See also bullion
slave trade, 104, 108
slavery, 57, 153, 156
Slavic studies, 4–6, 8–9, 12, 203
*sloboda*s, 122. See also *nemetskaia sloboda*
Smolensk War, 28, 90, 114–15, 117, 145
smuggling, 47, 127
Smutnoe vremya (*Smuta*). See Time of Troubles
soldiers, 24, 51, 53, 61, 87, 89, 94, 117–18, 145, 148, 176, 201
Solov'ev (Soloviev), S. M., 1
Sont. See Sound (Danish)
Souhay, Elisabeth, 176–77
Souhay, François, 28, 176, 178
Sound (Danish), 68, 193
Sound toll, 68, 193
South America, 39, 104
southern Netherlands, 8, 24–27, 43, 46, 50, 52, 73. See also Antwerp; Artois; Belgium; Brabant; Flanders; Hainault
Soviet POWs (Second World War), 202
Soviet Red Army, 202
Soviet Union, vii, ix, xi, 2–8, 14, 16, 202–203, 207
Spain, 10, 25–28, 31–32, 38, 41–42, 52, 69, 78, 89, 103, 106, 115, 118, 138, 154, 183, 194

spal'nik, 172
Spanish Fury (1576), 41, 46
Spanish Netherlands. See southern Netherlands
Spanish silver fleet, 39
spices, 41, 44
Spies, Marijke, 12
Spranger, Gommert, 86, 114
Sri Lanka, 104
Stanislavsky, Konstantin, 206
staple, 26, 35
state (government), 4, 10, 21, 23, 28, 32, 39, 44, 46, 51–52, 55–57, 62–63, 67–69, 80–81, 87, 89, 91, 98, 100, 107, 109, 124, 127–29, 133–34, 136–37, 147, 161, 169, 171, 183–84, 203, 207 See also *d'iak*; Estates-General; tsar
state, strength of, 51–53
State Department (US), 153
Stavoren, 26
Stellingwerff, Arent Claeszoon van, 91–92, 96–97
Stellingwerff, Jacob Arentszoon van, 91, 94, 96–97
Stockholm, 71, 75, 77, 89, 135, 161–62
Stoltz (Goncharov), 124
Strahlenberg, Philip Johann von, 160, 166
Stravinsky, Igor, 206
strel'tsy, 30–31, 137, 181, 183
Stroganov family, 25–26, 42
Struys, Jan Janszoon, 5, 7, 14, 16, 30, 60, 117, 125, 143–44, 153–54, 205
Stuart dynasty, 29–31, 107, 110, 132, 148
Sublime Porte. See Ottoman Empire
sultan, of Ottoman empire, 73, 104, 138, 148, 151, 169
surgeons, 92–96, 100, 144, 160
Surinam, 57, 104, 156
Surinam Society, 156
Swaen, Thomas de, 102, 114
Sweden, 7, 9, 25, 27, 29–32, 48, 52, 67–69, 71, 74, 76–77, 86, 100, 103–105,

137–38, 151–52, 158–59, 169–70, 172, 184, 188, 193, 201
Sweeden, Jan van, 29–30, 63, 80–81, 85, 99–102, 106, 110, 116, 124, 134–35, 144–45, 147, 149, 161, 182, 189, 204–205
Sweeden, Suzanna van, 161
Sweeden-Ruts, Maria van, 99
Swellengrebel, Erdman, 113, 118
Swellengrebel, Heinrich, 118, 155
Switzerland, 175, 178
Synod of Dordt (Dordrecht), 76, 152

Tabbert, Egidius, 99
tar, 45, 82, 130, 137, 188
tariffs, 29, 56, 58, 80, 86, 128, 136, 147
Tatars, 23–24, 31, 38–39, 69, 100, 114, 125, 137, 143, 151, 157, 159–60, 170–71, 176
Tavernier, Roger, 5
taxation, 29, 46, 55, 76, 80, 109, 128, 187
Tchaikovsky, P.I., 206
technology, 86, 114, 149, 151, 157, 171–72
Tensini, Octavio, 100, 102
Termu(o)nd(t), Jan van, 93–95, 143–45, 154, 205
Teutonic Knights, 37
Texel (island roadstead), 86, 202
textile, 82, 88, 99, 101, 189
texts, 2, 7, 18, 28, 50, 60–62, 109, 121
Thesingh, Jan, 161, 163, 187–88
Thesingh, Hendrik, 161, 187
Thirteen Years' War, 28, 103, 115, 152, 204
Thirty Years' War, 29, 68, 76, 103, 118
Thyret, Isolde, 8
timber. *See* wood
Time of Troubles (*Smuta*), 27, 45–47, 55–56, 59, 63–64, 73–74, 92, 114, 127
Timmerman, Frans, 1, 3, 31, 95, 160, 162–65, 170, 188, 205
tobacco, 63, 123

tolerance, 26, 30, 68
tolls, 26, 55, 68, 77, 80, 193
Tolstoi, Lev, 206
Tolstoi, P. A., 7
Torbay, 31, 170
torgovaia kniga, 21
torture, 91
Tot'ma, 56
trade, 3, 4, 6, 8–10, 12–14, 20–21, 23–29, 35–50, 56–59, 62, 67–69, 73–91, 96–97, 100–10, 116, 124, 127–36, 144, 148–49, 152–53, 155–56, 160–67, 171, 176, 178, 182, 184–85, 189–91, 197–99, 102, 205. *See also* bulk trade; Iran; merchants; rich trade; tariffs; tolls; trading privileges
trading privileges, 47, 55, 58, 67, 73, 76–77, 79–80, 128. *See also* monopolies; tariffs
translators, 2, 75, 93, 100, 136, 139–40, 144, 153–54, 158, 163, 204. *See also* Asperen; Vinius
transport routes, 35, 55, 73, 79, 85, 88, 93, 105, 116, 138
Transylvania, 104
travel accounts, 6, 16, 18, 59–60, 123. *See also* Bruin; Coyett; Danckaert; Fletcher; Goeteeris; Ides; Jenkinson; Olearius; Struys
Treaty of Copenhagen (1660), 29, 68
Treaty of Dover, 137
Treaty of Kardis, 136
Treaty of Karlowitz, 31, 157, 170
Treaty of Nerchinsk, 31, 160
Treaty of Nijmegen, 30, 156, 178
Treaty of Nystadt, 32
Treaty of the Pyrenees, 103
Treaty of Ryswyck, 31, 157, 170, 184
Treaty of Stolbovo, 27, 76
Treaty of Utrecht, 9, 32, 105, 183
Treaty of Westminster (1654), 29
Treaty of Westminster (1674), 30
Trip, Elias, 85–86, 89, 102, 108, 114
Triple Alliance (Republic-Sweden-Britain), 137

Tromp, Cornelis, 193
Troyen, Jeroen van, 155
Truce of Andrusovo, 9, 29, 105, 160
Truce of Deulino, 27, 77, 89
Tsvetaev, D., 1
Tuchthuys (Amsterdam prison), 59
Tula, 28, 82, 85, 99–100
Turgenev, Nikolai, 206
Turkey. *See* Ottoman Empire
Turks. *See* Ottoman Empire
turners, 189
Tver', 24
Twelve Year Truce, 27, 152

Ugra, 24
Uhlenbeck, C. C., 4, 12
Ukraine, 29–31, 37, 159–60, 207
Ukraintsev, Emel'ian, *dumnyi d'iak*, 137–38, 141, 154, 157–58, 169, 178, 182
Ulozhenie, 29, 127
United Kingdom. *See* Great Britain
United States of America, 54–56, 149
University of Amsterdam, 4, 203
University of North Carolina at Greensboro, vii, ix
Unkovskaya, M., 94
Ural mountains, 160
Ural (Iaik) river, 160
urbanisation, 35
Ushakov, Stepan, 67–69, 182
Ustrialov, N. V., 1, 13
usury, 56
Utrecht (city), 9, 105, 161, 183
Utrecht (province), 28, 32
Utrecht University, 4, 14

Valckenburg(c)h, Elisabeth van, 56
Val(c)kenburg(c)h, Margaretha (Margriet) van, 55–58, 90
value, 37, 41, 88–89, 154, 198
Vanderbilt family, 149
Vasily III, grand-duke of Russia, 24, 39
Vasily IV Shuiskii, tsar of Russia, 27

vats, 187
Veltdriel, Johan van, 28, 86–87, 89
Veluwenkamp, Jan-Willem, 5–6
Venice, 78, 86, 103, 138, 174, 181, 183
Vermeer, Johannes, 104
Verpoorten, Philips, 100–102, 109
Vienna, 31, 67, 110, 138, 151, 156, 159, 161, 183–84, 201–202
Vinius, Andrei Andreevich, 3, 10–11, 28, 32, 63, 93, 95, 98, 100, 116, 137–40, 144–45, 147, 149, 154–58, 160, 163–64, 166–67, 169–70, 172, 174, 178, 181, 194, 204–207
Vinius, Matvei Andreevich, 63
VOC (*Vereenighde Oostindische Compagnie*, United East India Company), 27, 46, 50, 57, 79, 164, 182, 188, 193
Vogelaer, Daniël Marcuszoon de, 55
Vogelaer, Jan Marcuszoon de, 55, 97
Vogelaer, Joost de, 42, 48
Vogelaer, Marcus Marcuszoon de, 55
Vogelaer sr, Marcus de, 26, 46, 49, 55
Vogelaer (-Glissenberch), Margaretha de, 42, 56
Vogelaer, de, family, 26, 28, 47, 55–57, 59, 80–81, 89, 99, 102, 124, 135, 166. *See also* Margaretha van Valckenburch
Volga, 24–25, 30, 32, 36–37, 39, 74, 79, 87, 100, 105, 116, 145
Vologda, 87, 161
Vondel, Joost van den, 97
Voronin, Vladimir, 137, 184
Voznitsyn, Prokofii, *dumnyi d'iak*, 181
Vries, Jan de, 7

Waarheid, De, 202
Waegemans, Emanuel, 6
wages, 61, 113
Walle, Jacques van de, 42, 46, 48, 78, 83
Walle, Jan van de, 25–26, 42–44, 48–50, 56, 78, 83, 204

Wallerstein, Immanuel, 6
Wallhausen, Johann Jacobi von, 115
Wallonia (French-speaking provinces of Netherlands), 26
Wapenhandelinghe, 115
War of the Reunions (1683-1684), 156
War of the Spanish Succession (1702-1713), 32, 52, 183–84
warehouse, 26, 55, 85, 117, 144, 165
warfare (manner of fighting), 6, 114–16, 118, 163, 175, 204
warships, 189. *See also* navy
Wasa dynasty, 51–52
watches, 171
Waterloo, 3
watermills, 171
waterpower, 171
waterways (inland), 35, 90
Waugh, Daniel, 6
wax, 88
weavers. *See* textile
Weber, Max, 124, 148
weather, 90
West India Company, 27, 188
Westerkerk (Amsterdam), 161
Western Europe, 2–3, 6, 9, 10, 16, 23–26, 29, 31–32, 37–39, 41–42, 45–46, 48, 51, 61–63, 74, 80, 82, 88, 92, 95–96, 100, 103, 109, 111, 113–16, 121–27, 130–31, 137, 139, 144–45, 148, 152, 154–55, 157–58, 160–64, 171, 175–76, 178–79, 181–84, 189, 193, 195, 197–98, 203
whale hunt (whaling), 27
White Sea, 1, 8, 25–27, 41–42, 44, 48, 81, 85, 130, 189
WIC (*Westindische Compagnie, Geoctroyeerde Westindische Compagnie, GWC*). *See* West India Company
Willem (Willum), Paul de, 114
William I (*Willem I van Oranje-Nassau*, the Silent/*de Zwijger, Guillaume le Taciturne*), stadtholder, 26

William II (*Willem II van Oranje-Nassau*), stadtholder, 28
William II of Orange-Nassau, king of the Netherlands, 3, 202
William III (*Willem III van Oranje-Nassau*), king-stadtholder, 30–32, 36, 52, 107, 138, 156–57, 170
wine, 41
Winius Jr, Andries. *See* Vinius
Winius (Vinius), Andries Denijszoon, *gost'*, 28–29, 80–82, 85, 99–102, 134–35, 147–48, 164–65, 182, 189, 204
Winius, Deni(j)s Tjerkszoon, 165
Winterkoning, Filips, 25, 42
Witsen, Cornelis Janszoon, 164
Witsen, Gerrit, 73, 77, 164
Witsen, Nicolaas Corneliszoon, 4, 6–7, 9, 13, 18–19, 28–31, 60, 63, 80, 101, 109, 111, 122–23, 154–56, 160, 163–65, 167, 182, 189, 194, 203–207
Witsen family, 73, 164–65
Witsen Project, 203
Witsen's diary, 4, 7, 9, 109, 164, 204–205
Witt, Cornelis de, 30, 152
Witt, Johan de, (*raadspensionaris*), 30, 103–104, 108, 110, 152
Wladimiroff, Igor, 6
women, seclusion of, 154
wood, 122
World System, 6
World War One. *See* First World War
World War Two. *See* Second World War
Wijk, Nicolaas van, 4, 12
Wijnroks, Eric, 5–6, 8, 41, 43–44, 47–48, 55, 68, 82–83, 87–88, 106, 131–32

xenophobia, 123, 127, 130

Yankees, 149
Yugoslavia, 203

Zaandam, 182
Zabelin, I., 1
Zaborovskii, Semyon, 67–68
Zandt, Christiaan, 6
Zee(Zea)land (province), 10, 23, 27–28, 31, 43, 75–76, 106, 118
Zeevaartreglement (*morskoi ustav*), 1, 117
Zhdanov University (Leningrad State University), 4
Zitser, Ernest, 6
Zoe (Sofia) Paleologos, 24
Zürich, 202
Zutphen, 37
Zwolle, 23, 37, 118

About the Author

Kees Boterbloem has written a dozen books on the history of Russia, the Soviet Union, and the Netherlands. A professor at the University of South Florida in Tampa, he served as the chief editor of the peer-reviewed journal *The Historian* from 2008 to 2018.

www.ingramcontent.com/pod-product-compliance
Lightning Source LLC
Chambersburg PA
CBHW061710300426
44115CB00014B/2623